Felice Lifshitz

THE NORMAN CONQUEST OF PIOUS NEUSTRIA
Historiographic Discourse and Saintly Relics, 684-1090

This work examines the religious historiography of Frankish Neustria (once the Roman province of Secunda Lugdunensis and now what is Normandy) through narratives composed between the late seventh and the late eleventh century.

Two principal methodological premises underlie the study: first, narratives describing the activities of saints are fully historiographical; and second, the production of historical narrative and the institution of saints' cults stem from the same impulse, an impulse that is fundamentally "political." The historiographic monuments and saints' cults from Merovingian Neustria represent the region as outstanding for its Christian piety: together they reveal the discourse of "Pious Neustria." By contrast, both Austrasian-Carolingian princes and their successors in Neustria, the Vikings, also benefitted from discourses embodied in written narratives and in saints' cults but which represented inhabitants of the diocese of Rouen as having been "not-Christians" during the Merovingian period.

The earlier sections of the study deal primarily with representations of the past which seem to have united the inhabitants of Neustria along regional lines whereas the later sections, in analyzing the aftermath of both the Austrasian-Carolingian and the Viking conquests, deal with representations of the past that divided the inhabitants of Normandy along social lines. The Carolingian- and Viking-era narratives have tended to dominate in the subsequent historiography of Christianization of the region, and have resulted in a widespread conception of Merovingian Neustria as having been "pagan." It is to that triumph of the conquerors' discourse that this book owes its title: the Norman Conquest of Pious Neustria.

STUDIES AND TEXTS 122

The Norman Conquest of Pious Neustria

Historiographic Discourse and Saintly Relics 684-1090

by

Felice Lifshitz

PONTIFICAL INSTITUTE OF MEDIAEVAL STUDIES

The preparation of this volume was made possible in part by a grant
from the F.I.U. Foundation.

BR
847
.N67
L54
1995

CANADIAN CATALOGUING IN PUBLICATION DATA

Lifshitz, Felice, 1959-
　　The Norman conquest of pious Neustria

(Studies and texts, ISSN 0082-5328 ; 122)
Includes bibliographical references and index.
ISBN 0-88844-122-3

1. Normandy (France) - Church history - Historiography.
2. Normandy (France) - History - To 1515 - Sources.
I. Pontifical Institute of Mediaeval Studies.　　II. Title.
III. Series: Studies and texts (Pontifical Institute of
Mediaeval Studies) ; 122.

BR847.N67L54 1995　　　274.4'203'0722　　　C95-932180-2

Printed in the United States of America by
Edwards Brothers Incorporated

To my mother for reading to me,
and to my father for working so hard.

Contents

Acknowledgements

This book began as a dissertation at Columbia University. The research for and writing of the original dissertation was funded during 1986-87 and 1987-88 by a Columbia University Travelling Fellowship and a Whiting Foundation Fellowship. Further research in subsequent years was funded, through a variety of grants and mini-grants, by Florida International University. The book itself was written during the 1993-94 academic year, for the most part while I was a Visiting Fellow at the Pontifical Institute of Mediaeval Studies in Toronto, Canada.

This book has been long in the making. It is difficult to pin-point precisely when it began to become the book it now is, rather than some other, quite different book which would have required different acknowledgements. At Barnard College and Columbia University I had the privilege of learning from William Harriss, Elaine Pagels, Morton Smith, Suzanne Wemple, Robert Somerville, John Hine Mundy, J.M.W. Bean, Eugene Rice, Wim Smit, Nancy Leys Stepan and Isser Woloch. Training in "modern" European history and historiography has been crucial over the years as I have grappled with the image of the "middle ages" bequeathed to and propagated by twentieth-century scholars. Malcolm Bean, my primary mentor and the sponsor of the dissertation from which this book ultimately grew, has continued to support and encourage me over the past six years as he did during my years at Columbia. I had the great fortune as well to spend more than a year during 1986 and 1987 in Europe, and to be advised throughout that year of research by Baily Young, Jean-Charles Picard, Léopold Génicot, Martin Heinzelmann, Joseph-Claude Poulin and, above all, François Dolbeau, all of whom introduced me to technicalities of archeological, codicological and other types of research that cannot be acquired in a classroom while sitting on this side of the Atlantic.

Over the years I have discussed issues central to or connected with this book with, and received relevant off-prints and unpublished work from, Richard Abels, David Bates, Thomas Head, Gerda Huisman, Richard Landes, Kimberly LoPrete, Cassandra Potts, Rachel Schwartz, Leah Shopkow, and David Spear. Conversations with several present and former colleagues (Eric Leed, Jerma Jackson and, above all, my husband Joseph F. Patrouch) have been even more frequent and more intense and, therefore, more influential on the final shape of the book. Earlier stages of the present book were read in manuscript form by, and often significantly improved through the comments of, Benjamin Arnold, Bernard S. Bachrach, Kate Cooper, Sheila Delany, Nancy Gauthier, Patrick F. Geary, Walter Goffart, Yitzak Hen, J.N. Hillgarth, Alan Kahan, Paul Oskar Kristellar, Jacques Le Maho, Michael Pammer and Hugh Thomas. Elizabeth Dingman provided not only commentary but also the perfect locale in which to live, as I wrote, in Toronto. The errors which remain are entirely my responsibility.

Abbreviations

AASS   *Acta Sanctorum*, eds. Hagiographi Bollandiani (Antwerp, 1643 ff.)

AB   *Analecta Bollandiana*

Acta Archiepi-scoporum   *Acta Archiepiscoporum Rotomagensium*, ed. J. Mabillon Vetera Analecta II (Paris, 1675); repr. PL 147

AM   *Archéologie Médiévale*

Anglo-Norman Studies   *Proceedings of the Battle Conference*, eds. R.A. Brown (vols. 1-11), and M. Chibnall (vols. 12 ff.)

ASOSB   *Acta Sanctorum Ordinis Sancti Benedicti*, ed. Jean Mabillon, 5 vols. (Paris, 1668-1701)

Atsma, ed. La Neustrie   Atsma, Hartmut ed., *La Neustrie. Les pays au nord de la Loire de 650-850* (Colloque historique international; Beihefte der Francia 16/1-2, 1989)

BHL   *Bibliotheca Hagiographica Latina*, eds. Hagiographi Bollandiani I-II and Supplements (Brussels, 1989-1911, 1987)

BM   Bibliothèque Municipale

BN lat.   Paris, Bibliothèque Nationale, ms. latin

BN NAL   Paris, Bibliothèque Nationale, ms. Nouvelle acquisition latine

BR   Brussels, Bibliothèque Royale Albert Ier

BSS   *Bibliotheca Sanctorum*, 1-12 plus index (Rome, 1960)

CCHP   *Catalogus Codicum Hagiographicorum Latinorum Antiquiorum Saeculo xvi qui asservanter in Biblioteca Nationali Parisiensi*, I-III (Subsidia Hagiographica 2), eds. Hagiographi Bollandiani (Brussels, 1889-1893)

CCHR   *Catalogus Codicum Hagiographicorum Latinorum Bibliotecae Rotomagensis*, eds. Hagiographi Bollandiani (AB 23; 1903)

CCSL   Corpus Christianorum, Series Latina

CSEL   Corpus Scriptorum Ecclesiasticorum Latinorum

Dudo, De moribus   Dudo of St. Quentin, *De moribus et actis primorum Normanniae ducum*, ed. Jules Lair (Mémoires de la Société des Antiquaires de Normandie 23; Caen, 1865)

EME   *Early Medieval Europe*

Fauroux   *Receuil des actes des ducs de Normandie (911-1066)*, ed. Marie Fauroux (Mémoires de la Société des Antiquaires de Normandie 36; Caen, 1961)

Flodoard — Flodoard of Reims, *Les Annales de Flodoard*, ed. Philippe Lauer (Collection de Textes pour servir à l'étude et à l'enseignement de l'histoire 39; Paris, 1905)

Flodoard, HER — Flodoard of Reims, *Historia Ecclesiae Remensis*, eds. J. Heller and G.H. Waitz in MGH SS 13 (Hannover, 1881)

GC — *Gallia Christiana in provincias distributa*, I-XVI (Paris, 1715-1785 and 1856-1865)

Gérard de Brogne — *St. Gérard de Brogne et son oeuvre réformatrice* (Acts of the Millenary Conference on Gerard's Death, 1959) *Revue Benedictine* 70 (1960)

HLF — *Histoire Littéraire de la France*

"Il Secolo di Ferro" — *Settimane* 38 (1990)

Jumièges — *Jumièges. Congrès scientifique du XIIIe centenaire (Rouen, June 1954)* (Rouen, 1955)

MGH — Monumenta Germaniae Historica

MGH AA — MGH Auctores Antiquissimi

MGH SRG — MGH Scriptores Rerum Germanicarum

MGH SRM — MGH Scriptores Rerum Merovingicarum

MGH SS — MGH Scriptores

OV — Orderic Vitalis, *The Ecclesiastical History of Orderic Vitalis*, I-VI ed. and trans. Marjorie Chibnall (Oxford, 1968-1980)

PL — *Patrologiae cursus completus*, series latina, ed. J.-P. Migne (Paris, 1844-1864)

RHEF 62 (1976) — Riché, Pierre, ed., "La Christianisation des pays entre Loire et Rhin, IVe-VIIe siècles" (Actes du Colloque de Nanterre, May 1974; *Revue d'Histoire de l'Eglise de France* 62 [1976])

Richer — Richer of Reims, *Histoire de France, 999-995*, ed. and trans. Robert Latouche (Classiques de l'Histoire de France au Moyen Age 12 and 17; Paris, 1930)

"Santi e demoni" — *Settimane* 36 (1988)

Settimane — *Settimane di studio del Centro italiano di studi sull'alto medioevo* (Spoleto)

Ste. Gen. — Paris, Bibliothèque Sainte-Geneviève ms.

Vat. palat. lat. — Bibliotheca del Vaticano, ms. Palatinus latinus

Vat. reg. lat. — Bibliotheca del Vaticano, ms. Reginensis latinus

Vies des saints — Benedictines of Paris/Baudot-Chaussin, *Vies des saints et des bienheureux selon l'ordre du calendrier avec l'historique des fêtes*, I - XII (Paris, 1952)

1

Introduction: Discourse and Definitions in the Historiography of Religious Change

Despite nearly two millennia of historiography on the subject of Christian evangelization and conversion, we know almost nothing for certain about the process whereby Europe "became Christian."[1] The tremendous difficulty involved in the task of reconstructing so apparently complicated and multi-faceted a process has clearly never stopped historians from writing religious history, not in the tenth century and not in the twentieth. Historians have differed over every conceivable aspect of the conversion scenario.[2] For instance, the main cause of conversion has been presented as everything from preaching through miracles through example to coercion.[3] The leading actors in the process have sometimes been kings and queens, sometimes bishops, sometimes hermits, sometimes aristocratic lay individuals, sometimes women, and others besides.[4] Conversion has been

---

[1] Hans-Dieter Kahl, "Die ersten Jahrhunderte des missionsgeschichtlichen Mittelalters" in *Kirchengeschichte als Missionsgeschichte* II: *Die Kirche des Früheren Mittelalters* I ed. Knut Schäferdiek (Munich, 1978) pp. 23-31.

[2] For instance, see the recent debate over Ramsey MacMullen *Christianizing the Roman Empire, AD 100-400* (New Haven, 1984) pp. 1-9 and pp. 74-85 and R. MacMullen "Conversion: a historian's view" *The Second Century* 5 (1985/6) pp. 67-81: W. B. Babcock "MacMullen on conversion: a response" *The Second Century* 5 (1985/6) pp. 82-89; Mark D. Jordan "Philosophic 'Conversion' and Christian Conversion: A Gloss on Professor MacMullen" *The Second Century* 5 (1985/6) pp. 90-96; F. Parente "L'idea di conversione da Nock ad oggi" *Augustinianum* 27 (1987) 7-25; D. Praet, "Explaining the Christianization of the Roman Empire. Older Theories and Recent Developments" *Sacris Erudiri* 23 (1992-1993) pp. 5-119.

[3] J.N. Hillgarth, "Modes of evangelization of Western Europe in the Seventh Century" in *Irland und die Christenheit/ Ireland and Christendom: Bibelstudien und Mission/The Bible and the Missions* (Acta of the Conference "Irland und die Christenheit," Dublin, 1984) eds. Proínséas Ní Chatháin and Michael Richter (Veröffentlichungen des Europazentrums Tübingen: Kulturwissenschaftliche Reihe; Stuttgart, 1987) p. 326.

[4] Some examples: C. Grosset "Hypothèses sur l'évangelisation du Cotentin: III- Un Poitevin de bonne famille: Paterne" *Revue du Département de la Manche* XV (1973) pp. 41-59; K. F. Werner, "Le rôle de l'aristocratie dans la Christianisation du

perceived both as a gradual evolution and as a catastrophic and therefore datable event, while within both scenarios some authors have imagined that the process (or event) proceeded smoothly, others that it faced concerted resistance.[5] Some historians have considered the establishment of an organized institutional church a *sine qua non* of complete "Christianization," while others have not.[6]

Little of the literature on the religious history of Europe that was composed before the nineteenth century is taken very seriously by nineteenth- and twentieth-century historians. As long ago as 1944, Eva Sanford called for "a thorough appraisal of the medieval types of historical revisionism," and asked "modern critics" to take seriously their "medieval" predecessors.[7] To my knowledge, the present work is the first book-length study to do so. The present work examines the religious historiography of

---

nord-est de la Gaule" in "La Christianisation des pays entre Loire et Rhin, IVe-VIIe siècles" (Actes du Colloque de Nanterre, May 1974) ed. Pierre Riché (*Revue d'Histoire de l'Eglise de France* 62 (1976) pp. 45-72; Felice Lifshitz, "Des femmes missionnaires. L'exemple de la Gaule" *Revue d'Histoire Ecclésiastique* 83 (1988) pp. 5-33. Against the importance of women missionaries, see Michelle Renee Salzman "Aristocratic Women: Conductors of Christianity in the Fourth Century?" *Helios* 16 (1989) pp. 207-220.

[5]   G. Bonner "The extinction of paganism and the Church historian" *Journal of Ecclesiastical History* 35 (1984) pp. 339-357; Alain Dierkens "Quelques aspects de la christianisation du pays mosan à l'époque mérovingienne" in *La Civilisation mérovingienne dans le Bassin Mosan* (Actes du colloque Internationale d'Amy-Liège; August, 1985) pp. 31-33.

[6]   Roblin only defines the sacred spots in his study, and therefore the Oise region, as having been "Christianized" in the eighth century when the sacred springs and cemeteries of the area seem to have been incorporated into a parochial church structure, evidenced through the construction of stone church buildings (Michel Roblin, "Fontaines sacrées et nécropoles antiques, deux sites fréquents d'églises paroissiales rurales dans les sept anciens diocèses de l'Oise" *RHEF* 62 [1976] pp. 235-251). Patrick Geary rejects the equation "Christianity = Church" and argues that the fourth and fifth centuries were marked by a Christianity (centered around bone/relic cults of the dead) which had nothing to do with the Roman-style administration of "the Church," the absence of which has led many scholars to call the period "pagan" ("Cults Without Impresarios," Plenary Address to the Sewanee Mediaeval Colloquium, "Saints and Their Cults in the Middle Ages," April, 1993).

[7]   Eva Sanford "The Study of Ancient History in the Middle Ages" *Journal of the History of Ideas* 5 (1944) pp. 21-43. I owe this reference to Leah Shopkow.

what is now Normandy, which was before that Neustria, and before that the Second Lyonnais, using narratives that were composed between the late seventh century and the late eleventh century. A study of the historiography of Christianization raises, in the first instance, a question of definitions: what do I mean, for the purposes of this study, by "Christianity" and "Christianization?" (The question is also raised, what do I mean by "historiography?" I mean "representations of the past;" I will return, in the second part of this introductory chapter, to the question of "historiography.")

It seems impossible, despite Herculean efforts, to get a solid grip on "Christianity;"[8] the very attempt to find a unitary definition of something which was, in fact, not defined during much of the period under review, would be counterproductive to the enterprise.[9] The definition of which practices and beliefs are meaningfully Christian has not remained static over the centuries. The tremendous amount of conciliar legislation of the fifth, sixth and seventh centuries should suffice to indicate how much official Christian practice was just beginning to be established by the bishops and the princes who claimed the power to do so during those centuries.[10] Going a step further, the mere existence of authoritarian pronouncements made by bishops in council does not ever automatically translate into a lock-step acceptance of new definitions either by laypeople or even by the clergy. We would hardly be on safe ground were we to take conciliar legislation as a reliable index of generally-accepted norms of Christian behavior.

Because of the constant process of redefinition of Christian practice,

---

[8] See the hundred-page attempt at a definition in "Christentum der Bekehrungszeit" in *Reallexikon der Germanischen Altertumskunde* (2nd. ed, IV.5) pp. 501-599.

[9] In this regard, the present **historiographical** study is the polar opposite of the **scientistic** approach advanced by James Russell in *The Germanization of Early Medieval Christianity. A Sociohistorical Approach to Religious Transformation* (Oxford, 1994). There is a valuable discussion of a problem related to the central issue of the present study, namely that of the definition of "heresy," in Howard Kaminsky's "The Problematics of Later-Medieval 'Heresy'" in *Husitství-Reformace-Renasance* eds. J. Pánek, et. al. (Prague, 1994) pp. 133-154. The necessity to conceptualize one's definition of Christianity and Christianization in the broadest possible terms was also emphasized by Leonard P. Boyle in "Popular Religion: What is Popular?" (Plenary Address to the International Medieval Congress, Leeds 1994).

[10] C. de Clercq *Concilia Galliae, 511-695* (CCSL 148A; Turnhout, 1963) and C. de Clercq *La legislation religieuse franque de Clovis à Charlemagne* (Louvain/Paris, 1936).

an area that has been Christianized according to the definitions of one era, can suddenly find itself labelled as "pagan" against the yardstick of another. Take, for example, debates over the veneration of saints, a practice which has been assigned as frequently to "paganism" as to Christianity. The view that saints' cults are remnants of "pagan" practice and result from the polytheistic leanings of a besotted populace, is at the moment out of favor in the scholarly literature;[11] nevertheless, its effects have been deeply felt in much of the historiography of Christianization. Any author who believes the veneration of saints to be, essentially, a "not-Christian" practice, will inevitably write the history of the evangelization of Europe through that prism. As a general practice, a number of historians have measured whether or not Christianization has been achieved in a particular area against his or her own definition of Christianity.[12]

There is no guarantee that populations identified as "not-Christians," whether in a contemporary or near-contemporary source or in a twentieth-century history of Christianization, did not in fact identify themselves as Christians. Indeed, even a contemporary narrative purportedly describing how a given territory was initially "Christianized" may well mask another reality, namely how the Christians that area were persuaded to abandon their definition of Christianity in favor of a new one. For instance, we are privy to the thoughts of at least one Latin Christian missionary on the

---

[11]   Particularly after Peter Brown *The Cult of the Saints. Its Rise and Function in Latin Christianity* (Chicago, 1981) pp. 13-22.

[12]   For instance, Delumeau's provocative but misguided arguments have placed the Christianization of Europe in the eighteenth and even the nineteenth century; since his definition of Christianity was a modern definition, it is not surprising that he found Christianity finally to have arrived in Europe when modern Christianity did (J. Delumeau, *Le catholicisme entre Luther et Voltaire* [Paris, 1971]). The most blatant recent statement of this sort of anachronistic judgmentalism is Gurevich's assertion that "the Christian Middle Ages" is a legend-not because the "Middle Ages" is a historiographic construct, but because there was no "Christianity" in the "Middle Ages," only folkore, animism, naturalism and superficial faith (Aaron J. Gurevich, *Contadini e santi. Problemi della cultura popolare nel Medioevo* [Turin, 1986; Italian translation of Russian original *Problemy Srednevekovoj narodnoj Kul'tury* (Moscow, 1981)] pp. 345-346). Similar expressions of Gurevich's views can be found in his *Historical Anthropology of the Middle Ages* ed. and trans. Jana Howlett (Chicago, 1992) pp. 14, 28, 44. On the other hand, Gurevich himself has also called for a study of Christianization which takes into account changing definitions of Christian practice (*Historical Anthropology* p. 119).

subject of proper Christian practice, namely Martin of Braga, through his writings to his fellow missionary Polemius *circa* 574. Martin highlights a series of practices which he considers "not-Christian" and tantamount to Devil worship; at the top of the list is the following:

> Error, too, so deceives the ignorant, that they think the Kalends [1st] of January is the beginning of the year, which is entirely false. For, as Holy Scripture says, the eighth day before the Kalends of April [March 25], at the equinox, was constituted the beginning of the first year. For so we read: "And God divided the light and the darkness" [Genesis 1:4]. For every division entails equality, and so on [March 25] the day has as many hours as the night. And so it is false that the Kalends [1st] of January is the beginning of the year.[13]

According to Martin's definition, the inhabitants of twentieth-century Europe and North America would be considered "pagans" even though they might, for the most part, identify themselves as "Christians;" there is a very good possibility that the rustics of whom Martin wrote would likewise have identified themselves as already Christianized.

Somewhat more radical examples of concurrent and competing definitions of Christianization can also be adduced here. First, there is the revealing anecdote told by Gregory of Tours about his great-grandfather Gregorius, bishop of Dijon (†539/540).[14] Apparently the country-folk had long been venerating a certain Benignus, a local martyr, and their prayers were nearly always successfully answered. Therefore the new bishop assumed that the locals were members of a "not-Christian" sect, and so he attempted to prevent them from worshipping at the shrine of Benignus. In the end, the devotion was imposed upon Gregorius, but his initial reaction speaks volumes about the divergent definitions of a religion that can be in force at a single moment, and particularly about relations between officials and the (mindless?) "body" of the faithful. In this case, it seems that Gregorius was forced to alter his conception of Christianity to conform to local practice.

---

[13] Martin of Braga, *Martini episcopi Bracarensis Opera Omnia* (Papers and Monographs of the American Academy in Rome, 12; New Haven, 1950) ed. C. W. Barlow pp. 189-190; the text is quoted using the translation of J.N. Hillgarth in *Christianity and Paganism, 350-750. The Conversion of Western Europe* (Philadelphia, 1986) p. 59.

[14] Gregory of Tours, *Liber in gloria martyrum* (= *Libri octo miraculorum* 1; ed. B. Krusch MGH SRM 1.2 [Hannover, 1884]) c. 50 pp. 522-524.

A similar dynamic may underlie one of the missionary episodes in Fulbertus' biography of Romanus, a tenth-century history of the Christianization of Neustria that will be the centerpiece of Part II of the present study. According to Fulbertus' chronology, bishop Romanus of Rouen would have been a contemporary of Gregorius of Dijon. Fulbertus describes Romanus' evangelization of the rural areas of his diocese in terms of two temple exorcism scenes; it is the first of these scenes which particularly concerns us here.[15] Romanus came upon a church "which had been used as a temple by the original heathen inhabitants," and which was, at the time of his arrival, a church served by Christian priests.[16] The local priests had been assuring the populace that the edifice was, in fact, "kosher," yet when Romanus approached the church, "he saw the most hideous crowd of unclean spirits sitting atop the high gables of the temple, and they were hastening to resist him, eager to fight any enemy who tried to invade the interior chambers" (fol. 122r). The bishop courageously entered the sanctuary, only to discover golden idols, all of which

---

[15] Quotations from Fulbertus' *Vita Romani* are my own translations of the text as transcribed in Appendix 2 from Paris BN lat. 13.090 and Evreux BM 101; citations are to folios which match the transcription in that Appendix.

[16] Such reutilization of ancient religious sites was apparently common in the Christianization process. See Bede *Ecclesiastical History of the English Church and People* B. Colgrave and R.A.B. Minors eds. and trans. (Oxford, 1969) pp. 106-109; L. Michael White *Building God's House in the Roman World. Architectural Adaptation among Pagans, Jews and Christians* (Baltimore, 1990); Bryan Ward-Perkins *From Classical Antiquity to the Middle Ages: Urban Public Building in Northern and Central Italy, AD 300-800* (Oxford, 1984), especially ch. 10, "Spoliation and Reuse of Unwanted Buildings" pp. 203-229; V.I. Flint, *The Rise of Magic in Early Medieval Europe* (Princeton, 1991) pp. 254-273; Roblin, "Fontaines sacrées et nécropoles antiques;" J. Hubert, "Sources sacrées et sources saintes" *Comptes-rendus de l'Academie des Inscriptions et Belles-Lettres* (1967) pp. 567-573. One justification for the policy was formulated by Augustine: to take buildings and practices which are "good" from another group is only to take away what never really belonged to that other group in the first place (Augustine, *Aurelii Augustini Hipponiensis Episcopi Epistulae* ed. A. Goldbacher [CSEL 34; Prague/Vienna/Leipzig, 1895] Epistle 47, pp. 132-133). This same Augustine, it is worth remarking, has been accused of being a "Neo-Platonist" (or a "not-Christian") in "Christian's" clothing, when measured against nineteenth- and twentieth-century definitions of "Christianity" (James J. McEvoy "Neoplatonism and Christianity: Influence, Syncretism or Discernment" *The Relationship Between Neoplatonism and Christianity* eds. Thomas Finan and Vincent Twomey [Dublin, 1992] pp. 155-170).

fell in ruins to the ground at his approach. As a finale, Romanus caused the entire edifice to sink into the ground, "not without the admiration of the onlookers." He then moved on to a nearby temple of Mercury and Apollo, where "at his advent the whole statue-filled temple collapsed precipitously and dissolved into a powder" (fol. 122v). Romanus had, in a day's work, destroyed one "Christian" church and one "not-Christian" temple, both of which shared the identical offending characteristic: they contained "idols."

Fulbertus makes it clear that the local population and their priests, who worshipped in a church filled with "idols," considered themselves to be Christian. According to Fulbertus' own definition, Christianity could not embrace the veneration of any "idols" (or "demons"), and so the meaning he ascribed to Romanus' actions was Christian evangelization. But the veneration of "idols" seems to have been considered compatible with or part of Christianity for some people, and Fulbertus was at least able to conceive of such persons; he may have considered them grossly misguided, but he did not consider them to be a logical impossibility.

What is essential to Christianity, in terms of a practicable definition to be used by historians? At the end of the sixth century, at least one Latin missionary considered the date one celebrated the beginning of the New Year to be an important index of the success of Christianization efforts. Other Latin leaders, especially in the fourth and fifth centuries, had adhered to more minimalist definitions, for instance that a person be baptised.[17] Although having undergone baptism was considered a sufficient definition of a Christian in the post-Constantinian world, that had not been the case during the pre-Constantinian illegal phase when being a Christian could mean risking one's life, and tends also not to be the case for nineteenth- and twentieth-century historians of Christianization, who have frequently argued that "religion" is "interior" and requires private conviction, not ritual formality. Being a Christian can mean living a life

---

[17] Robert Markus *The End of Ancient Christianity* (Cambridge, 1990) p. 53. Markus' own solution to the problem of definition (pp. 1-17) distinguishes "sacred" and "secular" spheres; he argues that between 300 and 600 there was a narrowing among Christians of the "secular" sphere accompanied by a sacralization of every aspect of society. Yet Markus himself admits that, in the ancient world, "religion" was, or could be, directly relevant to every aspect of culture, and that ancient society did not distinguish sacred and secular spheres (p. 7).

totally distinct from that of one's neighbors, or it can mean conforming to mass practice.

The Christian tradition can veer from "Blessed are the peacemakers" to launching the crusades, and this is not in spite of but because of one of the top contenders for "essential" status, namely, the Bible which, in and of itself, provides justification for every conceivable stance. There are some definitions of Christianity according to which the Bible can be seen as both essential to the religion, and as itself providing a measure against which to judge Christianization; Martin Luther's *sola scriptura* dictum is the most famous of these theologies. But the Bible is an extraordinarily rich library of texts, open to manifold interpretations; *sola scriptura* has never prevented a plethora of interpretations from flourishing simultaneously.

The difficulty, however, runs deeper than variable interpretations of a single text, for *sola scriptura* presupposes a special attitude about texts, as well as the widespread circulation of standardized texts. I have seen very little evidence from the seventh through the eleventh century of bibliocentrism; that is precisely why so many ninth-, tenth- and eleventh-century historians could write histories of Dionysius the Areopagite, Martial of Limoges, Mary Magdalen and a host of other figures, histories which would be truculently attacked by Luther himself and by a host of other bibliocentrists of a later era, when the definition of Christianity was radically revised. Pre-thirteenth-century manuscripts testify to quite a different relationship with the written word from the one to which Luther ascribed.[18]

---

[18]   There can be no better illustration of the lack of veneration of a precise text during the period covered by this study than the ninth-century epic poem *The Heliand* (*Heliand und Genesis* ed. Otto Behaghel [9th ed, reworked by Burkhard Taeger, Tübingen, 1984]). The poet was a master of "...intercultural communication. He rewrote and reimagined the events and words of the gospel as if they had taken place and been spoken in his own country and time....in order to help the Saxons cease their vacillation between their warrior-loyalty to the old gods and to the 'mighty Christ'" (G. Ronald Murphy trans. *The Heliand. The Saxon Gospel* [Oxford, 1992] pp. xiii-xvi; also see G. Ronald Murphy *The Saxon Savior. The Germanic Transformation of the Gospel in the Ninth-century Heliand* [Oxford, 1989]). For instance, the poet used the image of warrior-companionship in a *comitatus* (for example, in Song 26 (trans. Murphy p. 72; ed. Behagel/Taeger pp. 82-84), rather than that of the disciple-group of a rabbi which had spoken to the world of Hellenized Judaism; the *magi* too, ancient middle eastern philosopher-astrologers, became foreign

Every scribe was apparently free to alter texts when copying them; that is part of the explanation for why there are no two identical breviaries, even for the same church or monastery.[19] It was not until the thirteenth century that there is any evidence of the simple re-copying of saints' biographies into legendaries without significant alterations.[20]

Among all the discussions of Christianization over the past ten years, among the boldest has been that by Dierkens, who shows how the evolution of ideals of precision concerning practice could mean that a particular custom might go from being considered non-Christian to being considered anti-Christian.[21] But the point is not simply to recognize that practices considered during a certain period or by certain groups to be positively "anti-Christian" can also, during some other period or in some other culture, be "tolerated" either as indifferent or as simply "non-Christian." Fulbertus' biography of Romanus indicates that some eventually-purged customs can be considered not as indifferent but as positively "Christian." Fulbertus rejected the incorporation of "idols" into Christianity though he knew some priests and faithful thought otherwise; sixteenth-century reformers rejected the incorporation of saints' cults and relic cults into Christianity,

---

warriors. The prophetic dimension of the Greek Gospels was suppressed: the Heliand poet never once presents an event as the fulfillment of biblical prophecy, whereas the leitmotif of the Gospel of Matthew, for instance, had been the rigorous logical subordination of every episode to some earlier biblical prophecy. In the Saxon context, the Hebrew Bible had no pre-existent authority, and it meant less than nothing that the episodes of Jesus' life could be shaped to conform to certain prophecies contained within that sacred text. Battles over the Mosaic Law, which had dominated the narrative in the Greek gospels, are absent, for the *Heliand* poet did not care about Jesus' pronouncements concerning sabbatarian observances, dietary restrictions and marital regulation. In other words, the poet did not take the Gospel as "gospel."

[19] Victor Leroquais *Les bréviaires manuscrits des bibliothèques publiques de la France* I-V (Paris, 1934) I pp. liii-lx.

[20] Guy Philippart *Les légendiers latins et autres manuscrits hagiographiques* (Typologie des sources du Moyen Age Occidental 24-25; Turnhout, 1977) p. 46.

[21] Dierkens, "Quelques aspects de la christianisation" pp. 32-33. I owe this important reference to Léopold Génicot. Others had touched upon the problem of definition, but avoided facing its implications squarely. Grosset, for instance, believed that the inhabitants of the Cotentin against whom Merovingian kings and queens sponsored "Christianizing" missions were not actually "païens au vrai sens du mot" ("Hypothèses sur l'évangelisation" p. 44).

although they knew that many priests and many of the faithful considered those cults positively part of the definition of Christianity.

Valerie Flint has shown how, during the sixth through tenth centuries, certain forms of ancient *magia* were actively rescued, preserved and promoted by prominent members of the ecclesiastical elite, after Roman-era elites had attempted to stamp out *magia* in all its manifestations.[22] "Magical" practices thus became a part of Christianity, they became a part of the very definition of Christianity. By the sixteenth century, however, "witches" were burned for engaging in the very same practices which had been prescribed by tenth-century clerics.[23] It is therefore not at all impossible that "idols" were, for many Christians, at times positively a part of the definition of Christianity.

"Idols" are not the only aspect of religious practice that have been in dispute. Consider the well-known sixth-century princely burials beneath St. Denis and the Cologne cathedral, burials which include traces of ritual fires and remains of animals.[24] To at least one twentieth-century historian, this evidence supports the conclusion that Christianity only very slowly drove out "paganism" because that author considers these particular mortuary practices essentially incompatible with Christianity, meaning that the princes in question cannot have been fully Christian.[25] Yet, again and again, similar food practices have been at the center of controversies over what constitutes "full" Christianization. St. Monica, Augustine's mother, was only persuaded by her respect for Ambrose of Milan to abandon her practice of bringing food to the cemetery.[26] Other examples can be

---

[22] Flint *Rise of Magic* pp. 4-12. Flint's conclusions have recently been both challenged by Richard Kieckhefer, "The Specific Rationality of Medieval Magic" *American Historical Review* 99 (1994) pp. 813-836 and seconded by Yitzak Hen "Popular Culture in Merovingian Gaul" (Ph.D. Dissertation, Cambridge 1994).

[23] Flint, *Rise of Magic* p. 83.

[24] J. Werner, "Frankish Royal Tombs in the Cathedrals of Cologne and St. Denis" *Antiquity* 38 (1964) pp. 201-216.

[25] Hillgarth, "Modes of evangelization" p. 328. It is true that Hillgarth's definition is not exclusively an idiosyncratic or personal one, but is in line with the stances of Gregory the Great and other observers contemporary with the events in question. Nevertheless, the opinions of a few powerful and prolific authors cannot realistically be allowed to stand as the sole standards for a historical understanding of Christian practice.

[26] Augustine *Confessions* VI.2 trans. R.S. Pine-Coffin (London, 1961).

found even closer to home. The late-nineteenth-century devotional forms of southern Italian Catholic immigrants to the United States were denounced as "pagan" and "sacrilegious" by American Catholic officials of the day,[27] while those immigrants' own word for themselves, used with pride, was precisely "cristiani."[28] The dual problem for the theologians and officials was the importance of food-and-drink-centered *feste* and of eating and drinking in the *domus* to the immigrants' definition of Christianity.[29] I hope that, by putting the St. Denis and Cologne burials in an accessible context, I have thrown serious doubt on any attempt to label those famous burials "not-Christian" on the basis of food remains.

If Christian practice always changes over time and space, as indeed it seems to, then any historian who is not conscientiously and vigilantly attending to changing definitions will, in effect, simply apply an anachronistic and culturally-irrelevant definition to his or her subject. The various authors whose histories I shall examine in this study all operated on then-current definitions of Christianity which, when applied to earlier periods, made those earlier periods appear to be "not-Christian." Both Carolingian princes and their successors in Neustria, that is the Vikings, benefitted from discourse which presented earlier inhabitants of the diocese of Rouen as "not-Christians." Whether or not the individuals in question had in fact been Christians became irrelevant, for there are few weapons more powerful than historiographic discourse. The "past" itself evaporates, and can hardly assert its own point of view; historical narrative, however, lives on, and the historian can assert whatever he or she wishes about the "past," effectively unimpeded. This study of the historiography of Christianization in the Second Lyonnais-Neustria-Normandy is therefore a study of the effects of changing definitions of Christianity and of changing political contexts on the complex interplay between concrete self-perceived reality and abstract historiographic discourse.

Neustria seems, in "reality," to have been Christianized by the Merovingian era; Carolingian- and Norman-era discursive strategies, however, sought to deny that reality altogether. Merovingian-era evidence testifies

---

[27] Robert Orsi *The Madonna of 115th Street: Faith and Community in Italian Harlem, 1880-1950* (New Haven, 1985) p. xvi.

[28] Orsi, *Madonna of 115th St.* p. xvii and 83-86.

[29] Orsi, *Madonna of 115th St.* pp. xxi-xxii, 75-77, 172-173.

neither to rampant "not-Christianity" ("paganism") nor to a decrepit, corrupt religious life in Francia; nevertheless, Carolingian- and post-Carolingian historiography has asserted such a "past" into existence.[30] That
particular discursive transformation will form the subject of Part I of the
present study. Part II of the study will focus on the Norman period. Norman historiography is a text-book example of the power of discourse.
Every indicator of concrete "reality" evidences relative continuity and minimal disruption, from Carolingian Neustria to Viking Normandy.[31] Yet
the narratives of various purveyors of the myth of Norman sacred destiny
were able to claim through mere words that what in fact was a complete
continuity should be considered an epoch-making transformation, in part
because the Viking settlement entailed, finally, the effective "Christianization" of the region. Within Merovingian and Carolingian historiography,
the greatest attention will be paid to the biographies and cult of bishop
Audoenus of Rouen, the principal patron of the diocese throughout its
"Neustrian" phase of identity. Within Viking Normandy and Norman
historiography, the greatest attention will be paid to the biographies and
cult of bishop Romanus of Rouen, who replaced Audoenus as principal
patron of the see and as principal symbol of regional identity.[32]

[30]   Similar arguments have recently been made by Yitzak Hen, on the basis of
liturgical sources of the Merovingian era, in "Popular Culture in Merovingian
Gaul" and in "Merovingian Liturgy in Cultural Perspective" (Paper presented to the
International Medieval Congress, Leeds 1994).

[31]   Felice Lifshitz, "La Normandie Carolingienne" (forthcoming Annales de Normandie); Felice Lifshitz, "Dudo's Historical Narrative and the Norman Succession
of 996" (Journal of Medieval History 20 (1994) pp. 101-120). For other recent work
tending to minimize the vision of rupture or discontinuity between the ninth and
tenth centuries in Upper Normandy, see David Bates, "Rouen from 900 to 1204:
From Scandinavian Settlement to Angevin 'Capital'" in Medieval Art, Architecture
and Archeology At Rouen, British Archeological Association Conference Transactions
(XII, 1993) ed. Jenny Stratford pp. 1-11 and Patrick Périn, "Les objets vikings du
Musée des Antiquités de la Seine-Maritime" Recueil d'études en hommage à Lucien
Musset (Cahiers des Annales de Normandie, XXIII, Caen, 1990) pp. 161-188.

[32]   A measure of the importance of Romanus, who is little known today outside
of France, during the period covered by this study may be found in the aftermath
of the third miracle ascribed to Romanus in an early-eleventh-century collection
of his wonders. A clerk of Rouen who, en route to Jerusalem, has been saved from
shipwreck by Romanus, does not even linger in Jerusalem itself, but rushes home
to Rouen: "For coming very expeditiously to the end of the road on which he had

The two principal methodological premises of this study are the following: that narratives describing the activities of saints such as Audoenus and Romanus are fully historiographical, and that the activities of producing historical narrative, on the one hand, and of instituting and elaborating saints' cults on the other, are generated by one and the same impulse, an impulse which is fundamentally "political." I use "political" in the broadest possible sense, to indicate the state of being enmeshed in those material and ideal power relations which have been the subject of philosophical musings at least since Plato and Aristotle. Humans are political animals, those denizens of the Athenian *polis* asserted so many centuries ago; any subject which requires attention to human relations is a political subject.

It must always be kept in mind as well that "historiae," during the period covered by this study, were not only literary narratives about the past, often prominently featuring saints and read by the learned both individually and in groups, but were also public liturgical offices performed according to a whole cycle of festivals in each local tradition.[33] It was through participation in traditional festivals that most people, including the clergy, acquired their identities and their visions of the past. Neither a compulsory public ritual in which historical identities are enshrined and disseminated, nor any historical narrative, can ever be removed from its social and political contexts.[34]

---

begun, as soon as he had completed his vows he went away from the Holy Sepulchre and returned to his natal soil, turning neither to the right nor to the left, not even waiting to say goodbye or to embrace or to receive the kisses of his friends, but made a beeline for the church of blessed Romanus" (fol. 34r). Quotations from the *Miracula Romani* (unknown to the Bibliotheca Hagiographica Latina [= BHL]) are from my translation of the text, which is transcribed in Appendix 2 below from Evreux BM ms. 101; citations are according to the foliation of the manuscript.

[33] Ritva Jonsson *Historia. Etudes sur la genèse des offices versifiés* (Stockholm, 1968; Studia Latina Stockholmensia 15).

[34] F. Lifshitz, "Beyond Positivism and Genre: "Hagiographical" Texts as Historical Narrative" (*Viator* 25 (1994) pp. 95-113); François Dolbeau, "Les hagiographes au travail: collecte et traitement des documents écrits (IXe-XIIe siècles). Avec annexe: une discussion chronologique du XIIe siècle (édition de BHL 5824e)" in *Manuscrits hagiographiques et travail des hagiographes* ed. M. Heinzelmann (Beihefte der Francia 24; 1992) pp. 49-76. It is not surprising that scholars from Baudouin de Gaiffier, beginning in 1926, to Thomas Head in 1990, have found so-called "hagio-

It has been remarked concerning the Anglo-Saxon context that the vast majority of extant tenth- and eleventh-century sources are "crisis-led," that is, they were originally produced in response to various critical moments, moments such as the Viking attacks which stimulated the historiographic outpouring of Alfred's reign, or the attacks on monastic lands after 975, or (most famously) the Norman Conquest of 1066.[35] The original Neustrian base of those victors of 1066 was no different: historiographic production in every case was engendered by invasion, conquest and crisis, or to a lesser extent by threats to churchmen. Written historiographic monuments were first produced in Neustria at the end of the seventh century, generated by the need to present a regional identity to the invading Austrasians. The Austrasian, or more precisely Arnulfingian, or for convenience Carolingian take-over of Neustria generated both saints' cults and historical narrative. The region of Neustria then bore the brunt of the "pagan" conquests during the "age of the Vikings,"[36] a moment of self-conscious "not-Christian" takeover and settlement, a crisis which provoked a second wave of local historiographic production and generation of saints' cults.

The majority of written tomes preserved and passed on through great manuscript collections languish in oblivion, unread, and have, therefore, to appeal to no one.[37] However, the correspondence between the atmosphere and the creator which Gurevich posits for oral genres and for

---

graphical" texts and cults of saints and of relics so permeated by present purposes for, as cultural anthropologists are eager to remind us, the aim of historical traditions is to justify the present, and "hagiographical" narratives express historical traditions (B. de Gaiffier "L'Hagiographie dans le marquisat de Flandres et le duché de Basse-Lotharingie au XIe siècle" (Thèse, Ecole des Chartes, 1926), in B. de Gaiffier *Etudes critiques d'hagiographie et d'iconologie* (Subsidia Hagiographica 43; Brussels, 1967) pp. 415-507; T. Head *Hagiography and the Cult of Saints: The Diocese of Orleans, 800-1200* (Cambridge, 1990); Jan Vansina, *Oral Tradition as History* (Madison, Wis; 1985) p. 92.

[35] Pauline Stafford *Unification and Conquest. A Political and Social History of England in the Tenth and Eleventh Centuries* (London, 1989) pp. 4-9 and 16-23.

[36] The best available synthetic survey is P.H. Sawyer, *Kings and Vikings. Scandinavia and Europe, AD 700-1000* (London, 1982).

[37] Guglielmo Cavallo, "Libri Scritti, Libri Letti, Libri Dimenticati" in "Il Secolo di Ferro" *Settimane* 38 (1990) pp. 765-770.

some written genres[38] unquestionably applies to the historiographical narratives treated in the present study. The content of the stories cannot have been idiosyncratic in the eyes of any of the participants, but provide a window onto the conceptions of the past not only of the "popular" classes (of whom Gurevich speaks), but also of the *literati*. The full-scale narratives of saints' lives that have been preserved in non-liturgical codices were, in abbreviated versions, read publicly during the special ceremonies of each local ritual calendar from the sixth or seventh century at the latest.[39] They were also used for daily readings in monastic refectories and other clerical contexts. Whether used liturgically or not, the codices on which this study is based do bear marks of readership, almost by definition: each textual subdivision is a "lectio."[40]

The "gulf" between the learned clergy who "read" the codices and the rest of the population was also not always as great as it has sometimes been made out to be,[41] and not only because of a "popular" element in the backgrounds of some clerics. Knowledge of local historiographic traditions was not confined to the literate clergy, who interacted constantly with their parishioners in a language that was comprehensible and accessible to the latter.[42] The issue of communication is crucial for a full

---

[38] Gurevich speaks of oral genres as subject to "preventive censure," meaning that they must be plausible enough to be repeated and listened to (Gurevich, *Contadini e santi* p. 8 and *Historical Anthropology* p. 39).

[39] Leroquais *Bréviaires* I pp. xxxvii- l; Pierre Riché *Education et culture dans l'occident barbare (VIe-VIIIe siècles)* (Paris, 1972) p. 540. The preface to the early-eighth-century biography of Eligius of Noyon-Tournai by an anonymous monk of St. Eloi of Noyon explains how and why one must read excerpts from the deeds of Christ and the saints to the people (BHL 2474 ed. B. Krusch MGH SRM 4 pp. 663-664).

[40] Even when no direct marks of use are observable on the extant manuscripts, that does not mean we can conclude they were not used; as Leroquais points out (*Bréviaires* I. pp l-liii), until the invention of the breviary form in the eleventh century, a director of the office would signal when and where the participants in an office were to begin and end their readings, so no mark would be required. Normally, however, there will be a roman numeral or some other indication of the use of the codex.

[41] Hillgarth, "Modes of evangelization" pp. 311-313.

[42] For the linguistic changes of the eighth, ninth and tenth centuries discussed below, see Roger Wright *Late Latin and Early Romance in Spain and Carolingian France* (Classical and Medieval Texts, Papers and Monographs 8; Liverpool, 1982) chapter 3, "Carolingian France: The Invention of Medieval Latin" pp. 104-144.

appreciation of the power and the role of the historiographic discourse embodied in the saints' cults of Francia. The present study is divided into two halves not only because of the political transformation represented by the Viking conquest, which turned Neustria into Normandy. The two halves of the study also fall on either side of a great divide in the history of communication. Throughout the period covered by the first half of the study, saints of "Pious Neustria" were celebrated publicly in the language of the public, a public which was therefore able to understand completely, and presumably to accept through the exercise of "preventive censure," the identities then in force in a given locality.[43] All of the narratives examined in the first half of the study contain explicit references to "hearers" and "listeners" among the audience. It is my impression that the "discourse" during this period matched the "reality."

However, after the middle of the ninth century, the effects of Alcuin's comprehensive program for the reform of learning and liturgy began to make themselves felt in Francia; new rules of orthography and of pronunciation of Latin made the liturgy, and other annexes of written culture, increasingly incomprehensible to those not educated in a formal way. It was recognized also from the middle of the ninth century that sermonizing would require clerics to use what we now consider "vernacular" rules of pronunciation in order to be understood by their parishioners; however, sermons are rarely historical. On the other hand the "historiae" used in public offices as part of the liturgy would no longer be part of the global self-conceptions of the entire population of a locale, but would increasingly represent only the visions of the past as held by the educated elites. Meanwhile the "discourse" moved ever farther away from the "reality."

---

[43] "Even" the Bible was never able to force standardized visions of "that which is holy" on all the regions of Merovingian Francia, for the uses made of the Bible were always tied intimately to cultural milieux and intended audiences, a point which brings to mind once more the problem of definitions (Marc Van Uytfanghe, "La Bible dans les Vies de Saints mérovingiennes. Quelques pistes de recherche." *RHEF* 62 [1976] pp. 103-111). Katrien Heene has argued that biographies of saints were utilized primarily for internal monastic consumption, rather than for recitation to the public, already by the ninth century ("Merovingian and Carolingian Hagiography: Continuity or Change in Public and Aims?" *Analecta Bollandiana* 107 [1989] pp. 415-428, but has recently indicated in private conversation that she is now reconsidering her views on the date at which the "illiterate" audience ceased to be a factor in the shaping of saints' biographies.

By *circa* 1000 there were two distinct languages in use in Normandy, one Latin and one Romance, one primarily written and the other primarily oral; therefore analysis of the cult of Romanus and of other Norman-era saints requires attention to tensions and even conflicts between the identities represented in written narratives, and the ones that seem to have been current in oral tradition. The fact that the region had just experienced a military conquest only exacerbated the potential conflicts between rulers and ruled inherent in the new structures of communication. In the first part of the study, therefore, I am dealing primarily with ideologies which seem to have united the inhabitants of Neustria along regional lines; in the second half, I am dealing instead with ideologies which divided them along social ones. The substance of the later written narratives has tended to dominate in the subsequent historiography of Christianization of the region. It is to that triumph of the conquerors' discourse that this book owes its title: the Norman Conquest of Pious Neustria.

2

Neustria Pia

A. CHRISTIANITY AND THE HISTORIOGRAPHY OF CHRISTIANIZATION IN NORTHERN GAUL BEFORE THE CAROLINGIANS: REMARKS AND HYPOTHESES

The narrative sources of pre-Carolingian Upper Normandy consistently bespeak a world in which "Christianity," however it had been implanted, was a given and "not-Christianity" a less than marginal concern throughout the late Roman and Merovingian eras.[1] The Merovingian realms seem in general to have been covered with churches, to judge from twentieth-century archeological studies; the edifices were small, in keeping with the low population levels of the fifth through the seventh centuries, but apparently covered with gold, mosaics and other ornaments.[2] Contemporary sources and Merovingian-era historiography are devoid of reference to actual missionizing, or to the perceived need for missionary activity. The religious practices of the populace at large, which presumably identified itself as Christian, were not seen by historians or by anyone else as "not-Christian."

The question then, is this: do the historiography and literary imagery of Upper Normandy correspond to or reflect an underlying "reality," or do we have here nothing more than a literary cycle, an ensemble of narra-

---

[1]   The identical point was made by Yitzak Hen in "Paganism and Superstition in the Time of Gregory of Tours: *Une question mal posée*" (Paper Presented to the 29th International Congress on Medieval Studies, May 1994).   Compare Lucien Musset "De S. Victrice à S. Ouen: La christianisation de la province de Rouen d'après l'hagiographie" *RHEF* 62 (1976) pp. 141-152: Musset calls the religion of the Merovingian period in Normandy "paganism" but with the qualification that it was "more folklore than credo," and really a matter of "rural superstition." I would prefer to dispense with the ideological and exclusionary constructs "folklore" and "superstitition" and call the religion of Neustria "Christianity," since that is what its adherents would have called it.

[2]   E. James *The Franks* (Oxford, 1988) pp. 148-152.

tives issuing from the same milieu and utilizing the same *topoi*, but bearing no necessary relation to "reality"?[3] It may be that the piety of Neustria is a *topos*, but there is no such thing as a "mere" *topos*: a dominant theme must always be at least plausible within its context.[4] The themes of Neustrian historiography and cultic veneration must especially have corresponded to local traditions, given the "preventive censure" exercised by the audience/participants before the effects of Carolingian linguistic reforms made themselves felt.

*

* *

Topographical studies show that the cities of northern Gaul acquired intramural churches and even cathedrals either before or immediately after the conversion of Constantine. A vision of Christian beginnings in peripheral suburban churches and even in cemeterial contexts, attested first in ninth- and tenth-century saints' biographies, is not applicable to northern Gaul. There certainly had been persecutions, and extremely humble and difficult beginnings for some Christian communities in the Mediterranean, but on the whole the story of romantic beginnings in tremendously adverse circumstances has little real application in northern Gaul, despite the fact that ninth- and tenth-century northern historians liked to model their local histories on Roman developments.[5] Recent archeological studies have challenged the notion of secret, persecuted Christian beginnings even in the Mediterranean world.[6] Finally, even where episcopal sees and organized institutional churches cannot be securely dated to the earliest Christian centuries, that does not preclude there from having been thriving Christian communities; in fact, there is significant evidence of such communities,

---

[3]   L. Van der Essen's *Etude critique et littéraire sur les Vitae des saints mérovingiens de l'ancienne Belgique* (Brussels, 1907) is the best-known example of a study of a regional or diocesan cycle as a literary whole.

[4]   *Contra* Frantisek Graus *Volk, Herrscher und Heiliger im Reich der Merowinger* (Munich, 1965) pp. 105-119 and pp. 148-157, where all the narratives of the period are argued to be driven by homogeneous "Heiligentypen."

[5]   Charles Pietri, "Remarques sur la topographie chrétienne des cités de la Gaule entre Loire et Rhin des origines au VIIe siècle" *RHEF* 62 (1976) pp. 189-204, esp. pp. 196 and 204.

[6]   White *Building God's House* pp. 102-139.

non-episcopal communities, in Gaul.[7]

If certain bishops such as Ambrose, locked in battle with the Roman emperors,[8] wished to enlarge to epic proportions the negative aspects of the secular government's treatment of early Christians, and to keep the memory of that past alive through the cults of martyrs, that does not mean we have to transfer Ambrose's romantic myth to every area of the Roman empire, particularly when the building record, combined with the absense of evidence of local martyrs, indicates a smooth and easy introduction of Christianity under the auspices of the imperial government or of its agents, like the caesar Constantius Chlorus (297-306), even before Constantine's conversion. The absence of martyrs in northern Gaul is not a function of an absence of Christians, but rather of the fact that Constantius Chlorus did not enforce the persecution decrees in Gaul.[9] Christianity was the preferred religion from the time of Constantine and the only legal religion of the Later Roman Empire...and Gaul was the center of the later Empire.[10] Furthermore, the demographic conditions and settlement patterns of northern Gaul in the later Empire (the third and fourth centuries) also would have facilitated evangelization, for the dispersed settlements of the first and second centuries had given way before fewer, sparsely-populated centers of habitation, making it all the easier to reach the ever decreasing number of citizens.[11]

We are fortunate in knowing quite a bit about the church of Rouen at the end of the fourth and the beginning of the fifth century, during the

---

[7]   Frank D. Gilliard, "The Apostolicity of Gallic Churches" *Harvard Theological Review* 68 (1975) pp. 17-33.

[8]   H.F. von Campenhausen, *Ambrosius von Mailand als Kirchenpolitiker* (Berlin and Leipzig, 1929); Jean-Rémy Palanque, *S. Ambroise et l'Empire Romain* (Paris, 1933).

[9]   René Herval *Origines Chrétiennes: de la IIe Lyonnaise gallo-romaine à la Normandie ducale (IVe-XIe siècles). Avec le texte complet et la traduction integrale du De laude Sanctorum de Saint Victrice (396)* (Rouen, 1966) p. 17.

[10]   Edith Wightman *Gallia Belgica* (Berkeley, 1985) pp. 191-218. Griffe argued for the full Christianization of northern Gaul in part on the basis of its centrality to Christianizing emperors (E. Griffe *La Gaule chrétienne à l'époque romaine* [Paris, 1964-1966] 3 vols; vol. I pp. 191-218). Wightman, on the other hand, argued that the region remained "not-Christian" because it was so full of "pagan superstitions" (pp. 282-289).

[11]   Wightman *Gallia Belgica* pp. 244-266.

pontificate of Victricius (†415), whose influence within his own diocese was exerted particularly in order to encourage the then-flourishing monastic movement, of which Rouen was among the very first western cities to partake.[12] Close study of Victricius' famous work, *De laude sanctorum*,[13] as well as of his career, reveals the diocese of Rouen to have been as "Romanized" and as "Christianized" as any Mediterranean town. In 385, Ambrose of Milan had "invented" the relics of Gervasius and Protasius at Milan, and had given fragments of those relics to Martin of Tours and to Victricius; ten years later, the bishop of Rouen received a new shipment of Mediterranean relics.[14] The preoccupations of the bishop as evidenced in his well-known panegyrical sermon, preached in 396/7 on the dedication of a basilica built to house the *minutiae* of those Roman martyrs, are absolutely not those of a prelate whose diocese is stained on any level by "not-Christianity."

It is more than the way Victricius assumes a knowledgeable audience, the audience of a fully-formed Christian community in cc. 1 and 3; what is most striking is Victricius' defensive posture concerning his beloved *minutiae*: the main concern of the sermonizer seems to be to persuade his traditional flock to accept the new-fangled innovation of some

---

[12] Nancy Gauthier, "Les premiers siècles des origines aux Carolingiens" in N.-J. Chaline *Le Diocèse de Rouen-Le Havre* (Paris, 1976; Histoire des diocèses de France 5, dir. J.-R. Palanque and B. Plongeron) p. 13; Pierre Andrieu-Guitrancourt "Notes, remarques et reflexions sur la vie ecclésiastique et religieuse à Rouen sous le pontificat de saint Victrice" *Etudes offerts à Jean Macqueron* (Aix-en-Provence, 1970) p. 7-20; J. Mulders "Victricius van Rouaan. Leven en Leer" *Bijdragen. Tijdschrift voor Philosophie en Theologie* XVII (1956) pp. 1-25 and XVIII (1957) pp. 19-40 and 270-89; Elpidius Vacandard "Saint Victrice, évêque de Rouen (IVe-Ve s.)" *Revue des Questions Historiques* 37, NS. 29 (1903) pp. 379-441. *Contra* Jacques Fontaine, "Victrice de Rouen et les origines du monachisme dans l'ouest de la Gaule (IVe-VIe siècles)" and "La culture carolingienne dans les abbayes normands: l'exemple de St.-Wandrille" in *Aspects du Monachisme en Normandie (IVe-XVIIIe siècles)* ed. L. Musset (Bibliothèque de la Société de l'Histoire Ecclésiastique de la France 15-16, 1982).

[13] Victricius, *De laude sanctorum* ed. Herval pp. 109-153; Victricius *De laude sanctorum* ed. Jacobus Mulders (CCSL 64; 1985).

[14] Herval, *Origines chrétiennes* pp. 39-54; M. Vieillard-Troiekouroff "Les monuments religieux de Rouen à la fin du VIe siècle d'après Grégoire de Tours et Fortunat" *Centenaire de l'abbé Cochet (1975)* (Actes du Colloque International d'Archéologie, Rouen 3-4-5 juillet, 1975; Rouen, 1978) vol. III pp. 511-520 at pp. 511-512.

up-to-date Mediterranean bishops such as Victricius' friend Ambrose of Milan, and to add to their dominical worship the veneration of saints. After praising his congregation for their sexual mores, ascetic practices and doctrinal purity (cc. 3-4), Victricius assures them that to embrace the *minutiae* of Roman martyrs will be the final step in their purification process (c. 5). He goes on to explain how and why reliquary-enclosed patrons are a good deal, how they can be guides, intercessors and models to lead the locals to heaven and, best of all, can stand firm as protectors against any and every enemy (cc. 5-7). Victricius is here the definitive episcopal *impresario* of relic cults, caught at the moment of the introduction of the practice.[15]

The *minutiae* brought to Rouen were foreign imports, and their veneration was not an organic development of the locale. On the Italian peninsula, episcopal orchestration of relic-cults has been charitably interpreted as intending to preclude "privatization of the holy," as church officials wrested control of the local "special dead," already spontaneously venerated, from the families of the deceased, who would otherwise have controlled access to the beneficent remains.[16] In Rouen, the episcopal importer of the new luxury items sought to create a new market, to create a new demand which had not existed before, and then immediately stepped forward as the one who could supply the desired goods. The introduction of martyrs' cults into areas which did not have martyrs is almost exclusively a matter of the establishment of episcopal control and episcopal power bases, particularly while the market was tight and relics not very easy to come by. Victricius in effect was telling his congregation: your ascetic practices and participation in the sacraments such as baptism are not enough; to complete your purification process, you also need the aid of these special items which I have just imported and will be housing here in this new building. In other words, he was attempting to change the current local definition of Christianity.

Victricius becomes particularly defensive in ch. 9, when he assures the congregation that he isn't implying the martyrs are anything like as

---

[15] Victricius, *De laude sanctorum* p. 113.

[16] Brown, *Cult of the Saints* pp. 31-39 and pp. 95-96. Brown reads Victricius' orchestration of the martyr cults at Rouen in an exclusively altruistic manner, although elsewhere Brown is keenly aware that the bishops were able to use the tombs, once in their control, as power bases.

good as the Trinity. We catch a glimpse here of an established northern Christian community, sufficiently integrated into the ceremonial forms of the Roman world to have appreciated Victricius' modelling of his sermon on panegyrical *adventus*-speeches delivered for triumphal rulers,[17] now suddenly faced with an episcopal innovation to which they do not appear to have been particularly receptive. A local hostility to, or at least a suspicion towards, the practice of relic cults may well be the best explanation for why figures like Victricius himself, so towering in his own day, and the "martyred" Merovingian-era bishop Praetextatus, were never rendered cults at Rouen.[18]

There is no sense in Victricius' sermon of any "pagan" or even diabolical threat to his flock, beyond the fear of loss of sexual purity,[19] though there are certainly hints of the doctrinal controversies which seem to have wracked the fourth-century churches; indeed, there is reason to believe that the very promotion of martyr-cults by Ambrose and Victricius was a part of the war against Arian Christians.[20] Victricius was concerned about "heretics," not about "pagans." The lack of evident concern with anti-"pagan" evangelization was not a result of any complacency on Victricius' part. The bishop of Rouen was one of the foremost anti-"pagan" missionaries of his age, well known as such even to the greatest luminaries of the time such as Paulinus of Nola. But Victricius' mission field lay far to the east of his own diocese, in present-day Belgium, and he is believed to

[17] Nikolaus Gussone "Adventus-Zeremoniell und Translation von Reliquien. Victricius von Rouen, De Laude Sanctorum" *Frühmittelalterliche Studien* 10 (1976) pp. 125-133.

[18] F. Lifshitz, "Eight Men In. *Rouennais* Traditions of Archiepiscopal Sanctity" *Haskins Society Journal* 2 (1991) p. 68. On the other hand, the case of Praetextatus' non-sainthood may be better explained by competing anti-Praetextatus local traditions of veneration for his replacement, Melantius, evidence which only came to my notice after the publication of my study of *rouennais* episcopal cults (Baudouin de Gaiffier "S. Mélance de Rouen, vénéré à Malmédy, et S. Mélas de Rhinocolure" AB 64 (1946) pp. 54-71.

[19] Victricius, *De laude sanctorum* ch. 12 pp. 147-149.

[20] Victricius' sermon as vigorously promoting Nicene Christology is the aspect most highlighted in Herval's study (p. 132); also see M. Simonetti *La crisi ariana nel IV secolo* (Rome, 1975) pp. 464-474 and Charles Pietri "Saints et démons: L'héritage de l'hagiographie antique" in "Santi e demoni" *Settimane di studi del centro italiano sull'alto medioevo* 36 (1988) pp. 74-82 for saint and relic cults as anti-Arian devices.

have been active in Britain as well.[21] Meanwhile Victricius' own diocese seems to have been already dominated by the type of asceticism that created so much enthusiasm among some sectors of late Roman society, and which served as a basis for later monastic movements.

The basic "Christianization" of the region had preceded Victricius' pontificate. The archeological evidence for the destruction of "not-Christian" houses of worship in Upper Normandy all pre-dates his episcopate. The dates at which the various temples of the region fell out of use, on the basis of the coins found in connection with their ruins, place four cases in the period 258-273, three cases in the period 306-340, and four cases in the period 364-388.[22] Yet the abandonment of these particular sanctuaries may be less significant in the long run than their existence in the first place: what we can discern about the "religious" predilections of Upper Normandy on the basis of its Roman-era monuments accords extraordinarily well both with the discourse of "Pious Neustria" and with the oral traditions of the region which seem to have survived even into the Norman period. First, there is the point that Upper Normandy was positively covered with sanctuaries, much more so than other regions of Gaul; the "piety" of the area is apparently deep-rooted, independent of any particular sacral regime (such as "Christianity"). Second, the type of sanctuary which so abounded in Upper Normandy during the Roman period was the water sanctuary; we will see that the core of the oral traditions associated with Romanus, patron saint of Norman Rouen, connected him with the waters of the Seine. Again, Upper Norman religiosity seems not to have been given particularly to relic cults, but to other forms of devotion.

Perhaps some of the credit for the evangelization of Upper Normandy should go to St. Martin who, according to the popular Norman saying, along with "Ste. Marie, se partagent la Normandie." However, for details of the evangelization process, we have to fall back on speculative connections with figures such as Martin of Tours, figures lucky enough to have found historians. Sulpicius Severus made Martin a household name, and

[21] Paulinus of Nola, *Sancti Pontii Meropii Paulini Nolani Epistulae* ed. G. de Hartel (CSEL 29; Prague/Vienna/Leipzig, 1894) Epistle 18 c. 4 p. 131; J. Corblet *Hagiographie du diocèse d'Amiens* (Amiens, 1868) vol. IV pp. 656-659.

[22] A. Grenier, *Manuel d'archéologie gallo-romaine* IV.2 (Paris, 1960) pp. 740-786; L. de Vesly *Les fana ou petits temples gallo-romains de la région normande* (Rouen, 1909).

not only in the Touraine, in part for selfish reasons.[23] Sulpicius needed an ally for his own embattled position. In contrast, it seems as though few historiography-generating conflicts arose in the Second Lyonnais; in the absence of conflicts or *coups*, there was little impetus to produce justificatory narrative. Pious Neustria was a calm place which seems to have been shielded not only from the sort of Roman imperial-era disputes which roused Sulpicius Severus to literary action, but also from the battles of the Franks as they advanced under Clovis.

The anonymous author of the earliest biography of St. Genovefa of Paris called his or her contemporary, Clovis: "rex bellorum iure."[24] Followed by some Franks who had settled around Tournai, Clovis took Soissons/Reims, Thuringia (past Cologne), Alamania (Alsace-Lorraine), Burgundy (to Lyons) and Gothia (through Toulouse and Bordeaux) between 486 and 506.[25] The Second Lyonnais was utterly shielded from this advance; there is no record of any battle having been fought in the region, which apparently accepted Frankish lordship as a result of negotiation (with whom? the bishops?) and was subject to nothing that would have caused hostility to the dynasty of Clovis. After Clovis' victory over the Visigoths at Vouillé (507), the Frankish leader received from the Eastern Roman emperor Anastasius the titles of patrician and honorary consul. In effect, he was made governor of Gaul, and began to strike coins with the emperor's portrait and his own new titles.[26] Gregory of Tours shows us Chilperic I of Soisson/Paris (561-584), one of Clovis' descendants, building amphi-

---

[23] C. Stancliffe, *St. Martin and his Hagiographer* (Oxford, 1983) p. 362.

[24] Anonymous, *Vita Genovefae* ed. B. Krusch (MGH SRM 2; Hannover, 1896) c. 56 p. 237 (= BHL 3335). For the speculation that the author of the *Vita Genovefae* may have been a woman, see the works of Nelson, McKitterick and Van Houts on female historians, and especially on authors of anonymous works (Janet Nelson, "Perceptions du pouvoir chez les historiennes du Haut Moyen Age" *Les femmes au Moyen Age* ed. Michel Rouche [Paris, 1990] pp. 77-85; Rosamund McKitterick "Frauen und Schriftlichkeit im Frühmittelalter" *Weibliche Lebensgestaltung im Frühen Mittelalter* ed. H. W. Goetz [Cologne and Vienne, 1991] pp. 65-118; Elizabeth Van Houts "Women and the Writing of History in the Early Middle Ages" *Early Medieval Europe* 1 [1992] pp. 53-68).

[25] James, *The Franks* p. 95; J. M. Wallace-Hadrill *The Long-Haired Kings, and Other Studies in Frankish History* (London, 1962) p. 163-185.

[26] Wightman *Gallia Belgica* p. 305; see pp. 305-311 for the continuity of Roman institutions under the new consul.

theatres, decreeing new taxes, making doctrinal and theological pronouncements, writing poetry in the manner of Sedulius, and forcibly converting
Jews to Christianity,[27] all activities which he rightly considered to be
what a Roman ruler does, and which must have been recognized as such
by his subjects.

Rouen was a prosperous and important town throughout the Merovingian period.[28] Although Neustria was never the Merovingian heart-
land in terms of settlement, it was effectively so in terms of support. No
deluge ever came to wipe out the Christian communities of Upper Normandy, not even in the persons of the Franks who, alone among the barbarian conquerors of the western provinces of the Empire, were "not-
Christians." It is clear, however, that the "not-Christian" status of the
leaders of the Franks was not considered a major threat by the officials of
the Catholic churches of northern Gaul. One might even imagine that
some of the bishops saw certain advantages to the government of non-
Christian princes; the interventionism of the Christian Roman emperors
had been extremely active, and it took Ambrose most of his episcopal
career to break the emperors, in part by rubbing their faces in the martyr
cults of which he was the original *impresario*. Bishop Remigius of Reims
apparently considered the rule of the non-Christians Childeric and Clovis
compatible with the spiritual health of the Second Belgic Province, for
Remigius wrote to the latter upon his entry into his father's position in
terms that implied religious difference would be no obstacle to a fruitful
relationship.[29]

---

[27] Gregory, bishop of Tours *Libri decem historiarum* ed. B. Krusch (MGH SRM
1.1) V. 17, V. 28, V. 44 and VI. 17.

[28] Nancy Gauthier, "Rouen pendant le haut Moyen-Age (650-850)" *La Neustrie.
Les pays au nord de la Loire de 650-850* (Colloque historique international; Beihefte
der Francia 16/2; ed. Hartmut Atsma, 1989) pp. 1-20, esp. p. 7; Vieillard-Troiekouroff
"Les monuments religieux."

[29] "There is nothing new in that you now begin to be what your parents
always were. First of all, you should act so that God's Judgment may not abandon
you and that your merits should maintain you at the height where you have
arrived by your humility....You should defer to your bishops and always have
recourse to their advice. If you are on good terms with them your province will be
better able to stand firm. Encourage your people, relieve the afflicted, protect
widows, nourish orphans, so shine forth that all may love and fear you...." and
much more along the same lines wrote Remigius of Reims to Clovis in approxi-

The leaders of the non-Christian Franks had been "Romanized" to the point of being recognized by the Emperors in Constantinople. Clovis himself had eventually been baptised into the Christian fold, and posed no serious religious threat.[30] However, that would not necessarily be the case with the rank-and-file of the Frankish armies. Any large-scale settlement of practicing "pagan" Franks would be very likely to affect the religious composition of a former Roman province in ways that paying tribute to a distant and assimilated barbarian prince would not. Here it is important to attend scrupulously to local and regional diversity. The religious history of the future "Normandy" cannot be written in the shadow of more easterly regions whose destinies differed radically from that of Rouen and the Seine valley. Again and again, the evidence for a significant Frankish, "pagan," settlement in post-Roman Gaul is concentrated between the Somme and the Rhine, while west of the Somme, the demographic continuity is stark and manifest.[31]

At Rouen itself, the image that emerges from the archeological evidence is one of stability and calm. The cathedral, along with its neighborhood, has been the object of intensive study over the past few years. There is, in the cathedral quarter, no sign of rupture or discontinuity, but only of elaboration and expansion from before the time of Victricius in the late fourth century, including at least six separate campaigns of construc-

---

mately 481 (*Epistulae Austrasicae* ed. W. Gundlach, CCSL 117 [Turnhout, 1957]) Ep. 2 pp. 408-9; quoted in the translation of J. N. Hillgarth, *Christianity and Paganism, 350-750* p. 76).

[30] G. Tessier *Le baptême de Clovis: 25 décembre* (Trente journées qui ont fait la France 1; Paris, 1964) and W. von den Steinen *Chlodwigs Übergang zum Christentum; eine quellenkritische Studie* (Libelli 103; Darmstadt, 1969; reprinted from *Mitteilungen des Österreichischen Instituts für Geschichtsforschung* XII. Ergänzungsband, 1932 pp. 417-501) are the classic studies; see also Mark Spencer "Dating the Baptism of Clovis, 1886-1993" *Early Medieval Europe* 3 (1994) pp. 97-116 and William M. Daly "Clovis: How Barbaric, How Pagan?" *Speculum* 69 (1994) pp. 619-664.

[31] Patrick Perrin and Laure-Charlotte Feffer *Les Francs* I: *A la conquête de la Gaule* (Paris, 1987) especially pp. 109-111 and *Les Francs* II: *A l'origine de la France* (Paris, 1987) especially pp. 138-151; P. Perrin, "A propos de publications recentes concernant le peuplement en Gaule à l'époque merovingienne: la 'question franque'" *Archéologie Médiévale* 11 (1981) pp. 125 -145; E. James, "Cemeteries and the Problem of Frankish Settlement in Gaul" in *Names, Words and Graves: Early Medieval Settlement* ed. P.H. Sawyer (Leeds, 1979) pp. 55-89.

tion between the seventh and the tenth centuries.[32] Therefore, despite the radical alteration of the political geography of the post-Roman world in the early sixth century, Upper Normandy was not affected on any deeper level. As Clovis and his followers brought the rest of Gaul under Frankish domination, the process of establishing a political hegemony did not translate into any level of effective Frankish colonization west of the Somme valley. The change at the "top" in general meant little change in the aristocratic and dominating classes of Gaul between the later Roman Empire and the sixth century.[33] At no point was the episcopal list of Rouen interrupted, and the bishops continued to appear at ecclesiastical councils.[34] Archeological and written sources are in accord in portraying an *encadrement* of the conquered populations that was more political than military, and that did not include the dispersion even of Frankish chiefs beyond the Somme.

The history of "pagan" Francia, and of Merovingian-era missionary activity, would therefore, logically, be the history of Picardy (the *départements* of Nord and Pas-de-Calais) and of Belgium. A map plotting the extant attestations of "pagan" beliefs and practices in early Merovingian Francia is strikingly blank throughout the Seine valley, as opposed to the "clutter" found farther north and east.[35] It is very possible that there was

[32]   The moment of dramatic destruction falls in the late ninth and early tenth centuries; see the series of bulletins by Jacques Le Maho in *Archéologie Médiévale* XVII (1987) pp. 213-214; XVIII (1988) pp. 333-334; XIX (1989) pp. 301-303; XX (1990) p. 389; XXI (1991) p. 326; XXII (1992) pp. 462-463 and his summary of findings, "Le groupe épiscopal de Rouen du IVe au Xe siècle" in *Medieval Art, Architecture and Archeology at Rouen* (British Archeological Association Conference Transactions for 1986) XII, 1993 ed. Jenny Stratford, pp. 20-29.

[33]   Martin Heinzelmann, *Bischofsherrschaft in Gallien. Zur Kontinuität römischer Führungsschichten vom 4. bis 7. Jahrhundert* (Zurich-Munich, 1976); Walter Goffart, "Rome, Constantine and the Barbarians" *American Historical Review* LXXXVI (1981) pp. 275-306.

[34]   Gauthier in Chaline, *Le Diocèse de Rouen-Le Havre* p. 15.

[35]   Perrin and Feffer II pp. 158-174. Nancy Gauthier's study of the Moselle region has emphasized the slow penetration of Christianity outside anything but the greatest towns during the Roman period (Nancy Gauthier *L'évangélisation des pays de la Moselle, IIe-VIIe siècles* [1980] esp. pp. 107-110). She has suggested to me in private correspondance that the same pattern of the slow impact of Christianity reigned in the future Normandy, despite the relative absence of barbarian "pagans," because the native Gallo-Roman population remained faithful to their

a total ecclesiastical disruption of the northeastern periphery of Gaul, a disruption which resulted from a massive Frankish installation. In the fifth century the episcopal catalogues are interrupted throughout all the Rhineland sees and in those beyond the Rhine, and some prelates, such as the bishop of Tongres who gravitated increasingly towards Maastricht, seem to have been forced to shift their residences westward.[36] Even the towns in the region were abandoned by prominent Christians known to have been active there, Victricius of Rouen most prominent among them; no known self-conscious missionaries or bishops returned to the coastal areas until the seventh century.[37] In addition, the archeological record at Thérouanne, just to take one example, shows tremendous destruction in the cathedral quarter during the later Empire (third-fourth centuries); the Merovingian episcopal group, built in the seventh century, sits immediately atop destroyed first- and second-century structures, indicating that the site was abandoned for centuries on end.[38]

To interpret (or impose a discourse on) this evidence of cultural change as indicating "paganization" *per se* (as opposed to organizational

---

ancestral, even non-Roman, cults. Through this prism it would be, she points out, the person of Victricius not the inhabitants of Rouen who was Romanized by the early fifth century. It would be possible to interpret the sketchy evidence for the late Roman period along such lines. However, the theoretical and methodological issues raised in the introduction above call into question the received view of evangelization, as described for instance by Gauthier, in that the evidence for thriving "pagan" practices is largely drawn from conciliar *acta* and other fulminations which may attest disagreement over definitions of Christianity rather than "survivals" of "paganism." Furthermore, the premise of "preventive censure" would preclude Victricius' sermon being meaningless to his congregation.

[36] Gabriel Fournier *Les mérovingiens* (Paris, 1966) pp. 79-80; P.C. Boeren "Les évêques de Tongres-Maestricht" RHEF 62 (1976) pp. 25-36.

[37] Michel Rouche, "Les Saxons et les origines de Quentovic" *Revue de Nord* 59 no. 235 (1977) pp. 457-473.

[38] H. Bernard, "Les cathédrales de Thérouanne" AM 10 (1980) pp. 105-135, to be read with reports by the same author on the Vielle Ville of Thérouanne in AM 11 (1980) pp. 290-292 and AM 12 (1982) pp. 315-318. A series of biographies of bishop Audomarus of Thérouanne portray him as evangelizing a region inhabited primarily by self-conscious "not-Christians" in the seventh century; those biographies are all, however, products of the ninth century and after, though they do seem to accord well with the archeological evidence (Van der Essen *Etude critique* pp. 400-409; BHL 763/764, BHL 767 and BHL 768; see esp. AASS Sept. III BHL 764 pp. 396-399 and AASS Sept. III BHL 767 pp. 402-403 and BHL 768 p. 407).

changes for instance) may not be the best route to take. Both Werner and Geary have begun to argue, from very different perspectives, for relative non-disruption even in the regions most exposed to Frankish settlement during the fifth and sixth centuries.[39] Hillgarth has settled on a non-religionist (and non-ethnicist, in so far as it avoids "Germanization") descriptor for the transformation of north-eastern Gaul, referring to the advance of a "warrior culture."[40] Fouracre and Wood have both addressed the issue of religious change in connection with narratives set in the seventh century, and have pointed out that Eligius, bishop of Noyon, located in the very center of Frankish settlement, did not battle "pagans" so much as opponents of his episcopal authority.[41] Eligius' opposition to diabolical games, wicked dancing and other "superstitions" current in a *vicus* near Noyon may well not be sufficient evidence to posit "not-Christian" inhabitants in north-eastern Gaul in the seventh century.[42] The evidence of the mid-eighth-century *vita Eligii* is equivocal; on the one hand, he is shown preaching to baptised crowds and urging them "ut nullus paganorum sacrilegas consuetudines observetis" (II.16), while on the other hand, he is said by his biographer to have been chosen to the post at Noyon because he was deemed capable of evangelizing the many "gentiles" who inhabited the diocese (II.2). What is significant is the very fact that both the archeological evidence and the earliest historiography of north-eastern Gaul are, on the subject of religious preferences, equi-

[39] K.F. Werner, "Conquête franque de la Gaule ou changement de régime?" in *Childéric-Clovis, rois des Francs, 482-1983. De Tournai à Paris. Naissance d'une Nation* (Paris, 1983) pp. 5-14; Werner may even underestimate the extent of the Frankish impact in the eastern regions. Likewise, Patrick Geary ("Cults Without Impresarios") seems to suggest that a strong level of "Christian" continuity reigned everywhere throughout the Roman world during the fifth through the seventh centuries when he speaks of the "myth of rupture caused by the barbarian invasions" or the "myth of discontinuity."

[40] Hillgarth, "Modes of evangelization" p. 312.

[41] P. Fouracre, "The Work of Audoenus of Rouen and Eligius of Noyon in Extending Episcopal Authority from Town to Country in Seventh-Century Neustria" *Studies in Church History* 16 (1979; "The Church in Town and Countryside" ed. D. Baker) pp. 77-91; I.N. Wood, "Pagans and Holy Men, 600-800" *Irland und die Christenheit* eds. Chatháin and Richter (1987) pp. 347-360.

[42] Anonymous, *Vita Eligii* ed. B. Krusch, MGH SRM 4 (= BHL 2474) II. 8 pp. 700-701, II. 16 pp. 705-708, II. 20 pp. 711-712. On the *vita Eligii* see Van der Essen *Etude critique* pp. 330-336 and Krusch MGH SRM 4 pp. 711-712.

vocal, whereas the evidence of Upper Normandy, whether archeological or literary, uniformly presents a "Christianized" face.

By way of more illustrative contrast, what is now Lower Normandy (namely, the Avranchin, the Bessin and the Cotentin) may have witnessed a still thriving "not-Christian" culture well into the Merovingian era. "Normandy" as a unit is geographically artificial, for Lower Normandy looks west, to Brittany, just as Upper Normandy looks south-east to Paris and, beyond Paris, to Rome and the rest of continental Europe. Only the Roman administrators who set up the *Notitia Provinciarum* in around 400 thought the Channel coast from Barfleur to Eu looked like a unit.[43] The artificial unit created by Roman administrators collapsed with the Empire itself, and would not be revived until Charlemagne's imperial administrators tried to recreate Roman units through the hierarchy of the Frankish Church. But, once more, only artificial imperial imposition could keep the Channel coast together. It is important, then, for the purposes of this study, not to reflexively treat Upper and Lower Normandy as a conceptual unit.

Like Picardy, Lower Normandy has never had a historiographic phase comparable to that of "Pious Neustria." Indeed, the Cotentin seems to have sometimes worn its past "not-Christianity" on its sleeve, as a badge of pride. The earliest narrative of the religious history of the Cotentin was contained in the Black Book of Coutances, a codex which had, by 1885, mysteriously disappeared, but whose contents were summarized on the basis of earlier framentary editions, by Pigeon in 1876.[44] The very first attempt to introduce "Christianity" into the Cotentin, placed by the late-eleventh-century author in the mid-fifth century, under Ereptiolus, a missionary said to have been raised at Rouen and sent to the west by bishop

[43] D.C. Douglas *William the Conqueror; the Norman Impact upon England* (London, 1964) pp. 7-19.

[44] E.-A. Pigeon, *Histoire de la Cathédrale de Coutances* (Coutances, 1876); L. Delisle, "Anciens catalogues des évêques des églises de France" *HLF* XXIX (1885) pp. 421-423. The codex seems to have been compiled from disparate sources in the thirteenth century and reworked in the fourteenth. Most of a late-eleventh-century history of the church of Coutances which was contained in the codex was published in GC XI, Instrumenta coll. 218-234, under the title "De statu huius ecclesiae ab anno 836 ad 1093." The "De statu" was basically a eulogy for bishop Gaufridus of Montbary (†1093; Pigeon, *Cathédrale de Coutances* p. 40). See also F. A. Delamare, "Essai sur la véritable origine et sur les vicissitudes de la cathédrale de Coutances" *Mémoires de la Société des Antiquaires de Normandie* 17 (1840-41) pp. 161-172.

Silvester of Rouen (†430), fails in the face of entrenched local "not-Christianity." The context of the episcopate of Possessor of Coutances in the early sixth century is still "not-Christian" when Marculfus of Nanteuil and his companions attempt once more to evangelize the diocese.[45] The cemeteries of Upper Normandy almost always display evidence of a phase of deliberate destruction during the periods that would correspond to the episcopates of Ereptiolus and Possessor,[46] the level of violence that seems to have been required to break with the past and "cleanse" the territory for a new beginning confirms the image of entrenched and durable "pagan" traditions. Finally, the episcopal lists of all the sees of Lower Normandy are very late and have univerally been judged to be totally fictional; the sees of Avranches, Coutances, Lisieux and Sées all seem to have been originally founded in the sixth century.[47]

On the other hand, as in Belgic Gaul, the evidence is just as likely to indicate regional independentism and lack of assimilation to the values and dictates of centralizing authorities in Lower Normandy as it is to indicate significant numbers of self-conscious believers in "not-Christianity."[48] The Avranchin, an area barely larger than the territory dominated by Mont-St.-Michel, is marked by a complete disinterest in historiography, including the historiography of Christianization. The archeological record indicates the presence, from the fourth century, of a cathedral and a baptistery on the spot of the present-day cathedral complex.[49] Documentary

[45]   Pigeon, *Cathédrale de Coutances* pp. 2-6.

[46]   Christian Pilet, in a review of H. Roosens "Reflets de christianisation dans les cimetières mérovingiens" *Les Etudes Classiques* LIII no. 1 (1985) pp. 111-135 in AM XVI (1986) pp. 281-282. Pilet cites the specific examples of Frénouville, Giberville and St.-Martin-de-Fontenay.

[47]   L. Duchesne, *Fastes episcopaux de l'ancienne Gaule* II. pp. 211-224 and 234-240; J. Dubois, "Les listes épiscopales témoins de l'organisation ecclésiastique" *RHEF* 62 (1976) pp. 9-23, esp. p. 12; L. Cristiani, "Liste chronologique des saints de France" *RHEF* 31 (1945) pp. 5-96, esp. p. 60.

[48]   Grosset, "Hypothèses sur l'évangelisation" pp. 44 and 52 interprets the "not-Christians" of the Cotentin as baptised resisters against Merovingian royal authority, although elsewhere (p. 43) he seems to treat the inhabitants of the region as real "not-Christians."

[49]   Excavations under the cathedral have unearthed a fourth-century monumental stone building, paired with another building which is endowed with a drainage system indicative of a baptistery and which lies under the site of a medieval chapel

evidence such as conciliar *acta* and chance references in narratives composed elsewhere provide the names of the bishops of Avranches throughout the sixth and seventh centuries.[50] Nevertheless, no written descriptions of evangelization were ever composed in the region. The Avranchin,
though placed by Roman and therefore by Carolingian administrators in
the metropolitan province of Rouen, belongs culturally with the Armorican
peninsula, which also disdained historiographic production throughout
most of the first millenium of the Christian era.[51]

In the absence of written monuments of local self-perception before
the end of the eleventh century, by which time there is reason to believe
that the changed structure of linguistic and liturgical communication
would have rendered Cotentin historiography alien to all but the learned,
how much credence ought we to lend to the perceptions of Fortunatus,
that famous Aquitanian poet who wrote, in c. 600, a biography of bishop
Paternus of Avranches and of the latter's companion, Scubilio (both †c.
564)? The *Vita Paterni* may, more than anything, evidence the difference
between Romanized Aquitanian culture and the Breton world which Paternus, born before the end of the fifth century to a senatorial administrative family of Poitiers, encountered in the Avranchin.[52] The "gentiles" encountered and battled by the Aquitanians Paternus and Scubilio in Fortunatus' view may well be a classic example of the misperceptions of an
outsider.[53] There is no Merovingian- or Carolingian-era evidence of local
acclamation of Fortunatus' perception of the Avranchin: the *Vita Paterni*
has been preserved and transmitted entirely through extra-Norman codices, and primarily by virtue of the fame of its author.[54]

---

of St. John the Baptist, all in conjunction with several rare cases of fourth-century
intra-mural burials (Daniel Levalet "The Cathedral Church of St. André at
Avranches" *AM* 12 [1982] pp. 107 -153, esp. 112-116).

[50]   Duchesne, *Fastes* II pp. 221-224.

[51]   Julia Smith, "Oral and Written: Saints, Miracles and Relics in Brittany, c. 850-
1250" *Speculum* 65 (1990) p. 313.

[52]   BHL 6477, ed. Bruno Krusch, MGH AA 4.2 pp. 33-37.

[53]   Paternus and Scubilio work so that "sua intercessione diabolica cultura quae
gentili sub errore male veneratur cessaret" (BHL 6477 IV. 14 ed. Krusch p. 34).

[54]   BHL 6477 is preserved in the Great Legendary of St. Stephen of Autun
(Montpellier H n. 55, fols 4-51, of the eighth century), the basis of Krusch's edition,
and in a series of extra-Norman codices, none of which contain biographies of or
readings for festivals of any other "Norman" saints, with the exception of the

On the one hand, there are no known accounts of translations, inventions or any other manifestations of a relic cult to Paternus or Scubilio in the Avranchin, nor are there any written records of miracles attributed to them, outside of the ones vaguely reported by Fortunatus (c. 54). On the other hand, there is a fountain of St. Pair associated with the saint's sixth-century burial church, along with a number of church dedications.[55] The Avranchin and surrounding areas did render some sort of fountain-centered cult to Paternus and Scubilio, a cult which did not require any written documentation, and this is perfectly in keeping with the cultic patterns of Brittany, as described by Smith.[56] One cannot, however, assume that the content of the local Avranchin-Breton fountain-centered cult to Paternus and Scubilio venerated them as "Christian" evangelists to a "pagan" region simply on the basis of the Aquitanian Fortunatus' belief that the two Poitevins had been missionaries to the Armorican world.

In both cases, that is Lower Normandy and Picardy-Artois-Belgium, there is reason to believe the issue was "ethnic" more than "religious," in so far as the two can be separated: both the Bessin and the Boulonnais, for instance, were key areas of intense settlement of Saxons, and these remnants of the *litus saxonicus* were unlikely to have been any more receptive to Frankish domination in the Merovingian period than they were to be later, in Saxony, during the Carolingian period.[57] The ethnic issue would continue to be a factor in Lower Normandy, where armies quite distinct from that of Rollo would conquer and settle in the late Carolingian period.[58] It is likely that the aggressively "not-Christian" self-conception of the Cotentin in the eleventh century was a function of the region's desire to remain independent of the aggressively "Christian" rulers of Upper

---

widely-venerated Audoenus. For the manuscripts, see B. Baedorf, *Untersuchungen über die Heiligenleben der Westlichen Normandie* (Bonn, 1913) pp. 1-12; the most important manuscript is Paris BN lat. 5666 (of the twelfth century; folios 126r-135r), which differs considerably from the Montpellier manuscript in the opening sections, and which served as the basis for the AASS and Pigeon editions.

[55]   Pigeon, *Vies des saints des diocèse de Coutances et Avranches* I pp. 35-36; Grosset, "Hypothèses sur l'évangelisation" pp. 48-49.

[56]   Smith, "Oral and Written."

[57]   Déchelette, *Manuel d'archéologie préhistorique, celtique et gallo-romaine* V (Paris, 1931) p. 389-397; Rouche, "Les saxons et les origines de Quentovic."

[58]   E. Searle, "Fact and Pattern in Heroic History: Dudo of St. Quentin" *Viator* 15 (1984) pp. 119-137; Sawyer, *Age of the Vikings*.

Normandy, the descendants of Rollo and his *fideles*. The evidence concerning episcopal organization and the like in Lower Normandy as well could "merely" witness an absence of Roman-style administrative methods (and thus be a function of regional independentism or ethnic separatism), rather than the presence of "not-Christians."

Whatever the explanation for the apparent "not-Christianity" of Lower Normandy and of Picardy-Artois-Belgium, the contrast with Upper Normandy throws the characteristics of the Seine valley into even higher relief: in Upper Normandy there is nothing which can even be stretched to indicate the presence of "not-Christians" during the Merovingian period, nothing which has to be explained as a matter of a foreigner's distorted perceptions. Nothing, in fact, contradicts, let alone outright disproves, the image of "pious Neustria" that emerges from the pre-Norman narrative sources of the Seine valley. By the time of Audoenus, to whom we will return in depth momentarily, Rouen could probably boast, besides the cathedral complex (St. Mary's and St. Stephen's), St. Martin du Pont inside the walls, and St. Gervais, St. Mary-St. Godard, St. Martin-de-Renelle and St. Peter-St. Audoenus outside the walls, certainly a respectable number of cultic centers given the low population figures of the epoch.[59]

There is no evidence in Gregory of Tours, to name the most well-known and frequently-cited source for sixth-century Francia, of a relapse into the practice of "not-Christian" religions. Gregory of Tours never presented any Merovingian rulers, nor any of their subjects of whatever status, as "not-Christian," though he does tell unflattering story after unflattering story about the monarchs. It would only be by "reading into" his stories of "barbarism" in the political realm that one could arrive at the conclusion of a decrepit and paganized Merovingian church. Gregory recounts only one incident concerning Rouen, which lay outside his usual area of knowledge;[60] in this instance, however, Gregory was personally involved. The conclusion to be drawn from Gregory's account of the running battle between bishop Praetextatus of Rouen (†586) and the kings

[59] Gauthier, "Rouen pendant le haut Moyen Age" p. 4.

[60] G. Kurth, "De l'authorité de Grégoire de Tours" *Etudes franques* (Paris, 1919) vol. II. no. XIV, pp. 117-206.

and queens of Neustria[61] is not that the diocese had seen a decadent Christianity give way before a "pagan" revival but that a normally-functioning diocese was being disrupted by political intrigues. The population was in touch with and under the influence of the bishop: how else the accusation that the latter had turned them against the king, Chilperic? The inhabitants of the diocese later took the opportunity of Chilperic's death to reinstate Praetextatus and to depose the royal "anti-bishop," Melantius.

Whatever evidence, archeological or literary, that can be mustered concerning the religious history of Neustria, indicates that the Seine valley was evangelized during the height of the Roman Empire, incorporated into the Roman ecclesiastical structure and assimilated into Mediterranean-style Christianity (saints' cults, etc.) in the course of the fourth and early fifth centuries, and remained undisrupted in its Romanized/Christianized ways of life despite major disturbances occuring elsewhere, disturbances from which it was shielded by its apparent docility under the new Frankish rule. It was probably precisely this detachment from all the great battles of the era which accounts for the absence of historiography in the region. Only in the face of the Carolingian takeover of Neustria did it become necessary to justify a position or legitimize claims to authority through the use of the past. Of all the possible permutations of historically-based legitimization and of the uses of the past, the one which would be most important at Rouen during the crisis of the Austrasian invasion would be the elevation of a local hero, or indeed of several: the promotion of local bishops as patron saints and as *foci* of local pride.[62] Which brings us to the seventh-century bishops of Merovingian Pious Neustria.

---

[61] Gregory of Tours *Libri Decem Historiarum* V.18; VII.16, 19; VIII.31 ed. B. Krusch, MGH SRM 1.1 (Hannover, 1884); De Gaiffier, "S. Mélance de Rouen" pp. 54-56.

[62] For a similar dynamic, T.S. Brown "Romanitas and Campanilismo: Agnellus of Ravenna's View of the Past" *Inheritance of Historiography* eds. Holdsworth and Wiseman pp. 107-114.

B. AUSTRASIANS AT THE GATES: THE "VIRTUS" OF AUDOENUS AND THE BEGINNINGS OF NEUSTRIAN HISTORIOGRAPHY

As we move to the study of late-Merovingian Neustrian historiography and the Austrasian take-over of Neustria, it is important to beware of the power of historiographic discourse, and not only the discourse of the Merovingian-era narratives themselves. Ninth-century Carolingian loyalists had a very different view of the final century of the rule of the Merovingian kings and queens than did those latter rulers' contemporaries. The most famous ninth-century historian of the late-Merovingian era is Charlemagne's biographer Einhard, who describes in the first three chapters of his *Vita Karoli* (written in the 830s) how the Merovingian rulers had degenerated into useless weaklings (the so-called *rois-fainéants*)[63] whose crumbling realms had had to be rescued by the Carolingian mayors of the palace, the *sub-reguli*.[64] The ninth-century views have long been known, and have become almost a part of the collective memory of the educated classes of nineteenth- and twentieth-century Europe and North America. Certain aspects of the ninth-century prism had become so naturalized by the middle of the twentieth century that historians could chide Carolingian-era authors for their uncreative mining and preservation of the past, perceived as a mere transmission rather than as an ideologically-loaded shaping.[65]

But Carolingian-loyalist historians such as Einhard and Alcuin were not historiographic innocents; they had a keen sense of the uses of the

---

[63] Wallace-Hadrill *The Long-Haired Kings* pp. 231-248.

[64] Einhard, *Vita Karoli* (BHL 1580) ed. G.H. Pertz, MGH SS 2 (1829) pp. 443-463. The same story can be found in the first part of the Royal Frankish Annals (Annales Regni Francorum, 741-795), which may (in both original and revised versions) have been commissioned by Charlemagne and written by Einhard (F. Kurze ed. *Annales regni Francorum 741-829 qui dicuntur Annales Laurissenses maiores et Einhardi* MGH SRG [Hanover, 1895] a. 749 pp. 8-9; *Carolingian Chronicles. Royal Frankish Annals and Nithard's Histories* trans. Bernard Walter Scholz with Barbara Rogers [Ann Arbor, 1970] introduction pp. 2-8). Also see the *Annales Mettenses Priores* (Hannover /Leipzig, 1905) ed. B. von Simson pp. 1-42.

[65] For instance, H. Fichtenau *The Carolingian Empire: the Age of Charlemagne* (Studies in Medieval History, 9; Oxford, 1957; translation by P. Munz of the introduction and cc. 1-6 of *Das Karolingische Imperium. Soziale und geistige Problematik eines Grossreiches*) pp. 95-103; for more references, Deug-Su I, *Cultura e ideologia nella prima età carolingia* (Rome, 1984) pp. 7-8 and 26-27.

past, and understood how subsequent ages would look backwards to their works just as they themselves were looking backwards.[66] Carolingian discourse has been analyzed critically over the past twenty-five years, and particularly over the past decade. Merovingian decrepitude, both political and religious, is increasingly seen as a matter of Carolingian propaganda.[67] Some authors have concentrated on the late Merovingian period *per se*, and on the difficulties faced by the Austrasian interlopers as they sought to make themselves rulers of Francia, first as *sub-reguli*, then as kings.[68] Other authors have concentrated on the historiographic monuments turned out by Carolingian loyalists.[69] The following chapters of the present study take the latter approach, and trace in particular the process whereby the religious historiography of Upper Normandy was transformed by the Carolingian discursive prism in the course of the eighth and ninth centuries.

*

* *

The very end of the seventh century, and the beginning of the eighth, witnessed throughout western Francia the establishment of shrine cults to recently-deceased heads of important Merovingian bishoprics and mona-

---

[66]   H.R. Bloch *Etymologies and Genealogies: a Literary Anthropology of the French Middle Ages* (Chicago, 1983) pp. 97-98; Marcia Kupfer *Romanesque Wall Painting in Central France: The Politics of Narrative* (New Haven, 1993) pp. 11-12.

[67]   P. Fouracre, "Merovingian History and Merovingian Hagiography" *Past and Present* 127 (1990) pp. 3-38, esp. pp. 4, 9-10 and 29-31; Hen, "Popular Culture in Merovingian Gaul." For a survey of recent literature, Reinhold Kaiser *Das römische Erbe und das Merowingerreich* (Enzyklopädie deutscher Geschichte 26; Munich, 1993).

[68]   Patrick Geary *Aristocracy in Provence: The Rhône Basin at the Dawn of the Carolingian Age* (Monographien zur Geschichte des Mittelalters 31; Stuttgart, 1985); Josef Semmler, "Die Aufrichtung der Karolingischen Herrschaft im nördlichen Burgund im VIIIe Jahrhundert" *Langres et ses évêques, VIIIe-XIe siècles. Aux origines d'une seigneurie ecclésiastiique* (Actes du Colloque Langres-Ellwangen, June 1985; Langres, 1986, dir. G. Viard).

[69]   Irene Haselbach *Aufstieg und Herrschaft der Karlinger in der Darstellung der sogenannten Annales Mettenses priores* (Lübeck/Hamburg, 1970; Historische Studien 42); Deug-Su I, *L'Opera agiografica di Alcuino* (Spoleto, 1983); Deug-Su I, *Cultura e ideologia nella prima età carolingia* (Rome, 1984); Giovanni Tabacco, "Agiologia e demonologia come strumenti ideologici in età carolingia" *Settimane* 36 (1988).

steries.[70] This sudden display of supernatural patrons took place against the background of the Carolingian penetration of the west, and was almost certainly intended to check that advance. The cult of Audoenus, who died in 684, was established by his immediate successor Ansbertus, also the abbot of Fontenelle, one of the great Neustrian houses. The two successive bishops of Rouen both came from powerful Neustrian families, and had served as Merovingian royal officials.[71] The oldest, anonymous, biography of Audoenus was composed against the background of the Carolingian take-over, probably by a monk attached to the monastery of St. Peter (later St. Ouen) that was then growing up around the new shrine to Audoenus.[72] Ansbertus' biographer was Aigradus of Fontenelle, writing under abbot Hildbertus, between 699 and the Carolingian take-over of Fontenelle in 701.[73] Ansbertus himself composed a Latin acrostic poem

---

[70] Alan Thacker, "Lindisfarne and the Origins of the Cult of St. Cuthbert" in *St. Cuthbert, His Cult and Community* pp. 106-108.

[71] Richard A. Gerberding, *The Rise of the Carolingians and the Liber Historiae Francorum* (Oxford, 1987) pp. 84-91.

[72] *Vita Audoeni* (BHL 750) ed. W. Levison in MGH SRM V pp. 553-567.

[73] BHL 520a, ed. W. Levison MGH SRM V. The *vita Ansberti* has always been judged to be an extremely trustworthy narrative, one from which intimate details of all sorts of seventh-century political intrigues have been mined. The author identifies himself as a monk of Fontenelle under Hildbertus, and that identification, when considered in the light of the tremendous reliability of the information contained in the narratives, had long been accepted, although it was noted that certain references in the *vita Ansberti* seemed slightly anachronistic and were understood to have been slipped in, along with certain stylistic changes, by copiests over the decades after 700 (Canon Legris, "Les *vies* interpolées des saints de Fontenelle" AB 17 [1904] pp. 265-306, esp. pp. 267-279). Wilhelm Levison, however, made a full-frontal attack on the early dating of even the core of Aigradus' biographies, primarily on the basis that the atmosphere in Merovingian Francia was so stultifying that no one could have written anything this intelligent during that period (Wilhelm Levison, "Zur Kritik der Fontaneller Geschichtsquellen" NA 25 [1899/1900] pp. 593-597; also see his introduction to his edition, MGH SRM pp. 614-615). Levison considered the *Vita Ansberti* to be a forgery of the ninth century, although he also agreed that every detail of information contained in it was completely accurate for the seventh century; the impossibility of such a thing having occurred without there being a near-contemporary core to the text does not seem to have carried much weight during the late nineteenth and early twentieth centuries with the MGH editors, whose hypercritical attitude towards the dating of texts is only slowly being rethought (Martin Heinzelmann and Joseph-Claude Poulin, *Les vies*

in honor of his predecessor.[74]

The near-contemporary biographies of Ansbertus and of Audoenus belong to a larger group of narrative histories that are marked by the discourse of "Pious Neustria." Patriotic authors sought to demonstrate that even very recently, even on the eve of the unjustified Austrasian takeover, the region had excelled in holiness. In contrast with the Orléanais, whose "fathers" were striking for their antiquity from the very beginnings of local historiography and cultic production,[75] there was not a shred of historiographical interest in the diocese of Rouen in any period other than the latter half of the seventh century during those years when political exigencies and historiographical vogues combined to produce the discourse of Pious Neustria. However, the superficial constrast with the Orléanais should not mislead us: the original establishment of the historiated inheritance of the diocese of Orléans took place several centuries before any crisis faced the diocese of Rouen. The Gallo-Roman patrons of the Orléanais were intended to justify and protect Gallo-Roman inhabitants in the face of Frankish aggression,[76] rather than to protect and justify Neustrian Frankish inhabitants against Austrasian Frankish aggressors.

The creation of the cult of Audoenus is described by Ansbertus' biographer, Aigradus of Fontenelle. Aigradus places the establishment of the shrine-cult to Audoenus at Rouen precisely in the context of Carolingian aggression: chapters 18-19 of the *vita Ansberti* describe the tremendous support always lavished on the house of Fontenelle, and on monastic foundations in general, by the pious Merovingian rulers; chapter 20 shows bishop Anbertus moving the body of Audoenus into a prominent spot in the church of St. Peter outside the walls of Rouen, placing it in an elaborate tomb, gathering a huge crowd for this solemn public event, and establishing the day as a mandatory festival in the diocese; chapter 21 shows the mayor of the palace, Pippin, an agent of the devil, exiling Ansbertus from Neustria. Yet, before being chased from the see of Rouen, Ansbertus had

---

anciennes de sainte Genevieve de Paris. Etudes critiques [Bibliothèque de l'école des hautes études, IVe section. Sciences historiques et philologiques 329; Paris, 1986] pp. 3-10).

[74] Ed. E. Vacandard *Vie de S. Ouen, évêque de Rouen (641-684). Etude d'histoire Mérovingienne* (Paris, 1902) p. 360; ed. W. Levison, MGH SRM V p. 542.

[75] Head, *Hagiography and the Cult of Saints* p. 7.

[76] Head, *Hagiography and the Cult of Saints* p. 22.

managed to erect a symbol of Neustrian pride and independence that would survive as a memento throughout the Carolingian period. Audoenus would not be toppled until the eleventh century when the Normans, more Carolingian than the Carolingians, completed the conquest of Pious Neustria.

The anonymous biography of Audoenus has already been analyzed, by Fouracre, in the context of missionary historiography. The semantically-scrupulous title of Fouracre's discussion is worth quoting in full: "The Work of Audoenus of Rouen and Eligius of Noyon in Extending Episcopal Influence From Town to Country in Seventh-Century Neustria."[77] Perhaps unwieldy, but oh so *juste*. Using conciliar *acta*[78] as well as Merovingian-era historiographic narratives such as the *vita Audoeni*, Fouracre describes Audoenus' attempts to increase his control of his diocese, against the opposition of local customs and local *seniores*; the introjection of any anti-"pagan" evangelizing motivations was unnecessary and would have been unjustified. If one does not impose a missionary discourse on the narratives on the assumption that "paganism" must have been rampant, the picture that emerges of Merovingian Neustria from contemporary sources is one that does not give a large role to "paganism."[79]

Quite the contrary. "In the times of the glorious prince Lothar, and of his son king Chilperic," noble couples who themselves were paragons of Christianity produced children who either went into the religious life (like the saint's brother Ado) or royal service (like Audoenus and his other brother Rado) (ch. 1). The bulk of the narrative, however, takes place in the reign of Dagobert, in whose court two bright candles, Audoenus and Eligius, future bishop of Noyon, shone simultaneously (ch. 3). The king

---

[77] Paul Fouracre, "The Work of Audoenus of Rouen and Eligius of Noyon in Extending Episcopal Influence From Town to Country in Seventh-Century Neustria," *Studies in Church History* 16 (1979; "The Church in Town and Countryside" ed. D. Baker) pp. 77-91.

[78] C. de Clercq, *Concilia Galliae 511-695* CCSL 148A (1963) and C. de Clercq, *La Legislation religieuse Franque de Clovis à Charlemagne* (Louvain/Paris, 1936).

[79] For the only possible passage which could even remotely imply a contemporary conception of "paganism" in seventh-century Neustria, see the anonymous *vita Audoeni* (BHL 750) c. 4 ed. Levison p. 556 lines 9-14, especially the phrase "relicto ritu gentilium"; but compare Nelson's discussion of the meaning of "ritus" in this period as "lifestyle" or "habits," rather than as a reference to any "religious" orientation (Janet Nelson trans. *Annals of St. Bertin* a. 864 p. 105).

and his friend Audoenus were both stern masters, who ruled with iron hands; both kept in check any high spirits which manifested themselves among their subjects, their strength evoking great admiration from our *rouennais* historian.[80] Audoenus, for instance, attempted to enforce the Lord's Day as a day of rest, although agricultors seemed inclined to work on that day like any other.[81] The author also emphasizes the strict asceticism of the bishop and his flock (e.g., ch. 6), a characteristic in keeping with Victricius' assumptions concerning his *rouennais* flock.

In Audoenus' diocese, it was not only the quality of the ascetic exertions but also the sheer quantity of monks and nuns that was remarkable:

> If anyone wishes to know precisely how many churches and how many monasteries of both sexes were founded by [Audoenus] and under his pontificate, let him wander through these parishes and, seeing the throngs of monks, he will wonder whether he is in Egypt.[82]

As the Austrasians worked to take over Neustria, at least one anonymous local historian challenged his readers and listeners to look around the diocese of Rouen, and to swell with pride at what they saw: they would almost think they were in Egypt! The tremendous crowds of priests, monks and nuns reappear in ch. 11 to welcome their bishop home from a pilgrimage.

Aigradus' biography of Audoenus' successor Ansbertus paints an equally rosy picture of Merovingian Rouen. The *vita Ansberti* is one of the earliest historical narratives ever produced in Normandy, although not the

---

[80] For Dagobert the "leo fervidus" see c. 2, BHL 750 p. 555.

[81] On the Sabbatarian issue in saints' biographies and other sources of the period, Joseph-Claude Poulin, "Entre magie et religion. Recherches sur les utilisations marginales de l'écrit dans la culture populaire du haut moyen age" in *La culture populaire au Moyen-Age* ed. Pierre Boglioni (Actes du colloque de l'Institut d'études médiévales, Université de Montréal, April 1977; Montreal, 1979) pp. 123-143, esp. pp. 126-128; Graus, *Volk, Herrscher und Heiliger* p. 484 ff.

[82] "Quantae ecclesiae quantaque monasteria utrique sexsus ab ipso et sub ipso pontifice sunt fundati, si quis uoluerit clare cognoscere, lustret per eius parrochias et videns se quasi Aegyptum mirare in agmina monachorum" (BHL 750 pp. 556-557); this sentence ought to follow the previous one immediately as it does in all the manuscripts, rather than begin a new chapter as it does in Levison's edition. It is clear from the entire unbroken passage that, when Audoenus inspired people to "place their necks under Christ's yoke and service" (as we are told in the previous sentence) that he did not inspire them to convert to Christianity, but to take up the religious life.

earliest, for the same author tells us he had already written a biography of Ansbertus' predecessor Lantbertus.[83] The *vita Ansberti*, like the *vita Audoeni*, is a witness to the first moment at which the need to justify an identity against external threats became a factor in the Seine valley. The *vita Landberti*,[84] on the other hand, seems to have preceded Aigradus' second composition by a number of years, and appears to have been composed before the crisis engendered by the Austrasian take-over, in response to a quite different sort of narrative-producing competition, namely a property dispute between the abbeys of Fontenelle and Jumièges (c. 4).[85] It is impossible to recognize in either of Aigradus' narratives decrepit Merovingian rulers or corrupt churchmen. Piety, military ability and the independent control of their realms are taken for granted in the cases of Clothar, Childeric and Theodericus, hardly the *rois fainéants* of Einhard's famous biography of Charlemagne; it is the Carolingians who are absent from his story, except as disruptive forces.

Aigradus describes Ansbertus as the vigilant pastor of a flourishing flock (BHL 520a cc. 16-17). Aigradus' world was one in which king Clothar III's officials were predominately holy men of noble background, Anbertus having served as his referendary, just as Lantbertus as well had served in Clothar's palace (BHL 4675 c. 1). Ansbertus was saved from the worldly cares of marriage by his equally high-born betrothed, the future St. Angadrisma, who became a nun and later abbess of Oroër, near Beauvais (BHL 520a cc. 2-3). Aigradus does not tell us what prompted Lantbertus to become a monk at Fontenelle, but he does tell us that the saint's uncles (also in royal service) themselves brought him to the monastery, and endowed it generously, though they would have preferred him to remain in the world (BHL 4675 c. 1).

---

[83] *Vita Ansberti* c. 11. The earliest biography of the founder of Fontenelle, Wandregiselus, is definitely an early text composed before the end of the seventh century, but it is not a product of Neustria as is normally supposed. See Appendix 1.

[84] BHL 4675, ed. W. Levison, MGH SRM V pp. 608-612.

[85] Only a fragment of the biography of Lantbertus has come down to us, preserved in a few folios which were copied during the twelfth century, and incorporated in 1639 by Augustin de Broise into the "Maius Chronicon Fontenellae," a collection of sources connected with Fontenelle. The *Chronicon* is ms. Le Havre, BM 332 (A.34); the *vita Lantberti* is on fols. 136v-137v. The text was still available in its entirety at Fontenelle during the early ninth century when it was used by a number of authors of the house (Levison ed. MGH SRM V p. 607 for references).

The very epitome of the discourse of "Pious Neustria" is embodied in the vineyard rendezvous between Ansbertus and king Clothar's younger brother Theoderic.[86] One day the monk Ansbertus, who had retired from his palatine career, was laboring in a vineyard planted by abbot Wandregiselus of Fontenelle. Theoderic, whom Ansbertus knew well from his days in the royal palace, came out to Fontenelle to visit the saint, and benefit from his holy teachings. Ansbertus predicted that Theoderic would have great difficulties when he became king, and Theoderic responded that he would then call on Ansbertus to help him as a bishop. Ansbertus, however, does not at the time think he is worthy of so exalted a position. There is nothing implausible in this story, which could have happened precisely as it was related. Whether or not the anecdote is "true," however, Aigradus' perception the extraordinary piety of Neustrian leaders is clear: both the king and the monk are humble, devout and hardworking, the former respectful of the latter's ability to guide, the latter of the former's ability to govern. Pious kings and pious nobles worked together to create a world of exemplary monasteries, as the Merovingian rulers endowed Fontenelle with material support (BHL 520a c. 9; BHL 4675 c. 3) and applauded the spiritual sustenance given the monks by the abbots, all personal friends and former officials of the royal persons (BHL 520a c. 13; BHL 4675 c. 2).

We have to think not only in terms of the content of the narrative biographies of these final two Neustrian bishops of Rouen, but also in terms of the political acts and public ceremonies connected with their bodies. In Aigradus' eyes, the days of Ansbertus marked the twilight of pious Neustria: the advent of Pippin recreated the conditions of the Neronian and Decian persecutions of pious Christians (BHL 520a c. 24). The exile of Ansbertus by Pippin to the heart of Austrasia (689-691), where the prelate would be surrounded by enemies and neutralized as an opponent in Neustria, forms the central dramatic point of the liturgical hymn that was chanted in public celebration of Ansbertus' cult.[87] Ansbertus had been allowed to return to Fontenelle, where he died in the odor of sanctity, and was buried by the Neustrian abbot Hildbertus in the church of St. Paul,

---

[86] *Vita Ansberti* (BHL 520a) c. 7 pp. 623-624.

[87] BHL 523, appended to all the oldest mss. of Ansbertus' biography; ed. Levison pp. 641-643, verses 14-17.

a shrine soon marked by miracles (BHL 520a c. 36). But the exile still loomed large in the local consciousness. Ansbertus was such a holy man that, according to his hymn, he took the opportunity of his exile to Hautmont, in Picardy, to evangelize the area. Austrasia, infested as it was with "not-Christians," was hardly a match for "Pious Neustria":

> Accused of no crime, but expelled due to hatred
> By the prince of the Franks, as Clement once from Rome,
> By the emperor Trajan, he became an exile for the
>   fatherland ("patria").
>
> Clement saved many peoples with his sacrosanct teaching,
> And this man [Ansbertus] led many straight along the path
>   to heaven,
> Teaching by words and example the Sicambrian people.
>
> Many, you say, were saved on the island under Clement,
> Many too as well under Ansbertus in the Belgic province,
> Many whom he urged on through his instruction towards
>   eternal rewards.[88]

---

[88] "Ob inuidiam expulsus a Francorum principe/ Uelut Clemens dudum Roma a Traiano caesare,/ Nullum adprobatus crimen, exsul factus **patriae**./ Plures Clemens saluat gentes sacrosancto dogmate/ Et hic multos recto ducit ad aethera tramite/ Uerbis et exemplo docens populo Sicambrico./ Quanti, putas, sub Clemente salui sunt in insula,/ Multique et sub Ansberto Belgica prouintia,/ Quos docendo ad aeterna excitauit praemia." We can constrast the perspective of this national anthem of pious Neustria with Aigradus' vision of "conversion" in Neustria itself: Ansbertus' merits had caused local people to convert from the world to Christ, and to take up the monastic life at Fontenelle: "Cuius doctrina et exortationibus plurimi **corroborati munitique**, ad conversionis festinantes gratiam, plurima deferebant dona in speciebus diversis pretiosorum metallorum, sed et possessionum praedia nonnulla, in diversis territoriis" (BHL 520a c. 13 pp. 627-628). BHL 519, which has sometimes been considered the original text of Ansbertus' biography ("Vita sancti Ansberti archiepiscopi rotomagensis ab interpolationibus pura nunc primum edita" AB I (1882) pp. 178-191) was printed from Brussels BR 9636-37 (3228) fols. 240r-242r. The manuscript is a legendary of the eleventh or twelfth century from St. Laurent of Liège, and BHL 519 is an epitome of Aigradus' biography made by the compiler of the legendary. If the text is to be studied, it must be studied in the context of the legendary itself, not of Merovingian Neustria. The same is true of another epitome in a seventeenth-century collection of abbreviated saints' biographies, BN lat. 17.635 fols. 293r-297v.

Despite the hymn, with its aspect of a national anthem for Pious Neustria, Ansbertus was not the principal patron of the region; that honor fell to Audoenus, a saint of monumental *virtus*, whose *post-mortem* life I will postpone discussing for a moment, in order to examine a third biography of the late-Merovingian diocese of Rouen, that of Filibertus of Jumièges. Filibertus belongs, with Audoenus, Ansbertus and Lantbertus, to that circle of saints who had been active in the diocese of Rouen during the decades immediately preceding the Austrasian aggression.

The earliest historiographical products of the abbey of Jumièges are quite as important as those of Fontenelle in terms of the expression of the self-conception of "Pious Neustria." A set of early biographies survives from Jumièges: an original and a "polished" version of the biography of the founder of the house, Filibertus.[89] As with Aigradus' biography of Ansbertus, or

[89] The author of the early biography of St. Austreberta (himself a monk of Jumièges), writing *circa* 724-730, knew and used both the original and the "polished" versions of the biography of Filibertus, the original having been dedicated to the third abbot of Jumièges, Coschinus, by a monk of that house, and thus having been written fairly soon after the saint's death. BHL 6805 and BHL 6806 are the class A and B versions of the biography, which differ in many readings and in their prologues. Class B is the "polished" version, referred to by the author of the *vita Austrebertae* (BHL 832), who expresses the desire to avoid a similar fate of finding his words rewritten. Hariulf also tells us that abbot Coschinus, who ruled St. Riquier as well, had had a biography of Filibertus written (*Chronicon Centulense* I.26). See the edition of the *vita Filiberti* by Levison (who hypercritically argues for a date of composition in the late eighth century [p. 573]), for how the A and B versions differ globally from each other (MGH SRM 5 [1910] pp. 577-581); the differences are entirely stylistic. However, within each stream (BHL 6805 and BHL 6806), there are many more variations in the manuscript copies than are reflected in Levison's apparatus, particularly when it is a question of how to expand an abbreviation; furthermore, the oldest surviving manuscripts (of the tenth century) all are full of scribal corrections and erasures. The difficulties which post-Carolingian scribes seem to have experienced in reading and copying the *vitae* of Filibertus indicate that they were working from very old, Merovingian-era exemplars. There is even a marginal tracing of a Merovingian ligature on f. 69r of Paris, BN nal 2261, a twelfth-century copy of the biography from Cluny. The completely nonsensical and ungrammatical readings of much of Paris, BN lat. 3809A (fol. 6r-8v), a copy made in the fifteenth century which nevertheless belongs to the A1a* family in Levison's stemma, may be a particularly good witness to the difficulties presented by Merovingian-era texts after the Carolingian transformation of the form of the written language. The class B version is much more widely known than the A version. All the oldest copies of class B survive in Picard manuscripts

the earliest biography of Audoenus, the biography of Filibertus, likewise written by a near-contemporary, includes all sorts of colorful political details. The competitive crucible of composition in this case, which began the production of historical narrative at Jumièges, included not only the very highest level politics of the Carolingian penetration, but also the more local problems caused for the house by the consistent favoritism shown by Audoenus, Ansbertus and the other powers that were, for Fontenelle. In the major litigation which had arisen between the houses of Fontenelle and Jumièges during Audoenus' pontificate, both the reigning king and the bishop of Rouen had supported Fontenelle, and gone so far as to despoil Jumièges of property and give it to Fontenelle.[90] Audoenus had, in that instance, according to Aigradus of Fontenelle, attempted to compensate Jumièges for its losses to some extent, but that was evidently not enough to make Jumièges authors fans of the powerful prelate. Abbot Filibertus of Jumièges himself had been at one point imprisoned and then exiled from the diocese by Audoenus.[91] The house of Jumièges, furthermore, is so very close to the city of Rouen that it would have found itself more open to resentment-producing episcopal control and intervention than would Fontenelle.

The image of Audoenus, emblem of pious Neustria, in Jumièges historiography is complicated by a certain local hostility towards the saint. But Jumièges historians did not reject the discursive prism of Pious Neustria; they simply sought to train its rainbow-bright beam on alternative candidates for national hero. The anonymous Jumièges historians both were less concerned to demonstrate the extraordinary sanctity of the entire *patria* of Neustria in general than to demonstrate the perfection of the monastic life at Jumièges in particular, which they wished to place at the top of the heap of local houses (read: above Fontenelle), and the perfection of the life of Filibertus, whom they wished to promote as a symbol preferable

---

(Boulogne BM 106 from St. Bertin; Arras BM 1029 [82] from St. Vaast; Arras BM 462 [573] also from St. Vaast); it was in the east that the narrative was incorporated into the *Liber de Natalitiis*, a Flemish legendary collection which circulated throughout Latin Europe.

[90] Aigradus, *Vita Lantberti* c. 4 (BHL 4675).

[91] *Vita Filiberti* BHL 6805 cc. 24-25, ed. Levison, MGH SRM 5 (1910).

to Audoenus.[92] Both streams of the Merovingian biography of Filibertus of Jumièges are concerned with describing the saint's retreat from the world and his search for perfection in a region characterized by a thriving monasticism; he is joined most especially by the monks of Jumièges, the very paragons of monkish perfection.[93] Though Filibertus did have certain advantages as patron of Pious Neustria, Ansbertus had been right to select Audoenus as the patriotic symbol: any figure, like Filibertus, who was associated particularly with a single monastic house rather than with the entire diocese would be bound to give the impression that his or her promoters were interested in issues of petty precedence.[94]

The earliest gemmetic historians showed Filibertus as the very motor of Neustrian monasticism: "multa monasteria per eius exempla sunt constructa in Neustria" (c. 22),[95] not through the example of Audoenus. Audoenus was not absent from this earliest monument of the Jumièges historiographic tradition. He played an important role in the early stage of Filibertus' career when, as the leader of a major circle of religious devotees then serving in the royal palace, he took Filibertus under his wing; furthermore, Filibertus' first full-fledged monastic experience took place at Rebais, Audoenus' foundation. Unfortunately, the experience had not been

---

[92] Like the late-seventh-century biography of Audoenus, as we will see momentarily, this contemporary biography of Filibertus emphasizes the saint's *virtus* (cc. 4, 11-21, 27). Filibertus's miracles were not only those required by an independent Neustria in general, but also those required by the house of Jumièges in its battles against officials who would despoil it in order to endow Fontenelle, as had happened during the abbacy of Lantbertus; one, for instance, describes his ability to perform revenge-miracles against those who steal his property (c. 16).

[93] When he is tonsured, it is "ut uiris perfectioribus imitabilis fieret" (p. 585); when he goes on a tour of monasteries, it is "quia perfecti semper perfectiora sectantur" (p. 587).

[94] Furthermore, Filibertus had (unlike Ansbertus) actually died in exile from the diocese of Rouen; after having been banished from the diocese by Audoenus (cc. 24-26), he ended his life in the diocese of Poitiers despite a reconciliation with Audoenus (c. 28) and became, in the first instance, a saint of Noirmoutier in the Vendée, where his first *post-mortem* miracles occurred (cc. 34-42).

[95] For the Filibertine rule, see BHL 181 I.8-13; BHL 6805 c. 23; L. Jaud, *S. Filibert, fondateur et abbé de Jumièges et de Noirmoutier, sa vie, son temps, sa survivance, son culte. Etude d'histoire monastique au VIIe siècle* (Paris, 1910). Filibertus founded and established his rule at least at Jumièges, Noirmoutier, Montivilliers, Pavilly and Quinçay.

a positive one: Filibertus had had to flee Rebais, where the monks had rebelled against his abbatial authority when he tried to impose strict regulation (c. 4). Audoenus then played no role in the foundation of Jumièges itself; in that instance the crucial aid was provided by the Merovingian king Clodoveus and his queen Baldechild, who are generally shown throughout the narrative as key stimulators of "pious Neustria." For, though the monks at Rebais were not as strict as they might have been, there were certainly no "pagans" in Francia; nothing seems in need of reform, except perhaps Rebais (but that is a dig at Audoenus), for Filibertus could tour the land finding nothing but good models for his planned monastery (cc. 4-5).[96]

Filibertus, Ansbertus and Audoenus all were described by their Neustrian biographers as leaders of "Pious Neustria," but it was the cult of Audoenus which became most important in Neustria. From the moment of its inception, the cult of Audoenus was one of the most solemn celebrations held at Rouen, and numismatic evidence indicates that his patronage overcame that of St. Peter in the church where he lay entombed before the middle of the eighth century.[97] We have already seen that the author of Audoenus' late Merovingian biography sought to mobilize the inhabitants of the diocese of Rouen behind the patriotic figure of the deceased prelate by urging them to tread the highways and byways of the region and to ponder its Egypt-rivalling sanctity. Likewise, he sought to involve them

---

[96]   The single passage in the biography which even recognizes the need to look outside the cloister walls explicitly describes how the brothers of the monastery would convert souls from the world to Christ, that is, to the monastic life, not from "paganism" to "Christianity": "Erat consuetudo sancti ad exortandas animas fratres de monasterio circumquaque transmittere, et confluebant ad eum uiri nobiles et potentes, propriis uoluntatibus respuentes, Christum dominum seruientes" (BHL 6805 c. 22 ed. Levison p. 595). There follows immediately an account of the foundation of the monastery of Pavilly. On the basis of this passage, L. Jaud made Filibertus an anti-"pagan" missionary (S. Filibert p. 188ff). Yet the only "conversion" Filibertus brings about according to his contemporary biographer is that of bishop of Ansoaldus of Poitiers, who "sub religionis norma episcopalem coepit inclinare potentiam" (c. 26), clearly a question of conversion from the world to Christ, not from "paganism" to "Christianity."

[97]   Jean Lafaurie, "Trouvailles de monnaies franques et mérovingiennes en Seine-Maritime, Ve-VIIIe s." Histoire et numismatique en Haute-Normandie (Caen, 1980; Cahier des Annales de Normandie 12A) pp. 111-116; Gauthier, "Rouen pendant le haut Moyen-Age" p. 12.

actively in the collection of memorials to the saint's *virtus*. The biography as a whole is primarily a collection of Audoenus' acts of power, an emphasis very much in keeping with what would have been required of the new supernatural patron of Neustria, with the Austrasians at the gates. Having established Audoenus in a see that it was possible to confuse with the deserts of Egypt, his biographer turns to narrating his miracles. The focus on the miracles distinguishes the biography of Audoenus from the near-contemporary biographies of Ansbertus and Lantbertus, whose author was much more concerned with describing the political intrigues of the day. The contrast points up how much Audoenus' character was, from the first, that of invisible patron.

First Audoenus ends a drought in Spain (ch. 7). Then he heals a man of Anjou who had been paralyzed when trying to work on the Sabbath, "unde terror in populo et stupor maximus inrueret." Audoenus does insist though that "Christiani" ought never to work on the Lord's Day (c. 9), for Audoenus, like Victricius before, took numerous stabs at changing the definition of proper "Christian" practice in the territories under his supervision; nevertheless, his biographer never implies that those peasants who had broken the sabbath were not Christians. Audoenus' vigor was even the main point of the description of the pilgrimage to Rome, which he made when his body was already weakened by age and ascetic practices (ch. 10); the author evidently considered the journey tremendously arduous, and we are suddenly reminded how long in the future lay the great age of pilgrimage. In Cologne to try to negotiate a settlement in the struggles between the Neustrians and Austrasians that erupted just before he died, he heals a mute (ch. 13). On the way home, he cures a possessed woman at Verdun (ch. 14).

Having narrated a mere fraction of the miracles performed by the saint while he still lived in this flesh, the author urges his readers and hearers to contact local observers throughout Spain, Italy and the Gauls for more examples (ch. 12, ch. 17). The author's final concern is to emphasize the power that Audoenus still exercises *post-mortem*, a power which, the author tells us in a most unusual passage, was not confined to the place of his burial but was active wherever Audoenus' relics had rested before burial.[98] In

---

[98] "Et non solum in eum locum, sed per plures prouintias, ubi ipse uir sanctus in corpore requieuit, tanta ad praesens miracula fulgent..." (ch. 17, p. 565).

effect, Audoenus' active patronage had been spread all over the diocese, for his body had been carried in a great, lamenting procession "per loca singula" before being buried at St. Peter's outside Rouen.

One particular locale in which the *virtus* of Audoenus had undoubtedly been concentrated was in a monastery dedicated to him, which had been founded, within a few years of his death, in the Mérey. The story of the foundation of the house was not put down in writing until a century after the event, by a monk of that house, La Croix-S.-Ouen, writing during the reign of Charlemagne.[99] Leutfredus, a noble Neustrian born near the city of Evreux, founded the monastery in honor of Audoenus on a spot where the sainted bishop was believed to have seen a vision of a cross, a spot Audoenus himself predicted would be the future site of true followers of the crucified Jesus (that is, monks who would mortify their flesh). Leutfredus, according to his biographer, had wished to settle in Rouen, but bishop Ansbertus sent him back to Evreux, feeling that Leutfredus could

---

[99] *Vita et miracula Leutfredi* (= BHL 4899 and 4901) ed. Mesnel, *Les saints du diocèse d'Evreux* VI (Evreux, 1922). The best copy of the *vita et miracula Leutfredi* is Rouen BM 1380 (U.55) fols. 91v-104v, a tenth-century manuscript from Jumièges, taken along with Paris BN lat. 5356 fols. 114r-121r, a twelfth-century manuscript from Fécamp. Either Mesnel's edition (based on Rouen BM 1388 [U.2]) or that in the AASS (ed. F.B. AASS June V pp. 92-97) is preferable to the MGH edition (MGH SRM VII ed. W. Levison pp. 7-18), for Levison excised sections of the text which seemed to him irrelevant from the MGH edition. Levison dated the text (both portions are by a single author) to the reign of Louis the Pious at the earliest and probably to c. 851 (MGH SRM VI p. 3), but Mesnel argued that it belonged to the reign of Charlemagne; in this he was supported by the review of M. Coens (AB XLI [1923] p. 446). There can be no doubt but that either the author of Leutfredus' biography borrowed his account of the foundation of La-Croix-S.-Ouen from the ninth-century B/C streams of Audoenus' biographies (BHL 751/753; see below pp. 87-94), or *vice versa* (BHL 4899 ed. Levison c. 10 pp. 12-13 documents the similarities). However, since the *Vita Leutfredi* is throughout an original work, including no known borrowings other than this potential one, while the B/C *Vita Audoeni* is a work of research including borrowings from many other narratives, it seems more likely that the author of the revised biography of Audoenus used the biography of Leutfredus than *vice versa*. Furthermore, it is unlikely that the author of the *vita et miracula Leutfredi* was using any biography of Audoenus, for nothing about him is described that can be traced to the "A" biography (BHL 750) at all, and the only overlap with the "B"/"C" biographies went in the other direction. As the revised biography of Audoenus was written in approximately 800 (see below pp. 89-90), then the *Vita Leutfredi* would date from soon before 800.

do more good there. Thus, against the background of the Carolingian penetration of Neustria and in the immediate aftermath of Ansbertus' establishment of Audoenus' cult at Rouen, a noble native Neustrian was sent off by Ansbertus to found an institution designed to keep alive the memory of Audoenus in the Neustrian diocese neighboring Rouen, namely Evreux.

The anonymous author of the *Vita Leutfredi* tells his listeners in the prologue that he is reporting oral tradition. The significance with which the late-eighth-century author invested the story of Leutfredus' late-seventh-century lifetime, and the latter's foundation of the monastery of La-Croix-S.-Ouen, is reminiscent of the patriotic hymn to Ansbertus, and of the *virtus*-laden biography of Audoenus, both composed at the end of the seventh century. The house of La-Croix-S.-Ouen, a small monastery which, unlike Fontenelle and Jumièges, was not to come under direct Carolingian control, preserved the memory of Audoenus, Ansbertus and all they stood for throughout the eighth century. Leutfredus himself only began to be honored with a cult in the lifetime of the author, who witnessed the translation of Leutfredus from his original burial spot in the church of St. Paul at La Croix into the basilica where Audoenus's relics lay.

The translation, along with the institution of a cult to Leutfredus, was performed by abbot John of La-Croix-S.-Ouen, who was also bishop of Dol.[100] Dol, in Brittany, was itself a center of resistance to the Carolingian Empire throughout the eighth century. It is striking that the connection between John of Dol and La-Croix-S.-Ouen itself constitutes the sum total of the evidence for contact between the Seine valley and anti-Carolingian Brittany;[101] the connection between Dol and a center of the cult of Audoenus should be seen as yet more evidence of the oppositional nature of Dol and Brittany.

What, then, were the oral traditions recorded by the anonymous monk of La-Croix-S.-Ouen concerning the pious Neustrian noble Leutfredus following the translation of the latter's relics by the bishop of Dol? The prologue (quoted below almost in its entirety) is resounding, and is almost literally a call to arms:

---

[100] AASS June V c. 29 pp. 96-97.
[101] Julia Smith, *Province and Empire. Brittany and the Carolingians* (Cambridge, 1992) p. 162.

We read in the book of Ecclesiastes: "Let us praise glorious men and our forebears in their generations, those who obtained glory in the great days of their nation, and thus will their name never be left behind"....Concerning men of this type, it is said through a prophet of the Lord: "Your javelins will go forth in brightness, your weapons in a flash of lightening." For the lightening flash of those weapons is indeed the splendor of their miracles. We are surely protected by those weapons, and have destroyed our enemies with those javelins; therefore miracles, with their qualities, are weapons like javelins. For holy men transfix the hearts of their adversaries by means of words as though they were some sort of javelin; moreover, by means of their arms, that is their miracles, they protect themselves, and so the extent to which they ought to be hearkened unto resounds clearly through the force of their javelins, and the extent to which they ought to be revered, is shown clearly through the weapons of their miracles.[102]

The militaristic ring is unmistakeable; one can almost hear the horns sounding. Those present at Leutfredus' festival in the church of St. Ouen were urged to remember their forefathers, and the great things the latter had done in earlier days. The miraculous powers of these patrons, Leutfredus and Audoenus, would protect their descendants, and bring egregious harm to the enemies of those descendants. At Rouen, the patronage of Audoenus in fact proved insufficient to stave off the determined Austrasians, despite the insistence of the saint's first biographer on his miraculous powers; after the 720s, the see of Rouen became an annex of the Carolingian-dominated abbey of Fontenelle. But off at La-Croix-S.-Ouen, where I have found nothing to connect the house during the eighth century with any of the key Carolingian office-holders or family-members, the protective power of a virtuous Neustrian patron must have seemed more realistic to laud at this late date.

---

[102] "Scriptum legimus in libro Ecclesiastici: 'Laudemus uiros gloriosos et parentes nostros in generatione sua, qui in diebus gentis suae gloriam adepti sunt, et nomen eorum non derelinquetur'....De huiuscemodi uiris per prophetam Domino dicitur: 'In lumine iacula tua ibunt, in fulgore armorum tuorum.' Fulgor namque armorum est claritas miraculorum. Armis quippe nos tuemur, iaculis aduersa destruimus, arma ergo cum iaculis sunt miracula cum praedicamentis. Sancti enim uiri uerbis suis quasi quibusdam iaculis corda aduersantium transfigunt; armis autem, id est miraculis, semet ipsos tuentur, ut et, quantum sint audiendi, sonent per impetum iaculorum et, quamtum sint reuerendi, ostendant per arma miraculorum" (MGH SRM VI p. 7).

The anonymous historian's vision of seventh-century Neustria is one dominated by its extraordinary piety. There seem to be monasteries and centers of learning everywhere. Leutfredus who, from birth, longs to devote himself to the ways of the spirit, can study first with the masters gathered in the suburb of St. Taurin at Evreux (c. 3),[103] seek "post-graduate" training at Condé and Chartres, soon realizing that he ought to be the master (c. 5), then set up an independent oratory and school near his parental home (c. 6), decide to give up everything (c. 7), take to the road and discover, in the immediate vicinity, a female house at La Varenne and a hermit at Cailly, with whom he settles for awhile (c. 9), then finally go to the big city, Rouen, where he studies with Sydonius, even joining the monastery which the latter had founded (c. 10). When he founds La-Croix-S.-Ouen (c. 12), the house grows unbelievably quickly, as everyone in the neighborhood rushes to devote himself to Christ (c. 11).

Having devoted the entire first half of the biography to establishing the spiritually-evolved state of Neustria, the author turns, in the second half, to describing the awesome power of Leutfredus. The first to get a taste of it is the bishop of Evreux, who attempts to interfere at the house and as a result finds his horse collapsing beneath him, its guts poured out on the road (c. 14). Finding himself in better temper, Leutfredus heals a monk (c. 15) and stops a fire (c. 16), before causing all the teeth of a man and of the man's descendants to fall out of their mouths because he had brought a law suit against Leutfredus (c. 17). When a woman challenged him over fishing rights in a local river, he cursed her and all of her seed to an eternity of baldness (c. 18). Now mollified, he created a spring for a community in need of a water source (c. 19), and then saved from death Charles Martel's son Grifo (c. 20), who presumably (and not incidentally) was thus enabled by Leutfredus' miraculous *virtus* to go to war against his brothers, Pippin and Carloman. Another healing (c. 21) precedes the exorcism of a demon from the monastic church (c. 22) and from a possessed man (c. 23). Nearing death, Leutfredus recovers a lost agricultural implement from a river with his abbatial staff (c. 24), curses with perpetual sterility the lands of some peasants who broke the sabbath (c. 25), and temporarily excommunicates a dead brother until the monk's sins were forgiven (c. 26). His *virtus* remains undiminished in death, for he turns up to cause a disre-

---

[103] Chapter citations are to the AASS edition.

spectful servant of a later abbot to bleed from all his bodily orifices (c. 31), to give sight to two blind people (cc. 32-33) and to liberate a demoniac (c. 33).

The Austrasian princes would hardly have been the only people the house of La-Croix-S.-Ouen wished to keep at bay during the eighth century, but they were probably principal among them. The graphic revenge-miracles in circulation in connection with Leutfredus' name may have contributed to the fact that we never hear of the Neustrian house of La-Croix-S.-Ouen being submitted to the control of any key pro-Carolingian institution or individual until 918 when Charles the Simple, desperate for supporters, granted some of its properties to the abbey of St. Germain-des-Prés.[104] La-Croix-S.Ouen remained an independent outpost of Pious Neustria until it almost didn't matter anymore.

It appears that the figure of Audoenus was flexible enough to serve as an anti-Austrasian symbol of "Pious Neustria" even outside the boundaries of what is now the ecclesiastical province of Rouen. Just as Ansbertus had established the cult of Audoenus at Rouen, and encouraged Leutfredus to install a similar center of Neustrian devotion in the diocese of Evreux, bishop Hermelandus of Le Mans, who took up the episcopate in 698/9, built an oratory of Audoenus near the walls of his episcopal city sometime before 712/713; to that oratory he attached a presbyter, a community of monks and a community of paupers.[105] The interest of the bishop of Dol, of anti-Frankish Brittany, in La-Croix-St.-Ouen, is mirrored here by the interest of the bishop of Le Mans in a sanctuary of Audoenus. Maine was the most difficult of all the regions of Neustria to bring under Austrasian control, and has the distinction of being the last bastion of resistance to the Carolingian *coup d'état*. The *virtus* of Audoenus, with which Hermelandus had hoped to protect Le Mans from the Austrasians,

---

[104] See the famous charter of March, 918: Archives Nationales K.16 no. 9; ed. P. Lauer, *Receuil des actes de Charles III le Simple* (Paris, 1940-1949) no. 92 pp. 209-212.

[105] *Actus pontificum cenomannis in urbe degentium* eds. G. Busson and A. Ledru (Archives Historiques de Maine II; Le Mans, 1901) pp. 231-234, the testament of Hermelandus, from Le Mans BM 224 of the twelfth or thirteeth century. The *Actus pontificum* was part of the corpus of forgeries produced by the cathedral chapter of Mans between 860 and 863, designed to aid in the restitution of the temporalities of the churches of Le Mans (Walter Goffart *The Le Mans Forgeries: A Chapter from the History of Church Property in the Ninth Century* [Cambridge, Mass, 1966]). The details of the endowment claimed for the oratory of Audoenus are therefore suspect; nevertheless, the existence of the oratory making the property claims is not.

failed in Maine as it had in Upper Normandy. In 724 the bishop's successor was deposed by Charles Martel, and the church of Le Mans suffered more than most from despoliations and usurpations of ecclesiastical property.[106] The Austrasian behemoth was in Neustria to stay.

The three most important local Neustrian institutions (the see of Rouen/St.-Pierre-St.-Ouen, Jumièges and Fontenelle) had failed at the end of the seventh century to present a united front against Austrasian aggression. Fontenelle was quickly recognized as a threat by the Carolingians, and was taken into their control from the very beginning of the eighth century. Jumièges, which seemed to resist the Neustrian independence cults of Audoenus and Ansbertus, was allowed to remain untouched for several more decades. The church at Le Mans had held out somewhat longer, perhaps inspired in part by the presence of the *virtus* of Audoenus, but Maine was the boulevard of Neustria, and could not be allowed to remain independent as the Austrasians tightened their grip on the west. By the end of the eighth century, only the tiny monastery of La-Croix-St.-Ouen in the Evreçin still celebrated, unimpeded, the memory of Pious Neustria.[107]

C. THE CAROLINGIANS AND THE WRITTEN WORD: AN IDEOLOGICAL APPRECIATION

i. Austrasians in the Cloisters: The First Decades of Carolingian Rule in Neustria

The Austrasian mayors of the palace took over Neustria at the end of the seventh century, and consolidated their political and military hold

---

[106] Goffart, *The Le Mans Forgeries*; Philippe Le Maître "L'oeuvre d'Aldric du Mans et sa signification (832-857)" *Francia* 8 (1980) pp. 43-64, esp. p. 45.

[107] The position and fate of Fécamp, one of the greatest of the Norman-era houses and originally a Merovingian-era foundation, are unclear. The house was founded late in the seventh century in the Caux region, one of a number of female houses there located, and its first abbess, Childemarca, is celebrated in martyrologies from the eighth century. Her biography, however, has been lost; excerpts which have survived through citation by later authors do indicate that *fécampois* historians likewise adhered to the discourse of Pious Neustria in the late Merovingian period. For the lost biography and various later citations, see V.D. Buck in AASS Oct. XI pp. 679-684.

on the Frankish kingdoms over the course of the first few decades of the eighth century, particularly during the reign of Charles Martel. As everyone knows, the position of *sub-regulus* under the Merovingian monarchs was not sufficient for the ambitions of this particular family, which had risen from its ancestral lands in the Meuse-Moselle-Ardennes in the course of the previous century to within what seemed to be a mere heartbeat of the kingship. But appearances can be deceiving. When the Merovingian king Theodericus IV died in 737, Charles' sons Carloman and Pippin attempted to succeed in their own names. Facing a loss of loyalty in region after region, the brothers were forced to accept the accession of Childeric III, a Merovingian, to the throne (743). The prize of royal status would not be so easy to come by. The Merovingian rulers had on their side not only centuries of traditional loyalties (particularly in the diocese of Rouen, which had always benefitted, and never suffered, under the Frankish polity), as well as the civil recognition of the emperors, but also their own sacred blood, embodied visibly in their long hair.

Just as the crisis of the Austrasian takeover had stimulated historiographic production in Neustria, the burning need to circumvent Merovingian legitimacy and to substitute for it a new basis of Carolingian authority would, from the middle of the eighth century, engender a whole series of historiographic and discursive strategies on the part of loyalist historians. The "prodigious output of the written word at every level of Carolingian society" has already been explored by Rosamond McKitterick in a book-length study. This prodigious output was seen in "an impulse to the recording of the past in writing, in the exploitation of the written word in government and administration, and in a marked impact on the character of aristocratic and lay culture in general."[108] Her masterful study does cover the latter two spheres of literacy, but barely touches the first, the "impulse to the recording of the past in writing"; indeed, she calls for a separate study of the historiographic aspect of the Carolingian project, on which she is presently engaged.[109]

While awaiting McKitterick's synthesis, this bi-partite chapter should serve to connect Upper Norman narratives of the eighth and ninth centur-

---

[108] Rosamond McKitterick, *The Carolingians and the Written Word* (Cambridge, 1989) p. 3.
[109] McKitterick, *Carolingians* p. 240 n. 101.

ies with Carolingian, historically-based legitimizing strategies which have already been noticed in various separate studies. Some of the techniques of Carolingian historiography and cultic manipulation would, along with so much else, strike deep roots in Normandy, eventually serving the Viking conquerors; it is also my intention to highlight those precedents, in preparation for the second part of the study.

*

* *

Pippin did not succeed in becoming king until the 750s, though not for want of trying. The royal coronation was as long in the making as the eventual imperial one would be.[110] Furthermore, the Pippinids of seventh-century Austrasia were already adept at combining "ecclesiastical" policies with other routes to advancement from their ancestral landed base in Meuse-Moselle-Ardennes.[111] Some early legitimizing strategies were pregnant with implications for the future religious historiography of the Frankish realms. The first appearance of sacrohistoriation may be the Concilium Germanicum, held in 741 under Pippin, Carloman and Boniface, the first official Frankish event commemorated by a text dated from the Lord's Incarnation. Thus did Pippin and Carloman, at the time usurpers and ille-gitimate kings facing resistance from every quarter, declare the dawning of a new and better age. Dating by dominical years appealed to metapoli-tics at a level far beyond the civil recognition which the Merovingians had received from the emperors to govern Gaul, and asserts a universalizing identity to the bargain: the Frankish realms were, thenceforward, to be conceived (by definition), as "Christian."

By definition, yes, "Christian." But what was to be the definition of "Christian" that would be in force? The Concilium Germanicum had been just the beginning for sacrohistoriation, and for the vision of secular his-tory which would increasingly underpin the Carolingian polity, while un-dermining the discourse of "Pious Neustria," rendering the latter a concep-tual impossibility. If the Carolingian princes were to be the saviors of Francia, the Merovingian world which they saved would have to be "not-

---

[110] Robert Folz *The Coronation of Charlemagne, 25 December 800* (London, 1974; trans. J.E. Anderson, revised by H. Maas, of *Le couronnement impérial de Charlemagne*; Trente journées qui ont fait la France 25: 25 décembre, 800; Paris, 1964) p. 73.

[111] Dierkens, "Quelques aspects de la christianisation" pp. 41-44.

Christian." Whether or not the strategy was fully deliberate in the 740s is irrelevant for the purposes of this study, which is concerned not with Carolingian politics but with the echoes of political struggles in historiographic narrative. The effect that policies adopted by the Austrasian *ambitiosi* in the 740s would have on visions of the Merovingian past into this century has been brought out by Dierkens, in the context of his innovative discussion of the definition of "Christianity" referred to above in the introduction.[112]

The twin councils of Estinnes and Soissons, held simultaneously in March of 744 under Carloman and Pippin III respectively, with Boniface attending the meeting at Estinnes, marked a major turning point in the definition of "Christianity." In the Vatican manuscript Palat. lat. 577 there has survived an annex to the *acta* of Estinnes, the *Indiculus superstitionum et paganiarum* (fol. 7rv).[113] In one fell swoop, the ambitious princes and their prelate sidekick defined as "pagan" a series of customs known to have been widely practiced (many of which would eventually be defined by other churchmen as "Christian"). But "eventually" doesn't matter here; what matters is that the Christians who acted in these suddenly proscribed ways, were now open to the accusation of being "not-Christian."

The official *acta* of the twin councils of 744 are the first known documents in the Frankish world to outlaw "paganism." This does not, however, mean that the Carolingian mayors of the palace were the first Frankish rulers to care enough about Christianity to battle "paganism." What it does mean is that the Carolingian mayors of the palace were the first Frankish princes to employ a definition of "Christianity" under which a whole series of common beliefs and practices were to be considered incompatible with the religion. It means that the Carolingian princes were the first Frankish rulers to believe that, if they were to go out into their domains and inquire along certain lines, they would find "pagans." They believed the "pagans" were there to be legislated against.[114] It was not

---

[112] Dierkens, "Quelques aspects de la christianisation."

[113] Ed. Werminghoff MGH LL, Conc. II (Hanover 1893) pp. 6-7 and 33-36; ed. Boretius, MGH LL, Conc. I (Hannover 1883) pp. 222-223; Alain Dierkens, "Quelques aspects de la christianisation" pp. 32-33.

[114] An interpretation inspired by the work of Moore on the twelfth and thirteenth centuries, a brilliant study that errs only in believing that the "heretics" of the twelfth century were the first non-existent group in Latin Europe to be sud-

that the Merovingian rulers had approved of "pagans," it was that they didn't think there were any around to worry about.

We can now grasp in a concrete example the dire historiographic consequences of applying uniform, essentialist definitions of "Christianity" to the process of evangelization, particularly when interpreting "mute" archeological evidence. For most of the nineteenth and twentieth centuries, archeologists defined a certain kind of burial as a "Christian" burial: oriented along an east-west axis, containing no objects, and preferably located in the vicinity of a church. Having determined that these and other features characterized "Christian" burials, archeologists and, following the technical specialists, historians then declared that Christianity had "penetrated" an area when they found these particular funerary practices in general use...and not before. Yet it is precisely funerary practices that were targeted for the very first time in the Carolingian legislation of the 740s and in the *Indiculus*. The fact that burials conforming to this new type, now defined by the authorities as "Christian," suddenly rise (which in fact they do) does not warrant concluding that Christianity has now finally penetrated the Frankish world; it warrants concluding that the Carolingians were willing and able to impose their wills over crucial *rites de passage*, traditionally considered to be under the control of families, about which Merovingian rulers did not feel it was their place to legislate.[115] But nineteenth-century archeologists were not the first scholars to be fooled by the ever-changing definition of "Christianity" that would continue to emerge from Carolingian legislation; by the height of imperial power in the early ninth century, definitions of "Christianity" were in force in the Frankish realms which would cause any historian to perceive the Merovingian past as, at a minimum, grossly in need of reform

---

denly defined into existence and then sought out as a pretext to facilitate the augmentation of princely authority (R.I. Moore *The Formation of a Persecuting Society: Power and Deviance in Western Europe, 950-1250* [Oxford, 1987] esp. pp. 106-112, but *contra* p. 67).

[115] For the older view, Edouard Salin, *La civilisation mérovingienne d'après les sepultures, les textes et le laboratoire* I-IV (Paris, 1949-1951) I. 213-248, II entire, IV. 421-426; for a ground-breaking but underappreciated revision, Baily Young, "Paganisme, Christianisation et rites funéraires mérovingiens" AM VII (1977) pp. 5-81; more recently, Patrick Perrin, "A propos de publications recentes concernant le peuplement en Gaule à l'époque mérovingien: la 'question franque'" AM XI (1981) pp. 139-145.

and, at a maximum, as "pagan."

Carolingian leaders asserted that "pagans" were out there, and that they needed to be combatted and converted to Christianity. The Merovingian kings and queens and their ecclesiastics were not so subtly reproached as negligent in the duties that pertained to "Christian" rulers in the service of God. Which brings us to Pippin's *coup d'état*, which succeeded in the 750s though it had failed in the 740s. Why did the Frankish world suddenly want a Carolingian king, and accept the deposition of the Merovingian dynasty? Few subjects have been as thoroughly researched as the constitutional transfer of authority from the Merovingians to the Carolingians; the most recent originally synthetic work is that of Noble who, by treating the Carolingian *coup* as an epiphenomenon in papal history, rather than *vice versa*, manages to appreciate fully the role of sacrohistoriation in the process of turning Pippin into a king. Given how much the constitutional fallout of the coronation favored the papacy, we may well wonder whether Pippin's decision to try again for a crown despite the dismal failure of his previous attempt was not ultimately the result of papal promptings and assurances that things would go better this time if the two leaders joined forces. Noble suggests that the alliance was initiated by pope Gregory, perhaps on Boniface's advice, rather than by the Franks.[116] The popes were, themselves, engaged in the 730s and 740s in the radical enterprise of carving an autonomous principality out of the Byzantine Empire, in the service of which a "splendid ideological apparatus [was] created to define the state and defend its existence."[117]

The key to the papal role in the success of the Carolingian *coup* was the royal unction.[118] In 754 at St. Denis, pope Stephen anointed Pippin and his queen with holy oil, a simple gesture whose multiple layers of meaning would have been well understood by all the advisors, ecclesiastics and

---

[116] T.F.X. Noble *The Republic of St. Peter: The Birth of the Papal State, 680-825* (Philadelphia, 1984) p. 46; for the character of the alliance of *amicitia* see pp. 260-274.

[117] Noble, *Republic of St. Peter* p. 94.

[118] Janet Nelson "Inauguration rituals" in P.H. Sawyer and I.N. Wood, eds. *Early Medieval Kingship* (Leeds, 1977) pp. 50-71, reprinted in J. Nelson, *Politics and Ritual in early medieval Europe* (London, 1986; History Series, Hambledon Press, vol. 42) pp. 283-308; J. Nelson, "Carolingian Royal Ritual" in D. Cannadine and S. Price, eds. *Rituals of Royalty. Power and Ceremonial in Traditional Societies* (Cambridge, 1987) pp. 137-180.

historians who would labor in the service of the new *reges Dei gratia*. On the simplest level, the sacred unction solved the dilemna of Merovingian staying-power: through the chrism an ecclesiastic transfers the charisma which had inhered in the hair and blood of the previous ruling family, providing Pippin and his descendants with a potential source of a holiness all their very own.[119] At the abbey of St. Denis, where the chrism had been applied, there was produced c. 767 under abbot Fulrad a tract explaining the significance of the unction: for one thing, Stephen had solemnly forbidden the Franks ever to choose a ruler from any other family than the one which he had consecrated.[120]

Beyond the sacral kingship, however, lay a sacrohistoriated kingship. The transfer of royal power through the application of chrism by a man of God relived the paradigm of David replacing Saul as king of Israel and Judah. The mimesis of metahistory is invoked. God changes His mind a series of times in the Hebrew Bible, but never more dramatically than when He decides to transfer the monarchy from the family of Saul, which had been negligent, lax, in his sight, to the family of David, through the agency of the prophet Nathan, who anointed the replacement king with sacred unction. The Merovingian rulers too had been negligent: they had failed as ministers of God's word, they had not fought the "not-Christians" with vigor. The Goliath of Merovingian-era ecclesiastical decrepitude required a David; the new Davidic line would defend "Christian" society.[121]

The effects of the new Carolingian ways of making meaning out of present and past were felt at first subtly, eventually with unequivocal harshness: the church of late Merovingian Neustria would appear in the historiography ever less "pious" and ever more decadent, corrupt, decayed, semi-"pagan," indifferent to "Christianity," in a torpor, and in need of external influence to move it in the right direction. Rouen itself, under Carolingian-Austrasian domination, entered a period of decadence, losing the splendor that had made it one of the principal towns of Merovingian Neustria, and its bishop one of the principal prelates.[122] A vision of decay in times

---

[119] Noble, *Republic of St. Peter* pp. 68-70.

[120] *Clausula de unctione Pippini regis* ed. B. Krusch MGH SRM 3 p. 465; Léon Levillain, "De l'authenticité de la *Clausula*" BEC 88 (1927) pp. 20-42.

[121] For the biblical paradigm, I-II Samuel.

[122] Gauthier, "Rouen pendant le haut Moyen-Age" pp. 17-19; Fouracre, "The Work of Audoenus of Rouen" pp. 86-90.

past must have seemed ever more plausible. Instead, the episcopal see of Rouen tended to become more and more an annex to the abbey of Fontenelle,[123] which flourished, under Carolingian rule, as never before. From 701, the abbey was always in the hands of some member of the Carolingian inner sanctum.

As the see of Rouen faded into the background, the loyal abbots of Fontenelle increasingly took on the character of Carolingian deputies. The new dynasty must have been thoroughly convinced of Fontenellian loyalism, for Fontenelle itself soon became a cornerstone of Carolingian attempts to bring the recalcitrant Bretons to heel. The abbey of St. Wandrille de Fontenelle was granted extensive landed holdings in Brittany as a way to gain a staunch and self-interested ally in the Carolingian battle to conquer the Armorican peninsula, a responsibility which the abbot and monks of the house shouldered with zealous seriousness.[124] Other ways in which the abbots of Fontenelle served the new dynasty included collecting tolls at and overseeing the major channel port of Quentovic, and diplomatic activities.[125] And, for a good part of a century, the atelier of Fontenelle would be one of the principal producers of Carolingian justificatory historiography.

The history of Fontenelle, once in Carolingian hands, can be easily reconstructed for, like all true Carolingian centers, Fontenelle didn't risk becoming dependent on the kindness of strange historians. Either abbot Einhard (817-823) or abbot Ansegis (823-833) commissioned a monk of the abbey to produce the *Gesta abbatum Fontenellensium*.[126] Einhard we have

---

[123] Gauthier, "Rouen pendant le haut Moyen Age" p. 17.

[124] Smith, *Province and Empire* p. 57.

[125] Susan Kelly, "Trading Privileges from Eighth-Century England" EME 1 (1992) pp. 3-28, esp. p. 18.

[126] *Gesta abbatum Fontenellensium* ed. G.H. Pertz, MGH SS 2 pp. 271-301; eds. Lohier-Laporte (Rouen, 1936). Ian Wood has recently argued that the Fontenelle *gesta* is a composite text, added to on numerous occasions; furthermore, the major impetus for recension he places in Charles the Bald's 841 visit to the monastery. None of this is impossible. Note, however, that his argument that Fontenelle was not always a pro-Carolingian house is rather problematic. Wood adduces the narrative of the *vita Ansberti*, with its emphasis on monastic correctness, as a denunciation of the policies of Charles Martel and Pippin III; however, Wood is accepting Levison's hyper-critical late date of composition for the text. If, in fact, the *vita Ansberti* were a product of the Carolingian period, it *would* imply that the

already met, not that he requires an introduction; Ansegis is somewhat less well known but was an important member of the Carolingian literary team, principally known as the author of a capitulary collection.[127] The historiographic prism of the Gesta, a product of the most developed period of Carolingian discourse, as a whole obliterates "pious Neustria," both "paganizing" and barbarizing the region; as such, it will be discussed in detail below. Meanwhile, we can reconstruct enough of the eighth-century history of Fontenelle on the basis of the narrative to discern how the Austrasian abbots handled the cultic traditions and historiographic heritage of Neustria.

We learn from the Gesta the following information, which reads like a shock of cold water after the biographies of Pious Neustria. The extremely praiseworthy and glorious duke Pippin, on his arrival in Neustria, made the equally loyal bishop of Bainus of Thérouanne rector of Fontenelle. Pippin also endowed the house with extreme generosity (ch. 2). Under Bainus, Fontenelle began to move forward on the cultic front, taking control of the memory of Ansbertus, and subordinating him to Wandregiselus,[128] the Austrasian answer to the cult of Audoenus. Bainus performed a triple translation of Wandregiselus, Ansbertus and Uulframnus, two former abbots and one former monk of the house (c. 2). The aim of the new shrine arrangement was to neutralize or at least dilute Ansbertus; in a figurative sense, the great Neustrian loyalist was once more exiled to Austrasia: his bones now lay in the shadow of the Austrasian, Wandregiselus, and of the missionary to Frisia, Uulframnus. No new biographies were written for Ansbertus, and in the Gesta he is not even acknowledged as having been abbot of Fontenelle.

Ansbertus was played down by Bainus of Thérouanne, as Wandregiselus was (literally) elevated, to the central spot in the central sanctuary

---

house of Fontenelle was less than loyal to the Carolingian dynasty. However, since it is a product of late Merovingian Neustria, it cannot be used as evidence that Fontenelle was not a pro-Carolingian center. On the other hand, the story of the return of abbot Wando, whom the Carolingian Pippin III had unjustly deposed and exhiled to Maastricht, may indicate that some level of anti-Carolingian feeling still lived in the memories of the monks of Fontenelle in the ninth century. See Ian Wood, "St. Wandrille and Its Hagiography" Church and Chronicle in the Middle Ages: Essays Presented to John Taylor eds. I. Wood and GA Loud (London, 1993) pp. 1-14.

[127] McKitterick, Carolingians and the Written Word p. 35.

[128] For the historical character of Wandregiselus, see Appendix 1.

of the monastery. Wandregiselus was not and could not have been a symbol of "Pious Neustria," for he was himself an Austrasian, born in Verdun, and the promotion of his cult as the central figure of Fontenelle was one of the ways in which the house served its Carolingian masters. But to use the word "promotion" is an overstatement. The Austrasian Wandregiselus was placed in a spot of honor by the Austrasian Bainus of Thérouanne, as a counterpoint to Audoenus and Ansbertus. But he was left there to moulder: there were no miracle collections, no biographies for local consumption, no spreading of the cult...indeed, it might be better to say that he was put in a safe place, where no one else could (easily) get to him. The aim in taking over Fontenelle had been in large part to shut down its independent operations.

Though Wandregiselus, the founder of the house, did not inspire historiographical interest at Fontenelle, Uulframnus did. Bainus, the Carolingian agent in the diocese of Rouen, instituted a cult to Uulframnus, former monk of Fontenelle and eventually archbishop of Sens, and commissioned a biography of the saint from the monk Jonas of Fontenelle. But Bainus was not interested in Uulframnus' life at Fontenelle, nor in his episcopate at Sens: the entire story of Uulframnus' life is the story of a missionary to the Frisians at the end of the seventh century, the saint's main claim to fame, as we are told in the very first line of the preface.[129] Bainus did not seek to sponsor historical narrative that would focus on pre-Carolingian Neustria; the *vita Uulframni* ignores the saint's time at Fontenelle and Sens. Instead, the historiographic spotlight was trained on the "pagans" of the enemy territory of Frisia, and on the need to convert them. Fontenelle, the Carolingian key to much of Neustria, quickly put its formidable atelier in the service of the Austrasian interlopers, and it may be that it is to Bainus of Fontenelle that the Carolingian princes owed the original appreciation of the value of missionary biographies.[130] In any case, we will see in the second part of this chapter that, by the latter part of the eighth century, biographies of anti-"pagan" missionaries to Frisia and elsewhere would become a stock theme in Carolingian historiography.

---

[129] *Vita Uulframni* (BHL 8738) ed. Levison MGH SRM V (Hannover, 1910) pp. 661-673, at p. 661. For the mission, see especially cc. 3, 4 and 6. For all of the narratives connected with Uulframnus, see E. Brouette in BSS XII coll. 1363-1365.

[130] For a completely different view of the *vita Uulframni* as an anti-Carolingian and pro-Merovingian document, see Wood "St. Wandrille and Its Hagiography" pp. 13-14.

When Bainus died in 707, he was succeeded by Benignus, whom the Fontenelle *gesta* present as having supported Charles Martel zealously in the "civil war" which began in 716 (ch. 3), althought it has been argued that Benignus, a Neustrian noble, was not a wholehearted member of the Carolingian camp until Charles crushed the Neustrian resistance at Soissons in 718.[131] In the full flush of victory, Charles took control of all Neustria. Even if some hesitation on the part of local *rouennais* nobles had previously marked their dealings with the Austrasians, after 718 crucial figures like Benignus definitely jumped enthusiastically on the bandwagon. One of the most enthusiastic was the grandson of Waratto, count of Rouen, through his Carolingian marriage alliance, that is Hugh.[132] By 723 Fontenelle, Jumièges, Rouen, Bayeux and Paris had all been given to Hugh, son of Drogo of Champagne and Adeltrude, grandson of Pippin of Herstal, nephew of Charles Martel, to have and to hold as best he could, in the interests of the new dynasty (ch. 8).[133]

As did Bainus at Fontenelle, Hugh sought out Austrasians who had been important in the religious life of Neustria, and focussed the cultic and historiographic spotlights on them. As Wandregiselus was the Austrasian answer to Ansbertus, Austreberta was the Austrasian answer to Filibertus. Hugh elevated and translated the relics of Austreberta, first abbess of Filibertus' foundation of Pavilly (located four leagues from Rouen), and stimulated the production of a biography of the saint, written at Jumièges.[134] The anonymous author of Austreberta's biography, who dedicated his work to the abbess Julia of Pavilly († circa 750),[135] adapted the themes of "pious Neustria," but transposed them so that "pious Neustria" stood second to "pious Austrasia."

The aptly-named Austreberta came from a noble family of the diocese of Thérouanne. The Jumièges historian, working under the Carolingian

---

[131] Gerberding, *Rise of the Carolingians* pp. 137-140.

[132] Gerberding, *Rise of the Carolingians* p. 144.

[133] *Gesta Abbatum Fontenellensium* c. 8 = BHL 4032; this "Fontenelle version" of Hugh's personality is accepted as "historical"; the later "Jumièges version" of his life (= BHL 4032a), which is discussed below pp. 130-133, is considered "fictional" (J. Van der Straeten, "La Vie inédite de S. Hugues" AB 87 [1969]).

[134] *Vita Austrebertae* ed. J. Bollandus, AASS Feb. 2 pp. 418-419 (= BHL 832); the elevation is commemorated on October 19.

[135] HLF IV p. 69; U. Chevalier, *Repertoire des sources: Bio-bibliographique*. I. 2690; Byeus, AASS Oct. 5 (1786) pp. 661-666.

abbot Hugh, makes the East the very center of the world in terms of religious genealogies. The locale in which the church had so flourished in the past, according to the Jumièges historian, was Austrasia. Chapters 4 through 10[136] describe the profoundly Christian society which existed in the diocese

[136] All citations are to the AASS edition, ed. J. Bollandus, AASS Feb. 2 (= BHL 832), although BHL 832 is a verbal reworking of Austreberta's original biography, a reworking which was produced at the time of the 1090 re-foundation of the priory of St. Austreberta, as a dependency of St. Catherine du Mont of Rouen (GC XI [1759] col. 127). BHL 836/7 (AASS Feb. 2 cc. 18-25), a series of miracles which took place in various Norman sites, was added at that time by the author of the reworking, who also dropped some of Austreberta's earlier miracles. BHL 832/836/ 837 can be found in four *rouennais* collections of the twelfth and thirteenth centuries (Rouen BM mss. 1392, 1401 [from Jumièges]; Rouen BM 1411 from St. Ouen; Paris, BN 5362 from Montivilliers), and in many later manuscripts, for this version of Austreberta's life and miracles was incorporated into the *Liber de Natalitiis*, a twelfth-century collection which circulated throughout the network of Cistercian monasteries in the twelfth and thirteenth centuries (the most important witness of the *Liber de Natalitiis* adaptation of Austreberta's story is Paris BN lat. 16.732, a twelfth-century manuscript from the Cistercian monastery of Châalis). A few copies of the BHL 832/836/837 complex add another set of Norman miracles (= BHL 838), also composed around the time of the 1090 refoundation by a monk of the abbey of Ste-Catherine du Mont de Rouen (especially Paris, BN lat. 5362; see Richard, "Les 'Miracula' composés en Normandie"). BHL 832 was printed by Surius in 1570 (an edition marked by all the faults for which Surius is notorious), and then reprinted by Bollandus from Surius' edition. Bollandus also printed the prologue, which Surius had omitted; however, the prologue as printed by Bollandus is riddled with typographical errors, and barely approximates his own transcription (see Brussels, BR 7763 [3443] fol. 102r-103r). Thus, the only available published versions of Austreberta's biography are extremely faulty editions of a late-eleventh-century reworking. Nevertheless, the verbal and stylistic overhaul did not change the substance of the narrative; scholars have been nearly unanimous in accepting BHL 832 as an early-eighth-century version of Austreberta's biography, and as a highly reliable narrative (HLF IV pp. 68-69; Bollandus, AASS Feb 2; Mabillon, ASOSB III p. 27 note 1; C. Smet, AASS Belg. V [Brussels, 1789] p. 426-427; Corblet vol. I pp. 230-261; Van Der Essen, DHGE 5 col. 791). Under the circumstances, it is convenient to cite BHL 832. However, something closer to the early-eighth-century version is contained in Alençon BM 12 (a legendary related to the Maine Legendary tradition) and Paris BN lat. 12.6005 (a legendary of Bec), that is BHL 831, plus BHL 834/5 (AASS cc. 1-17 of the miracles, all of which transpired immediately after Austreberta's death at Pavilly). The complex BHL 831/834/835 is a literary whole, marked by a unified style and set of assumptions. BHL 831/834/835 was quite long, and was circulating in an abridged version by the ninth century (= BHL 833), a version which a number of scholars have asserted to be the original, early-eighth-

of Thérouanne in the mid-seventh century; it is **there** that monasticism flourished, **there** that Austreberta lived as the venerated prioress of Port-en-Ponthieu (c. 9), **there** that she was veiled by the holy bishop Audomarus (c. 7). The roles of the two regions, of east and west, in the hymn to Ansbertus are here reversed. Now the saintly woman must come from the east to Neustria where, placed at the head of the new foundation of Pavilly, she faces a rebellion against her strict rule. Filibertus' "Pious Neustrian" biographer had shown Rebais as deficient in monastic virtue, but Filibertus had found serious and strict monks when he came to the diocese of Rouen. Like the inversion of the regional roles of the hymn to Ansbertus, the locales subject to monastic rebellions are inverted as well. In connection with the rebellion at Pavilly in Normandy, the author of the *Vita Austrebertae* draws parallels to early Christian times, just as the author of the hymn to Ansbertus had done: had Austreberta lived at the time of the idolaters, she would have been martyred, for she faced the comparable fury of her flock at Pavilly with such bravery (c. 12). Eventually, her example wins out, and "pious Neustria" looms into view (cc. 13 and 18), but it is a world created by Austreberta's Austrasian efforts.

The most extraordinary aspect of the anonymous gemmetic historian's vision of the past, however, was his transposition backwards of the activities of the Austrasian Austreberta and of her Neustrian sponsor Filibertus. The earlier biographies of Filibertus, to which the author refers, had recognized the pre-eminent role in Neustrian monasticism of king Clodoveus and queen Baldechild at the end of the seventh century. However, the *vita Austrebertae* is set long ago and far away in the reign of king Dagobert (†639); **that** is when "the holy Mother church flourished in the Gauls, adorned by the various virtues of holy priests and monks and of virgins dedicated to God" (c. 3).[137] Our anonymous monk of Jumièges, writing under Hugh, attributes the foundations both of Jumièges and of

---

century version, in opposition to BHL 832 (Malnory, *Quid Luxoviensis monachi* [1894] p. 39; Vacandard, *Vie de S. Ouen* p. 205 n. 1; Levison, MGH SRM 5 [1910] p. 595). BHL 833 circulated in two different streams, one in Flanders (as witnessed for example by Brussels, BR II.2309 and Brugge 403) as part of the Legendary of Flanders, and one which circulated in Italy (as witnessed by Vat. lat. 7810 and Vat. archivio S. Pietro A.2), a ninth- or tenth-century Italian legendary collection.

137 "...uelut palma in Galliis sancta Mater refloruit ecclesia, diuersis sanctorum sacerdotum monachorumque uirtutibus adornata ac Deo dicatarum uirginum."

Pavilly to the aid and generosity of Dagobert (c. 3). The author concentrates all the piety of the Merovingian era into the reign of the good (glorious, noble, mighty, powerful, vigorous, devout) king Dagobert.

The thrusting backwards of Austreberta's lifetime, and the shift in credit for the foundation of Pavilly from Clodoveus and Baldechild to Dagobert, are not nearly as inexplicable (or as insignificant) as they might at first appear, particularly not when examined in the light of abbot Hugh's own Carolingian familial connections, and of his simultaneous tenure of the bishopric of Paris. From the mid-eighth century, the Carolingian stronghold in the Parisian region, the house of St. Denis in the suburbs of Paris, began to focus on king Dagobertus, whose remains happened to be buried in that monastery, as the single repository of all that was "positive" about the Merovingian centuries. The house of St. Denis had not been a particularly extraordinary place in the Merovingian period, but it rose with the Carolingians, taking the reputation of Dagobert with it. The dionysian cult of St. Dagobert[138] strategically solved the vexing problem of explaining any good in the Merovingian past, while at the same time reinforcing the vision of the late Merovingian rulers as degenerate and ripe for Carolingian plucking. Obviously something had been good about the Merovingian era, which had certainly lasted long enough, and the cult of Dagobert, the only Merovingian buried in St. Denis, was a convenient repository into which to channel all positive, nostalgic feelings about the era and the dynasty. He was elevated, as a saint, as the last good Merovingian to have held the throne; "the good king Dagobert" was a concentrated ray of light in the darkness, whose reign could account for whatever

[138] The use of the cult and image of Dagobert as legitimizing tools by Carolingian and Capetian rulers has been brought out by Laurent Theis, "Dagobert, St.-Denis, et la royauté française au moyen âge" in Bernard Guenée ed. Le metier d'historien au moyen âge. Etudes sur l'historiographie médievale (Paris, 1977) pp. 19-30; also see L. Theis Dagobert. Un roi pour un peuple (Paris, 1982) pp. 75-84 and 115-118. All the relevant materials are catalogued and analyzed in Christoph Wehrli Mittelalterliche Überlieferungen von Dagobert I (Geist und Werk der Zeiten; Arbeiten aus dem Historischen Seminar der Universität Zürich 62; Bern and Frankfurt, 1982). Dagobert's biography was eventually composed by no less a personage than archbishop Hincmar of Reims (Gesta Dagoberti I regis Francorum ed. B. Krusch, MGH SRM II [1888-89]). For the house of St. Denis in general, see Gabrielle M. Spiegel The Chronicle Tradition of St. Denis: a Survey (Brookline, Mass., 1978; Medieval Classics: Studies and Texts 10).

positive features could not be denied, while the rest of the dynasty, and particularly his successors, could remain "degenerate."

Fontenelle and, to a lesser extent Jumièges under Hugh, were both important wedges into Neustria for the Austrasians. But it was St. Denis that was preeminent. Abbot Fulrad of St. Denis (749-784) was one of the few Neustrian figures to put their skills in the service of the rising dynasty, which was otherwise supported by a series of old Austrasian families. It was Fulrad, archchaplain to Pippin and later to Pippin's son Charles, who went to Rome to pose the infamous question concerning who ought to rule in Francia to pope Zachary, and it was at St. Denis, in July of 754, that pope Stephen anointed Pippin, his wife and his sons. From 741, with the burial of Charles Martel, till 884, at the death of Carloman, more Carolingian royality was buried at St. Denis than in any other single place, as it truly became the royal mausoleum.[139]

Abbot Fulrad and the first two Carolingian kings not only inspired historiographic changes which would destroy "Pious Neustria," they physically destroyed the Merovingian church of St. Denis, and built a new basilica, dedicated, as the "first actual Carolingian church," in 775.[140] The basilica was modelled on the early Christian basilicas of Rome, and was built "romano more" under the direct supervision of the monarchs. The basilica was built against the background of the replacement of local Gallican liturgies by the Roman liturgy. The pushing backward of historical interest away from the late seventh and early eighth century to a middle-distant Merovingian period was not the most radical transformation of the vision of the past to be precipitated by the Carolingian *coup*: at St. Denis in the mid-eighth century there began the "end run" around the Merovingian era entirely. Eventually, historiographic highlighting of Roman "Antiquity," and ignoring of the Merovingian centuries, by Carolingian authors would become known as the "Carolingian *renovatio*" or "renaissance." The revised vision of when mattered began slowly in the diocese of Rouen with the relatively small chronological adjustment made by the author of the *vita Austrebertae*; it was only the first step along a

---

[139] Alain Erlande-Brandenburg *Le roi, la sculpture et la mort. Gisants et tombeaux de la basilique de Saint-Denis* (Exposition de la Maison de la Culture et des Services d'Archives de la Seine-Saint-Denis; Paris, 1975) p.6 and p. 12.

[140] Sumner McKnight Crosby *The Abbey of St. Denis, 475-1122* (New Haven, 1942) vol. II pp. 87-96, 125 and 157.

long road which would leave "Pious Neustria" far behind, looking rather more like barbarous Neustria.

Why, then, does the present study not purport to trace the "Carolingian Conquest of Pious Neustria"? Because as much as their **surroundings** were re-imagined, the saints of pious Neustria themselves survived intact both the Carolingian *coup* of 754 and the imperial upgrade of 800. Audoenus, Ansbertus, even Wandregiselus, and the host of more minor figures... all may have been seen as surrounded by brutish subjects and boorish royalty but they themselves could be said to have risen to the occasion. They became even more magnified in their sanctity by way of contrast. They were great Neustrian local heroes who had overcome even the most adverse circumstances. They remained symbols of local pride. Every time the festival of one of these Merovingian-era saints was celebrated, the population was reminded of the glories of seventh-century Rouen. The "conquest," then, was never completed in the Carolingian period, for the Neustrian self-conception remained one initially formulated specifically in reaction against the Austrasian threat. It was the Normans who would fully conquer "Neustria." The historiographic prism of tenth- and eleventh-century Norman authors would take ninth-century Carolingian products as a point of departure, and develope the vision of a "paganized" and decrepit Merovingian world. Only then would "Pious Neustria" be obliterated.

The discourse of "Pious Austrasia," one early replacement for "Pious Neustria" which I have examined in the preceding pages, had little historiographic future; its appearance in Austreberta's biography is the fortuitous result of a conjunction of factors: a historian trained in the local gemmetic historiographic tradition, which at the time was thoroughly marked by the discourse of "Pious Neustria," wrote a biography of an Austrasian saint during the abbacy of a scion of the Carolingian dynasty, just when the new Austrasian rulers were beginning to thrust themselves forward as potential replacements to the Merovingians along "more Christian than thou" lines. Instead, the "not-Christianity," or at least the degenerate "Christianity" of the entire Merovingian era would become a legitimizing prism preferred to that of the piety of the special saviors from Austrasia. The historiographic route with the greatest future was neither the promotion of Austrasians nor the simple ignoring of "Pious Neustria"; instead, it was to be the historiographical transformation of the saints of Pious Neustria (saints who did continue to be venerated in the region) into "Columbanians" (followers of the *scotus* Columbanus) which would strike the deepest roots in the imagined European past.

b. *Insularophilia, "Paganism" and Mission: Historiographic Themes Across Two Millenia*[141]

The Austrasian dynasty of the Carolingians had been responsible, through its push into Neustria through Rouen at the end of the seventh century, for the very beginning of historiographic production in the future Normandy. The Neustrian self-conception then enshrined in the monuments of its past was one of extraordinary piety, of a region that rivalled the deserts of Egypt in its ascetic devotions to God. The piety of local rulers and local inhabitants was matched by that of the Merovingian monarchs of Neustria, who led with princely vigor yet were sensitive to the commands of God. Onto the waters of this Neustrian historiographic prism came an oil spill of catastrophic proportions. The insularophilia of Carolingian authors served, more than any other single strategy, to "paganize" the Merovingian world, and to depict it as at least degenerate and in need of reform. At the end of the eighth century, the history of Merovingian Rouen was revised to conform to the new discourse.

The insularophilic discourse in the historiography of Christianization has been, however, even more characteristic of nineteenth- and twentieth-century narratives than it ever was of Carolingian-era narratives. Anyone who has not been following the debate over what has been called "iromania" will need to be sensitized to the potential influence of "iromania" on their own vision of the Merovingian world, irrespective of what its own sources tell us about that period. Nineteenth- and twentieth-century historiography of Christianization has been marked by this particular thematic, which does have its roots in Carolingian-era historiography, but which has been amplified by the context of modern crises, both within the hierarchy of the Catholic Church, and between that hierachy and the rest of Europe and North America. A conjunction of nineteenth- and twentieth- century forces have combined to inflate the insularophilic aspect of Carolingian historiography to a veritable iromania.

---

[141] The concepts of insularophilia and iromania, used in the present chapter, were suggested by Johannes Duft's constructions in "Iromanie, Irophobie. Fragen um die frühmittelalterliche Irenmission exemplifiziert an St. Gallen und Alemannien" *Zeitschrift für Schweizerische Kirchengeschichte* 50 (1956) pp. 244-262. For another recent treatment of the issue, quite different from mine, see M.J. Enright "*Iromanie-Irophobie* Revisited: A Suggested Frame of Reference for Considering Continental Reactions to Irish *peregrini* in the Seventh and Eighth Centuries" in *Karl Martell in seiner Zeit* eds. J. Jarnut, U. Nonn and M. Richter (Beihefte der Francia 37; 1994).

In August, 1923, Pope Pius XI declared in a Pontifical Brief: "the revival of all Christian knowledge and culture in many parts of France, Germany and Italy was due to the labors and zeal of St. Columbanus."[142] There are not that many points of Frankish history on which the papacy has issued *obiter dicta* in the twentieth century; that Pius did so in this case should alert us to the high stakes surrounding the issue. In the latter part of the nineteenth century, and during the early decades of the twentieth century, the Roman bishopric was beseiged as it had never been before.[143] A direct military threat was posed by the new nation-state of Italy.[144] Descendants of Pippin and Charles, whose pact of spiritual *amicitia* (made at the time of the alliance of the 750s) would have obliged them to defend the Papal States against aggressors were, alas, nowhere to be found. In fact, the scholarly leaders of the French church were engaged in fueling the Modernist movement, pitting themselves against Rome in ways no less perilous for the papal monarchy than were the territorial claims of Italy. The Catholic Austrian Empire grew ever weaker through the same period, and ended up dismembered; little chance of help there. Perhaps the bishops of Germany, which was rising to the status of world military and industrial power as Austria weakened, might have been willing to help, but they had their own hands full trying to withstand the anti-Catholic *Kulturkampf*, and could hardly risk being seen as lacking in nationalist spirit.

The Holy See found itself relying, for its staunchest support, on the bishops of Ireland, and on Irish-American and Irish-Canadian bishops in North America. Not that the Irish didn't have their own problems, such as the establishment of Irish-American pride in the face of the anti-Catholic and ethnically-based discrimination imposed by the rulers of Protestant Anglo-America;[145] meanwhile, back home in the British Isles the move-

---

[142] "...Columbani labore et contentione factum esse, ut in Galliae, Germaniae Italiaeque nonnullis partibus christianae sapientiae humanitatisque cultus renasceretur..." (Pius XI, "Epistola ad Francisum, diaconum sancti Caesarei in palatio," *Acta Apostolica Sedis: Commentarium Officiale* Annus XV, vol. XV [Rome, 1923] pp. 445-448, at p. 445).

[143] For the embattled pope, see Robin Anderson *Between Two Wars: The Story of Pope Pius XI (Achille Ratti), 1922-1932* (Chicago, 1977).

[144] Samuel William Halperin *Italy and the Vatican at War, a Study of their Relations from the Outbreak of the Franco-Prussian War to the Death of Pius XI* (Chicago, 1936).

[145] Orsi, *Madonna of 115th St.* pp. 61-63.

ment for Irish independence from the English crown was reaching its greatest heights during the 1920s. We cannot consider the fundamental scholarship on the Merovingian Church and on Columbanus which was carried on during those decades outside the context of life-and-death battles that were then raging. The iromanaical historiographic discourse rewarded the Irish for their loyalty to Rome, and made the conjuring of Irish nationalist pride ever easier. The English, though unmentioned in Pius' Brief, would eventually discover that they too had been converted to Christianity, directly or indirectly, from Ireland.[146]

The major source for iromania, and to some extent even for insularophilia, is not difficult to pin down, since it is cited in every nineteenth- and twentieth-century discussion of the Christianization of Gaul: Jonas of Bobbio's biography of Columbanus, an "Irishman" (scotus) active on the continent from c. 589/90-615, written in approximately 639-643. Jonas wrote:

> A Brittanis ergo sinibus progressi, ad Gallias tendunt, ubi tunc uel ob frequentia hostium externorum uel negligentia praesulum religionis uirtus pene abolita habebatur. Fides tantum manebat christiana, nam penitentiae medicamenta et morificationis amor uix, ut, quaecumque loca progrederetur, uerbum euangelicum adnuntiaret.[147]

I would translate the passage as follows:

> Therefore, having gone forth from the coasts of Britain, [Columbanus and his companions] make for Gaul where, at that time, due either to the great number of external enemies or to the negligence of the prelates, the strength of the religion was almost completely destroyed. Only the Christian faith remained, for the medicaments of

---

[146] Henry Mayr-Harting *The Coming of Christianity to England* (London, 1972); James Campbell, "The First Century of Christianity in England" *Ampleforth Journal* 76 (1973) pp. 10-29; Annethe Lohaus *Die Merovinger und England* (Münchener Beiträge sur Mediävistik und Renaissance Forschung 19; Munich, 1974); James Campbell, "Observations on the Conversion of England" *Ampleforth Journal* 78 (1975) pp. 12-26; Freidrich Prinz, "Zum fränkischen und irischen Anteil an der Bekehrung der Angelsachsen" *Zeitschrift für Kirchengeschichte* 95 (1984) pp. 315-336; James Campbell, "The Debt of the Early English Church to Ireland" *Irland und die Christenheit* eds. Chathain and Richter (1987) pp. 332-347.

[147] Jonas of Bobbio *Vita Columbani abbatis discipulorumque eius libri duo* (= BHL 1898) ed. B. Krusch, MGH SRM IV p. 71.

penitence and the love of mortification were hardly to be found there, or only in a very few places. The venerable man was intending to proclaim the evangelical word wherever he went.[148]

A few things seem clear. First, Jonas does not say that Christianity had died out in Gaul; he says that penitential practices and extreme asceticism were not marked features of Christianity in Gaul. As far as we can tell, it seems that Columbanus made some effort to change practices in Gaul to bring them more in line with his definition of Christianity; he and others like him successfully introduced into Gaul a feature of insular spirituality, namely penitential practices.[149]

Apparently, in Columbanus' view, the proper definition of Christianity included penance as part of its essence. Equally obviously, a different definition of Christianity was operative in Gaul at the time. That the customs of Gaul were not identical to the customs of Ireland cannot be disputed, although recent work has tended to emphasize commonalities over differences.[150] To privilege one version with the label "Christianity" and refuse it to the other is not warranted by the evidence or by logic (or indeed by charity). Yet this is precisely how the passage in Jonas was treated during the wave of historiographic iromania at the end of the nineteenth and the beginning of the twentieth century. From a widely-used textbook for the teaching of "Western Civilization" we have the following

---

[148] The translation is literal, and is also in keeping with the interpretation of Knut Schäferdiek, "The Irish Mission of the Seventh Century: Historical Fact or Historiographical Fiction?" in *The End of Strife* ed. D. Loades (Edinburg, 1981) pp. 143-146.

[149] J. Laporte ed. *Le pénitentiel de saint Columban* (Tournai, 1958; Monumenta Christiana Selecta 4); Cyrille Vogel *Les 'Libri Paenitentiales'* (TSMAO 27; Brepols, Turnhout 1978); J.T. McNeill and H. M. Garner *Medieval Handbooks of Penance* (Columbia Records of Civilization; New York, 1938; repr, 1990); Mayke De Jong, "Power and Humility in Carolingian Society: the Public Penance of Louis the Pious" EME 1 (1992) pp. 29-52, at p. 43.

[150] Wood, "The *Vita Columbani*" pp. 73-74; Alain Dierkens, "Prolégomènes à une histoire des relations culturelles entre les îles Britanniques et le continent pendant le haut moyen âge: La diffusion du monachisme dit colombanien ou iro-franc dans quelques monastères de la région parisienne au VIIe siècle et la politique religieuse de la reine Bathilde" *La Neustrie* II ed. H. Atsma (Beihefte der Francia 16/2) pp. 371-394; Rosamond McKitterick "The diffusion of insular culture in Neustria between 650 and 850: The implications of the manuscript evidence" *La Neustrie* II pp. 395-432.

translation (and we ought to note the very fact that this Merovingian-era saint's life was chosen for inclusion in the first place):

> At that time, either because of the numerous enemies from without, or on account of the carelessness of the bishops, the Christian faith had almost departed from that country [the Gallic lands].[151]

Over the space of more than a hundred years, we can follow the insularophilic, and sometimes iromaniacal, theme in the historiography of Christian conversion. 1861: "Perhaps the lowest point [in degree of intelligence] for Western Christendom at large was the sixth and two following centuries...[evidenced by] the deterioration of piety as of arts and letters which is painfully prominent....Ireland was at this time conspicuous for its light; it was full of conventual houses, where the learning of the West had taken refuge and from which as from missionary schools, the gospel was transmitted far and near." The story then begins with Columbanus.[152] In 1887, the "barbarism," "corrupting influence," "deterioration" and "degeneracy" of the Merovingian lords once more confronted the vigor of the insular missionaries Columbanus, Willibrord, et. al.[153] 1929: "The rule of the Merovingians...was a rule of savages, and Christianity but a change of name for the Franks....the barbarian deluge nearly wiped out civilization altogether," the "first counter-attack" was led by Columbanus.[154] 1950: "I recall therefore with pride that to the church, hurled from the mountaintop of a great civilization and lying spent and wounded within its ruins, there came, at the end of the sixth century, help from the little island to which I belong."[155] In 1961, it was still only thanks to the efforts of the outsiders Martin, Columbanus and Boniface that Gaul had ever been converted to Christianity, as those saints battled against "the degenerate state

---

[151] C. D. Munro *Translations and Reprints from the Original Sources of European History* (Philadelphia, 1899) vol. II p. 6.

[152] C. Hardwick *A History of the Christian Church: the Middle Ages* (London, 1861; 2nd ed. 1883, ed. W. Stubbs) pp. 2, 16-18.

[153] G. P. Fisher *History of the Christian Church* (N.Y., 1887) pp. 97 and 150.

[154] C.P:S. Clarke *A Short History of the Christian Church, from the Earliest Times to the Present Day* (London, 1929; 2nd ed. 1950) pp. 106-108 and 113.

[155] J. Ryan, "The Church in the Sixth Century" *Mélanges Colombaniens* (Actes du Congrès International de Luxeuil, July 1950; Paris, 1951) p. 45. The collection in question, taken as a whole, may be the greatest monument of the iromaniacal prism.

of the Frankish church" and the "decadent clerical discipline of Frankish Gaul"; for "Irish scholars performed a priceless service to civilization by conserving Graeco-Roman learning while the continental centers of culture were paralyzed by the Teutonic invasions."[156] 1978: "Christianity, which had been bruised and beaten by the surging hordes of barbarians that poured out of the unknown to flood what had been the proud empire of the Romans, was given once more the breath of life by monks from Ireland....Never in human history has another nation as small as Ireland done so much missionary work in so many lands over so many decades as did the Irish in what, save for them, would indeed have been the unrelieved Dark Ages."[157] 1981: "Despite itself the Merovingian Church was saved by Columbanus and his monks. The Irish tonic spread and revived the sclerotic body."[158] As recently as 1983, Columbanus, definitive missionary to Gaul was still making appearances, and still almost entirely on the basis of the assumption that Christianity had been wiped out in the Germanic *Volkerwänderung*, which had brought with it the superficially-Christian Franks, saved only later by the insular activists Columbanus, Boniface and Willibrord; the only evidence cited in this particular treatment is the passage from Jonas which was quoted and translated above.[159] In every single work cited in the course of the present paragraph, the Jonas quotation was the centerpiece, and sometimes the totality, of the evidence adduced by the relevant authors.[160]

---

[156] Newman C. Eberhardt *A Summary of Catholic History* vol. I pp. 340-355 (St. Louis, 1961-1962).

[157] William Marnell, *Light From the West. The Irish Mission and the Emergence of Modern Europe* (New York, 1978) pp. 1-2.

[158] Pierre Riché, "Columbanus, His Followers, and the Merovingian Church" *Columbanus and Merovingian Monasticism* (Essays from the University of Dublin Colloquium, 1977; eds. H.B. Clarke and Mary Brennan; British Archeological Reports, International Series 113 [Oxford, 1981]) pp. 59-72.

[159] J. Koenig "Irlands europäische Mission" *Würzburger Diozese Geschichtsblätter* 45 (1983) pp. 15-25.

[160] Also see: J.M.A. Ebrard, *Die iroschottische Missionskirche des sechsten, siebenten und achten Jahrhunderts und ihre Verbreitung* (Gütersloh, 1873; repr. Hildesheim, 1971); Albert Hauck *Kirchengeschichte Deutschlands* (Leipzig, 1896; repr. Berlin, 1952); M. Malnory *Quid Luxovienses monachi, discipuli sancti Columbani, ad regulam monasteriorum atque ad communem Ecclesiae profectum contulerunt* (Paris, 1894); J. Guiraud, "L'action civilatrice de S. Columban et de ses moines dans la Gaule mérovingienne"

The insularophilic and iromaniacal theses were enshrined around the turn of the century not only in translated sourcebooks and general text-books intended for a wide public and for students, but also in collections of sources in the original Latin, intended for scholars, such as the *Monumenta Germaniae Historica Scriptores Rerum Merovingicarum* series. Authoritarian introductions and thick commentary accompany every text in the series, theoretically a source collection, not a monograph. That Irish missionaries had set a moribund Frankish church on the track back to life was argued throughout the MGH SRM by its editors, Krusch and Levison,[161] and in separate, admittedly argumentative literature, composed by the two scholars during the same period.[162] One example, examined in detail, should suffice to illustrate the dynamic: the treatment accorded the early-to-mid-eighth-century biography of Eligius of Noyon-Tournai (BHL 2474), friend and colleague of Audoenus.

One of the key themes of BHL 2474 is Eligius' staunch opposition to, indeed his persecution of, errant insular holy men.[163] Eligius' "Irish" opponent is a trouble-maker and arch-heretic according to the saint's Merovingian-era biographer. However, when the author of the revised Carolingian-era biography of Audoenus retold the same story of the two prelates' joint battle against an arch-heretic, he suppressed the Irish origin of the fomenter of disruption for, *circa* 800, this particular type of insular holy man was being credited with inspiring "reform" in the Merovingian church, rather than being charged with disrupting it.[164] What is extraordinary, and not a little ironic, is the fate of Eligius the persecutor of Irish disrup-

---

Thirty-First Annual Eucharistic Conference (Dublin, 1932); M. Henry-Rosier S. *Columban dans la barbarie Mérovingienne* (Paris, 1950); George Tessier, *Le Baptême de Clovis, 25 décembre* (1964); Gabriel Fournier, *Les Mérovingiens* (1966); I. Meyer-Sickendiek *Gottes gelehrte Vaganten. Auf die Spuren der irischen Mission und Kultur in Europa* (1980).

[161] For instance, Krusch opens p. 1 of vol. 4 by quoting the omnipresent Jonas passage, then continues: "Ecclesiae Gallicanae senescenti novus surculus insitus est mox late diffusus immigrantibus scottis." Krusch's evidence for the decrepitude of the Merovingian church consisted entirely of the writings of Gregory of Tours. Jonas' *vita Columbani* is the first source printed in the volume.

[162] For instance, W. Levison, "Die Iren und die Fränkische Kirche" *Historische Zeitschrift* 109 (1912) pp. 1-22; repr. *Aus rheinischer und fränkischer Frühzeit* (Düsseldorf, 1948) pp. 247-262.

[163] BHL 2474 I.35-36 ed. Krusch pp. 691-693; Van der Essen, *Etude critique* p. 332.

[164] BHL 753 c. 10; for discussion, see below pp. 87-94.

tive elements in nineteenth- and twentieth-century historiography: because Eligius was an active and committed bishop, he has been identified himself as a follower of Columbanus.[165] Throughout his edition of the Merovingian-era *vita Eligii*, Krusch argues in the notes against the author of the text itself, correcting that historian for not presenting Eligius as a Columbanian! Krusch based his critique on Jonas' claim that Eligius had founded Solignac according to the rule of Columbanus.[166] There was a tendency during the iromaniacal historiographic phase of the early twentieth century to privilege the perspective of Jonas over any other orientation, even in the absence of any independent evidence to confirm Jonas' assertions.[167] Jonas' own polemical purposes have, since the time of Krusch, been recognized: to defend Columbanus from charges of heresy, and to present him as having been approved by the important and the orthodox.[168]

The perspective of the generation to which Krusch belonged was nuanced in the mid-twentieth century, as Columbanus, Luxueil and the *scotti* in general were submerged within a wider current of "iro-frankish"

[165] Hauck, *Kirchengeschichte* I.280; Eberhardt, p. 359; Jaud, *St. Filibert* p. 89; Van der Essen, *Etude critique* p. 326.

[166] Jonas, *Vitae Columbani et discipulorum eius* II. 10 ed. Krusch MGH SRM 4 p. 128; Krusch MGH SRM 4 pp. 703 note 1 and 724 note 6. Van der Essen argued in a similar manner against Eligius' near-contemporary biographer (*Etude critique* pp. 327-331).

[167] The foundation charter for Solignac, dated 22 Nov. 632, presents the house as a dependency of Columbanus' foundation at Luxeuil, and as independent of local episcopal authority (see the edition by Krusch in MGH SRM 4 pp. 746-9). The condition of the grant is "ut uos uel successores uestri tramitem religionis sanctissimorum uirorum Luxouiensis monasterii consequamini et regulam beatissimorum patrum Benedicti et Columbani firmiter teneatis, et nullam potestatem nullumque ius episcopus uel quelibet alia persona in prefato monasterio neque in rebus neque in personis nisi tantum gloriosissumus princeps poenitus sit habiturus." Malnory had considered the charter inauthentic (*Quid luxovienses monachi*), and Krusch's arguments for its authenticity are not entirely convincing (MGH SRM 4 pp.743-45). The earliest manuscript dates from the eleventh century (Limoges, Fonds de Solignac 9116). The monks of Solignac admitted the "loss" of the original document in a fire at some point, and the re-creation of the contents of the charter could easily date from its "confirmation" in 866 at Soissons. The charter was not known to Eligius' eighth-century biographer, whose scenario contradicts it.

[168] I. Wood, "The *vita Columbani* and Merovingian Hagiography" *Peritia* 1 (1982) pp. 63-80.

monasticism, "iro-frankish" mission and "iro-frankish" reform.[169] The present generation of scholars has gone even farther. Major international conferences have been devoted to determining whether or not there is any truth in the proposition promulgated by pope Pius in 1923. Participants in the review of the issue have arrived at conclusions ranging from the assertion that the "Irish missionary church" is utterly mythic,[170] to the argument that there is a kernel of truth in the image of the Irish missionary, but one whose minimal significance has been blown far out of proportion, and which can only be propped up by historiographic fictions.[171] Some

---

[169] Eugen Ewig, *Spätantikes und fränkisches Gallien. Gesammelte Schriften (1952-1973)* ed. H. Atsma, 2 vol. (Munich, 1976-1979); E. Ewig "Die Christliche Mission bei dem Franken und in Merowingerreich" in Derek Baker, ed. *Miscellanea Historiae Ecclesiasticae* III (1970), reprinted with minor revisions in Jedin, *Handbuch der Kirchengeschichte* and in Schäferdiek, ed. *Kirchengeschichte als Missionsgeschichte* II/1; Friedrich Prinz *Frühes Mönchtum im Frankenreich. Kultur und Gesellschaft in Gallien, den Rheinlanden und Bayern am Beispiel der monastischen Entwicklung (4. bis 8. Jahrhundert)* (Munich-Vienna, 1965).

[170] Friedrich Prinz, "Die Rolle der Iren beim Aufbau der merowingische Klosterkultur" in *Die Iren und Europa im Früheren Mittelalter* ed. Heinz Löwe (Stuttgart, 1982) questions the theory of Irish influence even on monasticism. Edward James, "Ireland and Western Gaul in the Merovingian Period" in *Ireland in Early Medieval Europe* (Studies in Memory of Kathleen Hughes; Cambridge, 1982) ed. R. McKitterick p. 362-381 and H. Zimmer, "Über direkte Handelsverbindungen Westgalliens mit Irland im Altertum und frühen Mittelalter" part III *Sitzungsberichte der Königlich Preusissischen Akademie der Wissenschaften* XIV (1909) pp. 543-580 turn the scenario on its head, and have the Gauls influence the so-called "isle of saints," rather than *vice versa*.

[171] Wolfgang Müller, "Der Anteil der Iren an der Christianisierung der Alemannen" ed. H. Löwe *Die Iren und Europa im früheren Mittelalter* (Acts of the International Colloquium, Tübingen, 1979; Stuttgart, 1982) vol. 2 pp. 336-340; Heinrich Koller "Die Iren und die Christianisierung der Baiern" ed. Löwe *Die Iren und Europa* vol. 2 pp. 345-373; Heinz Dopsch, "Die Salzburger Slawenmission im 8./9. Jahrhundert und der Anteil der Iren" in *Irland und die Christenheit* pp. 421-44; Jersy Strzelczyk, "Irische Einflüsse bei den Westslawen im Frühmittelalter" *Irland und die Christenheit* pp. 445-460; Knut Schäferdiek, "The Irish Mission of the Seventh Century: Historical Fact or Historiographical Fiction" in *The End of Strife* ed. D. Loades (Papers from the Colloquium of the Commission Internationale Ecclésiastique Comparée, U. of Durham, Sept. 1981; Edinburgh, 1984) pp. 139-154. Löwe summed up the results of the 1979 Tübingen conference by noting that all the contributors reached negative conclusions; nevertheless, he suggested waiting a bit before rejecting the idea of Irish missionary influence entirely (*Die Iren und Europa*

authors have simply chosen to ignore the Irish completely, and to tell the story of the Merovingian church without them.[172] The revision has not been confined to the issue of mission *per se*, indeed, it could not have been, for the whole complex of theories concerning the insular preservers of culture, monasticism and religion must be treated as a unity.[173]

In contrast with the works of the various revisionist authors and conference participants noted in the previous paragraph, the present study concerns not so much the history of Christianization as it does the historiography of Christianization. My aim is not to determine how much "truth" there is to the Irish missionary, or to the vision of the Merovingian church as moribund, needing to be revived by insular evangelists; it is to study the discourse. We cannot doubt that Columbanus and others like him were present on the continent. The question is: what did that mean to historian-observers? To Eligius' Merovingian-era biographer and to other historians of the period it meant Trouble, with a capital "T." Likewise, seventh-century fontenellian, gemmetic and *rouennais* historians were pleased with the state of their local churches, and apparently had no political reason to present Neustrian religiosity as in any way decrepit; they therefore had no use for a discursive strategy that made the meaning of Columbanus and others of his ilk into bearers of salvation for Gaul.

However, the political context, and therefore historiographic exigencies, was transformed by the Carolingian *coup*. After 754 the papally-unctioned Davidic line of rulers, dating secular events from the Incarnation of the Lord, created a sacrohistoriated framework within which pro-Christian missionary activity would play a central role. At the same time, the Davidic line had replaced the negligent line of Saul, and that fact required a certain revision of Merovingian-era historiographic complacency and

---

vol. 2 pp. 1024-1026).

[172] J.N. Hillgarth, "Modes of evangelization of western Europe in the seventh century" *Irland und die Christenheit* pp. 311-331; Ian Wood, "Pagans and Holy Men, 600-800" *Irland und die Christenheit* pp. 347-361.

[173] Michael Herren, "Classical and Secular Learning among the Irish Before the Carolingian Renaissance" *Florilegium* 3 (1981); Rosamond McKitterick, "The *Scriptoria* of Merovingian Gaul" in *Columbanus and Merovingian Monasticism* eds. Clarke and Brennan (1981) p. 185; Alain Dierkens, "Prolégomènes à une histoire des relations culturelles entre les îles Britanniques et le continent pendant le haut moyen âge"; R. McKitterick "The diffusion of insular culture in Neustria between 650-850: The implications of the manuscript evidence" *La Neustrie* ed. Atsma, II pp. 395-432.

self-satisfaction. We can follow the progress of the theme of anti-"pagan" mission in Carolingian historiography from the aftermath of the 754 *coup* through the heady days of the Empire of Charles the Great and Louis the Pious, a theme which reinforced the sacro-ministerial basis of Carolingian kingship.

It would be possible to interpret the importance of the theme of missionary activity in late-eighth- and early-ninth-century historiography as a function of a changed "ideal of sanctity." Theologically and abstractly, such a conclusion could well be justified. Historiographically and concretely, however, the theme is hung about with ideological implications. Some missionary biographies were set in the Carolingian period, in the "pagan" lands to the east of Francia, lands which the Franks were, even then, as ministers of God, seeking to conquer/convert. The rest set the events in the Merovingian period, within Francia itself. The latter narratives necessarily implied that there were "not-Christians" present in the Merovingian kingdoms to be converted. Most of the rest of this chapter will focus on the work of Alcuin, the author of a number of missionary biographies.

Like Columbanus before him, Alcuin of York was apparently not a particularly flexible person. The Christianity of Gaul, in so far as it diverged from the insular Christianity in which he had been raised, was to his mind deficient. In the multi-pronged programme that produced the "Carolingian *renovatio*" the influence of Alcuin was paramount, including in reshaping the Bible and the liturgy.[174] His own historiographic *oeuvre*, to which the revision of the biography of Audoenus (discussed at length below) should be added, privileges either insular figures or individuals presented as having been influenced by insular figures, in scenarios describing the establishment of proper Christianity instead of the "negligent" kind. Alcuin wrote at least four works of history: a biography of St. Willibrord, and revised biographies of Sts. Vedastes, Richerius and Martin, all composed at Tours between 796 and 801, in the midst of planning for

---

[174] F. L. Ganshof, "La revision de la Bible par Alcuin" *Bibliothèque d'Humanisme et de la Renaissance* IX (1947) pp. 7-20; trans. Janet Sondheimer in F.L. Ganshof, *The Carolingians and the Frankish Monarchy* (1971); Donald Bullough, "Alcuin and the Kingdom of Heaven: Liturgy, Theology and the Carolingian Age" in Uta-Renate Blumenthal ed. *Carolingian Essays* (Andrew W. Mellon Lectures in Early Christian Studies; Washington, DC, 1983) pp. 1-69; McKitterick *Carolingians and the Written Word* pp. 11-12, 20, 165, 197-200.

the revival of the Western Roman Empire.[175] He bothered, as well, to emphasize the necessity of reading excerpts from his biographies aloud to the general public.[176] Such histories, composed around the signal year of 800, can hardly fail to be permeated by major ideological concerns.

Let us begin with Alcuin's biography of Willibrord, the first of his four works of history. The ideological implications of Alcuin's achievement in connection with Willibrord have been brought out by Tabacco, some of whose insights are summarized in the following paragraphs.[177] To appreciate Alcuin's procedure fully requires some background. We have already met Boniface, for instance at the Concilium Germanicum. Boniface sometimes worked in tandem with the Carolingian mayors of the palace; however, his own correspondance and his own biography, composed in the third quarter of the eighth century by his successor at Mainz, Willibald, are both highly critical of the Carolingian princes, who are not only perceived as responsible for the degradation of the church, but also as obstacles to the saint's missionary and reforming movements.[178] If some higher authority was responsible for Boniface's missionizing in Willibald's eyes, it was the papacy. Similarly, Arbeo of Freising's biography of his own predecessor Corbinianus, composed approximately at the same time as when Willibald was writing, also attributes to the papacy the creation of the authoritative missionary plan of which Corbinianus was a part, although Arbeo also puts the saint in contact with Pippin II, much in the

[175] Alcuin himself claimed that his purpose in writing was only to improve the Latinity of texts in circulation, but we can hardly believe such disingenuous assertions (Alcuin, *Vita Richerii* preface, MGH SRM 4 p. 389). For Carolingian rewritings as more than grammatical improvements, Deug-Su I, *L'opera agiografica di Alcuino* (Biblioteca degli "Studi medievali" XIII; Spoleto, 1983); Deug-Su I, *Cultura e ideologia nella prima età Carolingia* (Istituto Storico Italiano per il Medio Evo; Studi storici 146-147; Rome, 1984); Jean-Yves Tilliette, "Les Modèles de sainteté du IXe au XIe siècle, d'après le témoignage des récits hagiographiques en vers métriques" *Settimane* 36 "Santi e Demoni" (1988) pp. 387-388.

[176] Alcuin, *Vita Willibrordi* preface, MGH SRM 7 pp. 113-114.

[177] Giovanni Tabacco, "Agiografia e demonologia come strumenti ideologici in età Carolingia" *Settimane* 36 (1988) pp. 121-153.

[178] Boniface, Epistola 50 (MGH Epistolae Selectae I.82); Willibrord, *Vita Bonifatii* c. 7 ff (ed. Levison MGH SRG 57 (1905) p. 39ff and pp. 43-45.

same way that Willibald's Boniface had known Charles Martel.[179]

Willibald was a pro-Roman Angle, who had little interest in promoting the strength of the Carolingians. But, intentionally or not, he began a vogue for biographies of missionary bishops, biographies which publicized the negative characteristics of "pagan" enemies to the east, a historiographic perspective that would help to justify the wars of expansion being waged in those territories.[180] This expansion-legitimizing perspective is quite clear in Einhard's biography of Charlemagne, which includes descriptions of the war against the "devil worshippers," that is, the Saxons (II.7). The "devil worship" of the Saxons is, for Einhard, the legitimization for the war; it is in and of itself sufficient reason to attack a region. The author of the Royal Frankish Annals is even more firmly committed to explaining the wars as an attempt to force the Saxons to accept Christianity.[181] Frankish victories were seen as God's will, and in the end the Saxons were baptized.

How, then, does Alcuin's biography of Willibrord fit in? Willibald had written the history of Boniface's activity in Germany as completely

---

[179] F. Brunhölzl Bischof Arbeo von Freising. Das Leben des heiligen Korbinian in H. Glaser, F. Brunhölzl and S. Benker, Vita Corbiniani. Bischof Arbeo von Freising und die Lebensgeschichte des hl. Korbinian (Munich-Zurich, 1983); Tabacco, "Agiografia e Demonologia" p. 140.

[180] The many Carolingian histories of the anti-"pagan" missions are extremely well known, and have been studied from every possible angle. Some texts in which the theme of Carolingian royal support of anti-"pagan" mission in Germany is prominent are Eigil's biography of Sturm of Fulda (P. Engelbert ed. Die Vita Sturmi des Eigil von Fulda (Marburg, 1968), Liudger's biography of Gregory of Utrecht (Liutgeri, Vita Gregorii abbatis Traiectensis in MGH SS XV/1), Rimbert's biography of Anskar of Hamburg and an anonymous biography of Rimbert (Rimberti Vita Anskarii in Quellen des 9. und 11. Jahrhunderts zur Geschichte der hamburgischen Kirche und des Reiches [Darmstadt, 1968] and Vita Rimberti in Vita Anskarii auctore Rimberto; accedit Vita Rimberti ed. G Waitz in MGH SRG 55 [Hannover, 1884]). Ardo's biography of Benedict of Aniane, composed circa 821, applied the narrative structure which had served so well in the context of "paganism" to monasticism, presenting his subject's monastic reform movement as no less motivated by Louis "the Pious" than by Benedict, who is also shown being trained in Pippin's court, and working as a servant of Charlemagne (Ardo Vita Benedicti abbatis Anianensis MGH SS XV/1). For Tabacco's discussion of all these materials as ideologically-loaded Carolingian historiography, see "Agiografia et demonologia" pp. 141-150.

[181] Revised version of RFA anno 775 and 776, trans. Scholz pp. 51-55.

independent of the Carolingians. There was no way for Alcuin to rewrite, so very soon, the history of the Bonifatian mission itself, for it would have been impossible to claim that Willibald's Latin was corrupt. Alcuin's stroke of genius was to write, instead, a history of a certain Willibrord, whom he presented as in every way the predecessor of Boniface; Boniface, then, had merely followed in tracks established by Willibrord, and Willibrord, in Alcuin's biography, was a Carolingian lacky from the word "go." According to Alcuin's biography, Willibrord, himself from the area of Ripon, studied in Ireland for twelve years before deciding to evangelize the "pagans" of Frisia. Frisia in particular (under its evil ruler Radbod), and northern Francia in general were, when the insular missionary arrived in the late seventh century, terrible places, inhabited by obdurate inhabitants of little faith. Willibrord was sent by Pippin to change all that, a Pippin whose greatest desire in life was to support Christianity. Although Willibrord's mission was technically set during the period when Merovingians still ruled in Francia, Merovingian kings and queens are absent from Alcuin's history. After the death of Pippin, it was Charles Martel who sent Willibrord on evangelizing tours; Willibrord was neither independent, nor a functionary of Rome: he was a Carolingian servant.[182]

Thus, Alcuin, with his biography of Willibrord, determined the discourse through which Willibald's biography of Boniface would be read, so that even though no tight connection had been asserted between the Carolingians and saint Boniface in that saint's own near-contemporary biography, anyone reading in chronological order (as students of history tend to do), would mentally interpolate a strong role for the Carolingians into Willibald's text: had not the Carolingian princes been responsible for the beginning of Boniface's mission during the career of Willibrord? Furthermore, simply increasing the amount of attention paid in the historiographical literature to insular missionaries active in the late Merovingian period would in and of itself tend to reinforce the discourse of degeneration, for the Merovingian realm would seem to have been in such a bad way that it had to be revived by outsiders.

It was, similarly, the salvific role of the insular outsider that probably

---

[182] Alcuin, *Vita Willibrordi*, trans. C.H. Talbot, *The Anglo-Saxon Missionaries in Germany; being the Lives of SS. Willibrord, Boniface, Sturm, Leoba and Lebuin, together with the Hodoeporicon of St. Willibald and a selection from the correspondance of St. Boniface* (London, 1954) pp. 3-22.

attracted Alcuin to the life of Richerius († c. 654) whose biography, out of
the hundreds of available Merovingian-era saints, Alcuin decided to rewrite. The early-eighth-century biography of Richerius was one of the earliest biographies produced under the sponsorship of a loyal Pippinist,
namely Coschinus of St. Riquier and Jumièges.[183] Deug-Su I has already
emphasized how rewriting this particular early biography permitted Alcuin to attribute to Richerius, in a saintly harangue to king Dagobert, a long
verbal treatise on the proper relationship between wordly and spiritual
powers, a subject evidently much on Alcuin's mind in 800.[184] The same
plot possibility was inherent in Jonas' biography of Vedastes, whom Jonas
had shown as the primary catechist of king Clovis and then as the principal evangelist of Artois; Alcuin's revised *vita Vedastis*, which did not particularly emphasize insular characters, did focus on the need to re-evange-
lize the Artois after the Merovingian Franks had, according to Alcuin,
destroyed Christianity in the area.[185]

But let us return to the insularophilic discourse. According to his
earlier biographer, Richerius had been one of the "not-Christians" of Ponthieu. The turning point in the saint's life came when he happened upon
a crowd of local "gentiles...stulti" who were threatening two insular pilgrims, one a *scotus* and the other from Hibernia.[186] Richerius took the
two pilgrims back to his house, and sat up all night talking with them; in
the course of the night, he himself converted to Christianity and, for the
rest of his life, preached the word to all and sundry, though the two pilgrims themselves disappeared from the scene.[187] Writing a biography of

---

[183] Jean Laporte, *St. Riquier. Etude hagiographique* (1958) p. 16 (= BHL 7245).

[184] BHL 7245 c. 6 ed. A. Poncelet AB XXII p. 189; Alcuin *Vita Richerii* (BHL 7223-
7227) ed. Krusch c. 11 pp. 395-396; Deug-Su I, *L'opera agiografica de Alcuino*. Krusch's
explanation for Alcuin's seemingly odd choice of Richerius as a biographical
subject centered on Alcuin's desire to help his friend, abbot Angilram of St. Riquier, to gain certain local property rights (B. Krusch "Die älteste Vita Richerii"
Neues Archiv 29 [1904] pp. 15-48, esp. pp. 16-22).

[185] Jonas of Bobbio *Vita Vedastis* (BHL 8500-8503) ed. B. Krusch MGH SRM 3 pp.
406-413; Alcuin *Vita Vedastis* (BHL 8506-8508) ed. Krusch MGH SRM 3 pp. 414-427.

[186] BHL 7245 ed. Poncelet c. 2 pp. 186-187; Poncelet's edition, based on ms.
Avranches BM 167, a thirteenth-century legendary from Mont-St.-Michel, has to be
used in conjunction with the corrections published by Vielhaber from Vienna 420,
an eighth-century manuscript from St. Amand les Eaux (AB XXVI pp. 45-51).

[187] BHL 7245 ed. Poncelet cc. 3-4 pp. 187-188.

Richerius permitted Alcuin to focus attention on the rampant "not-paganism" of Ponthieu in the time of the Merovingian kings, who had done nothing to stamp it out; the evangelization of the region could, instead, be attributed to an individual who had had to be converted by insular pilgrims.[188]

Although Alcuin, in his insularophilia, chose to rewrite a saint's biography which included two insular characters, he did not depart from the discourse of the earlier biography concerning the significance of those figures: they remained pilgrims, not missionaries. It may have been Hariulf, the eleventh-century author of the Chronicon Centulense, who first moved in the direction of an iromaniacal historiographic thesis. For Hariulf, the meaning of the pilgrimage of the two Christians saved by Richerius in Ponthieu had been deliberate missionary activity in the first place.[189] In Hariulf's chronicle, furthermore, the insular missionaries do not drop from the picture but remain to evangelize Ponthieu. During the early-twentieth-century iromaniacal historiographic wave, the two insular pilgrims and Richerius were numbered by scholars among the throngs of specifically Columbanian missionaries who were believed to have relieved the Merovingian Dark Ages.[190]

To the historiographic efforts of Alcuin which have already been recognized, I would suggest the addition of the revised biography of Audoenus of Rouen, a symbol of Neustrian-Merovingian pride too potent to ignore. The revised biography of Audoenus has survived in two general streams: the so-called "B" vita (= BHL 751/752)[191] and the so-called "C"

---

[188] Alcuin vita Richerii ed. Krusch cc. 2-3 pp. 391-396.

[189] "De Aduentu et praedicatione sanctorum Hibernensium": "Ipso autem tempore quo isti, propria deserentes, Christum secuti sunt, multorum sanctorum examina produxisse scitur Hibernia. Ex quibus beatus quoque Columbanus homo scotici generis floruit, cuius laudabilis conuersatio uirtusque eximia totius Galliae loca respersit. Fertur uero quod cum ipso illi [the two Ponthieu pilgrims] quoque maria huc properando transmearunt...uerbum Dei praedicare" (Hariulf Chronicon Centulense I.6 (= BHL 7233) ed. F. Lot, Chronique de St.-Riquier [1894] p. 15).

[190] Jean Laporte St. Riquier pp. 3-6; Platelle, BSS XI cols. 155-157.

[191] BHL 751/752 is a popular family of relatively similar succinct abbreviations of the Carolingian narrative. Copies circulated in Western Francia and England where Audoenus was venerated as a saint: in eleventh-century legendary collections made in the Ile-de-France (Paris, BN lat. 15.437 from St. Marcel of Paris, and BN lat. 11.750 from St. Germain des Près) and in Maine/Anjou (Le Mans 227 from

vita (= BHL 753).[192] In both cases the complexity of textual transmission
has been collapsed into an oversimplified schema of a single "B" *vita*,
thought to have been later amplified by a second single author into a "C"
vita.[193] Although it is impossible to reconstruct precisely the "original"
Carolingian text from which both streams flowed, the impression given by
both the longer family of narratives (= BHL 753) and by the shorter family
(BHL 751/752) is sufficiently homogenous to clue us in to the main
features of the ninth-century historiographic prism. The BHL 753 family,
which has been preserved particularly in Austrasian circles, indeed in
major Carolingian centers, represents a fuller version, including for
instance the author's dedicatory epistle to the individual from whom he
received the commission to revise Audoenus' "antiqua historia," and is
likely to be more representative of the *renovatio*-period reworking of
Audoenus' biography into a full-length treatise on Merovingian Neustria.

It is extremely unfortunate that the salutation of the dedicatory

---

St. Pierre de la Couture), and in a number of Norman legendaries (Paris, BN lat
12.605 from Bec; Paris, BN lat 5296 from Fécamp; Rouen BM 1380 [U.55] from Jumièges; Rouen 1388 [U.32] from Fécamp; Rouen 1405 [Y.27], the Ivory Book of the
Rouen Cathedral; and Rouen 1406 [Y.41], the Black Book of St. Ouen of Rouen
[copy in Rouen 1411]). Because this family of narratives functioned often in liturgical contexts, many of the codices also include information on the whereabouts of
Audoenus' relics (BHL 751/2 c. 46; AASS Aug. IV p. 819). This abbreviation was
then thrown into extremely wide circulation due to its incorporation into the *Liber
de Natalitiis* in the thirteenth century (Paris BN lat. 11.758, BN lat. 17.005, Montpellier Bib. Fac. Med. 1 vol. IV; also Montpellier Bib. Fac. Med. 30, a legendary of Bur-
gundy/Franche-Comté made in the twelfth century, which served as a source for
the *Liber de Natalitiis*).

[192] BHL 753 is a family of relatively dissimilar, extremely long biographies of the
saint, preserved in a small number of scholarly manuscripts of the eleventh century
and earlier (Metz BM 652 [G56], from St. Arnulf of Metz, destroyed in World War
II, may have dated from the ninth or tenth century; Paris, BN lat. 9742 from St.
Maximinus of Trier; Paris, BN lat. 5607 from St. Maur-des-Fossés [Einhard abbot
of Fontenelle "reformed" that Norman house with the aid of abbot Benedict of St.
Maur-des-Fossés between 817 and 823 (see Laporte, "Fontenelle," DHGE 17 col.
918)]; Paris, BN lat. 10.852 from St. Willibrord of Echternach; Naples, BN XV.AA.13).
Copies belonging to this family were preserved mainly in scholarly centers where
Audoenus was not venerated as a saint.

[193] BHL 751/752 = AASS Aug. IV pp. 810-819 ed. G.Cointius; BHL 753 = "Vita
Sancti Audoeni Rotomagensis Episcopi auctore anonymo ex codicibus manuscriptis
quinque" ed. E. P. Sauvage, AB 5 (1886) pp. 76-146.

epistle in BHL 753 has not been preserved, for the author seems to have been one of the more respected, and sought-after, historians of his age; certainly he had a tremendous sense of his own importance! For a number of reasons, I believe this important personage to have been Alcuin. We know that Audoenus was on Alcuin's mind in the years during which the latter produced the four biographies already attributed to him. In 798/799 Alcuin produced a series of inscriptions for the churches of St. Amand-les-Eaux and St. Vaast of Arras.[194] At St. Vaast, he wrote inscriptions for the altars of Vedastes, Martin, Dionysius, Remigius, Audoenus, Lantbertus of Liège and Richerius, all of whom were presented in the inscriptions as having been inspired by an identical missionary spirit.[195] Audoenus therefore belonged to a group which also contained the three other saints whose biographies Alcuin is known to have re-written in precisely these years, and is known to have been conceived of by Alcuin as a missionary, an intrepretation of Audoenus' pontificate that is totally novel when compared with the saint's Merovingian-era biography. We can even identify at St. Amand in those very years a copy of the Merovingian biography of Audoenus (BHL 750) that was the source for the revised version: Vienna lat. 420 (Salisb. 39), a manuscript which also contains the oldest extant copy of the Merovingian biography of Richerius (BHL 7245), which Alcuin is known to have rewritten at the same time.[196]

The narrative of the revised biography of Audoenus is very close to

---

[194] MGH Poetae Latini aevi Carolini I pp. 305-312.

[195] MGH Poet. Lat. I p. 310.

[196] The manuscript has been identified as having been written at St. Amand, and as having come to Vienna *via* Salzburg (Vielhaber, AB 26 p. 45). In 785 the abbot of St. Amand, Arno, was promoted to the see of Salzburg. He kept in touch with his former house, and had at least one manuscript that later passed into the collections at Salzburg, then Vienna, copied for him in 795 (Wright *Late Latin and Early Romance* p. 128). Vienna lat. 420, which contains one of the oldest copies of Audoenus' Merovingian biography, was probably also compiled at St. Amand in the 790s, used by Alcuin for his revised versions of the biographies of Richerius and Audoenus, then sent to Arno in Salzburg. BHL 750 is also associated in two other codices with biographies rewritten by Alcuin, although we cannot trace his usage of them: The Great Legendary of Autun, Montpellier, School of Medicine H. 55 of the 8th or 9th century, included Jonas' biography of Vedastis (BHL 8502); and St. Gall 563 of the ninth or tenth centuries, included BHL 8502 and the oldest biography of Richerius (BHL 7245).

those in the other works produced by Alcuin around 800.[197] With Alcuin's recognized writings, the *vita Audoeni* shares the "generic" fact of being the revised version of a saint's biography, touted in the preface as having been undertaken because of the insupportable shortcomings of an "antiqua historia" which is merely being "ameliorated," and the fact of having been written with a specific view towards use in public readings (though clearly not *in extenso!*).[198] The *vita Audoeni* also features Alcuin's preferred dual-protagonist method of exploring ideal church-state relations, as Audoenus' relations with Dagobert mirror the Willibrord-Pippin, Vedastis-Clovis and Richerius-Dagobert pairs. The *vita Audoeni* also shares with Alcuin's works a marked tendency to moralize at length.[199] Finally, it shares with Alcuin's other biographies the utilization of the concept of the "enemy of the Church" (*inimicus* or *adversarius ecclesiae*), whether "heretic" or "pagan," as a way to solve the acute confusion in church-state relations engendered by the preparations for and achievement of the imperial coronation of Charlemagne.[200]

One problem faced by Alcuin and numerous other churchmen in connection with the imperial coronation was how to preserve independence for ecclesiastical authorities given the tremendous boost suddenly received by the secular power. To Charlemagne's hegemonic ambitions could be opposed the implications of the papal unction of 754, and of the papal coronation of 800. Alcuin's biographies of Willibrord, Richerius and Vedastis are all about the ecclesiastical *auctoritas*, about the honor and dignity of the prince of the church, which Alcuin asserted to be greater than those of the princes of the world.[201] The fact that the author of the *vita Audoeni* takes every opportunity (indeed, makes many opportunities) to dissertate upon precisely this aspect of Church-State relations, leads me to

[197] See the studies of those biographies by I: *L'opera agiografica di Alcuino* and *Cultura e ideologia nella prima età Carolingia.*

[198] Prologue, cc. 1-2 ed. Sauvage, pp. 76-78; the "B" stream seems to me possibly to represent the family of extracts made from the enormous treatise for use in public readings.

[199] I, *Cultura e ideologia* pp. 7-8.

[200] I, *Cultura e ideologia* pp. 119-125.

[201] I, *Cultura e ideologia* pp. 12-26, esp. p. 15.

attribute the text to Alcuin.[202]

The specific ways in which Alcuin's revision differs from the Merovingian version are in keeping with an insularophilic project to diminish whatever independent reputation for piety pre-Carolingian Neustria and the Merovingian monarchs might be enjoying. Anything resembling praise of a Merovingian ruler has been removed from this revision of Neustrian history.[203] When the royal palace is mentioned, it is as the equivalent of the "aula Babylonica," not a very nice place at all (c. 4). At the court of king Dagobert (who has been reduced to a cypher, from the "leo fervidus" of the Merovingian biography, BHL 750) Audoenus runs everything; indeed, it is to Audoenus' efforts alone that anything good in the kingdom is owed,[204] though ultimately Audoenus' own abilities must be traced back to a *scotus*, Columbanus (c. 7).

All would be darkness were it not for Columbanus, who is paralleled to Abraham (c. 4). Anyone who knows their Biblical antetypes (as this

---

[202] The extended "mirror of princes" diatribe preached by Audoenus at Dagobert in chapter 8 describes how God gave the books of the law through Moses (in whose stead princes of the church now stand) so that the princes of the world might govern according to His wishes, but never go beyond those wishes; how the job of the worldly prince is to enforce divine law and to defend the Church from its enemies; that a truly good prince also cares for the poor and other weak persons; and that everyone must love and venerate priests, who are the lights of the world and the "principes caelorum." A second treatise on the sacerdotal dignity fills cc. 27-32; in this case the focus is the ecclesiastical medicaments such as penance whereby priests, who hold the keys to heaven, can save those whom the wordly courts damn. This second section is an extended discussion of the relationship between the "two powers."

[203] The "B" stream, which after all circulated in Neustria, does not go as far as the "C" stream in suppressing every single, even off-hand, kind word about the Merovingians. Although the plot and the discourse are identical, the "B" stream occasionally attaches a word of praise, such as "glorious," to the royal names. Another semi-conscious resulting difference is how the "C" stream refers both to Neustrians and Austrasians as "Franks," some living in the west, others in the east (ed. Sauvage pp. 137-138 BHL 753 c. 63), whereas the "B" stream refers to Neustrians as Franks and the Austrasians as Austrasians (AASS Aug. IV p. 818, BHL 751/2 c. 37).

[204] In the succinct summation of the "B" stream (BHL 751/2), "Ispe autem rex supradictus, aurem Dei uiro libenter in omnibus, qua sausit, accommodabat. Quapropter et cunctis hostibus extitit fortior, et omnibus Francorum regibus, qui ante se regnauerunt, felicior" (AAS Aug. IV p. 811).

author shows he did) knows that Abraham has primacy among Hebrew patriarchs and prophets; Columbanus-Abraham is not just another prophet in a string of prophets, he is the first "Jew," the first man to bow to the will of the Lord, the human side of the original Covenant. Columbanus is shown blessing the child Dado, who would become the great prelate Audoenus, "nor could the blessing of so great a man be without effect" ("nec potuit tanti uiri benedictio inanis fieri" [c. 4]). Jouarre and Rebais, important Merovingian monasteries, are explicitly recognized as Columbanian foundations (c. 5 and 11). The figure of Columbanus was an extremely convenient historiographical device, for he could be used by Carolingian revisionists to explain any anomalous "holiness" that had crept into the Merovingian world.

One aspect of Alcuin's transformation of the character of Audoenus was to make him a Columbanian; the other was to strip him of his *virtus*. Alcuin's Audoenus is not a powerful saint whose relics are to be feared, he is a model of missionary activity directed against the enemies of the church. Chapter 10 and chapters 13-16 show Audoenus fighting "heretics," who seem to be rife in the Merovingian Church; "heresy" is equated explicitly with "idolatry" and demon-worship (c. 16). Audoenus also goes off to convert the many "not-Christians" who are shown to dot the pre-Carolingian landscape. The "rain in Spain" miracle of the Merovingian biography becomes an extended story of mission (cc. 18-23), in which the "miracle" itself is down-played to the point of seeming to be a metaphor, the absence of life-sustaining water having really been a symbol of the absence of the life-giving faith. The author turns the episode into a rationalizing narrative of anti-"pagan" mission.[205] The healing of the Sunday worker

---

[205] "...gentibus ut uerbum salutis praedicaret procul positas expetiuit regiones. Itaque euangelium praedicando Aquitaniam Hispaniasque perlustrauit....Itaque, transmisso Ligeris amne, cunctos in eisdem regionibus habitantes salutaris lumine uerbi quasi quidam sol irradiauit. Alios namque de gentilitatis errore ad uerae tramitem conuertit religionis, alios in fide corroborauit, alios haeretica priuitate corruptos ad catholicam ueritatem reuocauit....Quo miraculo uiso, Hispaniarum populi hominem Dei summis laudibus efferebant, summa deuotione uenerabantur, summa humilitate dictis eius obediebant. Gentiles idola deserentes ad Christi gratiam confluebant; credentes, secundum Apostolum, remissas manus et dissoluta genua erigentes, gressus rectos mentis passibus per rectum fidei callem faciebant; ad ecclesias diuersae populorum cateruae properabant, uerbum Dei tota cordis auiditate suscipiebant, hymnis, laudibus, orationibusque uacabant, moribus et

in Anjou (c. 24) is particularly diminished as a miracle, as it is immediately swamped by two chapters of meditations on how the merit is really due to the Cross (cc. 25-26).[206]

Alcuin's Audoenus is no longer the powerful miracle-working saint of the Merovingian biography, for fear of the prelate's remains was the last thing the author wished to inspire. In fact, Alcuin tells his readers and listeners outright that the relics of Audoenus in the church of St. Peter outside Rouen were no longer producing miracles.[207] One might be tempted to scoff, mere discourse! We could accuse Alcuin of attempting to assert the disempowerment of Audoenus into existence, of consciously inverting his character as Neustria's invisible patron of gargantuan *virtus*. But clearly there was more to it than mere discourse: the *virtus* of Audoenus **had** failed Neustria. His own see at Rouen grew more impover-

---

sanctae uitae studium componebant, operibus pietatis insistebant, sanctae legis meditationem, diuinorum monita praeceptorum agebant. Daemonum cultus nusquam, gentilis conuentus rarissimus aut nullus; templa denique cuncta destruebantur, arae subruebantur, luci succidebantur. Omnes ad Christi jugum mitia colla deferebant, omnes eius onus laetis humeris suscipiebant. Sic factum est, ut coelestis gratia per seruum suum potestate mortis liberatam totam prouinciam ad lumen uitae uocaret, atque, post longam sitis aerumnam, qua terra, pecudes hominesque deperibant, cum pluuia terras perfunderet, rore quoque sancti Spiritus mortalium mentes irrigaret" (BHL 753 cc. 18-21 ed. Sauvage pp. 97-100).

[206] Chapters 47-53, containing miracles worked by Audoenus in the Cotentin, do not follow the narration in the "historia antiqua" which the author of BHL 753 promises in his preface to follow scrupulously. Furthermore, they are miracles designed to demonstrate the saint's power, indeed even his power to harm people who show insufficient respect to his relics. These chapters must be an interpolation, because they contradict the spirit of the rest of the biography. The interpolation could have been made very soon after the text was written, but there is little chance they come from the pen of the original author. Chapters 61-62, likewise, do not follow the narration of BHL 750, and contain the report of a privilege given to Audoenus by king Theodericus, according to which the prelate would have exclusive jurisdiction over all things ecclesiastical in the diocese; counts are specifically mentioned, and then an unflattering story is told of the family of Waratto, count of Rouen. Both the Cotentin material (in showing Audoenus exercising power throughout the archdiocese) and this privilege (which is described as covering the whole province) favored the archbishops of Rouen. The archbishops at the time would have controlled St. Ouen, and were probably responsible for the interpolations.

[207] BHL 753 cc. 69-70 ed. Sauvage p. 142-143.

ished daily. The power of his relics had indeed been neutralized. By the ninth century, La Croix-St.-Ouen even changed its name, to La Croix-St.-Leufroy, in recognition of the patron whose relics had come through.

Alcuin's biography of Audoenus is a monument to the success of the Carolingian conquest of Neustria, but it is also a witness to the relative failure of the take-over. The strategy of channeling responsibility for "positive" features of the Merovingian world towards Columbanus, and through him, in the diocese of Rouen, to Audoenus, made of both of them absolute giants. For the fact is, there was an awful lot of "good" to account for! The greater the focus on Audoenus, the more monumental he became, growing ever more appropriate as a symbol of Neustrian pride. Alcuin tells us that Audoenus had to build new and repair old monasteries because his predecessors had all been negligent (c. 35). Audoenus had taken control of a decrepit diocese with crumbling churches about which not a single good word is said; by the time he was finished,

> So great a multitude of the religious, so great fervor for religion, so great a blessing of heavenly grace had filled the territory of Rouen, that one would think almost the entire region had taken up the religious habit;[208]

or, in the formula of the "B" stream:

> And during his lifetime, no diocese in all the provinces of Gaul could over come or even equal the diocese of Rouen in Christian devotion.[209]

Pious Neustria was not crushed, merely concentrated into the person of Audoenus.

Insularophilia was the historiographic vogue of the era at Fontenelle as well, the only major atelier of the diocese of Rouen which managed to produce at least one narrative under every discursive regime covered by

---

[208] "Tanta religiosorum multitudo, tantus feruor religionis, tanta coelestis gratiae benedictio Rotomagensium fines repleuerat, ut tota fere regio in religionis habitum transisse putaretur" (BHL 753 c. 36 ed. Sauvage p. 113).

[209] "Nullaque dioecesis in cunctis Galliarum prouinciis suo tempore diocesim Rothomagensem in devotione Christianae religionis superare, uel etiam coaequare potuit" (AASS Aug. IV p. 815).

the present study.[210] The early-ninth-century biography of Condedus is set in "Pious Neustria," a period otherwise ignored by Fontenelle authors, and specifically under the abbacy of Lantbertus of Fontenelle.[211] The twist, however, is this: whatever piety existed in Neustria was now to be laid at the feet of immigrants from the British Isles. It cannot be insignificant that the only history written about seventh-century Neustria by a Fontenelle historian during this period took as its main subject an insular missionary. The biographer of Condedus used the works of both Paul the Deacon and of Alcuin to paint his picture of a British hermit who comes with his disciples to the deserts of Francia not only for love of holy peregrination, but also because "it did not seem to him to be enough that he exert himself in the sanctity of religion if he did not also profit others by his preaching" (a quote from Alcuin's *vita Willibrordi*).[212] Subtle hints of missionary activity on the part of this insular hermit in his ninth-

---

[210] The interest in "Antiquity" of the Carolingian "renaissance" also found some reflection at Fontenelle: if we can believe the early-ninth-century *Gesta Abbatum Fontenellensium*, cultic promotion in the eighth century focussed on the relics of early Roman martyrs, as the Merovingian-era saints of Neustria were studiously ignored (*Gesta abbatum Fontenellensium* cc. xiii and xiv, concerning relics of Servatius and George [MGH SS 2 p. 288]).

[211] The *vita Eremberti*, which survives only in the Maius Chronicon Fontenel-lense, does not seem to me to be a Merovingian or a Carolingian text, for it is completely uncharacteristic of the character of Fontenellian productions during those centuries: the *vita Eremberti* is riddled with supernatural occurances, which otherwise find no place in seventh-, eighth- or ninth-century Fontenellian historiography (ed. Levison, MGH SRM 5 pp. 653-656). The narrative seems more likely intended to support a post-Norman property-restitution claim.

[212] "...non satis sibi uideri in religionis sanctitate sudare, si non et aliis quoque in praedicatione...prodesset" (*Vita Condedi* [BHL 1907] ed. Levison, MGH SRM 5); see Levison's introduction p. 644 for the author's sources, and cc. 1-4 and cc. 7-8 pp. 646-650 for his character, arrival and mission on the island of Belcinac. BHL 1908, a brief and dry epitome of BHL 1907 made for liturgical purposes, differs from the longer text in no appreciable way (ed. Victor de Buck AASS Oct. IX pp. 354-355; Levison, MGH SRM 5 p. 646; Benedictines of Paris, *Vies des saints* Oct. vol. IX). Though for the most part Condedus is modelled upon Willibrord the insular missionary, twice the author instead quotes the *vita Ermenlandi* (BHL 3851), former monk of Fontenelle who ended his days as abbot of Aindre in the diocese of Nantes, where his biography was composed, so that Condedus becomes a solitary devoted to monastic perfection, and renunciation of the world (BHL 1908 c. 4 p. 648 and c. 6 pp. 648-649).

century fontenellian insularophilic biography, swelled into unequivocally iromaniacal statements of self-conscious mission and "Columbanian" discipleship in the writings of nineteenth- and twentieth-century historians, the same pattern I have already traced for Eligius and Richerius.[213]

Of greatest importance for early-ninth-century Fontenellian historiography was the *Gesta* of the abbots of the house, a text of tremendous ideological depth, whose author not only used the prism of insularophilia to diminish pre-Carolingian Neustria, but even coopted the theretofore slightly dangerous figure of Wandregiselus for full-fledged Carolingian service. Wandregiselus, the founder of Fontenelle, had come originally from the region of Verdun, according to his contemporary biographer.[214] As such, he had been inappropriate as a symbol of Neustrian pride, and was not therefore thrust forward by anti-Austrasian forces at the time of the Carolingian penetration, when Ansbertus and Audoenus first received their public venerations. After the Austrasian takeover, Bainus of Thérouanne elevated the relics of Wandregiselus and instituted a cult to him, but no new biography was composed. Therefore the first hint we have of the character of the Wandregiselus who was venerated at Carolingian Fontenelle comes from the ninth-century *Gesta*.

By the early ninth century, the Wandregiselus who had founded Fontenelle had become a Carolingian himself,[215] rendering the Carolingian dynasty itself responsible for the main center of Pious Neustria even

---

[213] Jules Corblet, *Hagiographie du diocèse d'Amiens* (1868) I.545-553. The introduction and notes to Levison's edition of the *vita Ermenlandi* which was used by the author of Condedus' biography as cited in the previous note (BHL 3851; MGH SRM V pp. 674-678 and *passim* pp. 682-710), furnish extremely good examples of Levison's own iromania; see especially the first two sentences of the Introduction (p. 674) from which, before we even meet Ermenlandus, off being born in Noyon, we learn that Columbanus had been to Nantes, that Wandregiselus had connections with Columbanus' foundation of Bobbio, and that Audoenus was a Columbanian. What a contrast with the way Ermenlandus' eighth-century biographer chose to open his discussion of the saint: Ermenlandus is born in Noyon "cum fides sanctae ecclesiae, errorum caligine depulsa, luce euangelicae ueritatis corusca in omni dicione Chlottharii regis Francorum tranquilla uteretur pace" (BHL 3851 c. 1 p. 684).

[214] BHL 8804; see Appendix 1, pp. 220-224.

[215] "Cuius genitor, UUalchisus nuncupatus nomine, ut ueracium didicimus traditione seniorum, patruus gloriosissimi Pippini ducis Francorum, filii Anchisi, extitit" (c. 2).

before the Austrasian conquest! Though Fontenelle, the Carolingian foundation, is shown to have been a pious place during the Merovingian era, the diocese as a whole is not. At Rouen, the missionary bishop Audoenus busied himself

> administering the word of salvation-giving preaching to his citizens, a promoter and likewise a teacher of the catholic faith, he would intoxicate their barbarous and untameable minds with the nectar of evangelical doctrine, and he would teach that docile and subject nation, at one time so savage, to believe, and he would demonstrate with sedulous words of encouragement that the Lord God Christ ought to be worshipped with innumerable declarations.[216]

Audoenus' preaching might as well have taken place in a vaccuum, for all the positive response recorded by our Fontenellian historian.

More significant for the themes of the present study, however, is the *Gesta* author's use of the irophilic prism. The Burgundian author of the earliest biography of Wandregiselus, founder of Fontenelle, knew that his subject had visited Bobbio, a Columbanian foundation, in search of the true monastic life. But according to this monk of Romainmôtier, who knew Wandregiselus personally, the saint had not found what he was looking for at Bobbio; instead, he had found it at St. Romain in the Jura.[217] There is no hint in Wandregiselus' late-seventh-century biography that there was anything particularly special about Columbanus, despite the fact that, like many Burgundians, its author knew Jonas' *vita Columbani*. The foundation of Fontenelle in this earliest biography had been propelled by Wandregiselus' personal search for monastic perfection; no influence of either Columbanus or Audoenus was detectable. External interventions were restricted to God and His messengers.

God does not drive the plot in the *Gesta*. Wandregiselus is no longer led unconsciously to an unsatisfactory stay at Bobbio; instead, he makes a calculated decision to go to Bobbio, because he desires to visit particularly holy places. For the most part, the author of the *Gesta* cuts things out

---

[216] "...uerbum immortalitatis suis ciuibus administrabat, fideique catholicae fautor pariterque praeceptor, barbaricas ac indomabiles eorum mentes nectare euangelicae doctrinae debriabat, atque gnaram bene credere gentem docebat, sedulisque exhortationibus Christum dominum Deum esse colendum monstrabat" (c. 4); MGH SS 2 p. 272.

[217] BHL 8804; see below, p. 222.

of the *vita Wandregiseli*; but while cutting everything about the saint's early life, he bothered to add the Carolingian background, and to expatiate at length on the subject of Bobbio. The reader must know that this holy place had been founded by the *scotus* Columbanus, who had been expelled from Gaul by the evil Merovingian king Theodericus, and that the monastery was still being run by disciples of Columbanus, and that there in Bobbio did Wandregiselus gain his instruction in "the innocent life" (cc. 3-4). So the first series of divine interventions in Wandregiselus' life (miracles, angelic visitations) was replaced by the saint's respect for Columbanus as the major motivating force. By the ninth century, both Audoenus and Wandregiselus had been turned into Columbanians.

*

*   *

There may well be regions in which the "Irish" (or other insular missionaries) did play an important role in Christianization, and not just in changing the fashions of devotion. By the early ninth century, Columbanian missionary disciples were being fabricated wholesale.[218] A *topos*, I have repeatedly asserted, has to be plausible. Alcuin himself was an example of the real influence of insular individuals on continental forms. Furthermore, it would be difficult to argue against recognizing some kernel of truth in the religious historiography produced in Brittany in the late ninth century and after when, without exception, historians ascribed the Christianization of the region to insular (British or Irish) missionaries said to have crossed the Channel in the fifth and sixth centuries.[219] But the present study deals with Neustria/Normandy, where the Irish role was minimal at best.[220] At least, no insular role was recognized by Merovingian-era authors, and that is what matters, in a study of changing historiographic discourse.

---

[218] For instance, the apparently "mythical" Columbanian Serenicus of Spoleto, described by a monk of St. Martin of Séez in the early ninth century [= BHL 7590].

[219] Smith *Province and Empire* pp. 124-146 for the context; Smith, "Oral and Written" *Speculum* 65 (1990) pp. 315-334 for the dates and places of composition of the narratives.

[220] There is not a single sanctuary or cult center to Columbanus in Normandy (L. Gougaud, "Le culte de St. Columban" *Revue Mabillon* XXV [1935] pp. 169-178, esp. p. 172).

The discourse concerning the role of insular missionaries has shifted radically over the past fifteen years, from the iromania of the early part of the century, to something closer to the Merovingian era viewpoint. That change should reinforce the wider trend towards rejecting the pro-Carolingian vision of the decrepit state of the Merovingian church, and of its Merovingian rulers. The myth of the insular saviors, who helped the Carolingian princes revivify Christianity, began in the late eighth century and reached its apogee in the early twentieth; it now seems to be a thing of the past.

3

Entr'acte: To Every Force, Its Counterforce

In none of the Neustrian historiography so far discussed did "supernatural" events play a large role. Demons in particular were completely absent from the world-view of Merovingian- and Carolingian-era historians of religion. From the middle of the ninth century, however, angels and demons began to make ever more important appearances in Neustrian religious historiography. The vision of religious realities, past, present and omnipresent, which reigned among historians of late-ninth-century Francia, was generated in large measure by Viking activities on the continent. The Frankish interest in the archangel Michael, for instance, in the late ninth century can probably not be separated from anxieties over the Vikings who, from the 850s, became not so much an annual as a constant presence in Francia. St. Michael the Archangel, more than any other figure, was the metahistorical symbol and invisible patron of the Frankish empire, against enemies both piratical and demonic.

At the same time, the Vikings themselves could not remain impervious to the Frankish society around them, still less so given that Frankish society, far from being some pure autochthonous creation, was itself the result of dynamic interaction with the raiders. The principal cultic and historiographic trends of mid-to-late-ninth century Neustria were precisely what the Vikings of Rouen adopted, as Frankish culture, when they settled into the Seine valley. Almost every feature of the earliest Norman cultic and historiographic practices is traceable directly to the influence of ninth-century western Frankish precedents, as refracted through the specific traditions of Jumièges, the monastic house which would, from the late ninth century, replace Fontenelle as the premier atelier of the region.

The Vikings who settled in Francia at the end of the ninth century were therefore in a peculiar position. The Francia into which they had to integrate themselves, the only Francia they knew, was one organized around such principles as the eternal cosmic battle between the forces of Good, represented by figures such as the Archangel Michael, and the forces of Evil, represented by themselves. A complex process of negotiation was required in order for the Viking conquerors to situate themselves within that discourse. Their role in creating it had been fundamental: they were the demonic enemies against whom the hierarchical organizations of Pseudo-Dionysius the Areopagite and the angelic powers of St. Michael, both discussed below, had been supposed to protect Francia. Yet as Rollo and his followers assumed the reigns of power in late-ninth-century Francia, in order to assimilate into Frankish society, they had to see themselves instead as the earthly representatives of Dionysius and Michael.

An extraordinary mental transformation was required not only of the Viking conquerors, but also of the Neustrian conquered. One day, they had been praying to be liberated from the Viking peril; the next, they were paying tribute to and being judged by Viking lords. Perhaps they continued to pray for liberation, but no longer in official contexts. In any case, the official context was becoming alien and incomprehensible, as the linguistic reforms of Alcuin took effect in Francia. What a boon, though, were the changes in the structure of communication from the conquerors' point of view! When Hincmar wrote, in the final third of the ninth century, his biography of Remigius of Reims, he could still insist, as had Audoenus' biographer two hundred years earlier, on the importance of reading sections of the history aloud to the populace.[1] But by the tenth century the audience's powers of preventive censure would be drastically curtailed. The Norman conquerors and their advisors were left increasingly free to deal with the problem of transforming the Vikings from demonic enemies to saviors and defenders of hierarchy. The official context soon ceased to celebrate Pious Neustria.

Unimpeded by local comprehension or opposition, historians and cultic officials began with the negative view of pre-Columbanian and pre-Audoenian Neustria which had been developed by Carolingian-era historians, and created a vision of Neustria that was thoroughly unflattering to the conquered, and flattering to the conquerors. This new image was embodied by the new official patron saint of Normandy, the replacement to Audoenus: St. Romanus of Rouen. Romanus was an anti-"pagan" missionary and ally of angels, a great battler of omnipresent, infesting demonic hoards. The interrelated story of how he toppled Audoenus, and how the Vikings became, in part through the figure of Romanus, assimilated to Frankish and Christian values, forms the second part of this study.

---

[1]   Hincmar, *Vita Remigii* ed. B. Krusch MGH SRM III preface pp. 253-254 and 258-259 (= BHL 7153-7163).

A. Hierarchy: the Archangel, the Areopagite, and the Vikings

During the height of the empire of Charles and Louis, a favored historiographic theme had been the support by Carolingian princes for Christiza-
tion movements in enemy Frisia and hostile Saxony. The biographer of
Willihad, writing in the mid ninth century, believed that the empire had
been transferred from the Greeks to the Franks precisely because of such
Frankish support for the spread of Christianity.[2] Frisia, Saxony, and other
concrete regions covered by Frankish imperial expansionism were specific
places inhabited by specific "not-Christians." Both locale and population
could be, in every case, described realistically. Furthermore, the Franks
went to them, not *vice versa*: Carolingian war-leaders knew where to find
enemies of Christianity, and could lead the posse out to cleanse the landscape. They could gather their forces on the field of March, and stream
forward in organized annual campaigns to extend the dominion of God.

The Vikings changed everything. None of the Franks ever penetrated
their mystique: who really knew who "the Vikings" were, where they came
from, or where they were going? At any given moment, who even knew
for certain where they were? Except, all too horrifically, that they were in
Francia. Carolingian Francia meant "Christianity." The Concilium Germanicum, the papal unction, the imperial coronation all were part of the ideology of Francia, embodied in its historiographic monuments: Frankish
princes defend and extend Christianity as ministers of the Lord. What did
it mean that "not-Christian" Vikings were suddenly present in Francia itself? That a Viking band could, at any moment, attack a monastery?

Against the omnipresent and absolutely terrifying peril of the "pagan
Vikings," Francia required new ideological weapons. The force which
threatened to pull the empire apart was powerful and non-localized; a
counterforce of equal weight and equal mobility had to be pressed into
service. Against all the stresses of the mid ninth century, mere historical
discourse was insufficient. Indeed, even sacro-historical discourse was insufficient. With the middle of the ninth century, Frankish historiography
rose yet another notch: it became metahistorical. The message of the narratives produced by the major West Frankish ateliers and historians can be
summed up in a single word: hierarchy. The great irony is that this should

---

[2]   *Vita sancti Willehadi* c.5 MGH SS II p. 381.

be the core cosmic framework which the Vikings themselves would adopt.

The meta-historical figure of St. Michael, the Archangel and dragon-slayer, represented the triumph of Christianity over evil; he was the incar-nate battle spirit of "Qui ut Deus," the double of God, and as such was the saintly equivalent of the Carolingian dynasty itself, with its primary func-tion to defend the church and the faith through military action.[3] St. Michael was, on the metahistorical level, the equivalent of the work of rewriting the past that Carolingian historians such as Alcuin had undertaken:

> In the course of the eighth and ninth centuries, we witness an en-ergetic effort to remake Merovingian hagiography in a new spirit. The saints of Paris, Reims, Soissons had to have new "lives," lives that were ornamented, polished, adapted to the ecclesiastical and literary canon of the epoch, to its social and political philosophy. But this philosophy, with its cosmic scale, with its imperialist ideology, could hardly find its symbol in any of those local saints. On the other hand, it merged well with a religious image,-superhuman, but tied to terrestrial interests,-eternal, immaterial, but incorporated into a dramatic myth, in which there met both the battle and the tri-umph, both the past and the present.[4]

To quote an even more famous commentator, here is Henry Adams on the meaning of St. Michael:

> Standing on the summit of the tower that crowned his church, wings upspread, sword uplifted, the devil crawling beneath, and the cock, symbol of eternal vigilance, perched on his mailed foot, Saint Mi-

---

[3]   Olga Rojdestvensky *Le culte de Saint Michel et le Moyen Age Latin* (Paris, 1922) p. 6 and pp. 29-35; Tabacco "Agiologia e Demonologia" pp. 125-126.

[4]   "Au cours des VIIIe-IXe siècles, on assiste à un effort energique pour refaire l'hagiographie merovingienne dans un esprit nouveau. Les saints parisiens, remois, soissonnais devaient avoir des 'vies' nouvelles, ornées, polies, adaptées au canon ecclésiastique et littéraire de l'époque, à sa "philosophie" religieuse et sociale. Mais cette philosophie, à l'échelle cosmique, à l'idéal imperialiste, n'aurait pu trouver son symbole en aucun des saints locaux. Au contraire, elle s'unit admirablement à une image religieuse,-surhumaine, mais liée aux interêts terrestres,-éternelle, im-materielle, mais incorporée en un mythe dramatique, où la lutte et le triomphe, le passé et le futur se rejoignent" (Rojdestvensky *Le culte de S. Michel* p. 35). For the tension between local and universal cults, see Patrick Geary, "The Ninth-Century Relic Trade. A Response to Popular Piety?" in *Religion and the People* ed. J. Obel-kevich (Chapel Hill, N.C., 1979) pp. 8-19.

chael held a place of his own in heaven and earth....The Archangel stands for Church and State, and both militant. He is the conqueror of Satan, the mightiest of all created spirits, the nearest to God. His place was where the danger was greatest; therefore you find him here.[5]

At some point the Archangel, metahistorical symbol of the Carolingian empire, had found a terrestrial home in Francia, at the present-day Mont-St-Michel, in Lower Normandy. The traditions which have dated the foundation of the mount to the early eighth century do not appear before the twelfth century, and have no bearing on the Carolingian-era cult.[6] The first narrative texts concerning the mount date from the second half of the ninth century, when Michael was explicitly shaped to conform to the needs of late imperial discourse. It is not known for certain who first shaped the Archangel into a meaningful character; however, both the manuscript transmission of his *Apparitio in Monte Tumba* (also known as the *Revelatio ecclesiae sancti Michaelis*)[7] and the values in it point to St. Denis, at the time one of the most important ateliers in Francia, home to Hilduin and Hincmar.[8]

---

[5] Henry Adams *Mont-Saint-Michel and Chartres* (1st edition, 1904; cited in the Penguin edition of 1986) p. 7.

[6] B. Baedorf, *Untersuchungen über die Heiligenleben* pp. 21-23. The cult of Autbertus, who is the traditional founder of the house, was a development of the late eleventh century; his *miracula* BHL 859-860 (ed. Pigeon *Vies des saints du diocèse de Coutances* I.225-228 and 231-233) were composed at Mont-St.-Michel between 1066 and 1085 (Richard, "Les miracula composés en Normandie" *Position des Thèses, Ecole des Chartes*).

[7] BHL 5951, in Thomas Le Roy, *Livre des curieuses recherches du Mont-Sainct-Michel* ed. Eugène de Robillard de Beaurepaire (Mem. Soc. Antiq. Norm. XXIX, 1876) Appendix II pp. 856-863; AASS Sept. VIII pp. 76-78; Pigeon, I. 207-214; Jacques Hourlier, "Les sources écrites de l'histoire montoise antérieure à 966" in *Millénaire monastique du Mont Saint-Michel* 2 vols (Paris, 1966). The oldest complete copy of the *Revelatio* was transcribed by the monk of Mont St.-Michel, Hervardus, into what is now Avranches BM 211 (fols. 156r-210v) between 990 and 1015.

[8] The oldest, though truncated, copy of the *Revelatio* can be found in Paris, BN 2873A (fols. 110v-114r), a tenth-century collection which contains, in addition to the *Revelatio*, the central dionysian materials (correspondance between Louis the Pious and abbot Hilduin, Hilduin's *passio* of Dionysius, the *Clausula de unctione Pipini*). The codex also contains texts on Germanus of Auxerre; writings of Jerome on the paradigmatic universalizing saint, the Virgin Mary; a biography of Mary of Egypt;

The narrative is distinctly lacking in "historiation," (in the sense of concrete historical specificity), a characteristic totally in keeping with the metahistorical nature of the cult of the Archangel. The importance of the Archangel lay not in what he had done at a particular moment on earth, but what he always does at every moment in heaven. "Beatus archangelus," the author tells us, perhaps inspired by a reading of the *Celestial Hierarchy* of pseudo-Dionysius the Areopagite, is the heavenly being who

> ...is the one from among those seven, who always stand in the sight of the Lord, who is also the prior of paradise, who establishes the souls of those to be saved in the region of peace.[9]

The archangel represented the very concept of ordered hierarchy, which was at the core of the Carolingian imperial program. He was the invisible (and invincible) patron bolstering the authority of provincial governors and metropolitan bishops, themselves all earthly manifestations of the celestial hierarchies. The good angel, Michael, stood for subordination to his Lord, for proper recognition of his inferiority in the natural order of things; he was the antithesis of the fallen angel, Lucifer, who had sinned through rebellion, through refusing to accept submission to the *imperium* of God.

Michael's services were required in the late ninth century, as they had not been before, as the administrative structures of the empire threatened to break down. Through their anarchic, mobile military threat, the Vikings challenged the administrative hierarchies of the empire in the 850s and 860s. At the same time, the structure of the ecclesiastical hierarchy was under attack, most famously by Hincmar of Laon, whose battle with his uncle Hincmar of Reims over the limits of metropolitan authority was one of the major spurs to the latter's own historiographic oeuvre.[10] All of archbishop Hincmar's literary output has been described as being organized around the central notion of a hierarchical social structure, an orientation

---

miracles connected with another of the new Carolingian imperial-era universalizing cults, namely the Holy Cross; the *passio Benigni* of Dijon; and the *Revelatio corporis sancti Stephani.*

[9]   "....unus ex septem in conspectu Domini semper adstantium, qui etiam et paradysi prepositus salvandorum animas in pacis regione collocandas" (BHL 5951, c. 1; cited from BN lat. 2873A).

[10]   For the following remarks on Hincmar's political thought, see Jean Devisse *Hincmar, Archévêque de Reims, 845-882* (Travaux d'Histoire Ethico-Politique xxix.1-3; Geneva, 1975-1976).

in part traceable to his own education and apprenticeship at St. Denis. In the constant cosmic battle between good and evil, in which Christians must try to achieve salvation against the devil's attempts to sabotage them, the major weapon provided by God for Christians was, in Hincmar's view, a hierarchical social structure: only if each person remains in his or divine-ly-ordained place, without murmuring, would the stability and peace requisite for the pursuit of salvation be achieved. The *De ordine palatii*, for instance, composed when the archbishop was practically on his deathbed, described the glory of the reign of Charlemagne as a function of the em-peror having organized the officials of the palace and of the realm in a strict hierarchy. In this way, the *ordinatio* of temporal functionaries imitated the larger cosmological order which places God at the acme of the chain of being and requires that each link (the first being the archangels) love, fear and obey its superior in the hierarchy.[11]

The views of Hincmar may not be representative of all late-ninth-century historians and ideologues throughout the Frankish empire, but they are typical of the major figures of Neustria and particularly of the Dionysian tradition; it was precisely this complex of values that would exercise the greatest influence over the first few generations of Viking rulers in Neustria, through the end of the pontificate of Hugh of St. Denis, archbishop of Rouen till 989.

To stand in general for the proper hierarchical order of all things, and for the necessity for constant vigilance and mobility in the defense of Francia against the pagan Vikings, did not exhaust the functions of the polysemous Archangel. His permanent garrison on the Breton border gave primacy to a certain anti-Breton function. According to the *Apparitio*, the Archangel had appeared thrice to bishop Autbertus of Avranches and had commanded the bishop to build for him a habitation. The chosen spot in the Avranchin had been especially prepared by God to be a point of con-tact with the celestial world, an island to which popular access would be allowed twice a day, with the movement of the tides. Without denying the role of Divine Providence, we can still conjecture that, in temporal terms, the figure of Michael had been sent to the Breton march by Charles the

---

[11] Hincmar of Reims, *De ordine palatii* ed. and trans. Maurice Prou (Bibliothèque de l'école des hautes études 58; Paris, 1885); eds. and trans. T. Gross and R. Schieffer (Hanover, 1980).

Bald, who faced throughout the 850s and 860s the fiercest rebellions the Breton princes had ever mounted against the Carolingian Franks.[12]

In the ninth century the mountain of St. Michael represented the aspirations of the Franks to rule the craggy Armorican peninsula which stretched forth beyond the Avranchin, and it continued to stand for Norman ambitions to the same goal. That is what made Michael an ideal transitional or assimilation-facilitating figure for Viking devotions. Charles the Bald had, in the end, to cede the Avranchin to Solomon of Brittany,[13] but the Archangel stood on his island, a reminder that, in the proper order of things, Solomon was still a subordinate of the Frankish emperor, and that the Frankish inhabitants of the ceded territory, who rebelled against Solomon in 874,[14] must also keep their assigned place in the earthly hierarchies.

Adopting the Bretons as their own bosom enemies permitted the Vikings of Rouen to position themselves on the "Forces of Good" side of the dominant ecclesiastical discourse. Dudo of St. Quentin makes Rollo claim the Archangel as a principal patron of the realm from the moment of the conquest.[15] When Rollo and his descendants claimed the Mount, what they claimed, in effect, was that they had stepped into the traditional Frankish relational role vis-à-vis the Bretons. The Franks having abdicated, it would thenceforth be the obsession of the Norman dukes to bring the Bretons to heel. In fact, Norman control of the Mount was not achieved until the eleventh century, after a long and hard-fought battle.[16] But the Vikings of Rouen knew what the Mount symbolized from the beginning. The Norman princes, alone among late Carolingian potentates, kept the institutional hierarchies inherited from the Empire absolutely intact.[17]

---

[12] See the eye-witness account of the translation of the relics of Regnobertus and Zeno out of Bayeux and into Frankish control in 847, an account set against the background of the Breton occupation of the Bessin (BHL 7062, ed. Papebroch, AASS May 3 pp. 620-624).

[13] Smith, *Province and Empire* pp. 86-107.

[14] Smith, *Province and Empire* p. 120.

[15] Dudo, *De moribus* p. 171.

[16] Cassandra Potts, "Normandy or Brittany? A Conflict of Interests at Mont Saint-Michel (966-1035)" *Anglo-Norman Studies* (XII, 1990; Proceedings of the Battle Conference, 1989; ed. M. Chibnall) pp. 135-156.

[17] For institutional continuity between Carolingian Neustria and Viking Normandy, see Felice Lifshitz, "La Normandie Carolingienne" (forthcoming, *Annales de Normandie*).

The Archangel, the earthly guarantor of hierarchy, was conceptually in Norman service from the beginning.

Carolingian forms of all kind survived and flourished in Normandy in the tenth century as they did nowhere else. This meant more than the presence of a count in every *pagus*, and absolute ducal control of the profits of justice; it meant an understanding as well of the ideologies that bolstered the institutions. We may not know for certain whether the figure of the Archangel was first shaped as "the enforcer" at St. Denis or elsewhere, but we do know that the primary theorist of hierarchy, Dionysius the Areopagite, was a mid-century creation of that abbey. Like the figure of the Archangel, he was generated by the context of mid-ninth-century challenges to imperial hierarchies. Opposition to the emperor was a recurrent feature of the Carolingian polity after the death of Charlemagne. Twice Louis the Pious found himself publicly humiliated and forced to declare his penitence before an assembly of magnates. The first time, at Attigny in 822, Louis himself may have favored the use of the ritual, which enabled him to keep his grip on the Empire; the second time, at St. Medard of Soissons in 833, he was, all unwilling, stripped of his arms.[18]

Ideologically and historiographically, it was St. Denis to the rescue. Abbot Hilduin (814-841) put his own nose to the grindstone in the service of his lord. In 834, Louis was solemnly rehabilitated in a ceremony at St. Denis, an inversion of the ritual which had stripped him of his arms. The shattering events of 833 could have spelled the end of the dynasty, had not Hilduin and other ecclesiastical magnates rescued Louis. Hincmar declared that public penances were inappropriate for royal individuals; it will come as no surprise to discover that he appealed to the example of king David of Judah and Israel, who had confessed privately to the prophet Nathan.[19] Louis attributed his success to the patronage of Dionysius, and commissioned Hilduin to write a biography of the saint.[20]

---

[18] Mayke de Jong, "Power and Humility in Carolingian Society: the Public Penance of Louis the Pious" *EME* 1 (1991) pp. 29-52.

[19] Hincmar, *Ad Carolum regem pro ecclesiae libertatum defensione* PL 125 col. 1040-41.

[20] *Epistula Ludovici ad Hilduinum* (= BHL 2172), PL 104 col. 1326-28; *Rescriptum Hilduini* (= BHL 2173), PL 106 coll. 13-22. Hilduin's biography was not the first account of the mission and passion of St. Dionysius; a now-lost fifth-century *passio* and a mid-eighth-century revision of that *passio* (= BHL 2171) had already been

In Hilduin's biography (BHL 2175), and in another ninth-century *passio* of Dionysius also produced as St. Denis (BHL 2178), the saint was identified with Dionysius the Areopagite, pseudonymous author of a number of Neoplatonic tracts. Giovanni Tabacco has shown how both the life-story of the Areopagite, and the doctrines with which his name was associated, had clear-cut ideological functions in the attempt to maintain the Carolingian polity.[21] First of all, the saint's own peripatations summed up the genealogy of "Western Civilization," at the culmination of which the Carolingian rulers were eager to place themselves. Carolingian-era power structures at Paris hearkened back to an ancient and venerable development which had begun in Athens, where the Areopagite was said to have been born, had been fertilized through Jerusalem, where the Apostle Paul himself was said to have converted Dionysius to Christianity, and had moved on through Rome, whence pope Clement had sent Dionysius on to Paris. Once in Paris, Dionysius had worked tirelessly to unite Gauls and Germans in a single polity, under the umbrella of the cultural tradition which he himself represented, by converting them to Roman Christianity. How could anyone argue with those whom such a figure as Dionysius had chosen to place under his patronage?

The content of the Areopagite's numerous writings were no less ideologically useful for the Carolingian princes. Hilduin made these crucial writings available by producing the first known Latin translation of the entire corpus.[22] The name of the game for Pseudo-Dionysius, throughout his extremely repetitive corpus of writings, was HIERARCHY, described as a fundamental necessity in heaven and on earth, built into the very fabric

---

written. The earlier *passiones* were very brief, whereas Hilduin's (= BHL 2174-2175; PL 106 coll. 22-50) was a large-scale history (Heinzelmann-Poulin *Les vies anciennes* pp. 134-137).

[21] Tabacco, "Agiografia e demonologia come strumenti ideologici" pp. 121-153. This use does not preclude the mid-ninth-century dionysian writings from having also been aimed at establishing the apostolicity of the abbey, and therefore both its independence from the bishop of Paris and its hoped-for vice-papal status in Francia, the "pragmatic" aim which has long been emphasized (Crosby *The Abbey of St. Denis, 475-1122,* vol. I pp. 14-15 and vol. II pp. 80 and 165-167).

[22] For Hilduin's translation, see *Dionysiaca. Le Texte Latin des Oevres du Pseudo-Aréopagite (Recueil Donnant l'Ensemble des Traductions latines des ouvrages attribués au Denys l'Aréopagite* [Bruges, 1937]). Hilduin's translation was made in approximately 832 using Paris BN ms. gr. 437; the translation itself is Paris BN lat. 15.645.

of the cosmos.[23] Dionysius defined the guiding principles of the cosmos as follows: *vita* (life); *ipsum similitudo* (resemblance, similarity); *coadunatio* (unity); *ipsum coordinatio* (order). The four principles, working together, create hierarchy, as each creature, from angels through rational humans down to the lowest beasts, stays in its place along with other similar creatures, with the higher creatures caring for the lower, and the lower respecting the higher.[24] The entire ordered hierarchy of the cosmos, angelic and earthly, is "good," and comprehends every created thing; "evil" is not an extant substance, but disorder, insubordination, discord: to love that which has not been created by divine power, to turn away from being, is to turn to "evil." The ecclesiastical hierarchy and the imperial office were part of the necessary created order of things. The practical implications of Dionysian cosmology were not left to chance; Hincmar, for instance, explicitly justified the subordination of bishops to metropolitans by appealing to Dionysian theology.[25] There could be no greater sin, no more disruptive act, than to rebel against one's Lord, for the nature of things required submission.

In the ninth century, the devil suddenly became a common theme in artistic representations, depicted either in humanoid form, or as a tiny, misshapen being: an "eidolon."[26] Alcuin in particular made explicit the bi-partite nature of the cosmos: on the one hand, there was the sphere of Jesus, comprehending the Just; on the other, there was the sphere of Lucifer, comprehending "pagans," Jews and "heretics."[27] But it was only with Hilduin's translation of Pseudo-Dionysius that the Latin-reading audience gained access to a complete vision of the *taxis hiera*, the holy order, and

[23] The four main works attributed to Dionysius were: *On the Celestial Hierarchy*; *On the Ecclesiastical Hierarchy*; *On the Divine Names*; and *Mystical Theology*. Chapter IV of *On the Divine Names* gives a fairly complete picture of the main points of Dionysian thought (*Dionysiaca* pp. 145-320). The discussion below is based primarily on DN IV.20 (*Dionysiaca* pp. 260-299).

[24] *Divine Names* V.21, *Dionysiaca* p. 340.

[25] Hincmar, *Opusculum LV capitulorum adversus Hincmarum Laudunensem* cap. 12 (PL 126 col. 325 ff); for Hincmar's use of Dionysian theology in general, J. Devisse *Hincmar* II.pp 803, 1007 and III. pp. 1371, 1374ff, 1492.

[26] B. Brenk *Tradition und Neuerung in der christlichen Kunst des ersten Jahrtausends* (Vienna, 1966) pp. 102 and 196-197; Jeffrey Burton Russell *Lucifer. The Devil in the Middle Ages* (Ithaca, 1984) pp. 129-133.

[27] Russell, *Lucifer* pp. 99-100.

the role of evil within it. The aim of the devil is to suck creatures into the void of non-being, the void of the unreal, and away from ideal order of creation; any creature who disrupts the *taxis hiera* by turning away from it, creates the evil of discord.[28] Dionysius did not expatiate at any greater length than this on the role of demonic powers, but he did not need to; the point was simply that, with the appearance of Hilduin's Latin translation, a comprehensive cosmology which both accounted for and required angelic and diabolical forces became available.[29]

Dionysius is the sole extra-Norman saint (if Michael be defined as "Norman" since the Avranchin has long been considered part of Normandy) to whom Rollo is shown making baptismal gifts by Dudo of St. Quentin. From the moment of the Viking settlement, the Archangel and the Areopagite were a part of the new rulers' consciousness. The ideology of hierarchy was a necessary underpinning for maintenance of the strong Carolingian-style institutions of Viking Normandy. Without Dionysian cosmology it would have been that much more difficult to impose a strong "public" authority, both to appoint and to control a count in every *pagus*, as the Viking rulers did. That Dionysian cosmology was known in Viking Normandy is not a matter of mere speculation either; it was unquestionably known to the earliest biographer of Romanus, whose work will form the centerpiece of the second half of this study.

Fulbertus of Jumièges would be commissioned by archbishop Hugo of Rouen, newly arrived in Normandy from the abbey of St. Denis, to write a biography of Romanus of Rouen. Most of the narrative is taken up with describing Romanus' archangel-style battles against demons. However, on his death-bed the saint makes a speech to his disciples, enjoining peace, harmony and unity upon them. Before leaving his disciples Jesus himself had similarly enjoined concord upon them (John 14:27), and saintly death-bed scenes tended, more than any other part of a saint's biography, to become stylized along biblical prototypes.[30] However, Fulbertus

---

[28] *Dionysiaca*, DN IV. 18-34.

[29] The literary theme of the "pact with the devil," for instance, was suddenly popularized in the ninth century by those other Carolingian legitimist historians, Hincmar and Paul the Deacon (Russell, *Lucifer* pp. 80-81).

[30] Zoepf *Das Heiligenleben* p. 59. Examples comparable to Romanus' death-bed scene can be found in Bede's two biographies of Cuthbertus (Bede *Vita Cuthberti* ed. and trans. B. Colgrave *Two Lives of Cuthbert* (Cambridge, 1940; repr. NY 1969)

takes the opportunity to expand upon the simple evangelical theme, and
to display his own knowledge of philosophy. In Romanus' death-bed speech,
Fulbertus translates some of the main points of Dionysian cosmology into
terms comprehensible to the non-specialist, avoiding technical vocabulary.
He has Romanus say:

> Consider the winged creatures of the sky, how those which are of
> one type fly together in a group and do not desert one another, just
> like the very brute animals which are pastured together. If we saga-
> ciously consider all this, we see how irrational nature by living in
> concord indicates what a great evil rational nature commits through
> discord, when namely it intentionally loses what irrational nature
> naturally preserves. Nature has made you rational creatures; see that
> you not adulterate that dotal privilege of nature through the evil of
> discord....Furthermore do I admonish you to keep this, that you take
> care to love that which has been made and to inveigh against that
> which has not been made....[31]

The evil of discord, as we will see, was rife in mid-tenth-century Upper
Normandy, when Fulbertus wrote at Hugh's behest. The evil of discord
was equally rife in mid-ninth-century Francia, when Hilduin wrote at
Louis' behest. In the Norman case, the center would hold; hierarchy and
order would triumph. In the Frankish case, the much larger imperial unity
disintegrated, and all the Archangels and all the Areopagites could not put
it back together again.

    None of the elaborate justificatory devices of the Carolingian rulers
did them a shred of good after the age of Hilduin and Hincmar, and the
dynasty began to go under before the Robertians. What the Franks
wanted in a king at that time is indicated by a story told by the monk of
St. Gall in his *De Carolo magno*, written about 884.[32] King Pippin had just
returned from Italy where he had fought against the Lombards as part of
his pact with the Roman see. He discovered that some of the leaders of his
army were speaking contemptuously of him in private. So into their midst

---

ch. xxxix pp. 282-285 and Bede *Vita Cuthberti* ed. Werner Jaager *Bedas metrische vita
sancti Cuthberti* (Palaestra 198. Untersuchungen und Texte aus der Deutschen und
Englishen Philologie; Leipzig, 1935) ch. xxxiv.

[31] Fulbertus, *Vita Romani*, see transcription below fols. 123v-124r.

[32] MGH SS 2 ed. Pertz, II.15; trans. L. Thorpe *Two Lives of Charlemagne* (Penguin; Harmondsworth, 1969) pp. 159-161.

he released two savage animals, a bull and a lion, who were soon locked in combat. Pippin urged the on-lookers to break up the struggle, but all were terrified. So Pippin himself stepped forward and, with a single blow of his sword, severed the heads of both beasts. The leaders of the army then agreed that Pippin **was** their rightful lord and master. Carolingian military success was the salient point. In the second half of the ninth century, it was the Vikings who were winning the battles.

B. Historiographical Traditions in the Diocese of Rouen at the Time of the Settlement of the Vikings

Throughout the ninth century, the Christian Empire of the Franks was sporadically beseiged by "pagan" sea-borne pirates. At the end of the century, a group of those very same pirates conquered and settled in Neustria, in the diocese of Rouen. There can be little doubt but that the subjection of the population of the diocese to "not-Christian" lords was traumatic: this was Pious Neustria, whose Merovingian-era piety, however tarnished by Carolingian-era historians, would have been polished to gleaming brightness by an application Carolingian sacrohistoriation. Late-ninth- and tenth-century Norman literature must be understood in the psychological context of what can only have been a traumatic challenge to the world-view and self-conception of the inhabitants of the region. The Christians of Upper Normandy were ruled by "not-Christians." The transformation was something that would have to be worked out through a new historiographical discourse.

At the height of Viking activity in the late ninth century there was **greater** literary output, "crisis-led" output in Stafford's phrase, than had been seen in earlier periods.[33] The ecclesiastical province of Reims seems to have been the very hardest hit area in all of the Frankish Empire during the 850s: the dioceses of Thérouanne, Amiens and Beauvais all experienced Viking pirates on numerous occasions during the 850s, and witnessed the few instances of confirmed physical destructions at St. Bavo of

---

[33] Stafford, *Unification and Conquest* (see above p. 14).

Gent, St. Valery, and Noyon.[34] A mentality of terror concerning the Vikings dominated the liturgical sources of the province during the latter part of the ninth century.[35] Yet, or rather, therefore, the province of Reims, and particularly the archiepiscopal seat itself, was a major literary and historiographic center throughout the decades in question. The Orléanais, the only region whose narrative production has been scrupulously dated on the basis of codicological and contextual factors, invariably reacted to its three Viking raids (c. 854, 865 and 879) with narrative output.[36]

I would argue that the literature alluded to in the previous paragraph was generated by the need to come to grips with the meaning of events. The need to find a discursive strategy can have been nowhere more burning than in Normandy: in the province of Reims the danger passed; in the province of Rouen, it took over. In Rouen at the end of the ninth century, the demonic entities from whom the archangel Michael was supposed to protect Francia took over the apparatus of government.

a. The Memory of Bishops at Rouen

The memory of bishops seems to have been, with very few exceptions, neither cherished nor cultivated at Rouen in any written or official form. The relative penury of the diocese in written memorials concerning its prelates was not a result of losses incurred during the Viking conquest;[37] if anything, the conquest had the opposite effect: the moment of crisis precipitated historiographical production and cultic orchestration at Rouen. We have already examined the results of the Carolingian-Austrasian conquest of Neustria, which likewise stimulated historiographic interest in the occupants of the see of Rouen; in the Norman segment of the present study, we will see how the Viking conquest of the 880s, the chaos unleashed by the assassination of William Longsword in 942, and

[34] Dom Jacques Hourlier "Reims et les Normands" *Memoires de la Société d'Agriculture, Commerce, Sciences et Arts du Département de la Manche* 99 (1984) pp. 87-96.

[35] Hourlier, "Reims et les normands" p. 98.

[36] Head, *Hagiography and the Cult of Saints* pp. 50-53.

[37] Sober accounts of the period of the raids and the conquest can be found in E. Searle, *Predatory Kinship and the Creation of Norman Power* pp. 15-58 and Carroll Gilmore, "War on the Rivers: Viking Numbers and Mobility on the Seine and Loire, 841-886" *Viator* 19 (1988) pp. 80-109.

the pitched battles between the cathedral church and the abbey of St. Ouen in the eleventh century, generated both historiographical narrative and cultic orchestration.

In the normal course of daily affairs, outside of moments of crisis, the memory of the bishops of Rouen was left by the cathedral clergy to other keepers and creators of traditions, some of those being oral traditions. The monks of Fontenelle had, in the late ninth century, compiled the first known episcopal catalogue of the see.[38] Only in the middle of the tenth century, in connection with the crisis following William's assassination and the elaboration of the cult of Romanus, did an archbishop of Rouen seek and receive a copy of the list of occupants of his own see: a version of the Fontenelle list had to be sent to Rouen by Gerard of Brogne, all the way from Flanders.[39] Even then, the list was never elaborated or updated by the secular church of Rouen, but by monks of St. Ouen of Rouen who, at the end of the eleventh century, would use the skeleton of the list to compose a full-fledged narrative history of the archiepiscopal see.[40]

---

[38] At the end of the ninth century, refugee monks of Fontenelle compiled catalogues of the bishops of Rouen and of Sens as a way to situate historically the lifetimes of two saints, Ansbertus and Uulframnus, both former monks of the house who had risen to the episcopal dignity. The lists are now preserved in an eleventh-century copy in the *Maius Chronicon Fontenellensium*, Le Havre BM 332 (A.34) fol. 61v-62r. Romanus is designated as a saint on this copy of the list, but that cannot be used as unequivocal evidence for his having been considered a saint by fontenellian historians in the late ninth century. Romanus does not appear on the list on fol. 110r of Angers BM 275 (266), a ninth-century manuscript from St. Aubin of Angers containing, with the exception of this episcopal list, only Patristic treatises (Cat. Gen. XXXI p. 275; Jean Vezin *Les scriptoria d'Angers au XIe s.* [Bibliothèque de l'école des hautes études, IXe section, Sciences historiques et philologiques 322; Paris, 1974] pp. 88, 152 and 217). The fact that Romanus' name does not appear on this copy of the list does not mean he was an invention of later Fontenellian historians; the scribe of the Angers manuscript was not particularly interested in the people on his list, not one of whom is called "sanctus" and many of whose names are garbled (for instance Innocentius is Dicentius). This scribe could easily have skipped a name during copying, which could be the explanation for the omission of the name Silvester as well.

[39] See below pp. 162-163.

[40] F. Lifshitz, "The *Acta Archiepiscoporum Rothomagensium*: A Monastery or Cathedral Product?" AB 108 (1990) pp. 337-347. This chronology follows the pattern found by Picard in Acqui, Altinum-Torcello and Aquileia-Grado where late-ninth-century lists were turned into developed chronicles in the eleventh and twelfth

Fulbertus undertook at Rouen to write a biography of bishop Romanus without the benefit of an episcopal catalogue. That biography itself
will be examined in detail in the next chapter; now, however, I wish to
focus on the broader issues of memory and memorialization in early Viking Normandy. Romanus was not the only saint whose relics were at Rouen
during the period of the Viking conquest and settlement, yet it appears
that it was to Romanus that the populace attributed the facts that the town
had been spared the horrors often associated with a conquest, and that
peace and prosperity had followed soon after the conquest. The stories
that were told about Romanus to Fulbertus, his biographer, though shaped
by Fulbertus to serve his own particular ends, indicate that Romanus was,
like Audoenus, primarily conceived as a protective patron of the town of
Rouen. However, specific chronology does not keep well in oral tradition,
and Fulbertus had to take a wild guess when Romanus had lived. Fulbertus, lacking a structure for episcopal memorialization, placed the saint's
birth and career in the reign of Clothar I (†561), said to have succeeded
Clovis, husband of Clothild and first Christian king of the Franks. However, all other narratives (beginning with the earliest reference to Romanus
in Alcuin's biography of Audoenus) and episcopal catalogues (beginning
with the Fontenelle list) treat Romanus as the immediate predecessor of
Audoenus.[41]

There are other indications of a lack of interest in episcopal memorialization on the part of the see of Rouen. Sometime between 844 and 847,
the relics of three bishops of Rouen were transferred to St. Medard of Soissons. An account of that translation was composed a few decades after the

---

centuries (Jean-Charles Picard, *Le souvenir des évêques. Sépultures, listes épiscopales et
culte des évêques en Italie du Nord des origines au Xe siècle* [Bibliothèque des écoles
françaises d'Athènes et de Rome, 268; Rome, 1988] pp. 397-426). For a survey of
rouennais episcopal catalogues, E.P. Sauvage "Elenchi episcoporum Rotomagensium
quos ex codicibus manu scriptis et libris editis" AB 8 (1889) pp. 406-427. The *Archiepiscoporum Rotomagensium Chronicon* on folios 2r-7r of Paris BN lat. 5195, a fifteenth-century manuscript, is not a copy of the eleventh-century chronicle, but is
an original work which might be of interest to those who work in the later period.

[41] His having placed Romanus' lifetime in the sixth century is one point that
militates against Fulbertus' having written anytime after the middle of the tenth
century and particularly after the early eleventh century, for by then there would
have been numerous sources available at Rouen to help place Romanus chronologically.

event by Odilo of St. Medard (BHL 3540).[42] King Charles the Bald, eager to satisfy the relic-collecting fervor of the monks of one of his favorite residences, declared that the relics of Gildardus, believed to have been the twin brother of Medardus, should be taken from Rouen, even against the will of the citizens of the town, and brought to Soissons. The people of Rouen fought bravely in order to keep Gildardus with them, but when they saw they could not resist Charles, they made a deal with the monks of St. Medard:

> "...that in the place of the head of the venerable Gildardus, it be permitted that they carry off with them the head of most holy Romanus, archbishop of the same city, and the entire most holy body of saint Remigius, who among us is called similarly lord Remigius, prelate of that very same town.[43]

Romanus, and particularly Remigius, were clearly considered of secondary importance next to Gildardus.

At least until the middle of the ninth century, St. Gildardus was indeed a popular saint at Rouen, popular enough that the church of Mary in which he was buried had become known as St. Godard. In a tenth-century updated Flemish copy of the fontenellian episcopal catalogue for the see of Rouen, only three individuals are "sainted": Audoenus and Ansbertus, the most important saints of Merovingian Neustria whose cults and biographies we have already examined, and Gildardus.[44] Neither the living Gildardus nor his relics had ever had any connection with Fontenelle or with St. Bertin (the source of the Flemish version); we can infer, therefore, that Gildardus was in fact an important figure in Neustria, whose status was recognized even by those who stood to gain nothing from encouraging or acknowledging his veneration.

---

[42] F. Lifshitz, "The 'Exodus of Holy Bodies' Reconsidered: The Date of the Translation of Gildardus of Rouen to Soissons" AB 110 (1992) pp. 329-340.

[43] "...ut pro capite uenerabilis Gildardi, caput sanctissimi Romani eiusdem ciuitatis archiepiscopi, ac totum sancti Remigii sacratissimum corpus qui apud nos fertur domnus Remigius similiter ipsius urbis presul secum deportare liceret" (Paris, BN lat. 13.345 fol. 149v = BHL 3450; ed. A. Poncelet, "Vita Sancti Gildardi episcopi Rothomagensis et eiusdem translatio Suessiones anno 838-840 facta" AB 8 [1889] p. 403).

[44] St. Omer BM 764 fol. 52r, of the tenth century, from St. Bertin. Gildardus is also commemorated in a tenth-century Missal of St. Bertin, St. Omer BM 252.

Yet, even the popular veneration of a sainted bishop of Rouen did not result in written memorials on his behalf on the part of the archiepiscopal see. The entire time that Gildardus had rested in the church of the Virgin (later St. Godard) in the Beauvoisine suburb of Rouen, from the early sixth century through the middle of the ninth century, no bishop of the see ever seems to have cultivated the saint's memory in written form. Gildardus' head remained at Rouen even after the 843/847 translation, but still no historiography was produced concerning his pontificate. The first time a biography of bishop Gildardus of Rouen would become available locally would be at the very end of the eleventh century, when the saint's body was brought back from Soissons by the abbot of St. Ouen of Rouen;[45] at that time the new owners of Gildardus' body would receive from St. Medard a copy of a *vita Gildardi* which had been composed by Odilo approximately two centuries earlier (BHL 3539).[46]

Odilo's biography of Gildardus was, to say the least, flimsy, and was evidently the result of the complete ignorance which had reigned even in the ninth century concerning the details of Gildardus' life. When the flimsy text was brought to Rouen, the monks of St. Ouen added to it, verbatim, an extract from a tenth-century *vita* of Laudus of Coutances, which referred to Gildardus as having consecrated Laudus.[47] Odilo had explicitly chastized his predecessors for having so carelessly neglected to write

---

[45]   See below pp. 203-204.

[46]   Lifshitz, "The 'Exodus of Holy Bodies' Reconsidered"; both the *vita* (BHL 3539) and the *translatio* (BHL 3540) can be found in Paris BN lat. 13.345 fols. 142r-150r, part of some tenth-century materials from St. Medard of Soissons (fols. 117-184) now in this artificial collection from St. Germain-des-Prés. The eleventh-century St. Ouen copies of the *vita* and *translatio* can be found in Paris BN 5565 fols. 93v-105v. See Lifshitz, "The 'Acta Archiepiscoporum'" pp. 345-347, and "The 'Exodus of Holy Bodies'" p. 334 for the ascription of the manuscripts to St. Ouen and St. Medard respectively.

[47]   For the St. Ouen interpolation to the *vita Laudi* (BHL 4728), see Paris BN lat. 5565 fols. 99v-100v; L. Delisle ed. BHL 3539 p. 46 where it is published from the later copy in Paris BN lat. 5296; and CCHP I pp. 496-498, where the relevant portion of the original *vita Laudi* is published from Paris BN lat. 5283. The monks of St. Ouen also interpolated a *carmen* to Gildard and Medard, "corpore fratres," asserted to have been composed by Audoenus in the seventh century (see Paris BN lat. 5565 fols. 101v-102v (= BHL 5869) and ed. Surius III (1572) pp. 565-566) as well as two other *carmina* on the two saints (see Paris BN lat. 5565 fols. 105v-106r and L. Delisle's edition from Paris BN lat. 5296 fols. 49v-50r).

anything down about Gildardus; for lack of any specific information about Gildardus, Odilo had simply adapted pseudo-Fortunatus' biography of Medardus (BHL 5865) for Gildardus, assuming that they had led twinned lives.[48] Therefore, the secular church of Rouen at the end of the eleventh century accepted a recycled version of the biography of Medardus, completed by an excerpt from the *vita Laudi* (an even later text), as the definitive description of Gildardus.[49]

Odilo, in his Carolingian-era *vita Gildardi*, assumed that sixth-century Rouen could be paralleled with sixth-century Noyon-Tournai, where Medardus had presided: in other words, that it was missionary diocese, full of "pagans."[50] The notion could scarcely have seemed strange at Rouen by the late eleventh century (when the text became available there), since

[48] Odilo: "Uita beati et uenerabilis patroni nostri sancte sedis Rothomagensis ecclesie archiepiscopi Gildardi antiquorum incuria hactenus latuit postposita; quam, annuente Dei misericordia, exordiar posterorum pro posse tradere notitie. Cuius uite virtutes licet nequeam fideli specialiter sicut uellem stilo declarare, tamen dubium non est quod ceteris Dei electis cum ei generales extiterit, cum quibus etiam sortitus est premia regni celestis" ed. Poncelet, "Vita sancti Gildardi" pp. 394-395; Odilo goes on to use the Medardus materials, having little other choice.

[49] The St. Ouen interpolated version of the *vita Gildardi* was used for liturgical readings for Gildardus' festival by the cathedral church of Rouen (Rouen BM 1405 (Y.27) pp. 42-58, copied from Paris BN lat. 5565 in the eleventh century), for readings at table by the monastery of Fécamp in the twelfth century (Paris BN lat. 5296 fols. 47v-50r) and, in an abbreviated version, for liturgical readings at Fécamp in the twelfth century (Rouen BM 1388 [U.32] fols. 45v-46r). For later copies, see Poncelet "Vita sancti Gildardi" p. 390.

[50] Odilo first used BHL 5865 to describe how the saintly twins' Roman-Christian mother converted her Frankish-pagan husband and gave birth to Medardus who, along with bishop Remigius of Reims, then converted king Clovis and the rest of the Franks to Christianity (BHL 3539 ed. Poncelet cc. 1-5 pp. 394-398 and ed. Delisle pp. 44-45). For the theme of female missionaries working through familial relationships as it appeared in many late ninth- and tenth-century narratives, see Lifshitz "Des femmes missionnaires." Odilo then described how Gildardus became bishop of Rouen, where he "colloquebatur cum paganis quibus illa semper affluxit ciuitas, ita quoque ut satis superque execraretur eorum superstitiones, et quam plures illorum ad nostre sacramentum fidei tam familiaritate et amicitia quam caritate maxima prouocaret" (BHL 3539 ed. L. Delisle in A. Cheruel *Normanniae Nova Chronica* [Caen, 1850]; *Mémoires de la Société des Antiquaires de Normandie* VIII [1851] IV p. 45 and ed. Poncelet c. 7 p. 399-400). Otherwise he simply listed Gildardus' virtues, then returned to following pseudo-Fortunatus' *vita Medardi* for his account of Gildardus' death.

Romanus' biography by Fulbertus also (as we will see) depicted the diocese of Rouen as "paganized" in the sixth century. Odilo's biography of
Gildardus was yet another link in the Carolingian chains which have
weighed down the memory of the Merovingian era. The see and town of
Rouen were, as a general rule, outside periods of crisis, so indifferent to
the memory of their own rulers and leaders, that they ended up at the
mercy of fortuitous coincidences such as the fact that Gildardus shared a
feast day with Medardus; this simple fact set in motion a long chain of
events, at the end of which a stranger's vision of sixth-century Noyon-
Tournai became part of the official version of sixth-century *rouennais*
history.

Even Gildardus, whom the monks of Soissons desired, whom the historians of Fontenelle sainted, whom the populace of Rouen feted, and
whose head was ransomed at the cost of most of Romanus and all of Remigius, even he did not have a locally-written biography. Other Gallo-
Roman and Frankish occupants of the see who might have been likely
candidates for biographies or cults, figures such as Victricius, Praetextatus
and Remigius, had not been memorialized in writing either.[51] Another
regional study of episcopal historiography also consistently came up
against this same negative finding, namely how little interest there seems
to have been, in that case among the cities of northern Italy, in memoriali-
zing the bishops of the sees in question. The author of the study, Jean-
Charles Picard, found himself having to hypothesize about why there was
not a strong memory of bishops in the area, when it might have seemed
"natural" that there should have been. He found the answer, for northern
Italy, in the presence of extremely strong "pre-Christian"/civic memorials
of identity which rendered the memorialization of local episcopal heroes
superfluous, and perhaps even subversive.[52] But "not-Christian" civic traditions cannot explain historiographic indifference to the memory of the
bishops of Rouen, who were central both to the civic history and to the
"religious" history of the town. Why, then, at Rouen, did episcopal cults
and episcopal historiography find such limited enthusiasm when, in contrast, Odilo of St. Medard considered it crucial to provide Gildardus with
a written biography once the saint's relics arrived in Soissons? The answer,

---

[51]   F. Lifshitz, "Eight Men In."
[52]   Picard, *Le souvenir des évêques* pp. 567-576 and p. 713.

it has seemed to me throughout this study, lies in the absence of crises, crises which would have stimulated historiographic production.[53]

The last quarter of the ninth century was dominated in and around Rouen by the issue of the conquest by and the religious preferences of Rollo and his followers.[54] Five archbishops came and went through those years until, from 892 onwards, archbishop Wito felt secure enough to stick it out at Rouen for decades on end. He may have complained about his flock's propensity for multiple baptisms and other "irregularities," but he was not so intolerant as to find the situation unbearable.[55] If the ninth-century bishops, other than Wito, were somewhat squeamish, the relics of a former bishop, Romanus, stayed put through it all, through the difficult years of Rollo's reign and Wito's pontificate too, about which we know so little. The headless body of Romanus, which we last saw resting in the suburban church of St.Mary-St. Godard, was moved into the *intra muros* zone during the second half of the ninth century, to a chapel placed in one of the towers of the antique wall.[56] To Romanus' protective power did the inhabitants of Rouen attribute the smoothness of the transition to

[53]   Nancy Gauthier is currently planning a synthetic study similar to Picard's for all the bishops of Normandy. Her preliminary hypothesis is that the eighth, ninth and tenth centuries were devastatingly destructive for the region, and that everything concerning the bishops of the archdiocese of Rouen was lost at that time; the eleventh century, in contrast, was a dynamic period during which traditions were constructed from scratch (Nancy Gauthier, "Quelques hypothèses sur la redaction des vies des saints évêques de Normandie" *Memoriam Sanctorum Venerantes* [Miscellanea in onore di Mons. Victor Saxer; *Studi di Antichità Cristiana* XLVIII, Vatican City, 1992], pp. 449-468, esp. pp. 465-468).

[54]   For detailed discussion of the arrival of Rollo at Rouen, including the date, see Lifshitz, "La Normandie Carolingienne." For alternative, earlier scenarios, see Olivier Guillot, "La conversion des Normands peu après 911. Des reflets contemporains à l'historiographie ultérieur (Xe-XIe s.)" *Cahiers de Civilisation Médiévale* 24 (1981) pp. 101-116 and 181-219 and Walter Vogel *Die Normannen und das frankische Reich bis zur Gründung der Normandie (799-911)* (Heidelberger Abhandlungen zur mittleren und neueren Geschichte 14; Aalen, 1973) pp. 358-359.

[55]   Sources related to Wito and his work with the newcomers have been admirably collected by Guillot, "La conversion des Normands"; for an alternative interpretation of their significance, see Lifshitz, "La Normandie Carolingienne."

[56]   I am extremely grateful to Jacques Le Maho for sharing with me, in private correspondance, these unpublished details of his excavations at Rouen. The tower chapel was located at the entrace to the town corresponding to the present rue S. Romain.

Viking rule, and the continued relative absence of "crisis."

Soon the comital-episcopal pair of the immigrant Viking Rollo and the overtaxed but committed Wito would give way before that of William Longsword and Hugh of St. Denis. The Rouen of William and Hugh was not more calm and secure than the town had been in the late ninth and early tenth centuries, but less so. Rouen and its archbishops would be thrown, in the middle of the tenth century, out of the frying pan and into the fire. It was to be only in the years of the very darkest crisis of the see's existence that the memory of bishops would become a priority at Rouen. However, before turning to the tenth-century crisis of Norman power and the beginnings of episcopal historiography, especially in connection with Romanus, we must consider the related question of local abbatial and monastic historiography.

b. The Memory of Bishops and Abbots at Jumièges: The First Monuments of Norman Historiography

We cannot leave the subject of episcopal historiography during the period of Rollo's settlement without considering the related issue of the memory of abbots at Jumièges, a monastery located in the immediate vicinity of Rouen.[57] Dudo of St. Quentin describes the arrival of Rollo and his followers at Rouen as including a stop at Jumièges; there, the Viking army made its first camp near the chapel of St. Vaast, across the Seine from Jumièges.[58] Jumièges seems to have been, in the Merovingian and Carolingian periods, a minor monastic community, particularly when compared with the mighty house of Fontenelle. However, Jumièges would become the most important monastic community and historiographic atelier

---

[57] The conclusions I am able to draw in the following pages are based on the exemplary study of the manuscripts of the Jumièges abbatial lists by Jean Laporte, "Les listes abbatiales de Jumièges" *Jumièges. Congrès scientifique du XIIIe centenaire* (Rouen, June 1954; Rouen, 1955) pp. 435-466. The earliest list can be found on fol. 36r of Rouen BM 1409 (Y.189), an artificial collection of texts from Jumièges. There it forms a single unit with an eleventh-century copy of the *vita Aichardi* (BHL 181) on fols. 2r-36r. See Laporte for the other witnesses. The author of the *Vita Austrebertae* (see above pp. 66-69) may well have been the author of the first brief abbatial list of Jumièges compiled in around 733.

[58] Dudo *De moribus* pp. 151-153.

of tenth-century Normandy. Everything written in Normandy before the latter part of the tenth century was composed at Jumièges, including Fulbertus' biography of Romanus who was effectively, in his earliest literary manifestation, the composite product of the library resources available to a gemmetic author in the middle of the tenth century. We must begin, therefore, by looking more closely at the house of Jumièges.

The house of Jumièges had been founded by St. Filibertus, during the pontificate of Audoenus, just around a bend in the Seine from the diocesan capital. The house was not at the time a major foundation, and it may well be that Filibertus simply moved his followers into a pre-existant Roman fort, one of the many *castra* that remained from the Saxon shore system.[59] As we have seen, Filibertus supported the Austrasian party then attempting to take over Neustria, a position which pitted him against the Neustrian patriot Audoenus; Filibertus ended up imprisoned and then exiled by Audoenus. During Audoenus' lifetime the Neustrian party had held its own, but after his death the Austrasian Pippinids took the victory at Tertry (687). The house of Fontenelle was quickly seized by Pippinids, and turned to the service of the conquerors. But the house of Jumièges and its leader Filibertus were now vindicated. Filibertus could have returned to Neustria, but chose not to: Jumièges was of minor concern to him, compared with his much greater later foundation at Noirmoutier. The fact that Filibertus did not return to Jumièges indicates that it was a less than majestic community to begin with; the result of his own prolongation of his exile at Noirmoutier was that Jumièges was deprived of possession of his relics, something which could have made the monastery a more important place.

Instead of returning to Neustria, Filibertus sent an Aquitanian, Aichardus, to rule at Jumièges in his place (688-697). When Aichardus, Filibertus' appointee, died, Pippin gave the administration of Jumièges to Coschinus, abbot of St. Riquier.[60] Under Coschinus the atelier of Jumièges produced its first narrative, a mildly anti-Audoenus biography of Filibertus. That Jumièges was a bit of a cultural backwater is indicated by the

[59] Edward James, "Archeology and the Merovingian Monastery" *Columbanus and Merovingian Monasticism* (BAR Int. 113 1981) pp. 37-39.

[60] Paul Logié, "Jumièges and St.-Riquier" *Jumièges* I pp. 199-207, at p. 204; Jean Laporte, "Etude chronologique sur les listes abbatiales de St.-Riquier" *Revue Mabillon* XLIX (1959) p. 107.

fact that this monk's efforts were immediately judged to be unsatisfactory, and Coschinus was forced to have the narrative re-written in a more eloquent style.[61] At the death of Coschinus, Pippin of Herstal gave the administration of Jumièges to another *fidelis*, Godinus, bishop of Lyon. After the death of Godinus, Charles Martel confided Jumièges, along with Rouen, Bayeux and Paris, to his relative Hugh, who made the abbacy of Fontenelle his primary power base. From the time of Coschinus and Hugh, with the exception of a few decades in the late eighth century, Jumièges would be held as an annex either of St. Riquier or of Fontenelle, both monasteries of tremendous wealth and importance during the Carolingian period.[62]

Just as the Austrasian penetration of Neustria had engendered the first spate of biographies of local saints, the settlement of the Vikings in the diocese of Rouen also served to spur historiographic production. At the end of the ninth century, however, it was not the monks of Fontenelle who presented monuments of the region's identity to its new rulers, for the Carolingian loyalist monks of Fontenelle fled from Neustria.[63] A number of non-gemmetic or much later texts record Viking activity in the Seine valley during the middle of the ninth century, and Jumièges appears

---

[61] See above pp. 46-49. Coschinus also was responsible for the production of the first biography of Richerius, founder of St. Riquier (Laporte, "Les listes abbatiales" p. 448).

[62] In the eleventh century, Hariulf of St. Riquier even claimed that Jumièges and St. Riquier were effectively one monastery and that Jumièges was never independent after the abbacy of Coschinus (Hariulf *Chronique de l'abbaye de Saint Riquier* [Collection de textes pour servir à l'étude et l'enseignement de l'histoire; Paris, 1894] ed. F. Lot I. 26 p. 43); see also Logié, "Jumièges et St.-Riquier" pp. 199-207. Laporte suggests that, after Hugo, Charles Martel gave Jumièges to one of his warriors to be exploited directly by him, but that Pippin returned the formal abbacy to an ecclesiastic, Hildegarius of Cologne. Droctegangus, Landricus and Adam all seem, between 753 and 815, to have been primarily abbots of Jumièges, and the first two were even mildly prominent on the Frankish political stage. All of the ninth-century abbots after Adam were abbots either of Fontenelle or of St. Riquier. For the abbots of Jumièges, Jean Laporte "Les listes abbatiales de Jumièges" pp. 448-455.

[63] Jean Laporte, "Fontenelle," *Dictionnaire d'Histoire et de Géographie Ecclésiastique* 17 col. 932; Jean Fournée, "Quelques facteurs de fixation et de diffusion du culte populaire des saints: exemples Normands" *Bulletin Philologique et Historique du Comité des Travaux Historiques et Scientifiques* 1982/1984 (Paris, 1986).

likely to have suffered some damage.[64] The monks of Jumièges had always had close relations with the diocese of Arras-Cambrai, where St. Riquier was located, and there is a chance that some of them fled east, like the monks of Fontenelle, at the time of Rollo's settlement. But a number of them stayed, and Jumièges remained a functioning, albeit small, monastery. Any dispersion of the monks could not have been more than partial.[65]

Dudo, at the end of the tenth century, describes Rollo as having landed at Jumièges, where the churches of St. Peter and of St. Vaast were going concerns; in his later description of Rollo's baptismal-morn gifts to local churches, Dudo shows Rollo giving land to St. Peter and St. Aichardus of Jumièges.[66] Furthermore, for Dudo the monastery was functioning throughout William Longsword's life, for that duke, Rollo's son and successor, is presented as having always wished to retire there as a monk; at no point does Dudo imply that William's construction of a **large** church at Jumièges was a refoundation rather than an improvement.[67] Dudo explicitly recognizes that the relics of Audoenus had been taken from Rouen for fear of Rollo's arrival, and throughout his narrative he does not hesitate to show Rollo's band as destructive (though justifiably so); there is no reason for Dudo to have pretended that Jumièges, a house with which he had no particular connection, was functioning at the time of Rollo's settlement if it was not in fact doing so. William of Jumiège's melodramatic assertion in the eleventh century that the place reverted to waste after 842 and became a habitation for wild animals is part of that era's retrospective magnification of the ninth-century calamity, a historiographic prism which I have examined in detail elsewhere;[68] charter evidence of 862 indicates

---

[64] *Histoire de l'abbaye royale de St.-Pierre de Jumièges par un religieux Bénédictin de la Congregation de St. Maur (1764)* ed. Julien Loth from Paris, BN Nouvelle acquisition française 470 (Société de l'Histoire de Normandie, Publications; Rouen, 1882) 3 vols, vol. I pp. 111-116; *Chronicon Fontenellense* ed. J. Laporte (Société de l'Histoire de Normandie, Mélanges, XVe serie; Rouen, 1951) p. 89.

[65] Jean Laporte, "La date de l'exode de Jumièges" *Jumièges* I: 47-48; for full discussion of the issue of movements of monks and relics out of Jumièges, see Lifshitz, "The Migration of Neustrian Relics in the Viking Age: The Myth of Voluntary Exodus, the Reality of Coercion and Theft" (forthcoming, *Early Medieval Europe*).

[66] Dudo, *De moribus* pp. 170-171.

[67] Dudo, *De moribus* pp. 180 and 200-202.

[68] See Lifshitz, "The Migration of Neustrian Relics in the Viking Age." William's calamitous vision was echoed in the verses inscribed on escutscheons around the cloister of Jumièges itself, which Du Monstier saw and printed in the seventeenth

that the house was a going concern at that date,[69] and the earliest abbatial list continues uninterrupted through Welf, who died in 881.[70]

The memory of bishops did not become an immediate concern at
Rouen at the time of Rollo's arrival; it was not judged important by the
guardians of the archiepiscopal see, men such as Wito, to present to Rollo
proof of a glorious past or an authoritative present. It may well be that the
authority and position of the archbishop were accepted without question
by Rollo and his followers, who after all permitted themselves to be baptised and married at his hands. The archbishop was the most important
local official, with whom negotiation was a necessity.[71] He was a powerful man and a secular man, whose role could be understood by the new-
comers, for episcopal lordship had long been entrenched in the cities of

century (*Neustria Pia* pp. 263-264; repr. PL coll. 394-398), and which were still
visible in 1764 when an anonymous Benedictine of St. Maur wrote his history of
Jumièges (see above note 64). Migne assigned the verses to the tenth century, but
aside from the use of the type of recherché vocabulary frequently associated with
tenth- and eleventh-century authors, there is little reason to believe the inscription
could have been made at such an early date, especially given that the great Gothic
cloister and churches of Jumièges were constructed over the course of the late
eleventh century and after. The poet describes an elaborate seige of Jumièges by
Hasting, an episode which could hardly have failed to show up in the works of
earlier historians, such as Dudo, had the poem been known to them.

[69]   J.J. Vernier *Chartes de l'abbaye de Jumièges (824-1204) conservés aux archives de
Seine-Inférieur* (Rouen, 1916) I pp. 5-10.

[70]   The earliest abbatial list jumps from Welf to Martin, a contemporary of
William Longsword. Both Musset and Laporte have posited the existence of abbots
during this period whose names were not recorded officially through Jumièges,
and Laporte suggests the possibility that the three unknown abbots of Jumièges
commemorated by the Necrology of St. Evroul, Vincent, Odo and Hugh, pertain
to this period (Musset, "Les destinés de la propriété monastique durant les invasions normandes [IXe-XIe s.]. L'exemple de Jumièges" *Jumièges* p. 51; Laporte, "Les
listes abbatiales" pp. 454-455). Laporte considers that the names could also belong
in the tenth century after Martin; however, given that contemporaries seem to
have been particularly struck by the longevity of Rodericus, we should probably
not diminish the period of his abbatiate by adding the three names during the
tenth century.

[71]   R. Kaiser, "Royauté et pouvoir épiscopal au nord de la Gaule (VIIe-IXe s.)"
in *La Neustrie* I pp. 143-160; also cf. M. Weidemann, "Bischofsherrschaft und Königtum in Neustrien vom 7. bis zum 9. Jahrhundert am Beispiel des Bistums Le Mans"
in *La Neustrie* I pp. 161-193.

Neustria, When contrasted with the major literary response on the part of Jumièges, to be examined below, the very non-response to Rollo's arrival from the see the Rouen may shed much light on the general absence of episcopal historiography at Rouen.

Given that written texts are used to legitimate and justify claims, the only people who would need to produce historiography would be those whose legitimacy was not already well-established on other, non-textual, bases. Episcopal authority was bolstered by many centuries of effective exercise of power and of civil recognition, going back to the time of Constantine; there can hardly have been the slightest motivation, in the absence of extraordinary challenges, for the production of episcopal historiography in the seventh, eighth or ninth centuries. As Farmer has shown, it was the monastic communities, the Benedictine house of Marmoutier and the canonry of St. Martin at Tours, which required and therefore produced narratives in the eleventh and twelfth centuries, when those communities sought to challenge the hegemony of the archiepiscopal see.[72] Monastic communities had no recognized "secular" or civil basis for their claims, and therefore had to resort to written texts.

In post-Carolingian Neustria the importance and authority of the archbishop of Rouen did not require any sort of elaborate explanation to be made comprehensible and acceptable to the Viking new-comers. The monasteries, on the other hand, did. There is no reason that Rollo and his followers should have accepted the function and prestige of the monastery of Jumièges, particularly given the small size and relative lack of importance of the house. The need to explain and justify monasticism in general (and Jumièges in particular) to the Viking rulers led to the first major historiographic effort on the part of the atelier of Jumièges, and the first historiographic effort of the Norman era: the production of a codex, now Rouen BM 1377 (U.108), explaining the historical background of monasticism, and the place of Jumièges within it, the latter through a focus on the two oldest tombs then available for veneration at the monastery, those of the second abbot, Aichardus, and of the fifth abbot, Hugh.[73]

---

[72] Sharon Farmer *Communities of St. Martin: Legend and Ritual in Medieval Tours* (Cornell, 1991) pp. ix-x and 3-4.

[73] The author copied a treatise by Jerome on the life of monks (BHL 6524, fols. 1-41), followed by biographies of two of the most famous founders of the monastic way of life, Paul (BHL 6596, fols. 41r-45v) and Anthony of Egypt (BHL 609, fols. 45v-56). To these highlights of fourth-century monasticism, the author added two

Not a single author who has written on the biographies of Aichardus or Hugh in this century has treated the information in them as anything other than completely suspect (perhaps the range is unsure to fictional).[74] The fictionality of the narratives is traditionally ascribed to massive losses caused by the Viking invasions. Yet there is no evidence of losses; everything which seems to have been produced before the arrival of the Vikings, namely the biographies of Filibertus and Austreberta and the abbatial list of Jumièges, were available to be used by this ninth-century author. A number of pre-Norman charters have also survived. The "fictionality" of these first two Norman-era biographies can be ascribed to the concerns of the author at the time of the settlement of Rollo and of the latter's *fideles*. The fact is, Jumièges seems always to have been a minor house. Yet that is precisely the impression that this first Norman-era historian is at pains to prevent the new-comers from contracting.

For one thing it was important to enhance the prestige of Aichardus, whose body Jumièges possessed, at the expense of that of Filibertus, whose body the house did not possess. Neither Aichardus nor Hugh is commemorated in any of the many martyrologies composed before the end of the ninth century, nor is there the slightest hint of a memory of Aichardus even in south-west Gaul, where he is said by his first gemmetic biographer to have had an illustrious forty-year career during which he founded and headed a monastery at Quinçay.[75] However, it is the second half of the biography, once Aichardus has arrived at Jumièges, that contains the most interesting narrative choices.

---

of his own compositions on the nature of the monastic life in the form of biographies of Aichardus (BHL 181, fols. 117-135v) and Hugo (BHL 4032a, fols. 135v-152). For the common authorship of the two gemmetic narratives, see J. Van der Straeten, "L'auteur des vies de S. Hughes et de S. Aychadre" AB 88 (1970) pp. 63-73.

[74]   The only information concerning Aichardus in the Merovingian biography of Filibertus is that he was chosen by Filibertus to rule as abbot of Jumièges when Filibertus was in exile at Poitiers with bishop Ansoaldus (BHL 6085 ed. Levison cc. 32-33); the entire edifice of the *vita Aichardi* is built on this incident. Levison (MGH SRM 5 p. 600 note 5) calls the *vita Aichardi* completely "fabulosa"; Roger Desreumaux (BSS I p. 147) says "unsure"; Vacandard (*Vie de St. Ouen* p. 280 n. 1) "tout à fait légendaire"; Fortia d'Urbain (ed. *Vita Aichardi* = BHL 182 p. 66-67) says "unreliable."

[75]   Claude Vion and Paul Massein, "Les témoins liturgiques du culte de saint Aychadre" *Jumièges* pp. 365-370; GC 2 cols. 1289-1290.

The late-ninth-century historian still envisions the age of Audoenus and Filibertus as Pious Neustria, although there is a new nagging evil presence lurking in the diocese: demons. In the next century, the piety would (historiographically speaking) disappear, leaving only the demons. Jumièges, in this ninth-century historian's view, was a monastery which had housed 900 monks, and 1500 persons in total, including the servants (c. 39)! The very first thing our ninth-century historian wished the new-comers to know about Jumièges is that it had been, at one time, populated by an extremely large number of monks, which would imply that it was one of the grandest of all local institutions, if not the very grandest. How, then, did the author explain the fact that Jumièges in the 880s was so lacking in grandeur? Indeed, the house must have been in a particularly reduced condition by that date. The considerably-reduced population of the monastery was conveniently explained by the major anecdote in the second half of Aichardus' biography: the story of how half of the monks of Jumièges died on a single night, called by the Lord to their final vocation as a reward for the degree of perfection which they had reached (cc. 56-65). This "Pious Neustrian" explanation for why Jumièges is no longer as grand as it ought to be occupies most of the narrative set in Neustria. The bodies of all those monks, as well as that of Hugh son of Charlemagne and former bishop of Rouen, are said to be still located at Jumièges, in hallowed ground on which "multa et inennarabilia sunt ostensa miracula." The arrival of foreign princes at Rouen offered the monks of Jumièges the opportunity to present their house as having had a much grander past than it in fact appears to have had.

The rest of the Neustrian portion of Aichardus' biography describes primarily demonic battles. The anonymous author's vision of the monastic life at Jumièges under Aichardus is modelled on Evagrius' translation of Athanasius' biography of Anthony, a text which that Norman-era author himself had copied into the codex.[76] According to both Athanasius and the anonymous Jumièges biographer, monastic life consists of a battle against the devil for control of one's soul. First, Aichardus saves the brothers from the devil when the latter attempts to crush them under a tree (c. 43). Then, Aichardus himself has a brush with damnation when a demon catches him sinning and records the sin; immediate application of penitential practices

---

[76] BHL 609, published by Rosweyde in his *Vita Patrum*, repr. PL 73 cols. 127-170.

brings a sign that the sin has been forgiven (cc. 44-46). Aichardus, a vigilant pastor, constantly instructs the brothers on how to arm themselves through prayer and abstinence against diabolical attacks (cc. 51-55).

The production of this Jumièges history of monasticism in Rouen BM 1377 (U. 108) marks the very first appearance of the theme of the battle against the devil in any Neustrian narratives, and it can hardly be a coincidence that the narrative was produced against the immediate background of the settlement of Rollo and his Viking *fideles* at Rouen. The settlement of the "pagan Vikings" suddenly made the presence of an implacable invisible enemy a plausible theme in the mind of a Neustrian historian.[77] The gemmetic historian's second biography, written after the *vita Aichardi*, took a slightly different approach to local legitimation in the eyes of the new rulers. The narrative choices of the ninth-century *vita Hugonis*[78] would be equally important as those in the *vita Aichardi* in determining Fulbertus' vision of Romanus' Neustria, when he came to Jumièges in the tenth century and used the codex which is now Rouen BM 1377 (U.108).

It could be that Hugh was displayed before Rollo, and as an inspiration to the monks who remained at Jumièges and who were now urged to identify with and venerate that saint, as a Carolingian protective patron, much the way Audoenus had been displayed before Pippin, as a Merovingian protective patron. Hugh had presided over all the key ecclesiastical institutions of Neustria during the lifetime of Charles Martel, and had been buried at Jumièges in 732/3. His grave was in some respects the most important tomb possessed by the monastery, given that Filibertus had died and been buried in exile. However, Hugh was not acknowledged by his late-ninth-century biographer as abbot of Jumièges, but as a simple monk; furthermore, he is not seen as the cousin of Charles Martel, *sub-regulus*, but

---

[77]   The theme was explored in detail in Felice Lifshitz, "A Real and Present Danger: Demonic Infestation in the Tenth Century," paper presented before the International Congress of Medieval Studies, Kalamazoo, May 1994.

[78]   For the *vita Hugonis* (BHL 4032a) see J. Van der Straeten, "La vie inédite de S. Hugues, évêque de Rouen" AB 87 (1969) pp. 232-260. Van der Straeten transcribes the biography of Hugo from Rouen BM 1377 (U.108) fols. 135r-150r; he gives variants for all the other extant copies in his apparatus. This ninth-century copy is divided into readings, and includes neumes for chanting; therefore it is clear that a cult of Hugh was in fact introduced at Jumièges in the ninth century. For Hugh, see Henri Platelle, BSS 12 coll. 773-774.

as the son of Charles the Great, emperor.[79] These errors must have resulted from the author's confusion about the form of the abbatial list, on which Hugh did not seem to be included; the name "Hugo," as it would have stood on the dyptich-plus-continuations by the end of the ninth century, would have implied a monk of the ninth century (which is what the gemmetic historian took him to be), not an abbot of the eighth century.[80]

The St. Hugh brandished by the atelier of Jumièges upon the arrival of Rollo was a composite of "high" Carolingian features, and a figure who bore little relation to the pluralistic nephew of Charles Martel who had held Neustria for the early Carolingians. The prologue enmeshes Hugh in metahistory. After establishing the hierarchy of the archangels, etc. in heaven, the author moves from Adam, through the age of the Law, to the age of Grace, with its chain of apostles and martyrs,[81] before introducing the subject of the biography. Hugh himself incarnates an idealized vision of the Carolingian past. He was educated at St. Denis (c. 4). The youth of Hugh was dominated by learning and education; all his most cherished ambitions seemed to be scholarly in nature, and the imperial palace, which he sometimes visited, was the locale for frequent academic disputations; it is the report of Hugh's "incomprehensibilis sapientia" that brings him to the attention of Charlemagne (cc. 3-7). As soon as he was old enough, he went on pilgrimage with an enormous retinue to the holy of holies, Rome, where he enjoyed the intimacy of pope Leo, who was locked in a special relationship with Frankish royalty (cc. 9-13). It was in Rome that Hugh was tonsured, ordained a deacon, and vowed to become a monk of Jumièges. He was sidetracked by being chosen as archbishop of Rouen. The first thing we learn about his episcopate, once installed, is that the em-

---

[79]   BHL 4032a c. 1 ed. Van der Straeten, pp. 235-236. Charlemagne did have a bastard son named Hugh, who died (after a rebellion) in 844, but he was never bishop of Rouen. The author places the beginning of Hugh's episcopate, under Charlemagne, in 762 (c. 19 p. 247), a chronological impossibility.

[80]   See the reconstruction of the list by Laporte, "Les listes abbatiales" p. 449.

[81]   The prologue theme of the historiated chain from the Incarnation/Crucifixion had already been used by the eighth-century author of the *vita Austrebertae* and, on a particularly sophisticated level, by Paul the Deacon, in his history of the bishops of Metz, commissioned by Angilram of Metz in 783 (Walter Goffart, "Paul the Deacon's 'Gesta Episcoporum Mettensium' and the Early Design of Charlemagne's Succession" *Traditio* 42 (1986) pp. 59-93). For Paul's prologue, see MGH SS II p. 261.

peror subjugated all the suffragan bishops to Hugh's metropolitan authority (c. 19). He remained ever mindful of his Roman vow (made to St.
Peter), and throughout his episcopate he spent Lent at Jumièges (c. 27).
Finally, after the death of his father, he abdicated the archiepiscopal office,
and retired as a monk to Jumièges (cc. 29-30). All his life he followed canon law in every way. After ten years as a monk, he died at Jumièges.

Hugh himself was the very embodiment of Carolingian ideology:
hierarchical, metahistorical, dionysian, Roman, canonical...and he reposed
in the vaults at Jumièges. But there was also the matter of his surroundings. Over a century earlier, another Jumièges historian had, in his biography of Austreberta, transposed "Pious Neustria" to "Pious Austrasia," eager
to be of service to the new Carolingian rulers.[82] At the end of the ninth
century, our anonymous gemmetic historian transposed "pious Neustria"
to "pious Francia." Under Charlemagne, the empire was a place where
scholars disputed doctrine in the palace, the emperor's own sons were de-
manded by the churches of Metz and Rouen as their bishops, large crowds
of magnates went on pilgrimage, even larger crowds turned out on all the
routes to sing psalms and rejoice in the passage of the emperor's holy son,
the whole ecclesiastical hierarchy under their appropriate metropolitans
deliberated with the emperor concerning church appointments, and new
bishops were installed at massive empire-wide gatherings at Aachen (cc.
14-18). Chapters 19 and 20 are particularly dense visions of Pious Francia:
Francia is a world suffused with religious cares.

Given the piety of Francia as a whole, the condition of the archdiocese of Rouen is as much of a shock to the reader as it must have been to
Hugh when he first arrived, especially to the reader familiar with Audoenus and "Pious Neustria." The entire archdiocese had never seen a happier
day than the day on which Hugh arrived (c. 21). The new archbishop immediately set out to ameliorate the corrupt situation of pre-Carolingian
Rouen, and to rebuild and restore a world which lay ruined; he began by
extirpating the prostitutes who were at the time rampant in the city (c. 22).
Then he moved on to the monasteries (cc. 23-24). And he turned out to be
the best bishop who had ever served at Rouen:

> ...indeed, the blessed Hugh was considered to have excelled all of his
> predecessors through his pious goodness just as he overshadowed

[82] See above pp. 66-69.

them by his high birth, and this opinion was held not only by the king and his magnates, but indeed by all those to whom his reputation became known.[83]

Hugh was an updated, imperial-era version of Austreberta, an earlier savior from the east.

Tenth-century Norman historiography, including Fulbertus' biography of Romanus, cannot be understood without Hugh, or without the rest of the narratives produced at and stored in the Jumièges library during the ninth-century transition from Frankish to Viking rule. Romanus was to be described by Fulbertus as an Austrasian, like Austreberta and Hugh before him; he would be a pious Austrasian savior from the east, whose family served the Frankish kings in their palace from the time of Clovis. His mother's premonitory dream is explicit on this point. She describes the dream to her husband:

> Immediately a fiery little torch followed [the angel's] moving hand, proceeding from out of my womb, and along that long road running through the upper air all the way to Neustria and finally stopped there and, encompassing the region entirely with infused light, all shadows were submerged, light was shed all over Neustria.[84]

Romanus, however, is not introduced to the reader without a certain amount of preparation. The opening folios of the *vita Romani* enmesh the saint in the great chain of metahistory that had appeared in the biographies of Austreberta and Hugh as well, though not in any other Neustrian works composed between the seventh and the ninth centuries. Fulbertus, however, was concerned with something beyond the grand sweep of metahistory from the time of Jesus; he was also concerned with the specifics of Frankish history around the time of Clovis. These he took from the opening sections of Alcuin's revised *vita Vedastis*, which seems to be the only text quoted verbatim by Fulbertus.[85] Although I have not identified

---

[83] "...beatus scilicet Hugo, quanto altior erat natalibus, tanto dignior et prepotentior in omni pietate bonitatis pre ceteris suis predecessoribus habebatur, non solum cum rege suisque optimatibus, uerum etiam ab omnibus quibus notus pro suis dilatatis affluentiis inerat" (c. 27 p. 253).

[84] Fulbertus, *Vita Romani* fol. 116r.

[85] Compare the stories of Clovis and Clothild in the *vita Romani* (fol. 114v) with Alcuin's *vita Vedastis* (= BHL 8506-8508 ed. Krusch, MGH SRM 3 c. 1 p. 417).

a manuscript of the *vita Vedastis* known to have been at Jumièges in the tenth century, the centuries-long connections between the Seine valley monastery and Artois (especially St. Riquier) would imply that a copy of Alcuin's work could have been easily procured; at least some biography of St. Vedastus must have been available at Jumièges for, as we have seen, the chapel of St. Vaast, mentioned by Dudo, was a central feature of the topography of the monastery in the ninth and tenth centuries. Otherwise, Romanus' youthful erudition and his education are comparable to those of Hugh and of Leutfredus of La-Croix-St.-Ouen, a copy of whose eighth-century biography was also present at Jumièges in the tenth century.[86] Finally, Fulbertus' assertion that Romanus' first act as bishop of Rouen was to battle prostitutes is very likely to have been inspired by the *vita Hugonis*.

One particularly striking thing about Fulbertus' world-view is his interest in demons. In all of the religious historiography produced before the tenth century, only four narratives contain demonic episodes which can be paralleled to some of Fulbertus' choices: the biographies of Anthony of Egypt, Aichardus of Jumièges, Leutfredus of La-Croix-S.-Ouen, and Martial of Limoges. Every single one of these texts turns out to have been in the library at Jumièges before the middle of the tenth century.[87]

---

[86] Rouen BM 1380 (U.55) fols.91v-103r (= BHL 4899).

[87] For the *vita Antonii*, see above p. 127; for the *vita Leutfredi*, see above pp. 50-55; for the *vita Aichardi*, see above pp. 127-130. Also see *Vita Martialis prolixior* (= BHL 5552) ed. W. Gray de Birch *Vita sanctissimi Martialis: The Life of St. Martial by Aurelianus* (London, 1877) pp. 6-38. The first *vita prolixior* of St. Martial has been dated to the mid tenth century, and codicological evidence indicates that it was known in Normandy by the end of the tenth or the beginning of the eleventh century (C. Lasteyrie, *L'abbaye de Saint-Martial de Limoges* [Paris, 1903] p. 15). Richard Landes argues that, although the story itself would have been current in oral tradition by the mid-tenth century, the written text as we have it did not crystalize in its present form until the 990s (Richard Landes, "The Dynamics of Heresy and Reform in Limoges: A Study of Popular Participation in the 'Peace of God' [994-1033]" in *Essays on the Peace of God: The Church and the People in Eleventh-Century France* eds. Thomas Head and Richard Landes (*Historical Reflections/Réflexions Historiques* 14 [1987] pp. 467-511, esp. pp. 473-478 and p. 482.) The presence of copies of the *vita prolixior* in late tenth/early eleventh-century manuscripts of Jumièges (Rouen BM 1378 [.40]) and Fécamp (Rouen BM 1400 [U.3]), militates against Landes' proposed later date of written fixing. Fulbertus himself may have come to Jumièges from St. Cyprien of Poitiers in around 940, perhaps even

In the *vita Aichardi*, an original late-ninth-century gemmetic composition, the devil's role had been limited to his attempts to entrap monks, and demons only appear one at a time. Building upon this original monument of Norman historiography, as well as upon biographies of St. Anthony (also in Rouen BM 1377 [U. 108]), Martial of Limoges (in Rouen BM 1378 [U.40]) and Leutfredus of La Croix (in Rouen BM 1380 [U.55]), Fulbertus of Jumièges would, during the crisis of the mid-tenth century, expand the theme to demonophobic proportions. Indeed, the theme of demonic infestation would seem plausible enough to Fulbertus for him to have used it on two occasions: Fulbertus of Jumièges not only wrote the first *vita Romani*, he also wrote a revised version of the *vita Aichardi* in which he elaborated on demonophobic themes in a monastic context.[88]

In the tenth century at Jumièges, the monk Fulbertus would cull the monastic library for motifs which were both plausible and useful in his own context, and would end up harvesting the entirety of possible demonic models. The single enemy of the late ninth century had been Rollo, who was reflected as the devil in the earlier, anonymous biography of

---

bringing a copy of the *vita prolixior* with him. Quinçay, believed at Jumièges to have been a foundation of Aichardus, is but 1/2 league from Poitiers (GC 2 cols. 1230-1232 and 1289-1290). That fact would explain Fulbertus' interest in Aichardus, whose biography he rewrote using the ninth-century manuscript, Rouen 1377 (U.108). I would suggest, in fact, that Fulbertus himself was the copiest/compiler of Rouen 1378 (U.40), made under abbot Anno of Jumièges c. 942/43 (Van der Straeten, "L'auteur des vies de S. Hughes" p. 70). Rouen BM 1378 (U.40) includes a copy of BHL 181 (fols. 52-75) made on Rouen 1377, as well as the oldest Norman copy of the *vita prolixior* of Martial.

[88] The most important manuscripts of Fulbertus' biography of Aichardus (= BHL 182) are two eleventh-century Jumièges codices, Rouen BM 1399 (U.2) fols. 33v-45v and Rouen BM 1409 (Y.189) fols. 2r-35r (where it is followed by the oldest copy of the abbatial catalogue of Jumièges). The text has found no modern editor. As it happens, the *vita Aichardi* was included by Jacob de Guisia, a late-fourteenth-century Franciscan, in his compilation of texts concerning Hainaut, namely the *Annales Historiae Illustrium Principum Hanoniae* (Valenciennes BM 784-786, of the fourteenth century). The *Annales* were printed in their entirety by Fortia d'Urban under the title *Histoire de Hainault par Jacques de Guyse* (Paris, 1826-1838), and the complete text of the *vita Aichardi* appears in vol. VIII (1830) pp. 40-137 (= BHL 182beta). However, the preface in which Fulbert names himself appears only in the otherwise highly-abbreviated version of the *vita* published by Laurentius Surius *De Probatis Sanctorum Historiis* V (1574) p. 239 (= BHL 182alpha). The text is discussed in Lifshitz, "A Real and Present Danger."

Aichardus; in the mid-tenth century, demonic enemies would be everywhere, and they would not be only Vikings, but Franks and Flemings as well. Those enemies are reflected in the scenes of demonic crowd action included by Fulbertus in his two known works of history: his biographies of Romanus and Aichardus.

4

St. Romanus of Rouen

A. A Typology of Sanctity? The Study of Saints' Biographies

Romanus of Rouen was the headless and ill-remembered corpse of a Merovingian-era bishop onto whom his earliest historian projected a character, in the tenth century, which was consistent with locally-available literary sources and models, and with contemporaneous circumstances and mentalities. Tenth-century Norman historiography was determined by, or at least developed within the framework of, both general late Carolingian intellectual traditions (such as Dionysian cosmologies), and specific historiographical traditions of Neustria (such as that practiced at Jumièges). An understanding of such traditions can go a long way towards explaining how Fulbertus, the educated historian, shaped Romanus in the tenth century when the mid-century crisis of Norman ducal and *rouennais* episcopal power stimulated historiographic production. But such analyses leave unexplained other aspects of Romanus' character as described by Fulbertus.

"Romanus" is not reducible to a pastische of late Carolingian and gemmetic literary remains. He is also a saint, the saint, of Viking Normandy. He is a particularly polymorphous saint, in that he is both a popular figure, and the official patron saint of the duchy and the ecclesiastical province centered on Rouen. By the 960s, Romanus had become the official patron saint of Rouen, capital of the Norman duchy. At least three different emissions of ducal coins were produced at Rouen during the reign of Richard I, all between the 960s and the 980s, marked with the legend "SCE ROMANE ROTOM CIVI."[1] In the following pages, I will focus on Roma-

---

[1] Dumas-Dubourg, *Le Trésor de Fécamp* pp. 98-100, nos. 6042-6044 of the coin hoard of Fécamp. Older reports of individual coin finds: the *denarius* of Richard I (found in St. Petersburg) inscribed "RCARD MARCHIS" on the obverse and "ROTOMA ROMANUS EPS" on the reverse (A. de Longpérier, *Monnaies normandes* R.N. VIII (1843) pp. 53-61 plate II.8); another ducal *denarius*, this time of the eleventh century, bearing the inscriptions "ROTOMAG" and "SC ROMAN" (A. Tougard, "La Vie de S. Romain" *Société des Bibliophiles Normands* 60 [Rouen, 1899]). By *circa* 1000, *rouennais*

nus *qua* saint, rather than solely as a historical figure/historiographical character, and attempt to elucidate both his popular and his official appeal.

Fulbertus' Romanus does not fall into any of the "types" of saints already recognized in the scholarly literature, nor does his biography by Fulbertus fit any recognized schemata for the lives of missionaries or bishops;[2] it may well be that the "types" and the "schemata" have no existence outside of scholarly analyses in any case. For the record, Fulbertus' Romanus is not a man striving to follow Jesus, to change his life completely, to become perfect, to follow the "type" of Anthony. Nor is Fulbertus' Romanus an active pillar of the visible church, engaged in service to others, a bishop of the "type" of Hilary, Ambrose, Augustine. Nor is Fulbertus' Romanus like either Fontaine's Sulpicius Severus' Martin, a *miles Christi* with a dual vocation, a complete monk who humbly washes the feet of his biographer and lives a monastic life at Marmoutier while remaining an episcopal miracle-worker,[3] or Lotter's Sulpicius Severus' Martin, a "confessor and ascetic" who is not in any important sense a bishop at all because, in Lotter's typology, there is no such thing as a "Bischofs-vita."[4] Nor is Fulbertus' Romanus a representative of the "Augustinian-Gregorian type," which synthesizes monastic and clerical lives through canonial organization, the "type" of Cuthbert.[5] Fulbertus' Romanus can be said to be closer to Heiric's Germanus of Auxerre, both being bishops possessed of some ascetic and some prophetic virtues, but even there the details of presentation hardly match.[6]

---

ducal coins inscribed with the name of Romanus were appearing in numerous treasure hoards outside of the Norman heartlands (Dumas-Dubourg, *Trésor de Fécamp* p. 99 note 5 and p. 100 note 1).

[2]   For instance, Zoepf *Das Heiligen-Leben* pp. 41-42.

[3]   Jacques Fontaine "Hagiographie et politique. De Sulpice Sévère à Venance Fortunat" RHEF 62 (1976) pp. 113-140; for the foot-washing see *Vita Martini* 25.3.

[4]   F. Lotter, "Methodisches zur Gewinnung historischer Erkenntnisse aus hagiographischen Quellen" *Historische Zeitschrift* 229 (1979) pp. 298-356, at pp. 315-316.

[5]   Clare Stancliffe, "Cuthbert and the Polarity Between Pastor and Solitary" *St. Cuthbert, His Cult and Community* eds. G. Bonner, DW Rollason and C. Stancliffe (Woodbridge, 1989) pp. 36-40.

[6]   Heiric of Auxerre, *Vita Germani* (BHL 3458), a metrical biography of the mid-ninth century; Jean-Yves Tilliette, "Les modèles de sainteté du IXe au XIe siècle, d'après le témoignage des récits hagiographiques en vers métriques" *Settimane* 36 (1988) pp. 398-399

Fulbertus' Romanus is an apparently celibate bishop who governs a local monastery, devotes most of his life to a militant anti-"pagan" activism and retreats to an isolated cell when he learns that death is near. Fulbertus seems to have envisioned Romanus as living in the monastery of St. Ouen, which the bishops of Rouen governed as titular abbots until the eleventh century, but he places no emphasis on Romanus *qua* monk/abbot, and Romanus is never more than a dabbler in ascetic practices. Fulbertus' Romanus does belong in the so-called "tradition of Irish thought" which included the idea of predestination and the concomitant static portrayal of the saint.[7] Fulbertus also drew on the common stock of images available to him when he, like thousands of other authors, included a prodigious conception and a portentious birth from an overage, barren mother in his description of Romanus' life.[8] Fulbertus drew on that same stock when he protested, humbly, his inadequacy for the narrative task at hand, and when he presented Romanus as a *puer senex*.

I will not, however, be undertaking the typological (or generic) analysis of the preceding cluster of motifs, an analysis which would, undoubtedly, prove that Fulbertus was a person who wrote literature. The obsession with identifying "models" has already led to the widespread overestimation of the influence of certain supposedly exemplary works;[9] all sorts of dissimilarities would have to be ignored in order to assimilate episodes in the *vita Romani* to broad *topoi*, or to claim "influence."[10] The point, in

[7]   J.M. Picard, "Structural Patterns in Early Irish Hagiography," *Peritia* 4 (1985) p. 78-79. Romanus' role in life as savior of "pagan" Neustria was pre-destined. Romanus is said to have become pontiff of Rouen "not by his own will nor by ambitious desiring, but by the royal will, nay rather he was called by a divine and angelic preordaining oracle" (fol. 114v), and at his election an angel reveals that Romanus "has been called by God, and chosen before even he was born" (fol. 117r). There is never any discussion of Romanus as a changing and developing human.

[8]   Fulbertus, *Vita Romani* fol. 115v, where the angel who informs the aged Benedictus of the imminent birth of a son to the old man's sterile wife Felicitas echoes the words of the angel who had informed Zacharias of the birth of John the Baptist (Luke 1:13).

[9]   Clare Stancliffe, *St. Martin and His Hagiographer* (Oxford, 1983) pp. 58-69.

[10]   I have not been able to find a single example of unequivocal borrowing or influence from any of the standard "models" in Fulbertus' biography of Romanus. One could list "parallels" for the saint's body being levitated during a mass as confirmation of his holiness (cf. the ball of fire emanating from Martin's head, or

any case, is to understand how a particular historiographic strategy functions in its context. It would not therefore matter for my puposes, beyond
localizing the composition of a text through the reconstruction of library
collections, where an author found his or her inspiration; what matters is
why the author deliberately chose the motifs which he or she did choose,
when so many others were also available but were rejected. Authorial utilization of certain motifs, rather than others, is not a passive process of
absorption, but is creative and meaningful.[11]

Lest we think that the typological analysis of the above motifs would
lead us closer to a definition of "Christian sainthood"[12] or of the genre
of "hagiography," we have to remember that the very themes noted in the
penultimate paragraph above also belong to the fund of ideas known as
"folklore," and are literary commonplaces in many different traditions.[13]
The typological approach, if pursued without some massive suppression
of evidence, can only be practicable on a global scale, as a study of "human nature" or the "human imagination," an imagination which has told
identical stories about tenth-century Latin Christians and about Buddha

his jewelled hand in Sulpicius Severus, *Dialogues* ed. C. Halm in *Sulpicii Severi
Opera* [CSEL 1; 1866] II.2, 1-2 and III. 10, 6), for the saint's predicting his own death
(cf. Stancliffe, "Cuthbert and the Polarity" p. 44), and so forth, but one can never
pass beyond "parallels" to citations.

11 Hanns Swarzenski, "The Role of Copies in the Formation of the Styles of the
Eleventh Century" *Studies in Western Art* I, *Romanesque and Gothic Art* (Acts of the
20th International Congress of the History of Art, New York 1961; Princeton, 1963)
pp. 7-18; Linda Seidel, *Songs of Glory* pp. 12-13 and p. 21.

12 "Christian sainthood" is most commonly defined as an *imitatio Christi*; for instance, Richard Kieckhefer "Imitators of Christ: Sainthood in the Christian Tradition" *Sainthood* pp. 1-42. Romanus, by this definition, would not be a "saint," because there is not a single way in which this particular bishop of Rouen is shown
to have imitated Christ.

13 C.F. Loomis *White Magic. An Introduction to the Folklore of Christian Legend*
(Cambridge, Mass., 1948) pp. 15-26; Francesco Lanzoni, "Il sogno presago della
madre incinta nella letteratura medievale e antica" AB 45 (1927) pp. 224-241; A.J.
Festugière "Lieux communs littéraires et thèmes de folk-lore dans l'hagiographie
primitive" *Wiener Studien* 73 (1960) pp. 123-152; P. Saintyves, *En marge de la légende
dorée* (Paris, 1987 reed) pp. 538-547. *Contra* the approach of Gregorio Penco, "Significato e funzione dei prologhi nell'agiografia Benedettina" *Aevum* 40 (1966) pp. 468-
478; "L'imitazione di Christo nell'agiografia monastica" *Collectanea Cisterciana* 28
(1966) pp. 17-34, esp. pp. 17-19; "Le figure bibliche del *vir Dei* nell'agiografia
monastica" *Benedictina* XV (1968) pp. 1-13.

in 600 B.C.[14]

The present work is not a study of "human nature," but of historical narrative in Neustria and Normandy. Each narrative is particular; if one reads them without the prior intention of assimilating the episodes to *topoi*, one will discover, as Paul Fouracre has, that they are in fact not so assimilable.[15] My approach is much like that of Thomas Head, who rejected the literary study of saints' biographies *qua* the study of concepts of sanctity, and focussed instead on the relic-possessing and text-producing communities which created the narratives.[16] My approach is the polar opposite to that of Gurevich, who argued that "medieval" literature was unchanging and homogeneous from the time of Caesarius of Arles to the time of Caesarius of Heisterbach; such a belief can only result from *a priori* assumptions, and not from looking at individual examples.[17] The "medium aevum" was not an unchanging unity; indeed, there was no "medium aevum" beyond what is created by sixteenth-century and later discourse. It is hoped that this detailed regional study of specific changes over time will help to explode the typological approach to the so-called "medium aevum." To attempt to force a vast spectrum of historiography and of literature into a few recognizable *topoi* is superficial, ahistorical and decontextualized.

B. Written Text and Oral Tradition at Rouen: Romanus as Popular Saint

The Benedictines of Paris have noted that Romanus is a very popular saint

---

[14]   Loomis *White Magic* p. 13.

[15]   Paul Fouracre, "Merovingian History and Merovingian Hagiography" *Past and Present* 127 (1990) pp. 3-38, esp. pp. 12-21 and p. 37; he asserts that the texts he knows are not at all "typical" but continues to assume that the texts produced in other periods, periods which he does not know, **are** typical. It may be that after the twelfth century a formulaic genre of "hagiography" develops, but at no point covered by this study have I encountered texts that are "typical"; rather, it is complete variety which reigns. *Contra* L. Zoepf *Das Heiligenleben* pp. 40-108, who sifted out a few "biographies" as real and effectively collapsed the rest into a single legendary melting-pot.

[16]   Head, *Hagiography and the Cult of Saints* pp. 14-15.

[17]   Gurevich *Contadini e santi* p. 19.

at Rouen, although "l'historien ne voit guère la raison de cette grande vogue."[18] The entry for Romanus in their multi-volume guide to saints consists primarily of the repeated assertion that his biographies are all worthless, so it is no wonder the good monks were mystified by the saint's popularity. However, it may be that his written biographies are not particularly valuable for understanding Romanus' popularity. Were we to limit our investigation to the confines of learned narrators, we would never understand why Romanus is so popular. It is necessary, therefore, to undertake the extremely hazardous enterprise of conjecturing about oral tradition and popular memory, and we must do so largely on the basis of the extant written narratives, which are, unfortunately, practically the only source we have.

It would be naive to treat the generation of historiographical texts as though they transpired in an interpersonal vacuum, all the while pointing out the socio-cultural and political contexts in which the authors lived. Clerical historians did not live their lives within the hermetically-sealed walls of their scriptoria conversing only with dead or distant colleagues by means of books. No one lives exclusively within a literary tradition; it would probably be possible to detect in all texts an interaction between author and oral milieu.[19] Hippolyte Delahaye argued as early as 1906 that the production of saints' biographies was a matter of clerical editing of popular images and motifs; for instance, the ecclesiastic modifies the character and structure of the legend to accentuate its "religious" significance.[20] Thus, the influence of "oral," or "folkloric" or "popular" culture

---

[18]   Benedictines of Paris, *Vies des Saints et des bienheureux selon l'ordre du calendrier avec l'historique des fêtes* (Paris, 1952) vol. X pp. 790-791.

[19]   For instance, the canonical Evangelists have been seen essentially as redactors of oral traditions, rather than as creative authors: "Wie Dibelius und Bultmann überzeugend nachwiesen, sind die Evangelisten im wesentlichen als Redaktoren eines in mündlicher Überlieferung bereits ausgeformten Erzählgutes anzusehen, eine Beobachtung, die weitgehend auch für die Autoren hagiographischer Schriften Gültigheit besitzen dürfte" (F. Lotter, "Legenden als Geschichtsquellen" *Deutsches Archiv* 27 [1971] p. 197, referring to M. Dibelius, *Die Formgeschichte des Evangeliums* [1919] and R. Bultmann, *Die Geschichte der synoptischen Tradition* [1921]).

[20]   Hippolyte Delahaye *Les légendes hagiographiques* (Subsidia Hagiographica 18; Brussels, 1906; 3rd ed., 1927) pp. 12-100.

cannot be ignored.[21] Written culture can never be more than an islet in a sea of oral genres.[22]

The oral world could still have contained, after the ninth century, important traditions concerning a sixth- or seventh-century figure. However, it does not seem that the oral traditions told to Fulbertus about Romanus did in fact go back beyond the middle of the ninth century, when Romanus' head was shipped off to Soissons. Nevertheless, the way Romanus has "ascended" in time from his place on the episcopal lists to the era in which Fulbertus places him is precisely the type of confusion which apparently characterizes long-term oral transmission of information.[23] The very possibility of long-term oral transmission of tales is most famously exemplified by the figure of Roland, that contemporary of Charlemagne whose exploits in a battle dated 778 were finally immortalized in textual form in the eleventh (or perhaps even in the twelfth) century.[24] Fulbertus, like the Roland poets, would then have "fixed" in written form one version of his hero's exploits, exploits which had lived and would continue to live in a fluid oral tradition, always "shaped" according to the needs of the moment; the written version too would be "shaped" according to the concerns of author and audience.

Thus, we have to attend to the oral milieux in which Fulbertus would have spent most of his time. Yet there are few analytical methods

---

[21] For more theoretical issues surrounding clerical and "folkloric" interactions in the creation of Christian religious culture, J.-C. Schmitt, "'Religion populaire' et culture folkorique" *Annales E.S.C.* 31 (1976) pp. 941-953, especially p. 948, and R. Manselli "La Religione popolare nel medio evo: prime considerazione metodologiche" *Nuova Rivista Storica* 58 (1974) esp. p. 33. The Marxist perspectives of Schmitt and Manselli are useful correctives to Peter Brown's *Cult of the Saints*, which goes too far in the direction of attributing cultic creation exclusively to clerical elites. Julia Smith, "Oral and Written: Saints, Miracles and Relics in Brittany, c. 850-1250" *Speculum* 65 (1990) pp. 309-312 pp. 308-312 critiques an unfairly oversimplified version of the Marxist view, but nevertheless makes balanced points about the constant osmosis between oral and written traditions.

[22] The phrase is Gurevich's, who applies it only to the so-called "middle ages" (*Contadini e santi* p. 8). The generalized implication in the scholarly literature that "orality" is a feature of the past but not of contemporary culture is, to my mind, utterly mysterious.

[23] Vansina *Oral Tradition as History* pp. 177-178.

[24] S. Farrall "Sung and Written Epics: The Case of the Song of Roland" *Oral Tradition in Melanesia* ed. D. Denoon and R. Lacey (Hong Kong, 1981) pp. 101-114.

which need to be treated with more caution than this one. When one has at one's disposition both oral and written contemporaneous traditions, it is possible to compare and contrast them.[25] However, for early Normandy we have access only to the written traditions, and there is no one we can ask about the oral traditions. That is what renders the absolutely unavoidable subject of oral milieux so hazardous. On what basis can the reader of the preserved written text guess how its elements relate to oral tradition?

Deciding in advance what "type" of image we wish to dub "oral" and which we wish to dub "learned" reveals much about an analyst, but tells us little about the texts being analyzed.[26] It is not acceptable, for instance, for a rationalizing analyst simply to assign to oral tradition whatever seems "superstitious," such as a dragon-slaying.[27] Nor is it acceptable to reject as "oral tradition" whatever can be traced to an "important" person. Stancliffe once hypothesized that much of the material in Sulpicius Severus' Martinian writings came from oral tradition because of a number of strong resemblances to popular folktales, but in the end concluded that no oral or folkloric "interference" had taken place because Sulpicius gives his sources as Martin or the monks of Marmoutier![28] If this is not an example of "oral tradition," what is? Were Martin, the monks of Marmoutier and Sulpicius deaf-mutes, communicating by telepathy and scraps of parchment scribbled with anecdotes? What is the point of excluding Martin and

[25] R. Fourasté, "St. Exupère d'Arreau" in *Les saints et les stars* ed. J.-C. Schmitt (Paris, 1979) pp. 101-132.

[26] My approach to the oral/written question in the present chapter is precisely the opposite of that practiced by Gurevich, for instance in his study "Oral and Written Culture of the Middle Ages: Two 'Peasant Visions' of the Late Twelfth and Early Thirteenth Century" in *Historical Anthropology of the Middle Ages* pp. 50-64. In that study, whatever content Gurevich himself considers intelligent and sophisticated he assigns to the influence of a clerical redactor, and whatever content he considers superstitious he attributes to the peasant visionaries themselves (see especially pp. 60-61).

[27] Loomis considered everything mystical-magical-miraculous as "representative of the folk imagination" (*White Magic* p. 8 and passim). Festugière also sifted out from literary texts that which logically had to be folklore on this basis: "S'il est une partie de nos recits hagiographiques qui ressortisse au folklore, c'est assurément les miracles. Ici la fantaisie populaire se donne libre cours...." ("Lieux communs littéraires" p. 145).

[28] Stancliffe, *St. Martin and his Hagiographer* pp. 160-165.

his monks from "oral tradition" simply by virtue of their clerical status? Even within circles entirely composed of persons of elevated income, power and prestige, there is still an oral culture; there is no basis on which to assert that the stories exchanged by the tenth-century wealthy were any more "rationalistic" than those exchanged by tenth-century fishermen. It is not that there were points of intersection and exchange between clerical elites and the populace, it is that the former were part of the populace.[29]

What, indeed, is the point of ideologies which, for example, consider the "popular" psyche (unlike the "elite" psyche) "semplice ed elementare, amante del concreto e dell'evidente," while "cultivated" religion is characterized by "complesse formulazioni dogmatiche, [e] discussioni teologiche."[30] The relative "concreteness" of Latin "popular" Christianity is fully in keeping with the relative "concreteness" of the classical Latin tradition, from which few were exempt; Tacitus and Cicero were as "cultivated" as one could get, but both disapproved of drinking at the well of Greek (oriental) speculative and metaphysical philosophy. We need hardly abuse "Germanic" adherants of Christianity and their "mentalità primitiva,"[31] to find the cause of the "concreteness" of western religiosity, any more than we have to look to the humble social origins of much of the lower clergy to account for "folkloric" material in written texts.[32]

With all of these hazards and caveats in mind, we must nevertheless proceed to try to reconstruct, on the basis of the written texts, some part of the oral tradition concerning Romanus as it was passed on in early Normandy. It seems as though the episodes in Fulbertus' *vita Romani* which

---

[29] However, simply to replace the older social dichotomy of "popular" versus "elite" with a geographic dichotomy of "local" versus "universal" fails to take into account differences within a locality, personal leanings and preferences (William Christian, *Local Religion in Sixteenth-Century Spain* (Princeton, 1981) pp. 1-3). Vauchez's two-tiered model of "mentality" (which everyone shares) and "mental structure" (which distinguishes the population from the clerical elite) may be a step in the right direction, but I am unclear about how to put the distinction into practice (André Vauchez *La Sainteté en occident aux derniers siècles du moyen âge d'après les procès de canonisation et les documents hagiographiques* [Rome, 1981] pp. 625-629).

[30] Manselli, "La religione popolare" p. 33, in part citing Benedetto Croce *Poesia popolare e poesia d'arte. Studi sulla poesia italiana dal tre al cinquecento* (Bari, 1957; 4th edition).

[31] As Manselli does ("La religione popolare" pp. 34-37).

[32] As Gurevic does (*Contadini e Santi* p. 10).

include both Romanus and the entire populace of Rouen were related to oral traditions current at the time of Fulbertus' written "fixing." Each of these stories is extraordinarily rich, each abounds in discursive meaning; it is not simply a matter of an interpreter imposing or recognizing polysemy in an episode, for Fulbertus' "fixing" already overflows with polyvalent symbolism. The fact that each story already has several meanings, all packed into Fulbertus' narrative, indicates that the stories were living products of a fractured milieu, stories which were told in different ways by different people, and sometimes by the same people, at different times, and sometimes at the same time. The stories are not the product of a single authorial, authoritarian imagination.

Once Romanus has arrived at Rouen, Fulbertus immediately begins the first story, describing the danger from which the new bishop will save the town:

> There was, just to the north of the town, a high walled frame constructed in stone in the shape of an amphitheatre, in which a narrow pathway led to a subterranean cave. There the subterranean house was surrounded by lateral arches. They called this house the "domicile of Venus" because it was used by those who frequented prostitutes. In fact, inside the periphery of the exterior wall, there was at the top a spacious area, in the middle of which loomed a skillfully-constructed sanctuary, in which priestly place there stood an altar and above it the inscription of Venus. They said that the murmuring of unclean spirits was often heard from that place, and it was as though they had come from the far-flung regions of the earth to some sort of gathered council, in which each and every one was forced to give an accounting of his work, and each was honored highly according to the magnitude of his evil deeds, but beaten if he had been lazy. Just beyond the sanctuary there was a horrible cavern in a certain dark place, within indeed very spacious, but it hid its incalculable depths with a narrow inlet. Nor could any man see it for himself, since a sulphurous whirlpool emitted noisome vapors and intolerable stenches from the hole, as well as a pitch-black flame, so that the edifices of the neighboring town were frequently devasted by a cruel fire, and many were killed by its smoking odor....they were also beleaguered from the other side, that is from the south, by frequent flooding which, expelling the inhabitants, reached their homes and high palaces, and spread out through the whole town.

And this happened every two or three months without respite![33]

There is no "the" problem in this story. Fulbertus has collected, and himself refused to privilege any one over the other, all the explanations for why Romanus was remembered to have led an attack on the amphitheatre north of town. Fragments of the walls of the destroyed amphitheatre, at the time just north of Rouen but now in the center of town, are unearthed everytime any construction is done in the area. It is a "fact" that the Roman amphitheatre at Rouen was violently toppled, and that the rubble was never cleared.[34] The question is why?

The answer is manifold. Because Romanus was hostile to the prostitution trade which flourished in the neighborhood of the amphitheatre. Because Romanus was hostile to the presence of non-Christian religious edifices, the former amphitheatre/brothel suddenly ceasing to be a former amphitheatre/brothel and becoming a temple of Venus. Because the former amphitheatre/brothel/"pagan" temple was a place of habitation for demons, and not lazy demons either but vigilant ones who were goaded on through peer pressure to tempt as many people as possible into sin and to cause as much calamity as possible. Because the former amphitheatre/brothel/"pagan" temple/demonic lair was associated with a natural hazard, a cavern which emitted noxious fumes and also flames. In sum, the former amphitheatre/brothel/"pagan" temple/demonic lair/sulphur pit threatened the entire fabric of human life at Rouen, which must already have been extremely precarious since Fulbertus adds, for good measure, that the Seine flooded the town every few months. This jam-packed polyvalence continues throughout Fulbertus' narrative; the former amphitheatre/brothel/"pagan" temple/demonic lair/sulphur pit is always "all of the above," and never "A," "B" or "C." Furthermore, Romanus' destruction of the former amphitheatre/brothel/"pagan" temple/demonic lair/sulphur pit is also the fulfillment of a particular Biblical antetype: Christ's ejection of the money-changers from the Temple at Jerusalem, which story introduces the episode at Rouen.

When the *rouennais* structure is pulled down by the inhabitants, with their own hands but at Romanus' urging, the town seems finally rid of all dangers. Fulbertus the historian then steps in to make the event meaning-

---

[33] *Vita Romani* fol. 119r-119v.

[34] Nancy Gauthier, "Rouen pendant le haut Moyen Age" p. 2; *Bulletin de recherches archéologiques de Haute-Normandie* 1 (1984).

ful on historical, metahistorical and sacro-historical levels. In local oral tradition there were many stories of how Rouen had "become Christian," "become virtuous," "become safe," "become healthy," all associated with the
name Romanus and with the striking remains of the ruined amphitheatre.
Fulbertus integrated "the" story into a wider narrative, which began with
the Incarnation and the apostles, and passed through the conversion of
the Franks; now, having passed through the "purification" of Rouen, the
next step is articulated by Romanus in a prophetic rapture: the salvation
of the Viking conquerors. As a historian, Fulbertus is concerned that each
event be seen in its wider framework, so that its true significance can be
appreciated; thus, he has Romanus predict, at this moment, both the
conquest by and the conversion of a sea-borne nation.

Which brings us to the flooding river. In fact, destroying the former
amphitheatre/brothel/"pagan" temple/demonic lair/sulphur pit had not ended all problems at Rouen, for the town was equally beleaguered from the
south, by the flooding Seine. The former amphitheatre/brothel/"pagan"
temple/demonic lair/sulphur pit is picturesque, but it seems that even more
important for Romanus' popular reputation was his taming of the river.
Romanus' massive annual festival is celebrated, literally, above the Seine
river, on the bridges which connect the right and left banks, on the islands
in the Seine, on the quays along the banks. Attendees at the *Foire S.-Ro-
main* soar high above the river on the mechanical rides, whether the simple ferris wheel or the more stomach-churning contraptions, higher up
than it is possible to get from any other point in the city of Rouen, including the St. Romanus tower, the high tower of the cathedral. Romanus'
taming of the river is a key episode in his earliest biography by Fulbertus,
it is a key element (in a transmuted way) in the popular Golden Legend
version of his biography and in his iconography, and it is a key element
in the location of his present-day fair on the river, rather than on any of
the fair-grounds, churches, squares or exhibition halls in and around
Rouen.

In this case, as in the case of the explicitly polysemous former amphi-
theatre/ brothel/ "pagan" temple/ demonic lair/ sulphur pit, Fulbertus' story
is far from simple, as the flood of the river, which had already been associated with the problems described in connection with the amphitheatre,
also appears to mean everything from divine punishment for the sinful-
ness of the population to a foreshadowing of the Norman invasions and
the Christianization of the Vikings, and to mean all of those things at

once. Fulbertus the historian particularly steps in to make sure the reader/
listener is aware of the *longue durée*, by giving Romanus another long
prophetic harangue.[35] However, the gripping power of this particular
riverine image depends upon its ability to comprehend all the meanings
of the former amphitheatre/brothel/"pagan" temple/demonic lair/sulphur
pit episode, and more besides. At the same time, the riverine episode
avoided the unpleasant aftertaste of an architectural demolition. It would,
indeed, be a strange urban agglomeration that commemorated a patron
primarily because he had destroyed a cultural institution of the town; the
taming of the river, on the other hand, is a suitable symbol for urban life.

After the crowd of citizens from Rouen destroyed the former amphi-
theatre/brothel/"pagan" temple/demonic lair/sulphur pit,

> ...an unexpected inundation of waters from the western sea flooded
> the plain surrounding the town. And then to this marine surge was
> added a watery infusion from the eastern side, which reached all the
> way to the highest fortifications of the town, and the inhabitants es-
> caped from that deluge only with great difficulty, for deep in sleep
> at the first vigil of the night and expecting no adverse incursion of
> any type, they were resting in sweet peace....Quickly they took up
> their children and whatever of their property the opportunity al-
> lowed, and fled to the hills ringing the ramparts of the town, and
> from there they watched their houses and high palaces be devastated
> by the boiling deluge, consoling themselves for the loss of all their
> things with this alone, that they themselves were able to escape un-
> harmed from the perils of the furious deluge. By chance the vener-
> able pontiff was not there....And when he caught sight from afar of
> the town covered with the raging sea-swell...he said: "....Command,
> I beg you [Lord], the waters of the infesting deluge to turn back into
> the maternal breast of the ocean, that its turbid stream never again
> cross our borders." Having said this, grabbing the cross of the Lord
> which he always had carried before his eyes, he fearlessly forced his
> way through the raging waves, which immediately sought refuge as
> though overcome by fear and began to flee before his face, relinqui-
> shing the town and the fields which they had so maliciously occu-

---

[35] For the paralleling of Romanus to various biblical prophets such as Elijah
and Elisha, see Gregorio Penco, "Le figure bibliche del *vir Dei* nell'agiografia monastica" *Benedictina* 15 (1968) pp. 1-13; for biblical and especially prophetic analogues
to tales of saintly power over water, Loomis *White Magic* pp. 37-43.

pied. The holy man stood by the fleeing waters, and urged on those which lingered, until erupting through the open gates they flowed back into the river bed of the overflowing Seine. And the apostolic man constituted a boundary against them in the very entrance of the gates, that they never proceed beyond there again, and we see that these limits have been preserved with manifest signs all the way to today....[36]

The only way to understand how this superficially simple story can be at the root of the most magnificent and well-attended urban festival held in Upper Normandy in the twentieth century is to accept that "popular" symbolism can be semiotically rich, indeed, must be semiotically rich to speak to a large crowd of people at a single time, and cannot ever survive by giving in to the sort of authoritarian unidimensionality and concrete exactitude that is permissible in a learned tome.

Literary/historical narrative as it is practiced in the twentieth century and as it was practiced by the creators of "Pious Neustria" labors under a major limitation: it must be made to seem "realistic." From the end of the ninth century, "realism" ceased to be so much in fashion, and discursive possibilities became, accordingly, much less limited. We have seen in particular how demons and angels became common themes in literature, philosophy and historiography. Even within an expanded framework of discursive possibilities, Fulbertus had stretched the limits of narrative in his first depiction of what Romanus meant to Rouen by combining in a single breath demons, pagan temples, classical culture, prostitutes and certain types of natural disasters. He did refer to the flooding Seine in conjunction with the former amphitheatre/brothel/"pagan" temple/demonic lair/sulphur pit, but within the limits of verbal imagery there was no way to continue to treat the water as equivalent to the other dangers, though all the motifs probably circulated in a bundle at Rouen. Fulbertus separated the water from the earth and the fire because quite different remedies had to be engineered for the two sets of perils, logically speaking that is. However, in the imagination, in visual imagery, in a group (where many people can speak at once, rather than bowing to the linear narrative of a single author), the motifs would not have been separated; the two stories told by Fulbertus about Romanus and the entire crowd at Rouen were really one story.

[36] *Vita Romani* fols. 121r-121v.

When Fulbertus sought to fix in writing the life of Romanus, and the story of what the bishop had done for Rouen, he had to describe Romanus as having protected everything that matters; as a learned historian, he put his own interpretive spin on the story and enmeshed it in a metahistorical discourse about, among other things, the progress of salvation on the earth. But Fulbertus could have given the life of Romanus historical significance without having the prophetic-interpretive historiographical glosses take off from stories already so explicitly polysemous; a simple flood, a single sacred grove, one demon-infested temple, any one of those images would have done as the "evidence" for Fulbertus' *longue durée* thesis. The fact that Fulbertus' Romanus already stands for everything that matters indicates that the historian was privy to an extremely rich oral tradition about the saint at Rouen, none of which he felt comfortable omitting from the biography.

A saint about whom such polysemous stories were told could not have existed at this level in the near-anonymity in which Romanus lived from the sixth (or seventh) century until after the ninth century. Furthermore, a saint who aroused such passion at Rouen would not have been offered up to the monks of St. Medard with the alacrity that Romanus' head changed hands in the 840s. Romanus' reputation for having protected everything that matters at Rouen clearly post-dates the 840s translation, and given that the period of the Viking conquest and settlement in the late ninth century surely threatened to imperil everything that mattered at Rouen, the various stories, or the various ways to express the same story, all indicate that the relics of Romanus in the chapel in the tower of the ancient Roman wall were considered to have been responsible for the minimalization of the potential destructiveness carried by the Seine river.

The danger to Rouen in the late ninth century had been posed both by the river itself, and by the pirates carried on that river. Several inundations of Rouen by the Seine have been recorded by archeologists; the greatest of these reached precisely the level of the St. Romanus chapel in the town wall.[37] Apparently, the former amphitheatre/brothel/"pagan" temple/demonic lair/sulphur pit/river "bundle" stands also for the Viking

[37] Once again, I am extremely grateful to Jacques Le Maho for having shared with me this information, through personal correspondance, in advance of the publication of his study of Rouen and the Vikings.

invaders. It is without a doubt this semiotic lushness which enabled Romanus to become the patron of a Neustrian town whose defining moment was its conquest by "pagan" foreigners.

The individual shards of meaning in this bundle of dangers would eventually find a single symbol that could stand for all of them in a manner that would have been crystal clear to any imagination: the "dragon" named the *Gargouille*.[38] "Dragons" do not exist in "scientific" reality, only in semiotic reality, where they stand precisely for a number of things which otherwise would have to be designated with such unwieldy and narrationally limiting phrases as former amphitheatre/brothel/"pagan" temple/demonic lair/sulphur pit/river. All roads lead to the "dragon." The great "draco" of the Apocalyse envisioned by John, with its seven heads and ten horns, in the text of Revelations 12: 1-9 itself = the "magnus serpens antiquus" = the "diabolus et Satanas" who seduced the world in Genesis 3. The serpent of Genesis 3 = the devil = evil for the author of Jubilees III,17.23 and for Paul (2 Cor 11:3). The serpent = the dragon = the devil; serpents = dragons = demons. The preferred habitation for the dragon = devil and for dragons = demons is water.[39] At the same time, on two compatible symbolic planes, dragons = demons = "paganism," and dragons = water = "nature" = "dangers of the natural world."[40] The saint who over-

---

[38]   The earliest written version of the story of how Romanus tamed the dragon with his stole and the aid of a prisoner appears in a *livret* printed by Jean le Bourgeois between 1492 and 1498 for the *rouennais* bookseller Pierre Regnault. The cover of the *livret* showed Romanus and the prisoner, the latter holding the end of a stole wrapped like a leash around the neck of a fire-breathing, winged creature. A copy of this *livret*, "La Vie de S. Romain," was discoverd by Tougard bound into the back of the *Officium s. Gildardi Rotomagensis Archiepiscopi (1702) by J. Commirius; Tougard published a facscimile in Société des Bibliophiles Normands: Miscellanées* 4e série (1909). The bookseller Regnault also commissioned a "Norman Appendix" to Jacobo de Voragine's *Legenda Aurea* in 1507. In 1511, Richard Goupil printed a vernacular translation of the *Légende Dorée* for booksellers of Rouen (Richard Macé), Caen (Michel Angier) and Rennes (Jean Macé), and included translations of the saints in the "Norman Appendix"; in Romanus' case, instead of translating the 1507 *Legenda Aurea* text (BHL 7317), Goupil inserted the text from Jean le Bourgeois' *livret* (fols. 234-235). However, everything indicates that "everyone knew" that Romanus had tamed a dragon named the *Gargouille* for many centuries already.

[39]   P.-P. Joannou, *Demonologie populaire-demonologie critique* p. 12.

[40]   Alba Maria Orselli, "Santi e Città. Santi e demoni urbani tra tardoantico e alto medioevo" *Settimane* 36 (1988) pp. 788-791.

comes a "dragon" (as a number of saints did), conquers diabolic temptations to sin = evil = demons = "paganism" = "nature"; in other words, he or she conquers the former amphitheatre/brothel/"pagan" temple/demonic lair/sulphur pit/river. The "dragon," who spits fire and breathes smoke and slithers along river beds, is the neat semiotic device that permits a storyteller or visual artist to say all of these things at once, things which Fulbertus and the population of Rouen, who were not yet in the tenth century familiar with the device, had to express in long, lumbering narrations and multiple stories.

The earliest known use of the dragon device has been made famous by Le Goff: Fortunatus' sixth-century biography of Marcellus of Paris († c. 436).[41] In c. 10 of Fortunatus' biography, written a century after the saint's death, Marcellus tames a dragon which had terrorized the population around Paris by placing his episcopal stole on the nape of the dragon's neck, and leading it away from the city. As a visual symbol, the dragon seems first to have been used during Rogation processions at Vienne, under bishop Mamertus (†470), and to have spread from there during the pontificate of Avitus. During the three Rogation days, a "dragon" is paraded through the streets of a given town; on the first two days, the dragon's tail is arranged in an elevated position, but on the third day the tail is twisted downwards. What happened between the sixth century at Paris and Vienne and the twelfth century is a complete mystery. Yet by the twelfth century practically every major town in Gaul could boast a dragon-taming saint, and mounted Rogation Festivals with processional dragons.[42] There were two things very special, however, about the dragon at Rouen, the *Gargouille*, tamed by Romanus and paraded through the streets of the city.

The dragons slain and tamed by civilizing saints, the mock dragons

---

[41] Jacques Le Goff, "Culture ecclésiastique, culture folklorique au Moyen-Age: St. Marcel de Paris et le dragon" *Richerche storiche ed economiche in memoria di Corrado Barbagallo* II (Naples, 1970) pp. 53-90; English translation by A. Goldhammer in J. Le Goff, *Time, Work and Culture in the Middle Ages* (Chicago, 1980) pp. 159-188. Le Goff denies the polysemy of the symbol in its early centuries of use, and treats the later period as one of implacable hostility over two distinct, hermetically-sealed sets of meanings between the clergy and the folk; this interpretation is not borne out by the *rouennais* situation.

[42] A. Van Gennep *Manuel de folklore français contemporain* 3 (Paris, 1937) pp. 423-424; R. Devigne *Le Légendaire des provinces françaises à travers notre folklore* (Paris, 1950) p. 152.

paraded through the streets of Poitiers, Reims, Metz, Verdun, Douai, Tarascon, Nîmes, etc., seem to have stood in all these places for a bundle of motifs, for the triumph of the city over the countryside and the dangers of nature, for the triumph of the "true" religion, Christianity, over the soul-endangering religious forms of the *pagani*, the country-folk, for the triumph of virtuous living over sinful desires, and so on and so forth. Only in Rouen was the polysemy of the dragon so explicitly evoked in the name of the creature itself; all had names, but the *Gargouille* of Rouen was literally "the gargoyle," the grotesque spout which had begun to appear on buildings to carry rainwater clear of the walls. So Romanus' nemesis was not only the dragon carried by the water, but was the water-spout which carried the water too. The gargoyles of contemporary architecture possessed the same bundle of meanings as did the dragons;[43] to come full circle to Romanus' original bundle of problems, faced upon taking up the episcopal office at Rouen, those gargoyles were made to depict demons, sins, prostitutes...they were just another version of Fulbertus' former amphitheatre/brothel/"pagan" temple/demonic lair/sulphur pit/river.

It is also only in Rouen that the dragon also stood for the population of the town itself. At Rouen, semiotic lushness runs amok, and the "dragon," like so many autophagic serpents in the margins and historiated initials of manuscripts, turns back on itself. At least by the twelfth century, the "draco Normannicus" was a commonly-used metaphor for the "Normans," particularly as popularized in the poem of Etienne of Rouen, monk of Bec.[44] After all, had not the "Normans" been washed up, like a serpent/dragon, onto the shores of Rouen by the Seine river? Romanus of Rouen had tamed/destroyed the former amphitheatre/brothel/"pagan" temple/demonic lair/sulphur pit/river/Vikings. Every year over the three Rogation Days, at Romanus' massive festival, and, in later centuries also on Ascension Day when the so-called "privilege of St. Romanus" was exercised in commemoration of the saint's taming of the *Gargouille* and the feretory of

---

[43]   Michael Camille *Image on the Edge. The Margins of Medieval Art* (Cambridge, Mass; 1992) pp. 78-93.

[44]   Etienne of Rouen (†1149), *Le Dragon normand et autres poèmes* (Rouen, 1884); J.S.P. Tatlock, "Geoffrey and King Arthur in Normannicus Draco" *Modern Philology* 31 (1933-34); Le Goff, "St. Marcellus and the Dragon" p. 176.

St. Romanus paraded through the streets,[45] the people of Rouen celebrated how Romanus had conquered "all of the above," including the Norman conquerors.

Reporting current oral traditions holistically did not prevent Fulbertus from using the stories as a platform for his own ends, particularly by adding prophetic interpretations through which stories originally told about the salvation of Rouen from the Vikings became stories about the salvation of the Vikings at Rouen. He also emphasized the ever-present and continuing dangers of demon-infestation. Fulbertus was able, through the power of discourse, to transform the apparent meaning of the bundle of images from that of the salvation of Rouen to that of the salvation of the Vikings. The historian's discursive power was, by the middle of the tenth century, much greater than it had been for many centuries: the new structures of communication meant that the uses made by Fulbertus of oral traditions would not necessarily any longer have been known to or understood by the population as they celebrated the cult of Romanus. Both conquered Neustrians and Viking conquerors could celebrate Romanus, their savior, though each simultaneously was in fact celebrating a different side of the same event: salvation from the Vikings and salvation of the Vikings. The Latin/vernacular dichotomy gave free reign to cultic orchestrators.

The non-realistic narrative style of Fulbertus speaks volumes about the tenth century. His approach to the past and to historical narrative is one which clashes mightily with nineteenth- and twentieth-century scientistic conceptions; as a result, his synthetic masterpiece, embodying all the meanings of Romanus and of regional identity in the immediate aftermath of the Viking conquest of Neustria, as been either ridiculed or ignored. As early as the eleventh century, Fulbertus' discursive strategies would become impossible and incomprehensible. The middle of the tenth century was an extraordinary moment in the history of communication, and Fulbertus' biography of Romanus is a monument to that moment. The two separate spheres of oral and written cultures were beginning to coalesce, as written Latin and spoken Romance finally diverged to the point of being distinct languages. Yet this transformation would have taken place in the

---

[45]   Felice Lifshitz, "The 'Privilege of St. Romanus:' Provincial Independence and Hagiographical Legends at Rouen" AB 107 (1989) pp. 161-170.

course of Fulbertus' own lifetime, and his attitude towards oral traditions, learned and literate cleric though he be, could never reach the level of distaste which would characterize the learned clergy's orientation from the eleventh century.

The movement from memory to written record in the course of the eleventh century would devalue orality almost beyond the hope of rehabilitation. It has been argued that, by the early twelfth century, literate culture was independent of and segregated from oral culture;[46] such a thing is not, I think, ever possible, but it is possible for clerical anti-laicism to raise artificial discursive barriers between the two, and to assert the superiority of information supposedly gained "purely" from written sources. Fulbertus, on the other hand, respected oral traditions, so much so that he dared not trim Romanus' exploits *per se*, even if he did step in to impose a discourse on them *ex post facto*. From the eleventh century, historians became altogether less humble. The development of techniques of critical textual scholarship in the eleventh century led historians to approach the past as knife-wielding "correctors" of corrupt traditions, rather than as collectors of oral traditions.

*

*   *

The Romanus of *rouennais* oral tradition was a thoroughly militant figure. In effect, he was a regional version of the Archangel Michael. Michael himself would have been a very uncertain patron for a regional power. At any moment, the Archangel could have become universalizing or, worse yet, disconcertingly "French" or "Breton." But Romanus was a militant saint (and not one bit a thaumaturge) of the spirit of St. Michael, and he was of the Normans alone. Just as Michael, the paradigmatic militant saint, had been generated by the military struggles of the Carolingian Empire, struggles against Bretons, Vikings, and rebellious forces, so also was Romanus, the regional version of Michael's militancy, generated by a moment of acute military stress. This militant figure became both the popular and the official patron of Normandy. It is time to turn to Romanus' function as official patron of Viking-era dukes and archbishops.

---

[46] M. T. Clanchy and B. Stock *The Implications of Literacy* (Princeton, 1983).

C. DOCUMENTARY EVIDENCE AND POLITICAL EXIGENCIES:
ROMANUS AS OFFICIAL SAINT

So far, I have dealt only with Fulbertus' *vita Romani* itself, to the exclusion of other types of evidence concerning its composition. A complete copy of Fulbertus' *vita Romani* has been preserved in Evreux, BM 101, where it is accompanied by a collection of miracles of the saint; an incomplete copy (damaged due to fire and water) also exists in Paris, BN lat. 13.090.[47] The transcriptions in Appendix 2 below are based on these manuscripts. However, other codices also memorialize Romanus in one way or another, and it is to them that we must turn in order to understand the elaboration of Romanus' cult as the official patron of Viking Normandy.

a. Technicalia

The oldest extant manuscript copy of any text devoted to Romanus is contained in Paris, BN lat. 1805. The codex is an artificial collection containing various texts, all of which were copied during the tenth or eleventh centuries, and which were bound together during the seventeenth century by Jean Bigot. A total of eleven such artificial collections of texts entered the collection of the Bibliothèque Royale from Bigot's library, all of which contain some material which has been identified as having come from the Norman monastery of Fécamp.[48] Verbatim citations of the Romanus folios in BN lat. 1805 were made by François Farin in 1659; Farin referred to his source as a manuscript which he had consulted both in the collection of Bigot, and in the archives of the monastery of Fécamp.[49] The provenance of the oldest manuscript copy of a text related to Romanus is therefore the monastery of Fécamp, on the Channel coast of the diocese of Rouen.

The Romanus material in BN lat. 1805 is of two types. Folios 42-46

---

[47]   BHL *vacat*; see pp. 229-234 below for discussion of the manuscripts Evreux BM 101 and Paris BN lat. 13.090.

[48]   Gaston Lecroq, *Les manuscrits liturgiques de l'abbaye de Fécamp* (Extrait du *Bulletin de l'Association des Amis du Vieux-Fécamp*, 1934; Fécamp, 1935) p. 51; Betty Branch, "Inventories of the Library of Fécamp" *Manuscripta* 23 (1979) p. 172.

[49]   François Farin, *La Normandie Chrestienne, ou l'Histoire des Archevesques de Rouen* (Rouen, 1659) *passim* pp. 410-473.

form a gathering unto themselves: the gathering is a *libellus* containing nothing but the morning office for the festival of Romanus, that is, the office for the canonical hours beginning at the fourth vigil of the night (approximately 2:30 or 3:30 A.M.), which passed through three "nocturns" and culminated with "lauds" at sunrise (around 5:30 A.M.). The *libellus* includes the plainchant responses and psalmody for Romanus' office. Before the invention of breviaries in the twelfth century, the offices for saints' cults were contained in a series of individual notebooks such as this, notebooks which were frequently bound together at some later date to form passionaries and lectionaries. The office is divided into nine readings or *lectiones.* Therefore, it dates from before the Benedictine reform of the house by William of St. Benigne in 1001, for Benedictine houses divide their offices into twelve or eight readings. This same tenth-century *fécampois* version of Romanus' morning office remained the one in widest use throughout Normandy at least until the fifteenth century; many copies dating from the eleventh through the fifteenth century can be found in a number of later lectionaries and breviaries of both secular churches (where the nine-fold division of BN lat. 1805 was preserved) and of monastic houses (which adopted a rearranged twelve-fold division).[50] Thus, before

[50] Rouen BM 1383 (Y.80), from Jumièges (11th c.); Rouen BM 1404 (U.20), from Fécamp (12th c.) fols. 96v-97v; Rouen BM 209-210 (Y. 175), from Jumièges (12th c.) fols. 202v-203v; Rouen BM 1414 (A.53), from Jumièges (12th c.) fols. 113r-114r [for the attribution to Jumièges, see the end of the list of attestations]; Vat. reg. lat. 593 (12th c.), from St. Léger of Soissons fols. 148v- 151r; Rouen BM 207 (A.505), from Fontenelle (13th c.) fols. 400r-401r; Evreux BM 123 (13th c.), from Evreux fols. 246r-247r; Evreux BM 12 (14th c.), from Evreux fols. 443v-444v; Paris, BN nal. 388 (14th c.), from Evreux fols. 336r-337r; Rouen BM 195/196 (Y.95) from Rouen (14th c.) fols. 340r-341r; Paris, Ste. Gen. 2732 (14th c.), from Rouen fols. 229v-230v; Rouen BM 203 (A.572) from St. Catherine du Mont (14th c.), fols. 165r-166r; Rouen BM 198 (A.563) from Rouen (a.1474), fols. 482v-483v; Rouen BM 200-201 (Y.22) from Rouen (15th c.) fols. 270v-271v; Paris, BN lat. 1266A from Rouen (15th c.) fols. 279r-280r; Laon BM 255 from Bec (15th c.); Rouen BM 1415 (U.17) from Fécamp (15th c.) fols. 187v-190r. Rouen BM 1414 (A.53) must be ascribed to Jumièges on the basis of the sanctoral, the style of production of the manuscript, and the variants in the readings for Romanus' office. The most honored saints are Filibertus (founder of Jumièges), Aichardus (second abbot of Jumièges) and Benignus (patron of St. Benigne of Dijon, held in co-abbacy with Fécamp by abbots William and John throughout the early eleventh century, whose cult was introduced to Jumièges by abbot Theodericus, former monk of St. Benigne and prior of Fécamp), with twelve readings each,

the end of the tenth century there was an office to Romanus, complete with readings, in use at Fécamp.

Folios 30-41 of BN lat. 1805 are a separate *libellus*, devoted to St. Benignus, among other Burgundian saints. This *libellus* was produced at St. Benigne of Dijon, and brought to Fécamp by William's party when they came to reform the latter house.[51] On the blank back page of this *libellus* (fol. 41v), a different hand from that of the rest of the notebook has copied a letter of a certain Gerardus, "pater cenobitarum," addressed to archbishop Hugh (942-989) and the church of Rouen, informing them that he is sending to Rouen, at the prayer of the archbishop, both a verse and a prose biography of Romanus, although he is only giving the church of Rouen the original copy of the verse portion, substituting for the original copy of the prose portion (which he is keeping) an abridgement. The twinned biography had been given to him as a gift by his niece, a nun at a monastery of Notre Dame, who had purchased a copy through her agent, a clerk of Soissons, from a book-dealer who himself claimed to have "found" the manuscript (which had been "lost") in the *castrum* of Braine, a domain of the cathedral of Rouen.[52] The hand of this letter is somewhat later

followed by Bathild (who had granted the land for the foundation of Jumièges) with eight readings. The page lay-out and quire numbering systems match Rouen BM 1399, known to be a twelfth-century product of Jumièges. The text itself matches the copies in Rouen BM 1383 and Rouen BM 209/210, both from Jumièges. Another copy of Romanus' oldest and most popular office was also contained in a now-lost manuscript of Rouge-Cloître, from which it was copied into the Bollandist notebooks Brussels BR 11.987 (3234 vol. IV) fols. 81v-82v (16th c.) and BR 8919 (3485) fols. 49r-51r (17th c.) and then published by Van Hecke (AASS Oct. X pp. 91-94) [= BHL 7312].

[51] Bernard Prost, *Le trésor de l'abbaye St. Bénigne de Dijon* (Dijon, 1894) p. 319. We know from an eleventh-century letter of the prior of Fécamp to the prior of St. Bénigne that the two monasteries habitually exchanged manuscript books (Dom Lathenas, Paris, BN Collection de Bourgogne vol. XI f. 745rv).

[52] "Nouerit uolentiae uestrae sagacitas de uita sancti Romani patroni uestri, pro qua humillima memet exorastis prece, quoniam pactum quod pepigi uobiscum, nullo modo attendere quiui, ob aduersitatum uidelicet incommoditates qua undique presenti anno nostris in partibus perpessi sumus. Modo autem, dirigo uobis ueteranam uitam heroico editam carmine, ut omnino cunctis notum sit quod nulla inuentionum uobis dirigo mendacia. Illam, autem, que hystorialiter est stilo depicta, pro nimia uetustate penes nos retinens, hanc digestam stilo illius ad instar uobis transmitto....In Braina ergo, potestatis uestrae loco, eadem uita neglegentie causa

than that of the office on the following *libellus*, and is not the hand of someone educated in Normandy.[53] During the tenure either of William or of his nephew John, both simultaneously the reformed abbots of Fécamp and of St. Bénigne, the letter was copied onto the blank back page of the Burgundian *libellus* and bound together with the office of Romanus left over from the period of canonial occupation of Fécamp, and probably also with the next quire of BN lat 1805, which opens with the *passio* of Mary of Egypt.[54]

If we can determine the date at which Gerard sent his letter to arch-

---

fuit perdita....Quidem autem clericus Suessionis ciuitatis, ab inuentore mercatam, nostre contribuit nepte obtinendam in monasterio Dei genetricis Marie Deo sacrate, illaque post hec interiecto exigui temporis articulo eandem mihi muneris impertiuit gratia uitam" (BN lat. 1805 fol. 41v). For Braine's possession by the church of Rouen, see Flodoard, HER IV.23 p. 580 and Annals a. 931 p. 49, a. 933 pp. 54-55 and a. 950 p. 128.

53 François Avril, in private consultation. Folios 50v-61v of Paris BN lat. 11.624, a St. Bénigne manuscript of the eleventh century seems to have been copied by the very same scribe who was responsible for BN lat. 1805 fol. 41v.

54 At this time the Romanus *libellus* was cut down to match the size of the St. Bénigne *libellus*, and the original first folio of the Romanus *libellus* was lost, so that the antiennes and psalms of the first nocturn are missing, and some of the words on the outer edges of the page are now illegible, having been truncated. At least one copy of the *fécampois* readings was made before the trimming and binding of the folios, which served as an exemplar for the copy in an eleventh-century lectionary of Jumièges (Rouen BM 1383; see Nortier, *Bibliothèques*). That the readings in BN lat. 1805 were in fact an office, and that the Gerard letter and the text which followed it were not a unity, are both points which were disguised by the way the letter and the readings passed as a unity and without the plainchant portions of the office into the gemmetic tradition, probably during the abbacy of Theodericus, former monk of St. Bénigne and prior of Fécamp, who became the first reformed abbot of Jumièges in 1017, bringing the liturgical traditions of his former houses with him. The rubric introducing the letter on BN lat. 1805 fol. 41v reads "Incipit epistola in uita beati Romani episcopi," while the quite separate first reading of the office in the following *libellus* is headed "prologus siue prephatio." The Jumièges scribe introduced the letter with the rubric "Incipit prologus in uita sancti Romani archiepiscopi" and then, when faced with the actual prologue, headed that section with "Item prologus." Mabillon then published the texts from Rouen BM 1383 as a unity (*Vetera Analecta* (Paris, 1675) pp. 107-109) and that is how they have been treated ever since, as a single text (BHL 7312), namely a biography of Romanus rather than readings for his office, written by a certain Gerard, "of Soissons." The plainchant portions of the tenth-century *fécampois* office remain unpublished.

bishop Hugh of Rouen, that will provide a second chronological indicator, in addition to the existence, by the late tenth century, of the *fécampois* office readings. It will then remain to establish the relationship among the readings for Romanus' office which were in use at Fécamp in the late tenth century, the various biographies of Romanus referred to by Gerard in his letter (verse and prose *vitae* and an abridged version of the latter), and the biography composed by Fulbertus. Farin, who examined BN lat. 1805 not only when it was in Bigot's possession, but also when it was still in the possession of the church of Fécamp, suggested Gerard of Brogne as the author of the letter;[55] I have come, independently, to the identical conclusion.

The Gerard of the letter calls himself "pater cenobitarum" and is a sufficiently important personage to place his own title in the salutation before that of the archbishop of Rouen (for doing which he has scandalized scholars who have considered him a lowly and obscure dean)[56] and to insist that the archbishop command prayers to be said for him by the clergy of the church of Rouen, by the monks of St. Ouen of Rouen (before the eleventh century, governed by the archbishops), and by the clergy of all other places under the jurisdiction of the see of Rouen.[57] Gerard of Brogne was, depending on one's point of view, the lay abbot or restorer or reformer or the *Eigenklosterherr* of an extensive network of monasteries in the mid-tenth century in addition to his home base of Brogne.[58] Gerard of Brogne came from one of the most eminent families in Austrasia, that of Hagano, "Austrasiorum dux" and intimate counselor of Charles the Simple, and of Sancio, a powerful member of the entourage of king

---

[55]   Farin, *La Normandie Chrestienne* p. 463.

[56]   Jean Saas, *Notice des manuscrits de l'Eglise Metropolitaine de Rouen* (Rouen, 1746) p. 90.

[57]   "De cetero, humili efflagito quod cuncto illius loci fratrum contubernio pro me iubeatis ad Dominum preces fundere similiterque modo in monasterio sancti Audoeni fieri et in omnibus potestatis uestre locis iubete..." (Paris, BN lat. 1805 fol. 41v).

[58]   The *Historia monasterii Mosomensis* describes him as "a man of venerable life, who at that time due to the merit of his name and his religious behavior presided over many communities of monks in Francia" ("uir uitae uenerabilis, qui tunc temporis pro merito sui nominis et religione conuersationis pluribus in Francia preerat monachorum cenobiis") ed. W. Wattenbach, MGH SS 14 (Hannover, 1883) p. 610.

Robert.[59] Gerard of Brogne's alliance with the territorially-expansive Arnulf of Flanders brought him control of St. Ghislain (931), St.-Pierre-au-Mont-Blandin (941) and St. Bertin (945), but also allowed him in the 940s and 950s to extend his influence and his relic-collecting into Normandy, to St. Wandrille, Jumièges and Mont-St.-Michel.[60] The Gerard of the letter uses the word "milito" in the new and unusual sense of "to be in the service of God, the Church," a usage then current in Austrasia and among Carolingian officialdom.[61] Gerard of Brogne comes from precisely such a background. The Gerard of the letter requests that, in return for surrendering to the archbishop whose property Braine was, the texts which had been "lost" in Braine and bought by the former's niece, Hugh in return send Gerard some relics of Romanus.[62] Gerard of Brogne is known to have been an avid collector of relics, and a relic of Romanus, whose cult otherwise had minimal diffusion outside Normandy, was among those in the collection of the abbey of Brogne in the sixteenth century.[63] The Gerard of the letter had a niece who was a nun. Gerard of Brogne at least had a nephew who pursued an ecclesiastical carreer.[64] Gerard's letter in the Fécamp manuscript is followed by an episcopal catalogue of Rouen. This version of the list is identical to the episcopal catalogue of Rouen on fol. 52r of the codex St. Omer BM 764, a *libellus* concerning Wandregiselus, Ansbertus and Uulframnus of Fontenelle, which was produced in the

---

[59]   R. Wollasch, "Gerard von Brogne im Reformmönchtum seiner Zeit" in *Gérard de Brogne* pp. 224-225; *vita Gerardi* ed. L. de Heinemann, MGH SS 15.2 (Hannover, 1888) p. 656; P. Lauer, *Receuil des actes de Charles III le Simple* (Paris, 1949) p. 335; Richer I.16 and I. 21.

[60]   J. Laporte, "Gérard de Brogne à S. Wandrille et à S. Riquier," Albert d'Haenens "Gérard de Brogne à l'abbaye de S. Ghislain" and H. Platelle, "L'oeuvre de S. Gérard à S. Amand" in *Gérard de Brogne*.

[61]   *Novum Glossarium Mediae Latinitatis.*

[62]   "Preterea, flexa poplite oramus munificentie uestre modestiam, ut nobis re impendatis caritatis scilicet transmittendo nobis per gerulum nostrum ex eodem patrono uestro beatissimo Romano sacrorum pignorum munera utpote spopondistis, ut et nos eius condigne celebrare queamus memoriam" (Paris BN lat. 1805 fol. 41v).

[63]   Daniel Misonne, "Un écrit de S. Gérard de Brogne relatif à une relique de S. Landelin" AB 83 (1965) pp. 75-80; Daniel Misonne, "Gérard de Brogne et sa dévotion aux reliques" *Sacris Erudiri* 25 (1982) p. 26.

[64]   G. Gossiaux, "Le lieu de naissance et la famille de S. Gérard de Brogne" *Revue Diocésaine de Namur* 15 (1961) pp. 170-178.

tenth century at St. Bertin, where Gerard of Brogne became abbot in 945.[65]

The Gerard whose letter to archbishop Hugh of Rouen is preserved in connection with Romanus' tenth-century office must be Gerard of Brogne. Gerard of Brogne appeared on the scene in 919, and died in 959, and his correspondance with Hugh must date from between 942 (when Hugh arrived at Rouen) and 959. Gerard referred at the time to verse and prose versions of Romanus' biography and to an abridgement of the latter, and asserted that he was sending to Rouen the verse version and the new abridgement. Can texts answering this description be identified in the possession of the church of Rouen? Gerard's abridgement of the *vita Romani* and his copy of the metrical *vita Romani* were in the Rouen cathedral library as late as 1111-1128, when they were listed as free-standing *libelli* ("the *libri Gerardi*") in the library catalogue which is preserved in Rouen BM 1405, the Ivory Book of the Cathedral; however, by the end of the century they had either disappeared or been incorporated into larger lectionaries, as we have seen Romanus' Fécamp office had already been, for they are not listed in the cathedral library catalogue in Rouen BM 1193 (Y.44) fols. 52v-53v.

The verse version in question has been irrevocably lost;[66] however,

---

[65] More of the names are "sainted" in the Norman re-copying of the early eleventh century on fol. 41v of Paris BN lat. 1805 than in the Flemish tenth-century copy on fol. 52r of St. Omer BM 764, which is copied verbatim in Paris, BN lat. 5296B p. 188, a twelfth-century legendary of the Flemish house of Bergues-St.-Winnoc (Francois Dolbeau, "Anciens possesseurs des manuscrits hagiographiques Latins conservés à la Bibliothèque Nationale de Paris *Revue d'Histoire des Textes* 9 [1979]); otherwise this Flemish tradition of the *rouennais* episcopal catalogue diverges widely from all other extant copies of the list. For St. Omer BM 764, F. Wormald, "Some Illustrated Manuscripts of the Lives of the Saints" *Bulletin of the John Rylands Library* 35 no. 1 (1952) pp. 250-262, esp. p. 256; J. Laporte, "Gérard de Brogne à S. Wandrille et à S. Riquier," *Gérard de Brogne*.

[66] The verse biography of Romanus in the St. Ouen codex Rouen BM 1406 (Y.41) fols. 51r-61v (= BHL 7310, in PL 138 coll. 173-184) is not the metrical biography sent by Gerard to Rouen. Rather, it was written at St. Ouen sometime after the Benedictine reform of the house in the early eleventh century; for discussion of the verse *vita*, see below pp. 204-205. It is impossible even to speculate about the lost verse biography; there is no guarantee that it was written by Fulbertus himself. Twinned works were quite popular in the Carolingian world; however, the two halves were not necessarily always composed by the same person (Gernot

a copy of Gerard's prose abridgement has been preserved in a cathedral manuscript, namely Rouen BM 1405 (Y.27) pp. 62-85 (= BHL 7313a).[67] This text has been available in print since 1609, when it was published by Nicolas Rigault (BHL 7313a/b). This particular abridgement was used for the readings for Romanus' morning office at the cathedral of Rouen

---

Wieland "Geminus Stilus: Studies in Anglo-Latin Hagiography" *Insular Latin Studies: Papers on Latin Texts and Manuscripts of the British Isles, 550-1066* (Papers in Mediaeval Studies 1; Toronto, 1981) ed. Michael W. Herren pp. 113-133.

[67] It is not possible that the longer Fulbertine text is the work of an interpolator, and that BHL 7312a is the original version of the biography. From a literary point of view, the longer text (including the preface) forms an integrated whole, marked by consistent language and themes. The abridged version, on the other hand, contains a number of confusions and redundancies as a result of the excised passages: the omission of the description of the *fanum* from BHL 7313a/b results in the loss of the hole from which the noisome stench then emanates (*Vita Romani* fol. 119r); the omission of the angelic messenger to the citizens of Rouen from the account of Romanus' election renders mysterious the later speech of the civic delegation to the king (*vita Romani* fol. 117r-117v); the substitution of a generic statement of redoubled enthusiasm for prayer and almsgiving instead of Felicitas' angelic visitation suddenly stands, redundantly, cheek by jowl with another generic statement that Felicitas and Benedictus threw themselves into prayer and almsgiving (*vita Romani* fol. 116r); the replacement of the extensive description of Romanus' entry to Rouen by the generic statement that the populace came and complained to the new bishop suddenly places the latter statement cheek-by-jowl with the repeated assertion that the populace came and complained to the new bishop (*vita Romani* fols. 119r-119v). The reworking of the opening section is utterly chaotic: the placement of Remigius's baptism of the Franks at the head of the narrative rather than after Clovis' battlefield conversion renders the later introduction of the Christian Clothild and the pagan Clovis both chronologically confusing and meaningless in terms of plot; the omission of Clothild's missionary efforts and Clovis' battlefield experience renders the appearance of the Christian Clothild and the pagan Clovis completely meaningless; the omission of the battlefield passage causes the sentence introducing Clothar to refer not to Clovis but to Clothid, "huic successit in regnum"; the omission of the long battlefield passage causes two references to Benedictus to appear in consecutive sentences, the second time accompanied by the now entirely unnecessary comment, "cuius mentionem paulo ante prelibauimus" (*vita Romani* fols. 114v-115r). The abridgement also destroys Fulbertus' more expansive literary conceits, such as his elaborate parallel between Romanus' entry into Rouen and Jesus' entry into Jerusalem (*vita Romani* fols. 118v-119r). No interpolator bothers to add lines such as that Fulbertus walked from his cell to the church to begin the mass, whereas this is precisely the sort of non-essential detail that an abbreviator omits.

during the eleventh century; the text itself gives the nine *lectiones*, and is followed by (rather than interspersed with, as in the tenth-century *fécampois* copy) the plainchant portion of the office (pp. 86-92).[68] Both in the readings and in the musical portions, the *rouennais* office differs from the earlier *fécampois* office in a number of ways.[69] The principal difference, as far as the text of the readings is concerned, is that the *fécampois* office (BHL 7312) is much shorter than the *rouennais* office (BHL 7313a). It is probably for that reason that the *fécampois* office was more widely used than the *rouennais* office (with the former eventually supplanting the latter even at Rouen); copies of the *rouennais* readings survive in only a few manuscripts[70] compared with the many copies of the *fécampois* readings listed above. At the same time, there are tremendous verbal and substantive similarities between the two sets of *lectiones*, and BHL 7312 is in fact an extract from BHL 7313a.

All of these relations, and the series of abridgements made from Fulbertus' long biography of Romanus for liturgical purposes, can be followed in detail in the appendix below, in which I print a transcription of Fulbertus' *Vita Romani* along with, *via* the apparatus, transcriptions both of Gerard's abridgement of Fulbertus' *vita Romani* (BHL 7313a, used for the *rouennais* readings as attested in Rouen BM 1405 [(Y.27)], and of some anonymous canon of Fécamp's abridgement of Gerard's abridgement (BHL 7312, used for the *fécampois* readings as attested in Paris BN lat. 1805). Because BHL 7312 (ultimately abridged from Fulbertus' *vita Romani*) was in existence by the end of the tenth century when canons were installed at Fécamp, and because BHL 7313a (an unmediated abridgement from Fulbertus' *vita Romani*) was produced and sent to Rouen by Gerard of Brogne between 942, when Hugh became archbishop of Rouen, and 959, when

---

[68]   The St. Ouen readings were also based on Gerard's abridgement, since Romanus' cult would have been introduced there when the cathedral still controlled the abbey; see the copy in Rouen BM 1406 (Y.41) fols. 36r-46v (= BHL 7313b).

[69]   The Rouen office is published and analyzed by Dom Pothier, "Note sur la musique sacrée en Normandie au onzième siècle" *Mémoires sur la Musique Sacrée en Normandie* (Vienne, 1896).

[70]   Paris, BN lat. 5290, Paris, Ste. Gen. 556, Rouen 1399, Rouen 1405 and Rouen 1406. All of the variants of all of these readings, and an attempt to reconstruct the transmission of this *rouennais* office, can be found by the interested reader in F. Lifshitz, "The Dossier of Romanus of Rouen: The Political Uses of Hagiographical Texts" (Ph.D. Dissertation, Columbia, 1988) pp. 160-232.

Gerard died, Fulbertus' biography of Romanus must have been written long enough before 959 for a copy to have been brought to the archiepiscopal domain at Braine, "lost" there (as the Soissons-connection book-dealer perhaps truthfully claimed), sold to Gerard's niece, sent to Gerard as a present and reworked by him or by someone in his employ.

In Gerard's abridgement, Fulbertus' introductory historical background is reworked so as to diminish the role of the Frankish kings and queens in sacred history. Fulbertus' original biography describes at length the Christian conversion of Clovis from the urgings of Clothild to its achievement on the battlefield, thus ascribing his conversion and that of the Franks to direct divine intervention. Clovis then proceeds to archbishop Remigius of Reims in order to be baptised.[71] In Gerard's abridgement, Clovis is converted by the teachings of Remigius, while the stories of Clothild's efforts and the battlefield triumph are entirely omitted. Not only is Fulbertus' rather glorious account of the conversion of the Franks omitted, but the passage which puts Frankish valor and military might on the level of those of the Roman Empire is also cut.[72] Other examples of the systematic expunging of the central theme of the royal majesty from the Fulbertine narrative are the suppression of Romanus' own royal lineage,[73] the excision of the passages in which the king invests Romanus with the office of archbishop,[74] and the removal of even off-handed remarks such as that the king, more than anyone, marvelled at the young Romanus' erudition,[75] or at his prudence.[76] Sometimes the reworking required addition rather than deletion, such as when Gerard's abridgement adds the citation "Quanto magnus es, humilia te in omnibus" (Ecclesiasticus 3:18) to the Petrine injunction to be subject particularly to the king, an addition which dilutes the concentration on royal authority.[77] The strong prophetic content of Fulbertus' vita Romani, which had served to situate the Normans as well as the Franks within a larger framework of

---

[71]   *Vita Romani* fols. 114v-115r.

[72]   *Vita Romani* fol. 114v.

[73]   *Vita Romani* fol. 114v.

[74]   *Vita Romani* fols. 118r-118v.

[75]   *Vita Romani* fol. 116v.

[76]   *Vita Romani* fol. 116v.

[77]   *Vita Romani* fol. 116v.

glorious sacred history, is cut as well.[78]

A certain lack of enthusiasm for Frankish royalty and for the idea of the Normans as a chosen people are absolutely understandable given Gerard's own political alliances. In Flanders he depended upon Arnulf who, with other magnates such as Herbert of Vermandois and Hugh the Great, was a constant thorn in the sides of Carolingian kings, princes and legitimists. In Lorraine, Gerard depended on the German Emperor Otto I, who also periodically schemed to remove king Louis of Francia. Other reasons besides anti-Frankish royalism may account for some of Gerard's excisions. For instance, his adherence to the values of the tenth-century Lotharingian and Cluniac reform movements, according to which the Carolingian emphasis on the high birth of saints (rather than on their spiritual nobility) was misplaced.[79] Furthermore, according to the reformers, a holy person was supposed to be useful in the world, and the biographies of saints written in connection with the movement did not include the "*topos*" of canonical resistance.[80] Accordingly, Romanus' concerted resistance to the idea of promotion to the see of Rouen, overcome in Fulbertus' biography only by a direct royal command, which cannot be disobeyed, was probably cut from Gerard's abridgement on the dual basis of anti-royalism and reformist values.[81]

An appreciation of how much royalist material could be removed from Fulbertus' *vita Romani*, brings with it a recognition of how much royalist material was in fact in Fulbertus' *vita Romani* in the first place. However, by the time Romanus' public cult was established at the ducal capitals of Rouen and Fécamp, the readings in use were those drawn from Gerard's non-royalist abridgement. Royalism was not a very long-lasting

[78] For some prophetic excisions, *vita Romani* fols. 115v, 116r, 117r, 118v-119r. Other changes such as the elimination of Fulbertus' indictments of ambitious prelates (two such passages are cut from *Vita Romani* fols. 116v-117r and fol. 117v), or the glossing over of Romanus' eremetical tendencies (*Vita Romani* fols. 27v, 116v and 118v) may also be significant for our appreciation of Gerard of Brogne's moral scheme, but are less important for highlighting Fulbertus' main themes.

[79] Lotter, "Methodisches zur Gewinnung" p. 325.

[80] Bruno of Cologne [Ruotger *vita Brunonis Coloniensis* MGH SRG n.s. 10 (Weimar, 1951) ed. Irene Ott = BHL 1468]; Adalbert of Prague and Bernward of Hildesheim do not reject their episcopal promotions but eagerly take on the burden (Lotter "Methodisches zur Gewinnung" p. 327).

[81] *Vita Romani* fols. 117v-118v.

phenomenon at Rouen, but it did mark the original biography of St. Romanus, and the original commission of that biography. Fulbertus' *vita Romani* was therefore written at a time when an extremely pro-royalist stance would have been required in the biography of the patron of the see of Rouen.[82]

The second series of major changes which Gerard made to Fulbertus' biography of Romanus concerns demonic and angelic action. Fulbertus' demonophobia in particular is stripped from the abridgement. For instance, the miracle of the broken chrism jar is edited so that the accident becomes a mere accident, the result of a priest's carelessness, rather than of the deliberate manoeuverings of a devil intent on snatching the *populus Dei* from the arms of salvation.[83] To pull off such a cosmological transformation required careful editing, although some changes were fairly simple; some angelic apparitions, for instance, could just be cut wholesale.[84] The interested reader can work through the transcriptions below for more details; but angelic and demonic agency is so completely stripped in the abridgement that one is left wondering whether Gerard believed in such things. One might at first think that, here too, Gerard is merely reflecting

---

[82] Fulbertus' type of royalism, as witnessed particularly by the royal investiture scene, is conservative, tenth-century Carolingian royalism, and is unlike the eleventh-century Capetian royalism represented by authors such as Helgaud of Fleury (*Vie de Robert le Pieux. Epitoma vitae regis Rotberti pii*; ed. and trans. R.-H. Bautier and G. Labory, Paris, 1965). Fulbertus' Carolingian brand of royalism assigned a major role to the secular prince in the life of the churches, a role born of considerations of efficiency and of Roman-inspired traditions; Helgaud's sacralizing Capetian-era royalism saw the rulers as pious *reges Dei gratia*, complete with thaumaturgical powers (c. 1 pp. 56-58; c. 6; c. 7; c. 17 pp. 94-96; c. 21; c. 27; c. 29). Nancy Gauthier is correct that Fulbertus' brand of royalism is not incompatible with the eleventh-century era of reform as it was carried out in Normandy, where the dukes kept strict control of the church and of the process ("Quelques hypothèses sur la redaction des vies des saints éveques de Normandie" p. 464); however, there is too much codicological and textual evidence pointing to the tenth century to assign the original composition of Fulbertus' biography to the era of the Gregorian reform. Perhaps, however, we might assign the interest in copying such a long text as Fulbertus' biography of Romanus circa 1090 (the copy now preserved in the lectionary of Evreux, Evreux BM 101), a text which would otherwise have been lost, to the Norman stage of the Gregorian reform.

[83] *Vita Romani* fol. 26r-27r.

[84] *Vita Romani* fols. 116r and 117r.

the values of the Lotharingian and Cluniac reformers, who wished to emphasize virtuous living not miraculous power as the mark of holiness, a holiness which was to be demonstrated through descriptions of "realistic" and mundane activities.[85] Yet Gerard does not suppress the miracles of Romanus, he merely drains their demonological content. The point here, then, is that Fulbertus wrote at a time when *rouennais* authors were acutely conscious of the presence around them of demons; at least, he wrote at a time when that was a plausible theme in *rouennais* historiography, for Romanus was shaped specifically as a battler of demons. When, in pre-959 Rouen, would such a figure have been required?

b. Context

The tenth century in Francia was a time when *principes* dominated the landscape.[86] The European Empire of Charles the Great and his son Louis the Pious was no more than a memory (though one cherished dearly in certain circles), and even the power of the West Frankish kings which had emerged from the 843 division at Verdun was looking increasingly fictional, particularly in southerly regions such as Aquitaine and

---

[85] Lotter, "Methodisches zur Gewinnung" p. 319. For instance, Odo of Cluny's biography of Gerald of Aurillac frequently polemicizes on this point, arguing that Gerald can be considered a saint even though he performed no miracles (Odo, *Vita Geraldi comitis Aurillacensis* from *Bibliotheca Cluniacensi* ed. D. Manier/Marrier repr. PL 133 coll. 639-703, esp. pref. col. 641-2 and pref. book II. coll 667-670). Odo writes: "Qui signa quidem quae vulgus magni pendet, non multa retulerunt, sed disciplinatum vivendi modum, et opera misericordiae quae Deo magis placent, non pauca" (col. 642).

[86] Olivier Guillot, "Formes, fondements et limites de l'organisation politique en France au Xe siècle" *Settimane* 38 (1990) pp. 57-116. There is little agreement over the meaning of *principes*. Some have equated it with quasi-royal levels of power, others have considered it a bland qualification with no technical content. The problem seems to me to lie in the desire to limit the word to a single meaning; in the writings of Dudo of St. Quentin, for instance, the word has a wide range of meanings and connotations, depending on the context. Horst Zettel, *Das Bild der Normannen und der Normanneneinfälle im westfränkischen, ostfränkische und angelsächsischen Quellen* (Munich, 1977) pp. 84-90 and p. 220 discusses the multiple meanings of *princeps* in the period. For summaries of specialized regional and royal-level researches relevant to the present chapter, see Jean Dunbabin *France in the Making (843-1180)* (Oxford, 1985) esp. pp. 1-16, 27-43, 58-63, 68-74 and 95-97; for the use of titles such as *princeps*, see pp. 44-49.

Burgundy. Aquitaine and Burgundy were instead ever more controlled by their dukes, while Neustria fell apart, slipping even beyond the possibility of Robertian control on the Aquitanian and Burgundian models. The kings who sought to rule in Neustria never really overshadowed the leaders of smaller Neustrian units of power, and at times royal power seemed about to go under entirely, particularly in the crises of the 920s, the late 930s-early 940s, and the 960s-980s. Fulbertus' Carolingian-style royalism would logically have surfaced during one of these critical periods for a dynasty in its death-throes; because the third period of crisis is too late to allow for Gerard of Brogne's involvement in the elaboration of a cult to Romanus, only the 920s and the late 930s/early 940s remain as plausible times for a Frankish author to display major concern over Carolingian-style royal authority.

Most of the non-royal *principes* "officially" held the title of "count," which theoretically made them local representatives of royal power. It was as count of Rouen that the Seine Viking Rollo had first been recognized as part of the landscape of the late Carolingian world and endowed, for the benefit of his office, with tracts of fiscal land in Neustria. Some powerful magnates received elevated titles such as "dux" or "marchio" from the Carolingian and other kings, but for the most part the *principes* gradually adopted those titles themselves without waiting for recognition from the royal chancery. The most independence-minded and most powerful princely figures in Francia during Rollo's reign were Arnulf I of Flanders (918-965), Herbert II of Vermandois (†943) and Hugh the Great of Paris (†956). All had been known to forget the royal superior altogether, and both Arnulf and Herbert could claim Carolingian blood themselves, being descendants of Charles the Bald and of Pippin of Italy respectively. Rollo, however, never chose to follow the example of those powerful contemporaries. Aside from the occasional raid on Frankish territory along traditional "Viking" lines,[87] he and his followers kept themselves aloof from Frankish political conflicts and nursed few grandiose ambitions of their own. Rollo can hardly have felt completely comfortable as count of Rouen, and he and his closest followers may well have even had language problems which prevented them from meddling in Frankish affairs. Robert the Strong failed to pull the count of Rouen into the conflicts of the 920s, and the first great

---

[87] Flodoard a. 924 p. 19 and a. 925 pp. 29-30.

crisis of tenth-century royalty came and went without leaving a mark in the future Normandy.[88] The 920s, then, are unlikely to have served as a background or spur to royalist historiography at Rouen.

The *rouennais* policy of isolationism disappeared completely under Rollo's son and successor, William Longsword. In 925, while Rollo was away from his county raiding in Picardy and Artois, both the Franks and the Bretons had been raiding in Normandy; the count of Rouen had to rush back home to protect his territories.[89] Evidently, the other local *principes* of northern Francia were no longer cowed by the formerly formidable Seine-valley Viking. Soon, the younger and more vigorous William would be given the reigns of power by his father. By 927, the differences between Rollo and his son and successor, William, would become palpable to all concerned. In that year, the character of Seine Viking involvement with the Frankish world changed markedly. First, William "committed himself" to Charles the Simple as the sign of his accession to his father's comital office, Rollo having retired; William immediately also established a "friendship" with Herbert of Vermandois.[90] The next year, at a conference at Laon, a son of Herbert whom Rollo had been holding as a hostage (Rollo having had yet to request anything other than cash from those he fought), was returned to his father by William on the condition that Herbert too "commit himself" to Charles.[91] William had turned his father's raiding practices to the advantage of his own "foreign policy." In 940, William married his sister Gerloc to William of Poitou, reaching out and making alliances even into Aquitaine. William actively opened Normandy to increased connections with Poitou, welcoming monks and the new abbot Martin from St. Cyprien of Poitiers, sent by Gerloc to Jumièges.[92] It was

---

[88] Neither Flodoard nor Richer picture Rollo as having been involved in the conflicts; Dudo explicitly asserts that he was not (*De moribus* p. 173). As Lair convincingly reconstructs the scenario from Flodoard and Richer, Rollo and his followers did fight back when invaded (for instance by Robert's sons) but were not involved in the general intrigues, unlike the Vikings of the Loire-Nantais, who were (J. Lair, *Etude sur la vie et la mort de Guillaume*).

[89] Flodoard a. 925 pp. 30-31.

[90] Flodoard, a. 927 p. 39; Richer p. 104.

[91] Flodoard a. 928 p. 41.

[92] "Lament" verses V-VI. The *planctus* survives only fragmentarily in two manuscripts (Clermont-Ferrand BM 189 (240) fol. 45r of the tenth century, and Florence, Biblioteca Laurenziana 83 fol. 21v-22v, of the eleventh century. The two

probably in Martin's party that Fulbertus came to Normandy.

Not a single one of Rollo's followers could have failed to notice that the world was changing around them, and not necessarily for the better. William had been born and raised within the former Frankish Empire, and never seems for a moment to have felt himself an outsider among the other magnates of his day. William did not even have to "assimilate"; he was born and raised as a Christian, clearly was committed enough to the role of the Christian prince to build a church at Fécamp adjacent to the ducal residence, to endow Jumièges with great generosity,[93] and was believed by the end of the century to have himself intended to retire to a monastery.[94] William was, in short, a Frank, whose mother had been the daughter of the Carolingian count of Bayeux. William's father, on the other hand, and by definition his father's *fideles* as well, seem to have lived openly as "not-Christians." Correspondance between archbishop Heriveus of Reims (†922) and archbishop Wito of Rouen († before 941) indicates that the latter was feeling distressed by persons who were being repeatedly baptised, yet continued to act "more paganico."[95] Ademar of Chabannes reported that, although Rollo had become a Christian and had been very generous to the church, the new count of Rouen had also continued to sacrifice to "pagan" deities.[96] This, however, is how Ademar described the transition from Rollo to William:

Then, after the death of Rollo, his son William, baptized from child-

---

copies are difficult to make sense of, and do not always agree with each other. There are facsimiles of both manuscripts in Jules Lair, *Etude sur la vie et la mort de Guillaume Longue-Epée* (Paris, 1893) and attempts at a composite edition in Lair, *Etude sur la vie* pp. 66-68 and in P.A. Becker, "Der Planctus auf den Normannenherzog Wilhelm Langschwert (942)" *Zeitschrift für französische Sprache und Literatur* 43 (1939) pp. 193-195. Also see Dudo *De moribus* p. 200; Bernard Le Blond, *L'accession des Normands de Neustrie à la culture occidentale (Xème- XIème siècles)* (Paris, 1966) pp. 19-20.

93   "Lament" verses V-VI.

94   Dudo, *De moribus* pp. 179-180.

95   Paris, BN lat. 4280A fols. 102r-106v, a contemporary manuscript from Reims, with copies in Vat. reg. lat. 418 fol. 75rv, another tenth-century *rémois* manuscript; O. Guillot, "La conversion des Normands"; Jacques Hourlier, "Reims et les Normands" pp. 101-111; PL 132 col. 662-672.

96   Ademar of Chabannes, Chronicon III.20 ed. J. Chavanon (Paris, 1897) p. 139 and MGH SS IV ed. Pertz p. 123.

hood, ruled in his place, and the entire multitude of those Normans, who lived near Francia, took up the Christian faith and, putting aside the gentile tongue, began to use the Latin language.[97]

More and more after 927, it had become clear to Rollo's *fideles* that their new lord, William, would demand of them tokens of loyalty to Franco-Latin culture which they did not wish to provide, all the while involving them more and more in Frankish politics, where they did not wish to be. From 929 to 933, the usurper king Radulfus who, supported by Hugh the Great, held the royal title in Neustria, was locked in conflict with Herbert of Vermandois, an aspirant to the throne, himself supported by the Saxon king Henry I. In 928 William had tried to force Herbert to submit to Charles the Simple, whose son and "legitimate" successor Louis IV was now in exile across the English Channel. Charles and Louis were not at that moment full players, and one imagines that William fell back on his alliance of friendship with the Carolingian Herbert when the usurper, Radulfus, grabbed the throne. Then suddenly, in 933, William changed sides, and promised his loyalty to Radulfus, in return for a grant of Brittany, the Cotentin and the Avranchin.[98] His aged father had just recently died, and William apparently found the event liberating, as though it freed him from any prior restraint concerning Carolingian loyalism which might have resulted from land grants or confirmations by Charles the Fat[99] or Charles the Simple. William could now manoeuvre freely, like any other Frankish *princeps*. Finally, 933 also saw the birth of William's son and heir, Richard, whom William immediately had baptized.[100]

Unfortunately for William, the death of Rollo had liberated the old

---

[97] "Tunc, Roso defuncto, filius eius Willelmus loco eius praefuit, a puericia baptizatus, omnisque eorum Normannorum, qui iuxta Frantiam inhabitaverant, multitudo fidem Christi suscepit, et gentilem linguam obmittens, Latino sermone assuefacta est" (Ademar, *Chronicon* MGH SS IV p. 127).

[98] Flodoard a. 933 p. 55. The large number of coins of Radulfus in the Fécamp coin hoard (as against a single *denarius* of Charles the Simple) indicates that William received more than Brittany from the usurper king (Françoise Dumas-Dubourg, *Le Trésor de Fécamp et le monnayage en Francie occidentale pendant la second moitié du Xe siècle* (Paris, 1971) p. 10).

[99] For the possibility that the original grant to Rollo had been made by Charles the Fat, see Lifshitz "La Normandie Carolingienne."

[100] Dudo, *De moribus* p. 219.

Viking's *fideles* just as much as it liberated his son. The former had stood by as William made his new Robertian alliance, and noted the arrival of his "Christian" heir. And then, in 934, they rebelled; they rebelled both because of William's Frankish involvements, and because of the alarmingly "Christian" character of his regime. The earliest account of the rebellion was composed within a decade of the event by a monk of Jumièges:

> He was born into the world of a father from overseas, still persisting in the error of the pagans, and of a mother who was sealed with the nourishing faith, so he was washed by the sacred water. All lament for William.

> When his father died, faithless ones (*infideles*) rose up in arms against him, and he subjugated them to himself with a strong right hand, mightily strengthened by God. All lament for William.[101]

The *infideles* were surely unfaithful in two senses, both by being treacherous against their lord, and by being "not-Christians," "infidels." The second account of the rebellion, written at the end of the century, is that by Dudo of St. Quentin:

> However, a certain Riulfus, cruelly filled with the vileness of treachery, seeing that his lord, namely duke William, was so very much strengthened and was growing stronger through the assistance of his friends, having called together very many of the Norman leaders, told them in a deceitful voice: 'Deprived of our counsel, and goaded by animosity for our reduced condition, our lord William, sired from the most noble stock of the Frankish race, is acquiring Frankish friends for himself. Truly, he is trying to drive us entirely out of the realm, and to weight down harshly the necks of those who remain under the yoke of servitude.'[102]

---

[101] "Hic in orbe transmarino natus patre in errore paganorum permanente, matre quoque consignata alma fide, sacra fuit lotus unda. Cuncti flete pro Willelmo. Moriente infideles suo patre surrexerunt contra eum belloquose, quos confisus Deo ualde sibi ipse subjugauit dextra forte. Cuncti flete pro Willelmo." For the "Lament," see above note 92.

[102] "Uidens autem quidam Riulfus, perfidiae nequitia atrociter repletus, UUillelmum ducem, scilicet dominum suum, amicorum praesidio confortari ualde et conualescere, conuocatis plurimis principum Northmannorum, fraudulenta retulit uoce: 'Noster senior UUillelmus, nobilissimo Franciscae stirpis semine genitus, Francigenas amicos acquirit sibi, nostro consilio priuatus, nostraeque afflictionis

Dudo does not describe the revolt itself as religiously motivated, preferring to concentrate on its more broadly cultural anti-Frankish character. But he hints at the importance of "religious" factors in the way he describes the immediate aftermath of the revolt:

> In him [William] there shone sanctity and discretion, especially there gleamed incessantly fairness and justice. With harshness he overpowered the proud and malevolent, with reverence he exalted the humble and the benevolent. By word and deed he brought pagans and unbelievers to the worship of the true faith, while urging believers to praise Christ.[103]

So the first attempt to prevent the complete assimilation of the Vikings into Francia, and the loss of their culture, was a military failure. William continued to act every bit the part of the Frank which he felt himself to be, marrying Herbert of Vermandois' daughter, allying with the counts of Poitou, and so forth. Like the other *principes*, William at first accepted the Carolingian restoration of Louis IV (936), but he waited no longer than they did to become fed up with Louis. In 939 we see him matter-of-factly swearing fidelity instead to king Otto of Germany, in the company of Hugh, Herbert and Arnulf, and then beseiging Louis' stronghold at Laon the next year, again a full member of the quartet of anti-royal Frankish magnates.[104] Just before 940, he began to act in complete independence of the west Frankish monarchy, minting coins in his own name, coins which were designed as a brand new type, owing nothing to contemporary royal coinage.[105] He was now the *fidelis* of the king of the Saxons,

---

animositate inuestigatus [*recte* "instigatus" in all the mss., esp. Rouen BM 1173 (Y.11) f. 21v and Berlin Philipps 1854 fol. 37v]. Nos uero conatur regno penitus extrudere, remanentiumque colla iugo seruitutis duriter opprimere" (Dudo, *De moribus* p. 187).

[103] "Refulgebat in eo sanctitas et prudentia, praenitebat incessanter aequitas et justitia. Opprimebat superbos et maleuolos seueriter, exaltabat humiles et beneuolos reuerenter. Paganos et incredulos muneribus et uerbis adducebat ad cultum uerae fidei, credentes urgebat ad laudem Christi" (Dudo, *De moribus* p. 193).

[104] Dudo, *De moribus* pp. 192-193; Flodoard a. 939 p. 73 and a. 940 pp. 76-77.

[105] Dumas-Dubourg, *Trésor de Fécamp* pp. 23-24 and p. 50; J. Renaud, *Les Vikings et la Normandie* (Ouest-France, 1989), plate between pp. 64-65, a gold *denarius* of William from the Musée des Antiquités de Rouen.

So we have arrived at the late 930s/early 940s, the next period of major crisis for royalists and for the royal office in Francia. Louis IV was being deserted, nay rather attacked, *en masse*, and the Frankish *principes* were playing their own series of games, independent of any checks from royal authority. It was one of those horizontal intrigues which would prove to be the beginning of William's undoing. His own ambitions were immense, and within "Normandy" he had found success, though not without encountering opposition. To the east, however, lay the lands of another equally ambitious *princeps*, Arnulf of Flanders. Arnulf had himself, through exploiting local rivalries and sporadic competitions for the royal throne, pressed outward to Artois, Ponthieu, Amiens and Ostrevant. The clash between William and Arnulf arose initially over the relatively minor matter of control of Herluinus, the castellan of Montreuil,[106] but it ended in William's death when the Norman duke overstepped the limits of his own abilities for pulling off sophisticated political machinations.

In 939, William had made an enemy of Arnulf of Flanders over the issue of Montreuil. He would have been smarter thereafter to try for a while to appease the wrath of his former ally in the anti-Louis quartet of *principes*; instead, William reversed his policy, overthrew his alliances, and suddenly became, from 940 to 942, the sole supporter of Louis IV in Francia.[107] William became the godfather of Louis' son Lothar, effectively assuming a portion of the responsibility for the boy's future as king of Francia.[108] In 933, William's sudden reversal of policy had provoked a rebellion in Normandy, one which he had managed to put down. This time, his abandonment of the plans of the princely quartet drew Arnulf's wrath down upon him. William had made new allies, persuading Alan of Brittany and William of Poitou to join the royalist cause in 942, and he must have imagined the solidarity of this new troika could overcome the *principes* whom he had betrayed, especially with the help of Louis' royal authority. He was mistaken, and in 942 was assassinated by henchmen of Arnulf.

The situation of crisis for royal authority went suddenly from bad to worse, as Louis was shorn of his supporter, William. But the crisis for

---

[106] Dudo, *De moribus* pp. 203-205; Richer cc. 13-13 p. 148; Flodoard a. 939 p. 72.
[107] "Lament" verse IV; Flodoard a. 940 p. 75, a. 941 p. 82 and a. 942 p. 84; Richer c. 20 p. 156, c. 28 p. 168 and cc. 30-32 pp. 170-180; Dudo *De moribus* pp. 193-200.
[108] Dudo, *De moribus* p. 199; but cf. Flodoard a. 941 pp. 82-83.

royal power was nothing compared with the crisis for *rouennais* ducal power. It is a miracle that Richard I, William's ten-year-old son, ever came into his inheritance. The assassination unleashed every possible reactionary force in Normandy. All the resentments of 933 were still active, and were exacerbated by those created by William's suppression of the rebellion, and by his redoubled efforts along Frankicising and Christianizing lines. Richard had been raised at Bayeux, a stronghold of the "pagan" traditionalists, as part of William's deliberate policy to acquaint his son with the culture of those who would be his *fideles*,[109] although Richard was probably raised to a great extent in the household of his Christian grandmother's family, important local leaders. The prospect of a partially-sympathetic new duke, who could speak the "Germanic" tongue of the Bessin was not enough to carry the day with Rollo's old *fideles* and their descendants.

Some of the Norman warriors rejected Richard and all he stood for, fighting for their own local autonomy, or for a setup more like the one which had obtained under Rollo. The better to guarantee success, this time they called in reinforcements, allies from back home in Scandinavia. The "Christian" lords of Normandy, the real *fideles* of William, would hardly consider living in a territory dominated by "pagans"; however, they were faced with a tremendous dilemma. Should they support the ten-year-old Richard, who would need more help for his cause than he could give them for theirs? Or should they abandon their fallen lord's son, and throw in their lot with more promising, at least, more adult, war-leaders? Some did remain loyal to Richard; other Norman warriors rejected Richard, but not all he stood for: there were those who continued William's recent policy of support for Louis IV, and those who turned instead to Hugh the Great. Louis attacked, descending on Rouen, to try to put down the "pagan" independentist faction and, as it turned out, to try to profit from Richard's youth to gain Normandy for himself. Richard ended up imprisoned in Louis' fortress at Laon, and the numismatic evidence indicates that Louis briefly exercised supreme authority in Normandy during the mid-940s, overshadowing Richard completely; Louis even occupied Bay-

---

[109] Dudo, *De moribus* pp. 221-222.

eux.[110] Hugh the Great descended on Evreux, like Louis invited in by local supporters, but also looking to extend his own Parisian territories through the addition of the Evrecin. The "pagan" reaction combined with the new "pagan" influx into Normandy to create a perfect excuse for both Louis and Hugh to try to exploit the situation.[111]

Meanwhile, cowering (probably) in the maelstrom that was Rouen in the mid-940s, recently arrived from Aquitaine, were the transplanted monks of St. Cyprien of Poitiers, now settled at Jumièges, and the new archbishop of Rouen, Hugh, whom William had promoted to the position out of the monastery of St. Denis only a short time before the assassination. Fulbertus, a monk of Jumièges, wrote a biography of the Romanus who was being vaunted in popular tradition at Rouen for having preserved the town from destruction during the last deluge, the Viking conquest and settlement of Rollo and his followers. However, Fulbertus' own shaping of Romanus addressed as well the concerns of the church of Rouen in the mid-940s: to reinforce the faith of the Viking leaders who had converted to "Christianity" and were remaining, stalwartly, in the camp of king Louis; to alienate from their "demonic" deities through illustrations of the superior strength of the Christian God and of his saints whoever might be wavering; to persuade his audience of the great good fortune that had accrued to an earlier and equally glorious and ferocious race of warriors, the Franks, when they embraced Christ; to convince the non-combatants as well of the need to support the "good guys" in the battle raging round their heads; to convince the Normans that the Providential Plan of Sacred History required them to choose, at this moment, the "Christian-Frankish" side. "Demons" (that is, "pagan" deities) were to be shunned, Frankish royalty was to be embraced.[112] When the dust cleared, "pagan demons" had

---

[110] Dumas-Dubourg, *Trésor de Fécamp* p. 10 and pp. 104-105; A. de Longpérier *Louis d'Outre-Mer en Normandie. Trouvaille d'Evreux* (R.N. nouv. série, IV; 1869-70) pp. 71-85 and plate IV-V.

[111] Dudo, *De moribus* pp. 224-226; Flodoard c. 943 pp. 88-90, a. 944 pp. 91-95 and a. 945 pp. 95-98; Richer c. 35 pp. 182-184 and c. 42 pp. 194-196; P. Lauer *Le règne de Louis IV d'Outremer* (Paris, 1900) pp. 87-143; J. Lair, *Etude sur la vie et la mort*.

[112] L. Fallue, *Histoire Politique et religieuse de l'eglise métropolitaine et du diocèse de Rouen* (Rouen, 1850) vol. I pp. 61-62 also placed the composition of Fulbertus' biography, which he knew only in Gerard's abridgement (BHL 7313a, ed. Rigault), "dans les premiers temps de l'occupation normande."

been shunned, Frankish royalty had been embraced, Richard I ruled with a firm grip a Carolingian-style duchy and St. Romanus was the patron of the dynasty and the duchy.

Fulbertus' preface to the *vita Romani* hopefully asserted his belief in *mimesis*: that if someone read or heard the deeds of another person, he or she would be moved to imitate those deeds.[113] That is why he is wrote: to inspire his audience, both those who read and those who heard his text, to imitate the virtuous deeds there recited, for in the mid-tenth century it was still possible to count on some comprehension of "Latin" by illiterate audiences. Presumably no one could be expected, by dint of reading or hearing Romanus' biography, to turn back the overflowing Seine or repair a shattered chrism jar, or to fill their own careers with angelic visitations, annunciations and rescues. But they could easily follow the directives of Romanus' long and impassioned speeches, in which he called on the people of Rouen to pull down the pagan temples with their own hands, and reject the worship of idols.[114]

Idols were rejected, and Romanus was embraced at Rouen. The Romanus who was officially celebrated at Rouen, the episcopal center, and at Fécamp, the ducal capital, has been described in this chapter, on the basis of the liturgical remains of those two locales. That Romanus, I have argued, is best understood as a creation of the 940s, a period of crisis for Carolingian royalty, Carolingian-style bishops, and for the Carolingian-style duchy William Longsword had worked to create. The historian who first shaped Romanus, that he might later be fêted in official liturgical contexts, responded (as we have seen) not only to that political moment, but also to the contemporary oral traditions and the sources available to him in local libraries. That is how the official Romanus was originally constructed. It remains to see how Romanus, in both his popular and his official manifestations, replaced Audoenus as the primary regional saint of Upper Normandy.

---

[113] *Vita Romani* fol. 113rv.

[114] *Contra* the extremely provocative assertion by Brigitte Cazelles that saints' biographies, despite superficial appearances, are not intended for imitation but rather "served to confirm the subordinate role of the average Christian" (B. Cazelles *The Lady as Saint: A Collection of French Hagiographic Romances of the Thirteenth Century* (Philadelphia, 1991) p. 26).

5

The Norman Conquest of Pious Neustria

Rouen was not the only tenth-century center of Romanus' cult. The ducal capital at Fécamp, situated less than 2 km. from the Channel, provides a particularly vivid image of the dynamics of the "Norman Conquest of Pious Neustria." Two separate eleventh-century histories of Fécamp, as well as the archeological remains of the town, testify to the importance of Fécamp.[1] Fécamp, one of the many female monasteries of "Pious Neustria," had originally been founded in the mid-seventh century, on the site of a settlement which had flourished continuously from the first century C.E. Both eleventh-century *fécampois* historians, who may not have written before the final decade of the century, assert that the monastery had been destroyed by "pagans" during the ninth century in campaigns of such horrible thoroughness that the whole area reverted to waste.[2] The archeo-

---

[1]   *De sancto Waningo et fundatione Fiscannensis monasterii* in Rouen BM 528 (A.362) fols. 185r-187v, of the eleventh century, perhaps as late as 1090 (= BHL 8812), but perhaps as early as the very beginning of the century; *Libellus de revelatione, aedificatione et auctoritate Fiscannensis monasterii* is preserved only through Arturus Du Monstier *Neustria Pia* (Rouen, 1663; repr. PL 151 coll. 699-724), and was written for abbot Guillaume de Ros (1079-1108), probably between 1090 and 1094. For the narrative evidence, see Mathieu Arnoux, "La Fortune du *Libellus de revelatione, edificatione et auctoritate fiscannensis monasterii*. Note sur la production historiographique d'une abbaye bénédictine normande" *Revue d'Histoire des Textes* 21 (1991) pp. 135-158. The PL/Du Monstier text must be used in conjunction with Arnoux's readings, based on a newly-discovered manuscript of the *libellus*. For the archeological evidence, Annie Renoux, "Fouilles sur le site du château ducal de Fécamp (Xe-XXe siècles): Bilan provisoire" *Anglo-Norman Studies* 4 (1982) pp. 133-152, and Annie Renoux, "Le monastère de Fécamp pendant le haut moyen âge (VIIe-IXe siècles). Quelques données historiques et archéologiques," *Les abbayes de Normandie* (Actes du XIIIe Congrès des Sociétés Historiques et Archéologiques de Normandie, Caudebec-en-Caux 1978; Rouen, 1979) dir. André Dubuc pp. 115-133.

[2]   BHL 8812 ed. V.D.B. AASS Oct. XI c. 4 p. 685 puts the destruction of Fécamp under Louis the Pious (†840), "ut idem locus ad solitudinem redigeretur, ita ut fieret ferarum habitatio;" *Libellus de revelatione* (c. 9) eschews a specific timeframe, since "Ignorantes omnino discutere non praesumimus, cuius igitur praecesserit, nobis occultatur. Uerum sacri loci confusionem, antiquarumque ueprium reuersionem, et solitudinem fuisse, et usque ad tempora Guillelmi, secundi Northman-

logical evidence, on the other hand, indicates that the period during which Fécamp was unsettled was either extremely brief or non-existent; life did not stop at Fécamp, but the **dominant** use of the site changed from a monastic center in the late ninth century to an aristocratic residence in the early tenth century.

The *fécampois* historians may have been eager to efface the memory of the female occupation of the site. It could be that the reformed, masculine homosocial community of the late eleventh century felt uncomfortable with the idea of centuries of female presence within their cloister, and preferred, emotionally, to believe that every last wall of their monastery was a new construction. It is equally possible that our historians' motivations were more sinister. Rather than desiring to efface the memory of a distant occupation by nuns, they may have wished to suppress the fact that the occupation by nuns had continued until rather more recently: that the nuns had not fled before the Vikings or, if they had fled, had soon returned, and were expelled not by "pagan" pillagers but by the Norman dukes themselves, when the latter gave the house over to male canons. The ravaging Normans then would be a convenient prism to disguise the unpleasant beginnings of male occupation of Fécamp, which had involved dispossessing the nuns.[3]

Du Monstier's research, in 1663, turned up a number of references to a transfer of the nuns of Fécamp from their own house to Montivilliers around 989.[4] Jacques Yver also believed the female monastic community to have continued to live at Fécamp until 989, when they were sent to Montivilliers; the latter house, also a seventh-century female monastery, near Le Havre, became at that time at dependency of Fécamp.[5] In 1658

---

norum ducis, perseuerasse cognouimus" (PL 151 col. 712, accepting corrections from Arnoux, "La Fortune du *Libellus*" p. 156).

[3]   Even if Arnoux is correct in his speculation that the Chronicle of ms. Rouen 528 was written in the late tenth or early eleventh century, perhaps even by Dudo of St. Quentin, specifically in connection with the canonial or Benedictine reforms of the house, my hypothesis that the story of a false ninth-century destruction was used to mask the dispossessing of the female religious would still be plausible.

[4]   *Neustria Pia* (PL 151 coll. 712-713).

[5]   Jacques Yver, "Autour de l'absence d'avouerie en Normandie: notes sur le double theme du developement du pouvoir ducal et de l'application de la réforme grégorienne en Normandie" *Bulletin de la Société des Antiquaires de Normandie* 57 (1963-64) p. 199.

there still existed, on what has been determined to be the site of the tenth-century church in William's palace complex, a "chapelle des Vierges," which the monks demolished in that year.[6] No Carolingian-era or early-Norman-era text records or alludes to the destruction of Fécamp, which was in a privileged, sheltered position in relation to sea-borne raids. The forbidding chalky cliffs of the coast at Fécamp cannot be approached, nor is the river navigable; the port of the Norman Channel coast is Le Havre. An 872 charter of Charles the Bald, likewise, indicates that the environs of Fécamp were safe and inhabited at that date.[7] Finally, the site also seems to have been fortified as an *oppidum* in the ninth century, and the fortifications were still intact to be used by William Longsword as the wall of the ducal palace complex, whose layout was in fact determined by the pre-existent structure.[8]

Whether or not the nuns of Fécamp continued to occupy the house throughout the ninth and tenth centuries, the town did become a ducal residence from the early tenth century. Both eleventh-century historians credit William Longsword with having constructed a ducal residence at Fécamp.[9] His early-tenth-century residence has been paralleled closely to Charles the Great's residence at Aachen both in methods of construction and in symbolism: a well-made *aula* or central hall constructed in stone as were all the "public" sections; wooden private apartments; a "winter room"; a "dining room"; a segregated building for the ovens.[10] It was at Fécamp that William showed the world he was truly an aristocratic Frank of the highest caliber, and not a parvenu. Richard I built a great church to the Trinity on the site of his father's chapel, installing canons to serve the church.[11] A major building campaign soon turned the site into a verit-able *palatium*, with political, religious, intellectual and economic functions. The association of the princely residence with a monastery was still very

[6]   Renoux, "Le monastère de Fécamp" p. 119; Arch. Dép. Seine-Maritime 7 H 61, a contract concerning the abbatial manor.
[7]   G. Tessier ed., *Receuil des actes de Charles le Chauve* II p. 387 no. 399; Renoux, "Le monastère de Fécamp" p. 125.
[8]   Renoux, "Le monastère de Fécamp" pp. 126-128.
[9]   BHL 8812 c. 5 p. 685; *Libellus de revelatione* cc. 10-12 coll. 713-716.
[10]   In sum, "l'ensemble demeure traditionnel dans ses conceptions" (Renoux, "Fouilles" p. 143).
[11]   *Libellus de revelatione* cc. 14-16 coll. 716-718.

much in keeping with Carolingian forms. Finally, Richard I instituted at Fécamp, among the duties of the canons, the praise of holy Romanus.

The cult of Romanus was introduced to this Carolingian-style palace complex by Richard I at least from the time of the establishment of the canonical community there, if not before, during its occupancy by nuns. Fécamp was itself in every way an emblem of Carolingian continuity in Normandy, and it was the first large-scale building project personally undertaken by the Norman dukes. Practically the only thing we know about the details of life at Fécamp in the late tenth century is that a cult was rendered there to Romanus of Rouen, for the *libellus* containing his office has survived.[12] There is no evidence that any of the earlier, Neustrian, figures in the Merovingian history of the monastery, such as Waning (its founder) or Childemarca (its first abbess), were rendered cults at all during the Norman period; Romanus had replaced them, rendered them unimportant. Childemarca's seventh-century biography was lost and no *vita* was written for Waning until perhaps the fourteenth or fifteenth century.[13]

This is the image to keep in mind: the canons of a Carolingian-style palace complex venerating saint Romanus. In its particular admixture of old and new, in its juxtaposition of tradition and innovation, it can be a symbol of Normandy itself. The physical milieu, the material base, of the palace complex was no different from that of any other princely center of the ninth or tenth centuries; but the discourse had changed, the meaning, the ideological superstructure. So in spite of the fact that little, concretely, had changed from Carolingian times, the change in the meaning of the palace complex through the introduction of a new patron saint, effacing the memory of Childemarca of Neustria and her nuns, meant that everything had changed.

---

[12] See above, pp. 157-159.

[13] For Childemarca, see Victor De Buck, AASS Oct: XI pp. 679-684. The mass to Waning called for in the late-fourteenth-century Missal of Fécamp (Rouen BM 292 [Y.181]) and the presence of readings for his festival in a fifteenth-century lectionary of Fécamp (Rouen BM 1415 [U.17]) are the earliest evidence of a cult. Had Childemarca's biography survived, it is likely that it would have adhered to the discourse of Pious Neustria (see above p. 56).

A. Romanus Triumphant: The Toppling of Audoenus of Neustria

I have emphasized repeatedly the general reluctance on the part of the see of Rouen to promote saints' cults, or to sponsor historiographic production. It took a tremendous crisis, either the Carolingian (Austrasian) takeover of Neustria, or the assassination of duke William Longsword, to rouse the archbishops of Rouen to cultic promotion and historiographical patronage. In both those instances, a good deal of the labor and of the energizing motivation as well was provided by local monastic ateliers: Fontenelle in the Merovingian and Carolingian periods, Jumièges in the Viking period. New circumstances and new crises faced the eleventh-century archbishops of Rouen. However, eleventh-century promotional thrusts of Romanus differed markedly from earlier stages of cultic development in the region. In the eleventh century, the archbishops of Rouen had to operate in a world increasingly dominated by monastic "reformers." Indeed, the monastic reform movement, in and of itself, became the greatest threat to the archiepiscopal see in the eleventh century. Not only did Romanus' cult develop, in the eleventh century, without the support of a monastic atelier, it was generated in opposition to such ateliers.

Fulbertus of Jumièges had displayed absolutely no consciousness of the ideals of the tenth-century monastic, still less of the eleventh-century ecclesiastical, reform movements. That the archbishops controlled the monastery of St. Ouen, he simply took for granted; nowhere is there the slightest hint of ideals of monastic independence from king or archbishop, while the dependence of the episcopal see on the king is repeatedly underlined. Likewise, Fulbertus' vision had been one of the unity of the urban locale at Rouen. Just as he wrote at the very last moment before the transformation in clerical views of oral tradition, he also wrote before all the fracturing urban competitions of the eleventh century. He showed the town as unanimous in its desires and actions; everyone worked and prayed together. Farmer has emphasized how tenth-century visions of Tours, before all the competitions of the eleventh century set in, likewise presented the town of St. Martin as unified under the authority of the archbishop.[14] In the tenth century the town of Rouen was, theoretically,

---

[14] Farmer *Communities of St. Martin* p. 32, with special reference to Radbod of Utrecht's *Libellus de miraculo sancti Martini* (MGH SS 15.2 pp. 1239-1244 ed. Holder-Egger).

archbishop Hugh's; from the turn of the eleventh century, the abbot of St.
Ouen would begin to stake his own claims. In the tenth century, however,
conservative Carolingian churchmen such as Fulbertus had not yet faced
with any real seriousness the type of new ideas that would so perplex,
even apoplex, their successors.

Equally telling is the way Fulbertus had shaped Romanus' early
career, and his passage into the episcopate. Romanus, like his eventual
successor Audoenus, was said to have been elected to the episcopate while
serving in the royal household, having had no background in holy orders
or sacerdotal functions until that point. Audoenus' election, as described
in Alcuin's biography, had offered his Carolingian-era historian the opportunity to praise Audoenus for the saint's decision to work his way proper-
ly through the ecclesiastical grades before permitting himself to be installed as bishop. In the case of Romanus, there is no hint that the saint's
direct promotion to high ecclesiastical office seemed inappropriate to Fulbertus, or to the saint himself. In this regard, Fulbertus was a "better" historian than Alcuin, for Merovingian bishops seem to have been regularly
promoted out of the royal palace without any intermediate ecclesiastical
training.[15] Fulbertus' world stood between two eras of "reform."

Fulbertus had accepted the power and importance of the Carolingian
episcopate. Romanus has no powers until his episcopal consecration; his
power to combat demons in the prophetic mode comes on him only after
he takes up the episcopal office. Romanus receives the episcopal office in
a manner reminiscent of the general run of such tenth-century promotions,
through the definitive intervention of the "secular" power, which alone
seems to be constitutive.[16] Romanus became bishop of Rouen "not by his
own will nor by ambitious desiring, but by the royal will, yea indeed he
was called by a divine and angelic preordaining oracle."[17] The king always planned to put Romanus on the see of Rouen, for he had long been
privy to the Divine Will, and it is for that reason that he had brought the
saint to the palace; there the king waited for the people of Rouen to receive (a bit belatedly) their version of the angelic oracle and request Romanus as pontiff, so that he can command Romanus to take up the office,

---

[15] G. Scheibelreiter, *Der Bischoff in merovingische Zeit* p. 101 and pp. 124-127.
[16] Parisse, "Princes laïques et/ou moines" pp. 450-455.
[17] *Vita Romani* fol. 114v.

confer the pastoral staff on him, and lead him to Rouen.[18] Fulbertus showed royal rather than ducal power as decisive in the episcopal election because of his particular concerns during the mid-century crisis; in fact it was William Longsword who had unilaterally appointed Hugh of St. Denis to the see of Rouen.[19] But such niceties aside, Fulbertus' assumptions concerning episcopal appointments had been thoroughly in keeping with tenth-century realities, down to the detailed point that tenth-century "lay" interventions very frequently worked in favor of relations of the prince:[20] Romanus in Fulbertus' biography is a relative of the king.[21]

In the eleventh century, however, both monastic and ecclesiastical reform came to Normandy. The rise of Romanus' cult, and the fall of Audoenus', both in the course of the eleventh century, was a dual process intimately connected with the history of those reforms.

Archbishop Robert was the son of Richard I and Gunnor. He took up the archiepiscopal office, in service to his family, in 989 at the age of no more than 19, while his father was still alive; he held the office until his death in 1037, outliving his brother, duke Richard II, by more than a decade, and outliving the Carolingian world in which he had been raised by even longer than that.[22] It had been standard Carolingian policy to ap-

---

[18] *Vita Romani* fol. 118v.

[19] Parisse, "Princes laïques et/ou moines" pp. 454-460. Normandy was, in this regard, completely "unreformed" until as late as 1050, both in terms of episcopal and abbatial appointments (Olivier Guillot, "A Reform of Investiture before the Investiture Struggle in Anjou, Normandy and England" *Haskins Society Journal* 3 [1991] pp. 81-100, esp. pp. 87-92).

[20] Parisse, "Princes laïques et/ou moines" pp. 461-464.

[21] Attributing royal blood to Romanus was also an inflation of status common among non-reformist tenth-century biographers: Merovingian-era bishops had, in fact, all been of aristocratic background (Martin Heinzelmann *Bischofsherrschaft in Gallien. Zur Kontinuität römischer Führungsschichten vom 4. bis zum 7. Jahrhundert. Soziale, Prosopographische und bildungsgeschichtliche Aspekte* [Beihefte der Francia 5; Munich, 1976]; Scheibelreiter *Der Bischof in merowingischer Zeit* pp. 9-36) but were never royal; however, during the tenth century historians tended to elevate the ancestors of Merovingian bishops to royal status (Scheibelreiter *Der Bischoff in merowingischer Zeit* pp. 41-45).

[22] For all details of Norman ducal familial history, office- and property-holding throughout this chapter, I am indebted to Searle, *Predatory Kinship* esp. pp. 193-234; for the political framework, I have followed Douglas, *William the Conqueror* esp. pp. 31-70.

point family members to important bishoprics; Richard I installed his two sons as archbishop of Rouen and duke of Normandy respectively, in the hopes that they could continue a Carolingian-style policy of cooperation and mutual advancement. For a number of years they did cooperate, and the churches of Normandy flourished.[23] Archbishop Robert also served as a family deputy in southern Normandy, where he held the county of Evreux; ever since the foundation of a monastery around St. Taurin of Evreux in the early 960s, the dukes of Rouen had attached major importance to a presence in the south. Robert would eventually pass that office on to his own son, Richard.

As archbishop Robert moved into middle age, the world changed increasingly around him. Robert belonged to the world of the so-called "feudalized" church, "l'église au pouvoir des laïques."[24] His nephews, Richard III and Robert the Magnificent, who succeeded Richard II (†1026) in the ducal office, adopted the life-style of eleventh-century, Capetian-era princes, Robert in particular making spectacular displays of his own piety through activities like pilgrimage, and espousing all the values of the new reform movements. Archbishop Robert suddenly looked like an unreformed throw-back to a different age, for that was what he was. He ended up in open rebellion against the dukes, fortifying his county seat of Evreux against them, as a result of which presumption he was eventually exiled to France. To come back to his see at Rouen, he had to renounce his "worldly" lifestyle, abandon his wife and children, and do penance for his "sins" for the rest of his life. As a result of his late-life conversion, he was looked on favorably by the reformist author of the first history of the see, the late-eleventh-century *acta* of the archbishops of Rouen.[25]

---

[23] Fanning, *A Bishop and His World* pp. 62-63 shows how bishop Renaud of Angers always saw his policies fail because he developed them independently of the counts of Anjou, whereas Hubert, Renaud's successor, met with success due to his faithful cooperation with Fulk Nerra and Geoffrey Martel.

[24] Augustin Fliche and Victor Martin, *Histoire de l'église depuis les origines jusqu'à nos jours* (Paris, 1948) vol. VII, *L'église au pouvoir des laïques.*

[25] "Hic uir magnae pietatis et honestatis fuit, et in mundialibus divitiis adeo laudatus a saecularibus uiris; sed carnis fragilitate superatus, quamplures filios procreauit. Plura etiam ecclesiae bona fecit. Ecclesiam enim praesentem miro opere et magnitudine aedificare coepit. Ante obitum suum, gratia Dei praeueniente, uitam suam correxit. Feminam enim reliquit, et de hoc caeterisque prauis actibus suis poenitentiam egit" (*Acta Archiepiscoporum Rotomagensium* PL 147 col. 278).

Archbishop Robert had himself been a proponent of the monastic reform movement; that it would become a full-scale restructuring of the secular church, biting the episcopal and princely hands which had fed it, could have been predicted by no one. Some unsuccessful, probably half-hearted, attempts to introduce the new monastic reformism into Normandy had been made in the tenth century; but archbishop Hugh and Richard I, whatever else they might have been, were not reformers but conservative Carolingian-style rulers. Archbishop Robert himself began to turn the tide, sponsoring the canonial reform of Fécamp, along with his father, in 990, immediately on the heels of archbishop Hugh's death; Fécamp became the basis for the successful reform movement of the eleventh century, which began in earnest after the death of Richard I, when archbishop Robert and his brother Richard II brought William of Dijon to Fécamp (1001).[26] Archbishop Robert encouraged the spread of the monastic reform movement, accepting its twin doctrines of regular abbacies and monastic exemption. No hypocrite, at some uncertain date (probably *circa* 1000) he extended the policy to St. Ouen of Rouen, which had theretofore been under the control of the archbishop of Rouen.[27] The first regular abbot, Hildebert, died in 1008.[28] At the same time, we begin to get the

---

[26] Neithard Bulst *Untersuchungen zu den Klosterreform Wilhelms von Dijon* (Pariser Historische Studien 2; Paris, 1973) pp. 178-179; Fauroux no. 4 p. 72 ff; *Libellus de revelatione, aedificatione et auctoritate Fiscannensis monasterii* (PL 151 coll. 699-724).

[27] *Recueil des actes de Charles II le Chauve* ed. G. Tessier nos. 259 and 407, of 863 and 876 respectively, take for granted the identity of the archbishop and the abbot. A charter of archbishop Riculf has the prelate call himself abbot of St. Pierre-St. Ouen (Pommeraye *S. Ouen* p. 399). Writing in the mid-tenth century, Fulbertus tacitly assumes, in his *Vita Romani*, that bishop Romanus used a monastery for his base (see folios 26r, 27r, 123r and 123v of the transcription below for interactions between Romanus and the brothers of his monastery). Finally, Musset's study of the property holdings of St. Ouen also led to the conclusion that the abbey of St. Ouen and the cathedral of Rouen had been ruled as a unit for many centuries. Such episcopal abbeys, with no abbot other than the local bishop, may have been a common Carolingian phenomenon; other Norman examples are St. Martin of Sées and St. Vigor of Bayeux. See Lucien Musset, "Ce qu'enseigne l'histoire d'un patrimoine monastique: St. Ouen de Rouen du IXe au XIe siècle" in *Aspects de la société et de l'économie dans la Normandie médiévale (Xe-XIIIe siècles)* (Cahier des Annales de Normandie 22; Caen, 1988) pp. 114-129.

[28] *Chronicon Rotomagense* (written around 1080) ed. Philippe Labbe *Nova Bibliotheca manuscriptorum* I (Paris, 1657) p. 366; Bulst, *Untersuchungen zu den Klosterreform* p. 161 ff.

first evidence of a developed cathedral clergy group, with the archbishops having lost the service of the monks of St. Ouen.[29]

The reform of St. Ouen inaugurated a phase of intra-ecclesiastical competition at Rouen which provided the impetus for further promotion of the cult of Romanus.[30] It is probably to Robert's patronage that we owe the production of the earliest collection of miracles attributed to Romanus.[31] Robert, like Hugh, attached a certain importance to literary patronage.[32] He had supported the satirist Warner, and more importantly, was the principal ongoing patron of Dudo of St. Quentin as that cleric labored to complete his massive history of early Normandy.[33] The miracles were authored by a clerk of the church of St. Romain.[34] One of the miracles, an event related to our clerk by the keeper of the sanctuary at St. Romain, positively reeks of the eleventh-century context of competition with the newly-independent abbey.[35]

One night, the sacristan of St. Romain had had an ecstatic vision of a celebration in the church. Four pontiffs were ranged around the altar,

---

[29] For the earliest known individuals see David Spear, "Les doyens du chapitre cathédral de Rouen durant la période ducale" *Annales de Normandie* 33 (1983) p. 96; David Spear, "Les archidiacres de Rouen au cours de la période ducale" *Annales de Normandie* 34 (1984) pp. 17-18; David Spear, "Les dignitaires de la cathédrale de Rouen pendant la période ducale" *Annales de Normandie* 37 (1987) p. 122; David Spear, "Les chanoines de la cathédrale de Rouen pendant la période ducale" *Annales de Normandie* 41 (1991) p. 136.

[30] Head has analyzed narrative productions and especially *miracula* collections of eleventh-century ateliers at Micy, Fleury and Pithiviers precisely in this context of competition between independence-minded abbeys and hierarchy-minded bishops (Head, *Hagiography and the Cult of Saints* pp. 202-281). Similar developments dominated local politics at Tours in the eleventh and twelfth centuries, where three communities jockeyed for position, rather than the two significant institutions at Rouen (Farmer, *Communities of St. Martin* pp. 17-20).

[31] Evreux BM 101 folios 29v- 33r; the miracles are transcribed below in Appendix 2.

[32] Jean-Michel Bouvris, "L'école capitulaire de Rouen au XIe siècle" *Etudes Normandes* 3 (1986) pp. 90-92.

[33] Dudo, *De moribus* pp. 123-125, 126-128, 215-217, 292.

[34] The author recounts one miracle, which took place in the church of St. Romain on the saint's October 23 feast day, as an eye-witness; this miracle is discussed below pp. 211-214.

[35] *Miracula Romani* fols. 31r-32v.

like the jewels in a crown, and a fifth was at the altar, attending to the service. The celebrant, pressed for information, informed the man that the four pontiffs were Mellonus, Nigasius, Audoenus and Ansbertus. Little was known of Mellonus, whose relics were not even at Rouen, and little is made of him here; his was, however, the first name on all the episcopal lists of Rouen composed before the latter part of the eleventh century, and so his inclusion in the "crown" was logical.[36] Nigasius was a shadowy figure as well; he was remembered as a martyr of the region, but he too reposed far from Rouen, and had not yet been privileged with a biography.[37] Nothing particular is said about Ansbertus either, who was venerated more at Fontenelle than at Rouen, and whose relics had been seized for St. Pierre of Gent in 944.[38]

Audoenus is the figure who stands out in the "crown," even though the very structure of the narrative knocks him down to the level of the three others. He may be equated with them through his physical position in the celebration of the mass, but the author does emphasize the local presence of Audoenus' relics (something which cannot be claimed for the other three jewels in the crown), his status as a special protector of Rouen, and describes some of the well-known aspects of the saint's life story. The venerable status of Audoenus was thus not unknown to the author, and we can imagine that the monks of St. Ouen would have been mortally offended to see their eminent protector given no precedence over three shadowy figures whose relics were not even in residence in the town. But the vision becomes more offensive still. The account continues:

> Once the individual members of the starry crown had been thus enumerated, since I had not yet heard mention of blessed Romanus, I guessed that this was truly blessed Romanus who spoke to me, and I was even more certain about it because he acted as a *pater familias*

---

[36]   Sauvage, "Elenchi episcoporum Rotomagensium."

[37]   For discussion of Nigasius, see Lifshitz, "The Migration of Neustrian Relics" and Lifshitz, "The Politics of Historiography: Bishops versus Monks in Eleventh-Century Rouen" (Paper presented to the Modern Languages Association, December 1994).

[38]   For Ansbertus, see above pp. 39-46; for the seizure of his relics, see Lifshitz, "The Migration of Neustrian Relics" and *Une translation de reliques à Gand en 944: Sermo de adventu sanctorum Wandregiseli, Ansberti et Uulframni in Blandinium* ed. N.-N. Huyghebaert (Brussels, 1978) [= BHL 8810].

to the others of the house, as I perceived the mystical order of things. Therefore, interrogating him with familiar daring, I said: "Are you not our venerable father, that advocate Romanus, who alone chose to keep this place safe for us?" But he said, "Do not say that I am this man. For there will be no need of another's indication to recognize him. The manifest signs will be sufficient: his face clearer than the sun, brighter than the stars, his eyes flashing with a starry light like precious gems....Truly, he is within the sacristy with the other pontiffs...who will lead him before this altar to perform the lordly sacraments, since we will in no way leave this place today until we have been blessed by him...and we are also awaiting his edict concerning when we must return for another divine council like this one."

Audoenus, it now becomes evident, is two steps from the top, along with the shadowy bishops; for the speaker is Victricius, not Romanus. Romanus is on a level far above the others, including Audoenus, and only Romanus is worthy to perform the sacrifice of the mass itself. He emerges, a new Moses, he performs the mass, he gives communion to the other bishops, he prays aloud while the others maintain a reverent silence...in short, he is the premier occupant of the see, and Audoenus has to sit with the crowd.

Robert's strategy involved building; he decided on the construction of a large cathedral in the new "Romanesque" style, such as were being constructed by contemporaries such as Hubert of Angers.[39] He himself had been consecrated, as his predecessors had been, in the abbey of St. Ouen, and had been able to use the facilities there when he needed an imposing structure;[40] however, since the installation of a regular abbot at St. Ouen, the archbishops had become *personae non gratae* there. Robert cannot have waited long after the reform of St. Ouen (*circa* 1000) to begin work on the cathedral, and there is every reason to believe he always planned to complete the construction and transfer the patron of the town, Romanus, into the lavish new structure himself. The archbishop also attempted to put the domain of the cathedral in order, apparently a top priority of all good prelates in the pre-ecclesiastical-reform era.[41] Orderic

---

[39] Fanning, *A Bishop and his World* pp. 65-67.
[40] Pommeraye, *S. Ouen* p. 172.
[41] Fanning, *A Bishop and his World* pp. 73-81.

Vitalis speaks well of Robert in this regard, but the known restitutions he could scrape together are minor compared with the massive donations the dukes were soon to begin making to the abbey of St. Ouen.[42]

Robert did come close to completing the cathedral, but in the end he fell short; his troubles with his nephew, the duke, and with reformists who disapproved of his lifestyle cannot have made his building projects any easier. Unable to transfer the relics of Romanus to an incomplete structure, he settled for an elevation and inspection of the saint's relics, carried out on the eve of his own death.[43] As it turned out, the cathedral was only completed and dedicated, by Maurilius, in 1063. So Romanus' body remained in the "very ancient chapel" just to the north of the present-day cathedral, on the street which today bears his name; both the (Carolingian-style?) chapel and Robert's romanesque cathedral were destroyed in the twelfth century.[44]

It was not only archbishop Robert's troubles with reformers that disrupted his plans for the cathedral; yet another succession crisis figured as well, but this time it was entirely of Norman making, for the Franks had withdrawn, chastened, in 965. Richard II's death in 1026 sent his two sons, Richard III and Robert I, fighting against each other; the latter emerged the victor in 1027, perhaps through fratricide,[45] then launched an attack against his uncle, the archbishop, in 1028. Archbishop Robert won that skirmish, if at the price of his wife and children and of his pride, and returned to Rouen where, as senior member of the ducal family, he was able to preside over much of the affairs of the duchy. Perhaps he would have completed his cathedral and whatever plans he had for Romanus had it not been for the death of Robert the Magnificent in 1035, leaving as heir only a seven-year-old "illegitimate" son. The final years of the archbishop's

---

[42]   For the cathedral, see Fauroux nos. 66-68; for the abbey, see note 47 below; for Orderic's praise, *The Ecclesiastical History of Orderic Vitalis* ed. Marjorie Chibnall, book II c. 1, vol. II p. 43.

[43]   Farin, *La Normandie Chrestienne* p. 456 and Pommeraye, *Archevesques* p. 246 both mention a charter, still preserved in the archives of the cathedral in the seventeenth century, attesting to Robert's inspection of Romanus' relics in 1036.

[44]   The revenues of the chapel, which was not rebuilt since Romanus had already been transfered into the cathedral, were attributed to the chancellor of the cathedral school by archbishop Hugh in 1140 (Pommeraye, *Archevesques* p. 131).

[45]   Orderic Vitalis charged that Richard III had been poisoned (OV book V c. 9 ed. Chibnall vol. III p. 84).

life were occupied with mustering support for William the Bastard, and dispensing with William's "legitimate" older cousin, the son of Richard III, Nicholas. Nicholas was persuaded to accept the abbacy of St. Ouen, a decision pregnant with consequences for the future of Romanus' cult.

Meanwhile, the Norman dynasty survived yet another extended crisis, with William eventually securing his inheritance, an inheritance which he later enlarged beyond anyone's wildest dreams. The 1020s-1040s mirrored the 940s-960s in a number of ways: both were periods of crisis for Rollo's dynasty, both times that dynasty emerged not only unscathed but strengthened. In both instances, we can only marvel at the evident strength of "public" authority in Normandy, that the ducal office could have held on through such periods of upset. Robert secured William's inheritance not primarily as a family member (he was not above engaging in open warfare with members of his own family), but as archbishop of Rouen. With archbishop Robert's death, the mantle of ecclesiastical buttressing fell to Nicholas of Normandy, now abbot of St. Ouen. His efforts on behalf of young William brought a shower of rewards to the monastery, and inaugurated a new era in the ecclesiastical politics at Rouen. Nicholas of Normandy, abbot of St. Ouen, was a formidable figure. Cheated of the ducal title on two occasions, after the deaths first of his father and then of his uncle, he turned the abbey of St. Ouen into a major power.

Almost simultaneously in the mid-1030s, archbishop Robert died and Nicholas became abbot of St. Ouen. The oldest living scion of one branch of the ducal house was at the head of the local monastic community (Nicholas was the grandson of Richard II and Judith, through Richard III), while the archbishopric fell to Mauger, oldest living scion of the other branch (Mauger was the son of Richard II and Papia). In lineage they were a good match, but Nicholas had the pen, Mauger the sword; in this case the pen proved far mightier than the sword. Archbishop Mauger was a warrior through and through who was worse than a babe in the woods when it came to sophisticated propaganda or the manipulation of things ecclesiastical. He would have to face, too, the radical juggernaut of the reform movement, as it headed now directly for the secular clergy, leaving conservatives like Mauger bobbing, lifeless, in its wake. Nicholas, on the other hand, came to St. Ouen from Fécamp, where he had been a monk under John. He was conversant with the ideals of the reform, such as monastic exemption from episcopal intervention, and was comfortable in the age that was dawning. Nicholas was not only inclined to insist upon his "rights" as regular abbot of the house, he was more than capable of doing so. Everything seemed set for the *revanche* of Audoenus, and for Romanus to dissolve into an antiquarian curiosity.

He did not. Orderic Vitalis tells us how archbishop William of Caen (1079-1100) succeeded where archbishop Robert had failed: he moved Romanus "from his very own temple into the metropolitan basilica" and instituted a mandatory public cult to the saint throughout the archdiocese:

> He had the body of Romanus, archbishop of Rouen, translated from his own church to the cathedral with splended ceremonies, and reverently placed it in a reliquary of gold and silver, thickly encrusted with precious stones. He ordained that his feast day should be solemnly celebrated throughout the diocese on 23 October; and established by general decree that the relics of the holy bishop should be carried in procession to a celebration outside the city, and that men and women from the whole diocese should be encouraged to attend by injunctions and indulgences and special blessings.[46]

How did this happen?

At mid-century, such an event would have seemed unlikely. Abbot Nicholas had succeeded archbishop Robert as primary promoter of dynastic interests, and in the new world of the reform he was doing a bang-up job, sailing along better than Robert with his outdated Carolingian-era lifestyle could have hoped to do. Nicholas took regular life and reform values seriously; there is no hint in the sources that he ever engaged in a "private" life and so he, unlike Robert, never found himself running afoul of the reigning duke. Also unlike Hugh and Robert, he has never run afoul of historiographic scholarship, dominated as it is by a pro-reform perspective.

Almost overnight, Nicholas turned St. Ouen into the single most privileged and well-endowed ecclesiastical entity in pre-1066 Normandy, eclipsing the older centers of Jumièges and Fécamp.[47] His services rendered well warranted the flood of ducal endowments. Nicholas had been on the spot, in a prominent position, and backed by his heavenly patron,

---

[46] OV book V c. 4 ed. Chibnall vol. III pp. 22-25.
[47] The number of authentic surviving ducal charters alone is enormous: Fauroux nos. 13, 19, 21, 24, 37, 39, 40, 41, 43, 44, 53, 78, 79, 103, 105, 107, 112, 158, 191, 193, 204, 204bis, 205, 210, 211 and 212.

Audoenus, at the definitive moment in the establishment of William's claims to the duchy of Normandy. At a council near Caen in October, 1047, the Truce of God was proclaimed in Normandy, and oaths of fidelity to William were sworn by all concerned. The oaths were sworn on relics of Audoenus, surely held by Nicholas, who proclaimed ecclesiastical penalties for breaking the peace or breaches of loyalty to the duke.[48]

Archbishop Mauger had stood by, and permitted Audoenus to become the guarantor of Norman political and social stability, letting Romanus and the unfinished cathedral gather dust, unused. Meanwhile, Nicholas began construction of a remarkably large and beautiful church at St. Ouen,[49] a church which would rival and perhaps even overmatch the cathedral, were it ever completed. Archbishop Mauger, on the other hand, had quite different concerns. With his brother, William count of Talou, he devoted himself to personal aggrandizement and to establishing a power base independent of duke William. In 1053 the fraternal pair resorted to rebellion. They lost. Mauger was deposed from the archiepiscopal see in 1055 by a council at Lisieux in the presence of representatives of the duke and the pope.

Duke William had made a single major change in Norman government before 1066: he moved the center of gravity from Rouen/Fécamp to Caen/Lisieux in an effort to better integrate Upper and Lower Normandy. The departure of the duke from the Seine valley, combined with the incompetence of Mauger, left Nicholas of St. Ouen a free hand at Rouen. The abbot used his freedom to return Audoenus to the spotlight. Between the 1047 Peace Council at Caen and the 1055 Reform Council at Lisieux the atelier of St. Ouen turned out a set of miracles of Audoenus, dominated by the twin personalities of duke William, imposer of PEACE, and abbot Nicholas.[50] William found Audoenus so useful as a support of his "peace," he took him along to England where he had gone to spread more "peace." Another set of miracles attributed to Audoenus, produced by the house of St. Ouen at Rouen between 1075 and 1087, feature prominently

---

[48] *Miracula Audoeni* AASS Aug. IV p. 834, 5.

[49] OV ed. Chibnall, book IV vol. II pp. 298-299; André Masson, *L'église abbatiale de S.-Ouen de Rouen* (Paris, 1927) p. 10.

[50] Rouen BM 1406 folios 182f-209v (= BHL 760).

manifestations of the saint's *virtus* in England.[51]

With the duke safely out of the way, Nicholas could set about taking over Rouen with a vengeance. The *miracula sancti Audoeni* (BHL 760), turned out in the aftermath of the 1047 Peace Council by the monk Fulbertus of St. Ouen, give a taste of what the cathedral was up against. According to this history of tenth-century Normandy, the monks of St. Ouen had persuaded Richard I as long ago as 944/45 to grant them complete independence from archbishop Hugh, in execution of a privilege that had originally been granted by Charles the Bald! Nicholas, however, wanted more than autonomy; he wanted St. Ouen to become a great pilgrimage center.[52] Fulbertus was shameless in the presentation of the abbey's wares: where Roman shrines had failed, Audoenus could succeed; where St. Michael at Monte Gargano had failed, Audoenus could succeed; and where St. Martin at Tours had been overtaxed, Audoenus could pick up the pieces.[53] Nicholas and Fulbertus of St. Ouen even tried to syphon off pilgrims from the traffic flowing to Le Mont-St.-Michel, urging them to stop instead at the far superior outpost of the archangel which had recently been established on the present-day Mont-Gargan in Rouen.[54]

Another monk of St. Ouen, this one anonymous but also working under Nicholas' direction, produced two more histories of tenth-century Normandy. One of the narratives described the 918 transfer of Audoenus' relics back to Rouen from Condé, whence they had been removed for fear of the Normans during the previous century; the other recorded a failed *furta sacra* attempt to rob Normandy of its precious patron, Audoenus.[55]

---

[51] BHL 761. For both collections, see Jean-Claude Richard, "Les 'Miracula' composés en Normandie aux XIe et XIIe siècles" *Positions des Thèses de l'Ecole des Chartes* (1975) pp. 183-189.

[52] To Musset, the narrative "a un caractère de propagande assez agressif et contient même un éloge de la Normandie qui conviendrait presque à nos brochures touristiques d'aujourd'hui" (Lucien Musset, "Recherches sur les pélerins et pelerinages en Normandie jusqu'à la Première Croisade" *Annales de Normandie* 12 (1962) p. 132, in reference to AASS Aug. IV p. 829 § 22).

[53] AASS Aug. IV pp. 826-831.

[54] AASS Aug. IV p. 831; Musset, "Recherches sur les pélerins" p. 134.

[55] Copies survive in Rouen BM 1406 and Rouen BM 1411, manuscripts of St. Ouen that date from c. 1100 and the thirteenth century, respectively (= BHL 756 and BHL 757). The copies in Rouen 1406 are both incomplete, as the ms. is now missing folios 214 and 215. These materials are discussed in even greater detail in

The first account describes how Rollo was so overjoyed by the return of the indispensable Audoenus to Rouen that he donated to the monastery the entire eastern suburb of Rouen and exempted the house from comital authority and all fiscal exactions; the second describes how Richard I was so relieved after the aversion of the near-disaster that the loss of Audoenus would have entailed that he promised to provide the monastery with perpetual lighting for the altars of Peter and Audoenus, as well as to endow the house with two near-by villas and a large amount of moveable wealth.

Economic and political claims were clearly a very important part of the reason for the composition of Audoenus' translation narratives, but most of the author's energy was spent emphasizing how Audoenus was the indispensible patron of Neustria. However, when it comes to the third narrative in the same author's triad of interrelated translation accounts, namely the account of the arrival at Rouen of relics of Nigasius, no secondary local economic or political aims are apparent; the entire point of the claims to Nigasius is to locate in the abbey of St. Ouen relics of the past which could not, no matter what the cathedral came up with next, be improved upon.

The abbey of St. Ouen under abbot Nicholas has deservedly been singled out as the single greatest collector of relics and master of matters cultic in all of eleventh-century Normandy.[56] The genius and audacity of the abbey is nowhere clearer than in the appropriation of Nigasius, priestly martyr of the Vexin at some uncertain date, who became, at Rouen, an auxiliary of Audoenus in the battle against Romanus, as the abbey of St. Ouen fought the cathedral for control of the imaginary heritage of the region.[57] From the perspective of the cathedral of Rouen, the defin-

---

Lifshitz, "La Normandie Carolingienne"; Lifshitz "The Migration of Neustrian Relics," and Lifshitz "The Politics of Historiography."

[56] Jean Fournée *Le culte populaire des saints en Normandie* (*Cahiers Léopold Delisle* numero spécial, 1973) p. 51.

[57] According to the *translatio Nigasii et socii* (ed. Martène and Durand, *Thesaurus Novus Anecdotorum* [Paris, 1717] III cols. 1677-1682 [= BHL 6084]), relics of the saint had been stolen from Wampach, a property of the abbey of St. Ouen in present-day Luxembourg, by a monk of St. Ouen, in 1032, under the abbacy of Henry of St. Ouen. Since the translation is not described as by an eye witness, and throughout seems to be cast into the past, Nigasius' first historian must have written under Henry's successor, Nicholas, but early enough in the new administration (probably the early 1040s) for there to be a number of extant eleventh-century

ing moments of local politico-religious history were, "religiously," the Merovingian-era pontificate of Romanus, when the town had been liberated from demons through that bishop's ferocious battling; and "politically," the Viking conquest, when phase two of the divine plan for Normandy had been fulfilled, in accordance with Romanus' predictions. By the 1040s, the abbey of St. Ouen was also able to answer with a bi-partite image, for Audoenus alone could not stand against the historiographically sophisticated and sacro-historically enmeshed edifice being promoted by the cathedral. From the perspective of the abbey, the defining moments of local history were nothing like those envisioned by the cathedral.

The divine plan for Neustria dated in the abbey's prism to the first century of the Christian era when, according to the monk of St. Ouen who composed a biography of Nigasius, "omnipotent God released the people of the Gauls from its noxious enslavement to the ancient enemy."[58] And so, Nigasius was sent to Gaul in the company of Dionysius, first bishop of Paris and student of St. Paul; both were ordained bishops by pope Clement, first-century bishop of Rome and follower of St. Peter. After helping Dionysius at Paris, Nigasius set out for his own see, Rouen, and began the work of liberating the diocese from the ancient enemy. The success of Dionysius and Nigasius was so spectacular, that it brought upon them the wrath of the secular princes of the day, by whom both were cruelly martyred. In answer to the historiographic prism of the secular church of Rouen, which placed the Norman princes in the center of sacred history, the reform abbey of St. Ouen offered an identity independent of worldy rulers; the divine plan, as seen from St. Ouen, did not require princes, who were sometimes a hindrance, as Rollo himself had been, when his savagery forced Audoenus into temporary exile. The second defining moment of local history was the pontificate of Audoenus, when the divine plan for Neustria had clearly been fulfilled, for (as we have seen) the saint's diocese was blanketed with monasteries, and was so dedicated to monastic

---

copies of Nigasius' *passio* (BHL 6081). For the manuscript evidence concerning Nigasius, see L. Goubert, *Notice sur s. Nigaise, apôtre du Vexin* (handwritten by the author, 1867) and Lifshitz, "The Politics of Historiography."

[58]	"...cum uero omnipotens Deus populum Galliarum ab hostis antiqui noxia seruitute erueret, et ueri solis fulgore lustratum suae ditioni mancipari decreuisset" (*Passio Nigasii* [BHL 6081] Paris BN lat. 15.436 fol. 43v; Rouen BM 1406 [Y.41]; Goubert, *Notice sur S. Nigaise* p. 38).

virtues that a casual observer would have confused it with the deserts of Egypt.[59]

It may be that the abbey was initially attracted to Nigasius, martyr of the Vexin, because the date of his festival was perfectly suited for pre-empting Romanus. Audoenus' festival had long been celebrated on August 25. Late summer and early fall is Ordinary Time, and once the Assumption of the Virgin had passed on August 15 there was little to capture the imagination of the faithful and the restless. Audoenus' festival fell nicely just after the octave of the great Marian feast, and would have tended to merge with that central marker of summer holidays. But then came the lull of Ordinary Time, and by October 23 the festival of Romanus would explode as the locus of the next great burst of celebratory steam. The festival of Nigasius' martyrdom, which fell on October 11, in connection with the local celebrations of September 29 and October 15 for St. Michael, whose new pilgrimage spot in the hills surrounding Rouen was also being promoted by St. Ouen, were designed to syphon enthusiasm away from Romanus' feast as surely as Mont-Gargan-de-Rouen was intended to syphon pilgrim traffic away from Le-Mont-St.-Michel. Though the cathedral was forced to acknowledge the festival of Nigasius, October 11 has for a millennium been a minor date on the ecclesiastical calendar of the secular church at Rouen, and Nigasius' putative historical identity as proto-bishop of the see has never been accepted; he is venerated with readings from the Common for Martyrs, as a little-known martyr of the Vexin.[60]

It was in the midst of archbishop Mauger's rebellion, and precisely as a counterweight to Romanus, that Nigasius had made his first unequivocal public appearance at Rouen. We owe our knowledge of the following events, which took place in 1053, to an eye-witness participant, the author of the *inventio* of St. Uulframnus of Fontenelle.[61] 1053 was a time of great trouble in Normandy, not only for political reasons but also due to drought and plague. The monks of Fontenelle packed their relics and came to Rouen. They were greeted, outside the city, by the canons of the cathedral, the latter bearing relics of Romanus, representative of Rouen.

[59] See above pp. 38-48.

[60] A. Collette, *Histoire du Bréviaire de Rouen* (Rouen, 1902).

[61] *Inventio et miracula sancti Uulframni* ed. Jean Laporte (Mélanges publiés par la Société de l'Histoire de Normandie, 14e séries; Rouen, 1938) cc. 38-41 pp. 56-60.

The two processions merged into one and began to return to the cathedral, each holding their standards, Romanus and Uulframnus, aloft. Archbishop Mauger, busy elsewhere on his rebellion, is conspicuous by his absence.

The arrival of the Fontenelle contingent was a signal for the community of St. Ouen to act. The author of the *inventio* relates what happened next:

> Thus, accompanied by this crowd of devoted people, we were advancing through the town and feeling no violence of immoderate pressure, when suddenly there came forward with the body of St. Nigasius a whole chain of monks of St. Ouen, whitened by their albs and cloaked in their habits, and they stood in our way holding before them candles, and crosses likewise, and incense-burning censers, and in this way they began to lead us away, chanting, with great honor. Moreover, once we had gone a bit further, there arrived a multitude of nuns, resounding with the sweet melody of their voices.[62]

The cathedral canons were powerless to stop the two-pronged advance of male and female regular clergy, and the Fontenelle visitors were led to St. Ouen, where they deposited their relics and rested.

Perhaps 1053 was a moment of balance of power at Rouen, but the tides seemed to be shifting in favor of the abbey, behind its new Roman-era patron, St. Nigasius. Mauger's successor on the archiepiscopal throne, probably chosen by William in consultation with Nicholas, was as unlikely to make trouble for Audoenus as Mauger had been, although for entirely different reasons. Archbishop Maurilius was a political non-entity. Like Nicholas, he had been a monk at Fécamp, where he had retired after failing completely in an earlier attempt to impose the Benedictine reform on a monastery in Florence. Abbots who failed to impose monastic reform in the mid-eleventh century were few and far between, as the entire weight of the powers that were was ready to support their efforts. Maurilius must

---

[62] "Hac itaque deuote plebis constipatione comitati, per urbem incedebamus, nullamque ingentis pressurae iniuriam sentiebamus, cum ecce omnis monachorum caterua santi Audoeni albis candidata et palliis amicta iam cum sancti corpore Nichasii processerat quae preeuntibus ceris ac crucibus simulque thuricremis odoribus nobis obuiam uenit, ac sic cum honorificentia magna nos cantando deducere cepit. Procedentibus autem nobis paululum agmen occurit sanctimonialium dulci persultans modulamine uocum" (*Inventio et miracula Uulframni* ed. Laporte c. 41).

have been a singularly ineffectual leader, though he may also have been a pious and gentle soul. He was originally from Reims, though nothing more is known of his background. He had no connections and no power base in the region over which he was supposed to preside, while his rival in Upper Normandy was the older cousin of the reigning duke. He believed in clerical celibacy, and devoted himself to enforcing it, but there he had Nicholas on his side. Otherwise he seems to have steered clear of the sort of guerilla-warfare-with-relics at which Nicholas excelled.[63] For ten more years, Audoenus stood unrivalled at center stage.

Indeed, Audoenus seemed so entrenched as the primary patron of the diocese, that Maurilius' archiepiscopal successor, an appointee again in the tradition of Robert and Mauger, chose to wage the battle with St. Ouen over Audoenus rather than against him. The new archbishop, John, should have been in his dotage by the time he received the call. John was the son of Ralph of Ivry, count of Bayeux and half-brother of Richard I; John then was of the generation of Richard II, who had died in 1026, and was the grandson of William Longsword! He had spent much of his life as a warrior, but when he became too old for that, he switched to the ecclesiastical branch of family service. He served as bishop of Avranches from 1061 to 1067, then moved to the metropolitan see. Unlike Mauger, he could read the writing on the wall, and his career change seems to have brought with it a concomitant mental transformation: he became a reform-era ecclesiastic extraordinaire.[64] Perhaps it was simply a function of age; whereas archbishops Robert and Mauger had been too young to renounce their appetites for war and sex voluntarily, John was old enough for worldly fun and games to seem a nuisance.

It is hard to say whether John's staunch metropolitanism was a relic of the late Carolingian age in which he was raised, or a premonition of

---

[63] For Maurilius, see René Delamare Le Liber de officiis ecclesiasticis de Jean d'Avranches (Evreux, 1923) introduction.

[64] OV book IV c. 1 ed. Chibnall vol. II pp. 200-201. Contra Searle, Predatory Kinship pp. 112-117, 194, 198, 233 and 292. William of Poitiers' notice that John became a prelate because of the wishes of others, not because of his own ambitions, is praise of his good demeanor, not criticism of his indifference; in any case, the comment follows other words of praise for John's wisdom and religious lifestyle (William of Poitiers Histoire de Guillaume le Conquerant ed. and trans. Raymonde Foreville [Classiques de l'Histoire de France au Moyen Age 23; Paris, 1952] p. 136).

the thirteenth century; he was either ahead of or behind his times, but through it all he toed the party line on clerical celibacy and other *causes celèbres* of the day, so he enjoyed a measure of success in his efforts to enforce metropolitan rights over suffragan bishops. Already as bishop of Avranches he had been pushing the politically inert Maurilius to engage in some pro-active management of the metropolitan see. During the 1060s he wrote, and dedicated to Maurilius, the *Liber de officiis ecclesiasticis*, a treatise on the modes of celebration of Christmas, Easter, Pentecost, the Marian festivals, and the festivals of various saints. He recommended that a uniform calendar and uniform modes of celebration be enforced throughout the archdiocese.[65] John highlighted two non-universal saints whose festivals he felt ought to be province-wide: Audoenus and Romanus.

The balance of power was about to be tipped. In a dramatic move, the old but vigorous archibishop tried to wrest Audoenus from abbatial control, rather than attempt to overcome the age-old patron through a new promotional thrust of Romanus. The festival of Audoenus came in 1073, as it had for many years, but this year archbishop John tried to make the cathedral a focal point of the celebrations; after all, Audoenus had been bishop of Rouen. This is how the Chronicle of Rouen, composed *circa* 1080, describes the reaction of Nicholas' troops:

> In this year, the monks of St. Ouen attacked archbishop John with an armed band of men while he was celebrating the mass during the festival of St. Audoenus, wherefore it was judged in a council congregated in that same city, under the presidency of William king of the English, that the monks who were guilty of this crime should be put in prisons in the various monasteries according to the pleasure of the archbishop, and therefore were many dispersed.[66]

And that was the end of Audoenus.

William had been absent from Upper Normandy for decades, and embroiled primarily in trans-Channel operations for the previous seven

---

[65]   John of Avranches, *Liber de officiis ecclesiasticis* ed. R. Delamare (Evreux, 1923).

[66]   "Hoc anno inuaserunt monachi S. Audoeni Ioannem Rhotomagensem archiepiscopum missam celebrantem in festivitate eiusdem sancti cum armatu manu uirorum, unde iudicatum est in concilio in eadem ciuitate congregato, praesidente rege Anglorum Uuillermo, monachos huius criminis reos per abbatias in carceribus retrudi ad placitum archiepiscopi, indeque plures dispersi sunt" (*Chronicon Rotomagense* ed. Labbe, p. 367).

years. Matilda acted as regent of Normandy when William was in England, and so the duke-king would have been even farther removed from the details of Norman governance than one might at first imagine. It is unlikely that he had a clue as to the intra-ecclesiastical rivalries that had been raging for most of the century at Rouen; it is certain that he expected his highly-placed relations in Upper Normandy to be keeping the peace like good little deputies, not encouraging disruption. Nicholas' services during the mid-century crisis were forgotten. Nicholas, after all, was only William's cousin, and William now was king of England, hardly scared of cousins, even older ones. John, on the other hand, spoke with the voice of Norman beginnings, and stood before king William as the grandson of William Longsword, for whom the king had been named. But this latter-day William had not been killed interfering in areas that were none of his business. He had gained a kingdom, and now he wanted PEACE. It is hard to escape the suspicion that John deliberately provoked the monastic *familia* of St. Ouen, provoked them to violent over-reaction, a degree of over-reaction which Nicholas would never be able to justify before the king. The constant harping of abbey historians on the translations of Audoenus out of Rouen for fear of William's ancestors cannot have helped, nor is there any reason to imagine William would have felt any fondness for the new arrival, Nigasius the martyr to ambitious princes. And that was that.

We have already seen what happened next. Archbishop William Bona-Anima, former abbot of Caen, took John's advice and imposed a single calendar of saintly celebrations throughout the archdiocese, but he was unhampered by the need even to be polite to the abbot of St. Ouen. The single non-universal saint who became the official patron of Normandy was Romanus who, at the same time, was installed in a place of honor in the cathedral. Orderic gave no specific dominical year for William's establishment of Romanus, but it must have taken place between 1079, when William took office, and 1090, when the chastened abbot of St. Ouen effectively admitted defeat by procuring for himself a relic of Romanus, without which it was now impossible to continue. Nicholas was still a smooth operator, and he was not about to content himself with a bone chip from the body in the cathedral (if, indeed, the archbishop would have given him one). Nicholas negotiated with the abbot of St. Medard of Soissons to retrieve the saint's head, which arrived at the abbey, with all pomp and circumstance, on April 28, 1090. The history of that translation tells us that the body of Romanus was already "in vicina beate Marie basilica" when Nicholas' messengers left for Soissons.

Nicholas' acquisition did not come cheap. The massive endowments which Nicholas had piled up in the middle years of the century, when he had duke William's ear, must have come in handy in this transaction. Nicholas offered to the abbot of St. Medard, his old friend Odo, quite fervent prayers in return for the head of Romanus; however,

> As further inducement he added to the prayers precious gifts for divine worship, namely two small reliquary houses made from gold and worthily decorated with purple, an extraordinary long priestly garment with an ornate overgarment of gold and precious stones, a goblet with a dish of gold and silver, two branched candlesticks also of gold and silver, also two capes made from the best brocade and ornamented with gold, a dalmatic of plain white silk and one of white silk worthily decorated with gold.[67]

The atelier of St. Ouen also turned out a collection of miracles of Romanus for the occasion, which were used as readings for Romanus' June 17 translation festival; if the monks had to celebrate the feast, as least they could do it with their own miracles, and shape the saint into a more pleasing appearance.[68]

At the end of the eleventh century, the house of St. Ouen tried to turn the Romanus devotion into a shrine-based cult to the benefit of themselves, who controlled the new shrine;[69] they even claimed to have some water of Romanus, useful against all ailments. Anyone who knew Romanus in his tenth-century incarnation, turning back floods and causing marble temples to dissolve into a powder at his very approach, would hardly have recognized him now. The bishop of *virtus* and vengeance had become for the first time in his career a thaumaturge! But that was not all. A St. Ouen author also composed a metrical biography of Romanus.[70] In

---

[67] "Addit etiam precibus munera ad cultum aecclesie preciosa duas scilicet ex purpura casulas auro decenter ornatas, poderem ornatu insignem cum superhumerali auro et lapidibus precioso, calicem cum patena ex auro et argento, bina candelabra similiter ex auro et argento, duas quoque obtimi pallii cappas et aurifrisio ornatas, dalmaticam ex albo serico auro decenter ornatam, et albam sericam" (Rouen BM 1406 ff. 47v-48r = BHL 7319a). Faulty transcriptions are published by Pommeraye *S. Ouen* pp. 413-415 and Van Hecke pp. 84-85.

[68] BHL 7319b.

[69] For shrine-based cults, Ward *Miracles and the Medieval Mind* pp. 33-65.

[70] Rouen BM 1406 fols. 51r-61v (= BHL 7310).

this incarnation, Romanus became a vehicle for reformist ideals: his election permitted comments on the evils of simony, his temptation on the virtues of chastity. This Romanus was a good pastor, the *fana* and flood episodes shrink to a minimum, Norman sacred destiny disappears completely, all in favor of the description of the saint's chastity and other key virtues. In closing, the author slips into praise of Audoenus, "quo tota Neustria fulsit."[71] As a pastoral-minded thaumaturge, Romanus never did capture the imagination of anyone; it just wasn't him. The monks of St. Ouen venerated a tamed Romanus who could be called on to resuscitate little boys who had fallen into wells;[72] meanwhile the cathedral chapter and the population of Rouen would gather twice a year to celebrate a patron who had himself tamed a dragon (the Gargouille).

The abbey of St. Ouen procured a relic of Romanus, and attempted to start up a cult to rival his cathedral-based devotions. At Tours as well, beginning in the eleventh century, the archbishops lost their monopoly on the cult of St. Martin. Both the monks of Marmoutier and those of St. Ouen sought to turn the cults of local episcopal patrons to their own anti-episcopal ends. That they could even nurture such ambitions, at Tours and at Rouen, was a function of the breakdown of Carolingian ideals of hierarchy in the course of the eleventh century.[73] At Tours, Carolingian hierarchies did break down and, in the 1080s and 1090s, the archbishops lost.[74] Violent incidents such as the attack on archbishop John of Rouen also took place at Tours, and over identical issues of where and by whom the cults of the region's patrons would be celebrated. Again, the archbishops of Tours lost, broken by the alliance of monks from "below" and the pope from "above." By 1100, then, the Carolingian age had definitively

---

[71] Rouen BM 1406 fol. 61r.

[72] Rouen BM 1406 contains the only medieval copy of BHL 7319b, a report of various miracles attributed to Romanus' head after its return to the abbey of St. Ouen. There are transcriptions, made from Rouen 1406, in Neustria Sancta, Arthur du Monstier's unpublished 1657 compilation of materials concerning all the saints of Normandy (see f. 170v of BN lat. 10.051) and in BR 8919, a Bollandist notebook (twice; see ff. 84 and 88). Like BHL 7319a, the text of 7319b in Rouen 1406 is incomplete, this time at the end. However, only a finite verb and the doxology seem to be missing. A transcription is given below in Appendix 2.

[73] Farmer, *Communities of St. Martin* p. 37.

[74] Farmer, *Communities of St. Martin* ch. 2, "Excluding the Center: Monastic Exemption and Liturgical Realignment in Tours" pp. 38-77, esp. pp. 38-49.

ended at Tours. At Rouen, on the other hand, the archbishops won. The legacy of the Archangel and the Areopagite never faltered. Through Hugh of St. Denis and Fulbertus of Jumièges that Carolingian legacy was concentrated in the person of Romanus. Romanus, unlike Audoenus, never failed the see. The center was never excluded at Rouen; instead, the suburban monastery of St. Ouen languished on the edge.

B. AFTER THE CONQUEST: CONTINUITY AND ASSIMILATION

Truly that nation by predetermination is striving towards the goal of regeneration by God, nor can the way of predestined salvation be closed off to them. And even though that nation first hasten to penetrate lands that do not belong to them, nevertheless...it will soon renounce you and your world and be imbued with the lordly sacraments. Moreover, that place which that nation will pervade with barbaric cruelty will be for it the effective cause of its hoped-for salvation, since the name of Christ which it would otherwise never had heard, it will soon hear there, and having heard it, will faithfully believe, and having believed, will magnificently worship, and thus will it become a chosen people (*genus electum*), a holy nation (*gens sancta*).[75]
    —Fulbertus' Romanus, to a demon at the ruined amphitheatre of Rouen (*circa* 945)

For those waters are merely a foretelling of the piratical army of enemy nations that will one day come against you, which will completely subjugate your inhabited territory with unheard-of savageness and subject your descendants to their dominion....However, know this, that that nation about which we are speaking, now still in the grip of the error of heathendom, as soon as it shall hear the name of Christ, will take up the worship of the Catholic faith and go on to foster its subjects in great peace.[76]
    —Fulbertus' Romanus, to the population of Merovingian Rouen (*circa* 945)

---

[75] Fulbertus, *Vita Romani* fol. 120v.
[76] Fulbertus, *Vita Romani* fol. 122r.

[Rollo] gave a guarantee of safety to all the nations desiring to abide in his land. He apportioned that land among his *fideles* and rebuilt it all, foreseaken for so long, and he restored it, crammed with his own warriors and with foreign nations, he enjoined upon the populace rights and eternal laws ratified and ordained by the will of the leaders, and likewise compelled them to abide in peaceful intercourse. He erected churches that had been utterly cast to the ground, restored sanctuaries that had been torn down by the crowd of pagans, remade and increased the walls and towers of cities, he subjugated the rebellious Bretons to himself and tread down upon the whole Breton realm, affluently granted to him as a source of victuals. And then he sent out a ban, that is an interdict, in the land under his authority, that is he prohibited anyone to be a thief or a bandit or to be an accessory to any person of ill will....And thus was the land at rest, without thieves and bandits, and it was still, stripped of all seditions. Consequently all men, safe under Robert's[77] authority, were rejoicing in uninterrupted peace and long-lasting rest and were opulent in all goods, not fearing any hostile army.
—Dudo of St. Quentin (*circa* 1000)[78]

...in our *pays*, paganism still endured in the seventh century. When St. Romanus arrived at Rouen, around 631, he found its inhabitants given to a crowd of idolatries. He himself overturned the citadel of the demons, built to the north of the town....then he travelled throughout his diocese in order to pursue, even into their very last retreats, the cult and altars of false Gods. With his powerful hand, he caused temples dedicated to Jupiter, Mercury, and Apollo to crumble and, in his sacred arms, he smothered the monster of idolatry, which a grateful posterity has depicted in the form of a dragon, and designated with the name *gargouille*.
—Abbé Cochet (1854)[79]

---

[77] Robert was Rollo's baptismal name.
[78] Dudo, *De moribus* pp. 171-173.
[79] "...dans notre pays, le paganisme durait encore au VIIe siècle. Lorsque saint Romain arriva à Rouen, vers 631, il en trouva les habitants adonnés à une foule d'idolâtries. Lui-même renversa la citadelle des démons, bâtie au septentrion de la ville....puis il parcourut son diocèse, afin d'y poursuivre, jusque dans leurs dernières retraites, le culte et les autels des faux Dieux. Da sa main puissante, il fit crouler les temples dédiés à Jupiter, à Mercure, et à Apollo, et, dans ses bras sacrés, il étouffa le monstre de l'idolâtrie, que la posterité reconnassante peignit sous la

Under the combined impact of Carolingian discourse and of the conquest and settlement of the region by Vikings, Pious Neustria was transformed, historiographically speaking, from a region full of monks and nuns to a region full of demons and "pagans." The narratives of historical identity produced in Viking Normandy, such as Fulbertus' *Vita Romani*, were melodramatic, often violent, depictions of the past. By the eleventh century, the Vikings had been completely assimilated to Frankish culture. The emblem of their assimilation is archbishop Robert, great-grandson of the "pagan" conqueror Rollo, and leader of the Norman church. We can see the assimilation, the taming, not only his person, who late in life "repented," rejected his family and turned to sponsoring miracle-collections about the saintly patron of the town; we can see it also in the new shape of that saint, Romanus. There is still some bite left in the saint, but he is a mere shadow of his former self. He is no longer in his boyhood or in his infancy, but at least he is still in his adolescence. Or rather, he is in St. Nicolas' adolescence, to borrow the life-cycle imagery of C. W. Jones.

Nicholas, like the Archangel Michael, was one of those oriental saints whose popularity had risen suddenly in the Latin west during the ninth century.[80] Like Michael, he is a definitively "Carolingian" saint, one who was not tied to specific locales or relics, but who was capable of interfering universally, and even of being in more than one place at the same time.[81] Like Michael, he had already functioned, before his immigration to the Latin west, as an imperial saint, as a saint for a unified empire, the symbol of Byzantium, standing against the Muslim world.[82] Finally, like Michael, he took refuge in Normandy as the capital of his cult, when the rest of the Carolingian world had crumbled around him. Surely it is meaningful that both the Archangel and the Myroblyte felt so at home in Normandy?

Saint Nicholas was popular everyplace in the Carolingian West during the ninth century, but there are few places where he was as popular

---

forme d'un dragon, et désigna sous le nom d'une gargouille" (Abbé J.B.D. Cochet, *La Normandie souterraine, ou, Notice sur des cimetières romains et des cimetières francs explorés en Normandie* [Brionne, 1854] p. 409).

[80]   P. Gerardo Cioffari *S. Nicola nella Critica Storica. Le fonti, la vita, la letteratura* (Bari, 1987) pp. 91-92.

[81]   Jones, *St. Nicholas of Myra, Bari and Manhattan. Biography of a Legend* p. 27.

[82]   Jones, *St. Nicholas of Myra* p. 74.

as in the future Normandy. The evidence of parochial dedications in the region places Nicholas, with his 91 dedications, in the select company of the Virgin, John the Baptist, Martin, Peter, Germanus, Audoenus and Albinus, saints whose patronage attests to the great age of the churches under their protection.[83] The oldest known manuscript copy of Nicholas' Latin biography by John the Deacon of Naples (c. 880), older by a century than any other known manuscript copy, is a Norman manuscript of the tenth century.[84] Nicolas' cult was being embraced and promoted in the very highest social circles in Normandy during the early decades of the eleventh century. Isembertus, monk of St. Ouen, composed the text and melody of a chanted office of Nicholas, a musical composition that was to enjoy great popularity, and perhaps accounts for Isembertus' promotion as the first abbot of St. Trinité du Mont, near Rouen.[85] Richard III, that ill-fated and short-lived duke, named his son Nicolas, making the latter the first to bear the name north of the Alps.[86] As we have already met Nicholas of St. Ouen, we can easily imagine the fervor with which he promoted the cult of his patron saint.

Nicholas then, is a saint whose veneration in Normandy was continuous between the Carolingian and Norman periods. His adoption by the Normans, to the point of taking the name into the ducal family, was itself a feature of the family's assimilation into Carolingian ways. But an even more extraordinary level of assimilation is indicated by Robert's collection of Romanus' miracles: in the early eleventh century, Romanus, the Norman saint, was remade in the image of Nicholas. Romanus had done little besides battle demons and destroy temples; it was not necessarily an obvious step to assimilate him to Nicholas,[87] at least not to the Nicolas vener-

---

[83] Jean Fournée *Saint Nicolas en Normandie* (Nogent-sur-Marne, 1988) p. 47.

[84] Paris, BN lat. 989 from Fécamp (the biography of Nicholas is on fols. 54r-95r); Cioffari *S. Nicola* p. 96 (see pp. 91-100 and 113-122 for all the Latin writings about Nicholas). The various families of transmission of John's *vita* are BHL 6104-6117.

[85] Fournée, *Saint Nicolas* p. 48; Jones, *St. Nicholas of Myra* p. 148.

[86] Jones, *St. Nicholas* p. 148.

[87] N* (as Jones prefers to call him), had once destroyed a "pagan" temple, dedicated in N*'s case to Artemis. But he had done so much more besides, and the simple destruction of the temple, an activity he shared with so many other saints, was never an important feature of his "legend." In any case, the elaborated temple-destruction episode is a feature of a tenth-century Greek biography by Symeon Logotheta, which was not written in time to be translated for Latin audiences by

ated in the Latin west. We can take as our standard of "Nicolas" the starring figure of the noted office by Reginold of Eichstätt (966-991) that caused such an artistic sensation in the Latin world; Reginold highlighted two gold-giving miracles, one rescue at sea, an infantile refusal of nurse's milk, a chastizing of Constantine, and the exuding of myrhh.[88] Many centuries later, Nicholas is a very popular saint, because he still performs the functions around which his cult first developed: he protects mariners by calming the seas when storms arise, and he brings gold to persons in financial need (in this latter arena he has obviously become more creative about what to bring and more egalitarian about whom to bring it to).[89] Ships and money. Perhaps the reason Nicholas remained so continuously popular in Normandy during the tenth century was his appeal to the seagoing merchants who made Rouen one of the greatest emporia of the day, in one of the most prosperous and commercialized regions of Europe.[90]

One of the four miracles attributed to Romanus in Robert's collection credits the patron of Rouen with calming a storm at sea. Yet miracles at sea, like exorcisms, sometimes seem to be a dime a dozen in the repertoire

---

John the Deacon, who transmitted a synthesized version of earlier biographies by Michael the Archimandrite and Methodios (Cioffari, *S. Nicola* pp. 91-100; Jones, *Saint Nicholas* pp. 20-21 and p. 47).

[88]   Cioffari *S. Nicola* pp. 97-100.

[89]   Jones, *St. Nicholas* pp. 24-27 and 54-57 describes "Mariners," "Grainships" and "Three Daughters" in the version of Symeon Logetheta, but they appear in nearly the same form in the Latin *vitae* (Cioffari, *S. Nicola* pp. 91-100); Jones pp. 76-77 lists more maritime rescues and gold donations.

[90]   Warner of Rouen accuses a monk of Mont-St.-Michel of having fled his monastery and come to Rouen in order to exercise a penchant for finance (Lucien Musset, "Le Satirist Garnier de Rouen et son milieu [début du XIe siècle]" *Revue du Moyen Age Latin* 10 [1954] pp. 237-266); for more on the economic prosperity of the region, see Lucien Musset, "La renaissance urbaine des Xe et XIe siècles dans l'Ouest de la France: problèmes et hypothèses de travail" in *Etudes de civilisation médiévale [IXe-XIIe siècles]: Mélanges offerts à E.-R. Labande* [Poitiers, 1974] pp. 563-575; L. Musset, "Les invasions scandinaves et l'évolution des villes de la France de l'Ouest" *Revue Historique de Droit Français et Etranger* 43 [1965] pp. 320-322; L. Musset, "Les conditions financières d'une réussite architecturale: les grandes églises romanes de Normandie" *Mélanges offerts à René Crozet à l'occasion de son 70e anniversaire* [Poitiers, 1966] pp. 307-314; Dumas-Dubourg, *Le Trésor de Fécamp* pp. 17-18, 27, 51-52).

of holy men and women,[91] and if Romanus had only been endowed with a sea-calming episode, there would be little compelling reason for us to connect him with Nicholas. But the dropping of gold coins into the hands of a needy person is a trick of Nicholas' that few have been able to duplicate. On one occasion, Nicholas gives cash to a seaman, with which the latter is enabled to buy grain and alleviate a famine; on another occasion, he gives cash to a father, who is prevented from "having to" hire his daughters out as prostitutes. "Three Daughters" was a particularly well-known story in the Latin west from the tenth century, when a dramatized version played to packed houses in Rome.[92] Another of Romanus' early-eleventh-century miracles credited him with miraculously providing gold pieces to an impoverished cleric of the town.

In shaping the new Romanus in the image of Nicholas, the author of the miracle collection almost necessarily had to tame the missionary saint; the violence of Romanus' tenth-century biography was unsuitable for a myroblyte. One senses that it was the audience at Rouen that had become sqeamish, for Nicholas, though never reaching the levels of Romanus, had obviously been involved in stories more exciting than those of Romanus' eleventh-century miracles. Our eleventh-century *rouennais* author not only made Romanus into Nicholas, he made him into less than Nicholas. In the tenth century, Fulbertus had set Romanus' life in Merovingian Gaul, and the vision of the past was both violent and exciting. By the early eleventh century, another author set Romanus' post-mortem miracles in the present, and the present looked distinctly placid. It is from this miracle collection, for instance, that we know of the existence of a school of liberal arts at Rouen in the reign of Richard I, where archbishop Robert had been educated.[93] The events are set in the author's immediate present, for he relates as an eye-witness a strange and marvelous event that took place one year during the celebration of Romanus' October 23 festival.[94]

Romanus' first miracle collection, composed early in the eleventh century, should by all accounts have been much more dramatic than it

---

[91] Loomis, *White Magic* p. 45 and pp. 164-165 note 1 for over one hundred examples of saints quelling storms at sea.

[92] Jones, *St. Nicholas* p. 57.

[93] *Miracula Romani* fol. 30r.

[94] *Miracula Romani* fol. 30v.

was. Romanus was still a new saint and, in keeping with the character of miracle-collections of the eleventh century and earlier, particularly those of new saints, the aim of the stories is to establish the power of the saint, to demonstrate his sanctity.[95] During this stage, it was normal to report miracles which demonstrated the saint's might, miracles for instance, that demonstrated his or her ability to take vengeance on enemies. Once the sanctity *per se* had been established, authors turned to aggrandizing a particular sanctuary, at which the power in question could be harnessed.[96] The Romanus of the Norman tenth century could cause marble buildings to dissolve into a powder; one would certainly have expected his first miracle collection, of all people's, to include stunning displays of *virtus*. All four miracles are indeed intended to demonstrate Romanus' sanctity, yet none make use of violent or dramatic themes. There is not even a single spirited conversational exchange, not a single example of the sort of quick-witted railery in which Romanus had engaged with his demonic adversaries, or in which Queen Jezebel, protagonist of an earlier *rouennais* poem, had so excelled.[97]

The first miracle took place one day in the church of St. Romain, where archbishop Robert had come to celebrate Romanus' festival. Our anonymous author was an eye-witness of the event. Robert finds himself doubting whether the hand of God had really appeared to Romanus, for that sign had, in Fulbertus' biography, apprised the saint of his own imminent demise. When Robert expresses his doubts aloud, he is reprimanded by his own former teacher of liberal arts: did not the patriarch Jacob, the prophets Isaiah and Micah, and the protomartyr Stephen all see the Lord, as Scripture attests? The archbishop, evidently well taught, counters with

---

[95]   Richard, "Les 'Miracula' composés en Normandie" pp. 183-189; Ward, *Miracles and the Medieval Mind* ch. 3.

[96]   As we have already seen (above pp. 203-206), the attempt by the abbey of St. Ouen to turn Romanus into a shrine-saint, for the monastery's benefit, was a failure; Romanus never became a thaumaturge, or a saint whose power could be concentrated at a shrine.

[97]   Jan Ziolkowski, *Jezebel: A Norman Latin Poem of the Early Eleventh Century* (Studies and Sources Relating to the Middle Ages and the Renaissance 10; Humana Civilitas 10; N.Y., 1989) p. 3. Perhaps it is significant that, at Rouen, the only community sufficiently charmed with Romanus' eleventh-century miracles to use them in the office for the October festival was the canonry of St.-Lô (Paris, Bibliothèque Ste. Geneviève mss. 131, 1265-66, and 2634).

his own scriptural evidence: did not the apostles Peter and Thomas both doubt? Rouen is nothing if not "civilized."

To settle the matter, the old school master calls for a sign,

> ...and behold suddenly there rang out a crashing and thundering of the air...and behold that flashing of frightening light, which had filled the whole space of the church from top to bottom was compressed into a single ray, and that ray poured directly into the reliquary where the sacred bones lay...and thus did the elements clearly testify to what human hearts had hesitated to believe.[98]

In stark contrast with Fulbertus' demonophobia (or demonophilia?), the natural elements have now replaced demonic causation as means to move the plot along. It is not even an angel who comes to set the doubter straight. But, according to the anonymous author, it is entirely appropriate that we learn from the natural world, "since the insensible stones mourned the death of Christ." The device of the natural elements turns up again in the third miracle, in which Romanus saves two clerks, on pilgrimage to Jerusalem, from shipwreck. The cause of the storm (here in contrast to Nicholas' storm-at-sea miracles) is not even specified by the author as demonic, although Romanus himself suggests to one of the clerks that the storm might be due to the ancient enemy. The absence of demonic causation here is striking, since more often than not in the hundreds of storm-at-sea miracles attributed to Christian saints over the ages the storms are explicitly asserted to have been stirred up by demons.[99] When Fulbertus had invested the natural world with a role in the narrative, he described deep chasms spewing forth fumes and catapulting dirt with crushing force at the inhabitants of Rouen; the author of the *miracula* gives us thunder and lightening.

Fulbertus' world had been infested with malevolent spirits. All his life, Fulbertus' version of Romanus did nothing but battle supernatural opponents, when he (or his parents) was not receiving visits from supernatural allies. At Rouen in the middle of the tenth century, all sorts of enemies and allies, visible and invisible, around the corner and just over the horizon, must have seemed very believable. Both angels and demons are

---

[98] *Miracula Romani* fol. 30v.

[99] J. Rougé, "Topos et realia: La Tempête apaisée de la Vie de Saint Germain d'Auxerre" *Latomus* 27 (1988) pp. 197-202.

equally missing from the eleventh-century miracles; the only "supernatural" motif in the entire text is the appearance of saints in visions. And when one asks what Romanus had done for his devotees lately, one cannot help but notice that there has been little call for dramatic protection against fearsome enemies. In the fourth miracle, the saint appears to a member of the community serving his church, who has fallen on financially ruinous times, and presents him with five gold coins.

The cultural shift that seems to be indicated by the contrast between Fulbertus' biography of Romanus and that same saint's first miracle collection, is consistent with everything we know about the situation at Rouen by the reign of Richard II, when Normandy was the most traditional, conservative, and Carolingian of all the regions of the former empire. The Normans had learned how to be pedantic and boring. Like those "unconquered Franks" before them, who had never bowed their necks even to the Roman Empire, the Normans went from greatest threat to favorite son of Holy Mother Church. In the middle of the tenth century, demons had been everywhere around Rouen, and Romanus fought them; by the early eleventh century, the toppler of idols was reduced to giving cash handouts to devotees. If that is not a sign of the settled state of affairs, religiously and commercially, of the reign of Richard II, nothing is. Romanus' October 23 festival has at times been seen as the special "fête des bourgeois et des marchands," and to this day all of his fairs, at Rouen, at St.-Romain-de-Colbosc, and at Vassy, are major commercial moments.[100] Romanus, it would seem, had done his job too well for his own good. But let us not underestimate the resilience of his semiotic power.

The definitive Norman saint had been remade in the image of a popular Carolingian saint; should we call it a sop thrown to the conquered Neustrians, to encourage them to accept the new patron, and to reject Audoenus? Emphatically, no. First of all, Romanus was a saint who had originally come to prominence at Rouen as a Neustrian protector against Viking attack. He was coopted by Fulbertus and Hugh and Richard in the tenth century, and made into the special patron of the conquerors. But it was an even further revised version of the patron, Romanus, revised to conform to the ideals of the conquered, that reigned in the eleventh century,

---

[100] Fournée, *Le culte populaire des saints en Normandie* (*Cahiers Léopold Delisle*, numéro spécial, 1973) pp. 102 and 141.

and that became the mandatory patron of the archdiocese. This eleventh-century image is the one that had to be accepted by the conquerors themselves. Assimilation is a two-way street, and in the end it is hard to say who conquered whom.

Similarly complex modalities of the assimilation process have emerged from other studies of historical identities as expressed through saints' cults. We have seen the very saints of "Pious Neustria," initially put forward in hopes of protection against the invading Austrasians, continue to thrive in the Carolingian period, albeit in revised forms. Such a development did not begin in Upper Normandy until the late seventh century, for the region had been shielded during earlier stages of the Frankish conquest. The Orléanais, however, had not been so lucky during the fifth and sixth centuries: there it was gallo-roman saints which the local populace brandished against the wrath of the invading Franks, and therefore it was gallo-roman saints whom the Franks themselves adopted, after the conquest, as their own special patrons.[101] The conquering Frankish elite adopted, venerated and promoted, one after another, the patron saints of their conquered gallo-roman subjects: Anianus of Orléans, Martin of Tours, Martial of Limoges, Saturninus of Toulouse, Germanus of Auxerre, Remigius of Reims, Quintinus of Vermandois. Martin of Tours, in particular, became the very symbol of the alliance between the "conquered" gallo-roman aristocracy and the new Frankish leaders after Clovis' victory in the Touraine.[102] Several centuries later, a similar process would take place in England, as the Anglo-Norman bishops after 1066 focussed their attention primarily on Anglo-Saxon saints.[103] We cannot help but ask who conquered whom, or how assimilation works.

A similar process marked Viking assimilation into Frankish society in the tenth century. The primary patron of the new duchy became Romanus, a Frankish (even royal) saint originally deployed as a protector of Rouen against the sea-borne pirates themselves. As we know, Romanus was not the only such Carolingian-era saint taken to the Viking breast: St. Michael, the sword-arm of Francia in its war against "pagans" also became

---

[101] Head, *Hagiography and the Cult of Saints* pp. 282-284.

[102] Farmer, *Communities of St. Martin* pp. 24-26.

[103] Susan J. Ridyard, *The Royal Cults of Anglo-Saxon England: A Study of West Saxon and East Anglian Cults* (Cambridge, 1988).

a great Norman patron. The Viking conquerors of the Seine valley became the assimilated "Normans" the moment they accepted that their destiny in life was to find salvation in the bosom of the God of the conquered, as Romanus had predicted, to stand in battle with, rather than against, the Archangel, and to become as Frankish as the most Carolingian Frank, as Dudo described. So the conquerors assimilated to native structures and values; but the natives too became "Normans." The conquered Neustrians became "Normans" the moment they accepted that the region had been "pagan" and infested with demons in the Merovingian period, demons whom Romanus had battled, and that (in accordance with Romanus' prophecy), transcendant, sacred-historical meaning had only been super-added to the region's identity when the Vikings arrived. Both the "pious Neustrians" and the "Vikings" lost their earlier identities, and became "Normans."

Romanus was successful as the patron saint of Rouen, is successful as the patron of Rouen, in whose honor the very grandest party of the year is always given, precisely because everyone had cause to believe he was really their saint. He was "Francia," but he was also the special prophet of the northmen. He was the patron who had protected Rouen from the dangers of the Vikings, and he was the special prophet of the salvation of the Vikings. It becomes very hard to say who conquered whom: the Vikings who took over the profits of the political machinery at Rouen, or the Neustrians who insisted the new-comers become carbon copies of themselves?

The Viking conquerors had assimilated so quicky and so thoroughly to continental norms that the memory of their arrival need not have survived historiographically, let alone been cherished, nurtured, dramatized. Throughout the ninth and tenth centuries a structural continuity reigned in the, as it were, material base, even at the level of the organization of rural domains, the most real and day-to-day level of experienced life for most people.[104] Against this fundamental continuity, the level of power politics was punctuated by several moments of crisis and accentuated struggle (the grant to Rollo, the aftermath of William Longsword's assassi-

---

[104] Jean Yver, "Les bases du pouvoir ducal en Normandie," plenary address before the 26eme Semaine d'Histoire du Droit Normand, 1950; published in *Revue Historique du Droit Français et étranger* 4 ser, xxviii (1951); Lucien Musset, "Les domaines de l'époque franque et les destinées de la régime domaniale" *Bulletin de la Société des Antiquaires de Normandie* 49 (1942-45).

nation, the Frankish intrigues of the 960s), none of which were extraordinary or exceptional in the context of the late Carolingian world. No rupture ever occurred, but the THREAT of rupture was quite real. "Not-Christian" elites settled within the Carolingian Empire; they might not have accepted native values quite as thoroughly as they in fact did.

The cost of assimilating the new conquerors to native values, and averting the threat of rupture, was high: the conquered Neustrians had to accept the historiographical myth of discontinuity. They had to accept that "Normandy" had begun when the Vikings arrived, and to forget "Pious Neustria." New patrons and new symbols of historical identity were brought forward. Certainly, Norman parochial churches have preserved their Carolingian-era patrons, the patrons of "Pious Neustria" among whom Audoenus was predominant; but many saints who stood for "pagan" Neustria and for the need to evangelize it by force, not only Romanus of Rouen, but also others modelled on Romanus such as Laudus of Coutances and Vigor of Bayeux, appeared in the religious historiography of the region after the Viking conquest.[105] Discontinuity exists primarily in the historiography of the region, in the ideological superstructure, which has been preserved in the written record. From Fulbertus' gemmetic biographies and Dudo's chronicle of the dukes, the historiographic discourse of new Christian beginnings for a paganized world, borrowed (like so much else) from the legitimators of the Carolingian *coup*, steadily imposed itself. Myth or not, the discourse has functioned as real, in the real world, and above all in the real world of the history classroom (from elementary to univer-

---

[105] Audoenus has 111 Norman parochial dedications, or 2.5% of the total. The only other local saints (that is, individuals besides Mary, Martin, Peter, etc.) to have become parochial patrons are, in descending order, Vigor (49), Paternus (27), Laudus (14), Filibertus (11), Serenicus (7), Wandregiselus (6), Ebrulfus (5), Romanus (4), Helerius (4), Marculfus (4), Austreberta (3), Gildardus (3), Leutfredus (2) and Sydonius (2) (Fournée, "Quelques facteurs de fixation" pp. 120-121; Fournée, *Le culte populaire des saints* p. 29). With the exception of Audoenus, the saints of "Pious Neustria" are hardly commemorated. The saints catapulted to the top of the list all represented an image of the Neustrian past as "paganized" and difficult to "Christianize." For Paternus, see above, pp. 33-34. For Vigor, see Lifshitz, "The Migration of Neustrian Relics." For Laudus, see Lifshitz, "La Normandie Carolingienne."

sity levels), where most people now get their ideas about the past.[106] So the millenary of the "foundation" of Normandy was celebrated in 911, the year that has traditionally been associated with the baptism of Rollo.[107] The history of Normandy from the eleventh century has been the history of the Viking conquering elites, the effective tenth-century converts of St. Romanus, and not of the devout Neustrian populace whose diocese had already flourished in sanctity more than any other in Gaul during the seventh-century pontificate of St. Audoenus.[108]

Dudo of St. Quentin's task, as the first major historian of those conquerors, was unimaginably complex. His frequent protestations of anxiety over how his work would be received in Normandy, the way he likened himself to a sole mariner floating in a puny rowboat out on the open main, his fear that at least half of the work was completely useless, should not be dismissed as mere literary commonplaces.[109] Dudo was faced with the formidable task of simultaneously demonstrating two superficially-contradictory theses; that he did so, against the conventions of academic, professional historiography, has contributed to his rejection in recent times. Oddly enough, however, the bifurcated thesis of his narrative is an accurate evocation of the process of conquest and assimilation: he really does describe continuity in structures and institutions (for which he

---

[106] Compare the influence of another great historiographic myth in the classroom and in popular French history books: Elizabeth A.R. Brown, "The Tyranny of a Construct: Feudalism and Historians of Medieval Europe" *AHR* 79 (1974) pp. 1063-1088, esp. pp. 1068-1069, pp. 1078-1080, and p. 1085. A similar and in many ways more thorough analysis has recently been presented by David Crouch, "Feudalism and the Historians" (paper presented at the International Congress of Medieval Studies, Kalamazoo, 1994).

[107] *Le Livre du millénaire de la Normandie, 911-1911* (Paris, 1911), published under the patronage of the Comité des fêtes du millénaire de Rouen et du comité parisien des fêtes du millénaire. The fullest statement of the thesis of complete rupture and rebuilding from 911 is Michel de Bouard, "De la Neustrie Carolingienne à la Normandie féodale: continuité ou discontinuité?" *BIHR* XXVIII (1955) pp. 1-14. The author adduces no evidence in favor of his view; his argument depends entirely on a series of assumptions about "feudalism."

[108] For the later historiography of regional identity, see F. Lifshitz, "St. Romain de Rouen: missionnaire franc dans la Normandie des vikings" *La France à l'Ouest: Voix d'Ouest en Europe, Souffles d'Europe en Ouest* (Actes du Colloque International d'Angers, May 1992; Angers, 1993) ed. G. Cesbron pp. 23-30.

[109] Dudo, *De moribus* p. 120.

has been savagely reproached as a liar), while at the same time recognizing the rupture, and the new beginning, which had been necessitated on a metahistorical level (for which he has been savagely reproached as a purveyor of myth). He achieved his goal in large part through the use of the prosimetrical form: in the prose he could describe, prosaically, the institutional continuity; in the verse he could gloss the events, putting them into a metahistorical framework in which they could acquire meaning. Post-"Enlightenment" linear sensibilities are not comfortable with Dudo's gloss of himself, as he simultaneously portrays the Norman dukes as indistinguishable from any other Frankish prince, yet waxes eloquent as he recoils, poetically, from a wailing Francia, where no land is cultivated, all roads deserted, and fields have become overgrown with bushes.

The conquest and settlement of Neustria by Rollo and his followers can only be comprehended in a shadowy form at this great remove, and even then we can see the process only from the perspective of the Franks, whose civilization did not eschew written traditions. Very few sources survive to shed light on the process; the narratives of Fulbertus and Dudo represent the earliest Frankish historiographic attempts to come to grips with the transformation of Neustria into Normandy. For both Fulbertus and Dudo, the Neustrians had to become irrelevant, in order for metahistorical meaning to accrue to the baptism of Rollo. After the negotiations which resulted in the cession of Neustria to Rollo, a much more complicated series of negotiations was required to assimilate the Vikings to the Neustrians, and *vice versa*; the negotiations were fraught with tension, a tension which has played itself out ever since in historiographic revisionism and in the conflicts between the cults of Audoenus and Romanus.[110] "Audoenus" may be a more accurate representation of Neustrian history, but "Romanus" is necessary to understand Normandy.

---

[110] Lifshitz, "S. Romain de Rouen."

Appendix 1

Rejected Biographies of "Pious Neustria"

Although the Austrasian penetration of Neustria did provoke a certain amount of historiographic composition, two of the biographies normally associated with the late-Merovingian diocese of Rouen were not in fact composed then or there: the biographies of Wandregiselus of Fontenelle and Geremarus of Fly.

A. THE EARLIEST BIOGRAPHY OF WANDREGISELUS OF FONTENELLE (BHL 8804)

Paris, BN lat. 18.315, an early-eighth-century manuscript of 31 folios, contains nothing but the unique exemplar of BHL 8804, the earliest biography of Wandregiselus of Fontenelle.[1] The biography was written after the death of Wandregiselus (circa 672) by a monk of Romainmôtier, in the Jura mountains of Burgundy, who had known Wandregiselus during his time as a monk of that house, and was dedicated to the bishop of Lyons, Lantbertus (†688), who had been abbot of Fontenelle before coming to Burgundy. We have only the single copy of BHL 8804, BN lat 18.315. One of the most common alterations made to texts in copying them is to leave off the prologue, especially dedicatory letters; it is unquestionably the great advance of printed books that such things are so much harder to lose. BHL 8805, manifestly a much later biography based on BHL 8804,[2] contains in some manuscripts a dedicatory letter addressed to Lantbertus from an author who knew Wandregiselus. The letter does not belong with BHL 8805; the fact of it having been connected with that version of the biography has led to much name-calling of the hapless author of BHL 8805. I see no obstacle to the letter having originally accompanied BHL 8804.

The author of BHL 8804 was a Burgundian, who knew almost nothing and cared even less about Neustria *per se*. The author knew and was

---

[1] *Vita Wandregiseli* ed. Bruno Krusch, MGH SRM 5 pp. 13-24.
[2] AASS July V pp. 272-281.

influenced by Jonas of Bobbio's *vita Columbani*, a text which in the Merovingian period was confined to Burgundian circles.[3] Wandregiselus, in his biographer's eyes, was a man always searching for a life of monastic perfection. First he went to a local community in the Meuse, now Montfaucon, where he didn't stay very long (c. 6). Then Wandregiselus set up his own retreat (c. 8), but again to no avail. In both places, though he tried to mortify his flesh, he was constantly annoyed by the temptations of the *antiquus hostis*. God did not wish to leave Wandregiselus to battle against the *adversarius* alone, so in a vision he showed him Bobbio, in Lombardy, as a possible habitation. The saint then travelled to Bobbio, but found that monastery also unsatisfactory (c. 9). Taking to the road again, he arrives at Romainmôtier:

> Qui ipse abba eum cum summa diligencia recoepit. Ubi iuxta moris consuetudinem mandatum Domini adimplentes ad lauandum pedes uenissent, cognouit ipsi sanctus Dei, quo ibi era illa uita arta, quam illi per desiderio Christi uolebat sectare, et cercius per spiritum Dei notum ei fuit, quod ad hoc eum Dominus adduxerat, ut sub relegionis habito conuersare debiret, et se in oboedienciam ibidem deligauit. Qui multis diebus ibidem sub institucione regulare habitauit (c. 10).

The monastery at Romainmôtier is the only place (and this includes Fontenelle itself) that is described in unequivocably flattering terms. Wandregiselus was happy at Romainmôtier, but through an angelic vision learns that he is to take to the road again, to be shown eventually the spot where he is to settle. The author tells us that this miracle was related to him by the saint himself (c. 12). The ninth-century rewriting of Wandregiselus' biography (BHL 8805) explicitly says when recounting this particular miracle that its source was an inhabitant of Romainmôtier.[4]

Neustria is in every way a far-off place to our Burgundian biographer, who provides not a single local detail, in stark contrast with the

---

[3]   I.N. Wood, "The *Vita Columbani* and Merovingian Hagiography" *Peritia* I (1982) pp. 63-80, at p. 68.

[4]   BHL 8805, c. 12 ed. Peter Boschius AASS July V. On the basis of this reference, both Mabillon (ASOSB Saec. II pp. 526-534) and Boschius (AASS July V p. 253) identified the author of BHL 8804 as a monk of Romainmôtier. Krusch simply called the author of BHL 8805 a liar, asserted that Mabillon and Boschius had been too "rash," and the identification of the author disappeared from the literature (MGH SRM 5 p. 19).

Merovingian biographies of Fontenelle. Verdun, the saint's birthplace, has seemed close and familiar enough, and so has Lombardy, but when God sends Wandregiselus off to the very ends of the earth to make his merits known to "universis gentibus," that is when the saint lands in Rouen (c. 13). The author is unimpressed with the two contemporary bishops who have dealings with Wandregiselus, Audomarus and, more significantly, Audoenus who has nothing at all to do with the foundation of Fontenelle, except in so far as his permission is required for Wandregiselus to retire from the priesthood, an office he has been fulfilling at Rouen (c. 14). The Audoenus in this biography of Wandregiselus is not the Audoenus that would have appeared had it been written by a monk of Fontenelle under Ansbertus, the traditional date. In fact, Wandregiselus' first biographer seems most of all amazed that the saint has managed to survive at all now that he is on the very edges of civilization (c. 16). The Meuse, though geographically closer than Rouen to the heart of Roman Gaul where the author of BHL 8804 lived, was also perceived as inhabited by dangerous and barbarous thugs who would kill a person at the drop of a hat (cc. 5 and 7).

The terms in which a second eyewitness anecdote is related in BHL 8804 also points to the author as a monk of Romainmôtier. The saint's life at Fontenelle is described in cc. 15 and 16; in the course of the two long chapters, the author refers many times to the abbot's flock, always as his *filii* (sons), and puts speeches in the saint's mouth in which he addresses the monks as his *filii*. The author then digresses. In c. 1, he had announced that, although he had seen many things he could relate, he would only pass on a few, which he finally does in c. 17. Here the author tells, as an eyewitness, a story in which the saint addresses his interlocutors as *fratres* (brothers). Our author is remembering events which took place in Romainmôtier, when Wandregiselus was one of the *fratres*, and not the *abbas*. On the other hand, the ensuing description of the events surrounding the saint's death at Fontenelle are then attributed to a monk of that house, who related certain miraculous occurrences to our author (c. 19). The author himself is indifferent to the relics of Wandregiselus, or to anything connected with a cult to the holy father, for he does not say where the saint is buried and adds, only as an afterthought (after the "Amen"), "Nosse qui velit" the date on which Wandregiselus had died (c. 22).

The spirit of this author is as far removed as it could possibly be from that of all the known products of the atelier of Fontenelle, which is famous for an emphasis on material enrichment of the house, for the insertion of documentary evidence, for highly politicized narratives such as the *vita Ansberti* and the *Gesta abbatum Fontenellensium*,[5] and for other such "secular" leanings. The background of Neustrian politics, which we have just analysed, is entirely absent from the *vita Wandregiseli*. It is not a text composed against the background of a conquest. Nothing produced at Fontenelle between the end of the seventh century and the middle of the ninth century is lacking in a clear-cut political stance. Either the Carolingians are servants of the devil, or they are the saviors from the east, but a stance is taken. The products of the atelier of Fontenelle are among the most important sources for the political history of the late Merovingian and early Carolingian periods. The author of the first biography of Wandregiselus knows nothing, cares not at all, about "politics."

Instead, the author of the first biography of Wandregiselus seems genuinely concerned with the real possibility of imitating the virtues of the saint, whose comportment evidently impressed him tremendously during the years they were together (cc. 1-2). The author explicitly does not relate the many miracles performed by Wandregiselus the thaumaturge, precisely because such things cannot be imitated. Instead, he concentrates throughout on describing the actions of the saint which can be emulated, and he ends by calling on his brothers to humble themselves and mortify their flesh in the ways demonstrated by the saint (c. 21).[6] This is not the spirit of Fontenelle. The earliest biography of Wandregiselus is in every way comparable in terms of "spiritual" values, in its focus on the search for monastic perfection amidst the constant low-level irritation of the ancient enemy's temptations, with three other biographies produced in the sixth century at Romainmôtier, the *Vitae patrum iurensium Romani, Lupicini, Eugendi*[7] In so far as there is a dominating spirit in BHL 8804, it is the values of the Benedictine Rule.[8]

---

[5]   See above, pp. 38-46, 63-66, and 96-98.

[6]   Laporte considered this biography of Wandregiselus "la meilleure, du point de vue spirituel et religieux, de celles qui sont sorties du scriptorium de l'abbaye.... On y sent une âme fervente, attentive à l'évolution spirituelle du bienheureux" (DHGE 17 col. 930).

[7]   *Vitae patrum iurensium Romani, Lupicini, Eugendi*, ed. B. Krusch, MGH SRM 3.

[8]   André Borias, "S. Wandrille, a-t-il connu S. Benoît?" *Revue Bénédictine* 89 (1979) pp. 8-28, at pp. 22-27.

B. The Biography of Geremarus of Fly:
The Foundation History of Fly (BHL 3437)

Geremarus founded some sort of monastery at Fly in the Beauvaisis during the Merovingian period. He himself appears in none of the many martyrologies composed before the eleventh century, and the first mention we
have of the house itself, described as a small and decrepit canonry, comes
from the early-ninth-century *Gesta abbatum Fontenellensium*, which tells us
that abbot Ansegisus, received Fly, founded by a certain Geremarus, "in
precarium" from Charlemagne.[9] The next we hear of Fly it had passed, by
gift of Charles the Bald, to the control of Hincmar of Reims, yet another major
Carolingian churchman, this time "ad vitam."[10] In this case the structure
is described as a "cella vel monasterium"; Hincmar, like Ansegisus, had to
undertake renovation and beautification projects. According to the Annals
of St. Bertin, Fly was then destroyed by the northmen in 851.[11]

With the danger past, Charles the Bald gave what remained of Fly
to bishop Odo of Beauvais; the bishop's control of the house was confirmed by pope Nicholas I in 863.[12] According to Nicholas, canons had
lived in the house before 851, and the pope wished for Fly to be restored
by Odo so as to serve once more for the divine service. According to the
office for Geremarus' translation festival in the Breviary of Beauvais, Odo
did not discharge his duty, but instead ignored Fly and left the body of
Geremarus in the cathedral of Beauvais, where it had been carried during
the Viking raid; its presence at Beauvais had saved the city from harm. Finally, however, in 1030, bishop Drogo of Beauvais refounded the house,
submitting it to "regular discipline"; the orders of Nicholas were explicitly
cited at the time.[13]

Everything about the oldest biography of Geremarus (BHL 3437)[14]
points to an initial composition which post-dates the refoundation of the

---

[9]   *Gesta abbatum Fontenellensium* (MGH SS 2) c. 17; the house of Fly is also mentioned in c. 3 when Benignus, abbot of Fontenelle, succeeds his relative Gennardus
as abbot of Fly in 723.

[10]   Flodoard HER 3.18.; AASS Sept VI p. 694.

[11]   *Annals of St. Bertin* trans. J. Nelson a. 851.

[12]   GC IX.2 col. 240.

[13]   AASS Sept. VI p. 698.

[14]   Ed. J. Perierus AASS Sept. VI pp. 698-703 (Antwerp, 1757).

community in 1030 as one of the major Benedictine abbeys of the region, at which time the historian of Fly sought to provide his patrons (who might, of course, have been his fellow monks) with a more glorious past, connecting Fly with one of the best-known figures of Neustrian monasticism, St. Audoenus of Rouen, and depicting it as having been a continuously-thriving commmunity living under the Benedictine Rule since the seventh century, and one which never had even the slightest dealings with the bishopric of Beauvais. Finally, the main plot of the work is to demonstrate that the location of Fly was itself predestined and chosen by God, who would not permit Geremarus to settle comfortably anywhere else,[15] and who finally revealed to the saint, through Audoenus and an angel, that he was to found a Benedictine monastery at Fly; the author notes that all donations made to Fly and to the nearby hospice of St. John were embodied in charters.[16]

The history of Fly provides an example of the battle between centralizing bishops and independentist monasteries during the eleventh and twelfth centuries. Audoenus is a constant figure in the narrative, present at every important moment of the father-son team's life; there is almost an obsession to connect Geremarus and Amalbertus to Audoenus, who functions in the narrative as the legitimator of Geremarus' activities. However, Audoenus is not, in BHL 3437, a bishop, not of Rouen, not of anyplace. Any reference to an institutional framework is studiously avoided by the author, who depicts Audoenus as a sort of monastic emperor on the order of Gerard of Brogne. There are, indeed, no bishops of any kind in this first history of Fly. Evidently, the author wished to deny, or avert the consequences of, episcopal control and refoundation of the house although, in

---

[15] Geremarus leaves Pentale where Audoenus had installed him as abbot after the monks make an attempt on his life, and is called back to the Beauvaisis from St. Samson, where he had taken up the eremetical life, by the news of his son's death (AASS Sept. VI cc. 12-19 pp. 701-702).

[16] The basic narrative of BHL 3437 was not changed in any of the later versions adapted from it. BHL 3441 (ed. B. Krusch, MGH SRM 4 pp. 626-633) from Paris BN lat. 5306 (Colb. 705, Regius 3654), folios 10r-11v, a manuscript of the late fourteenth or fifteenth century, is an abbreviated version from a late legendary containing two-page synopses of the histories of hundreds of different saints. BN lat. 5306 forms a massive legendary collection, in conjunction with BN lat. 3809A. There is also an epitome in BN lat. 9745 fols. 1r-4r of the fifteenth century (BHL 3438; PL 156).

the end, an independent Fly lost, as did most other houses, before the institutional growth of the twelfth and thirteenth centuries.[17]

Although Audoenus comes close to being a co-star of the foundation narrative of Fly, Geremarus and Fly are totally unmentioned in any of the biographies of Audoenus or histories of his pontificate, even in BHL 753, a major work of research composed *circa* 800, whose author sought to bring in information about Audoenus' activities in monastic foundation from every possible source, and who would have used the information concerning Fly had it been available.[18] There is no evidence that anyone had written a history of Geremarus or of Fly before the latter part of the eleventh century, the date of the codex in which the oldest copy of the text is preserved.[19] The codex, originally a product of the Beauvaisis, also contains biographies of other late Roman and Merovingian figures of Picardy-Artois-Flanders, such as Quintinus of Beauvais, Ebrulfus of Beauvais, Angadrisma, Medardus of Soisson, Firmin, Adrian of St. Riquier; Angadrisma, Ebrulfus and Geremarus are among the very most important and venerated saints of the Beauvaisis.

The biography of Geremarus was not only preserved and transmitted in a Picard context, it is also permeated by the narrative conventions of that region. Beauvais lies on the very edge of Picardy, towards the Parisian basin and removed from the Oise, Somme, Sambre and Escaut centers of ecclesiastical life. It is also on the very edge of Normandy, and the author's use of Audoenus (a widely-famed saint) has fooled many historians into assimilating the monastery and its histories to Normandy (though the bishop of Beauvais was not fooled). However, the *vita Geremari* shares the key characteristic of the saints' biographies of Picardy-Artois-Flanders: the tendency to sanctify, not just a single individual, but an entire family,

---

[17] According to BHL 3442-3443, a letter of Peter bishop of Beauvais followed by the account of a translation, in 1132 the entire body of Geremarus was moved into the cathedral in the diocesan capital, in exchange for which the house of Fly received but the radial bone from the saint's right hand (AASS Sept. VI p. 697).

[18] See above, pp. 87-94.

[19] The oldest copy of a biography of Geremarus is contained in Paris, BN 17627, folios 129r-138v, of the eleventh century (= BHL 3437). The codex was formerly Notre-Dame 101, having belonged to Claude Joly, a canon of Paris and, before that, to John of St. Just, a clerk of Beauvais. BHL 3437 was published from this codex by Mabillon (ASOSB II.475- 82 (Paris, 1669; 2nd ed. 455-62) and reprinted from Mabillon by Perierus, AASS Sept. VI.

many of whose members remain lay people throughout most or all of their lives.[20] Geremarus' biographer, in keeping with the norms of the region, is almost as much concerned to describe the special qualities of Geremarus' son Amalbertus, a warrior who dies a virgin, as he is to describe Geremarus himself.[21] Geremarus' wife (Domana) also has signs of a cult,[22] as do his parents (Rigobertus and Aga).[23]

Congenital sanctity is not the only reason to locate the composition of the history of Fly in the mid-to-late eleventh-century Beauvaisis. The bleeding nostril miracle (the only such episode related in the vita Geremari) is borrowed from the vita Eligii, a biography which exercised a major influence on the narratives of Picardy, Artois and Flanders.[24] But the bleeding nostril miracle is not even a miracle of Geremarus; rather, it is a divine sign, independent of the saint, leading to the foundation of Fly.[25] Indeed, the entire narrative leads to the foundation of Fly. There is overall very litte interest in any of the attributes of Geremarus in the biography, which should be considered a foundation narrative of Fly, not a biography of Geremarus.

---

[20] The following are entire families of saints: Amalberga of Maubeuge with her two daughters (Gudula and Reynilda), her son (Emebertus) and her husband (Witger); Aldegundis of Maubeuge with her parents (Gualbertus and Bertilia), her sister (Waldetrude), her brother (Vincent Madalgar), her uncles (Guerlandus and Landricus), and her nieces (Aldetrudis and Madalberta); Rictrudis of Marchiennes with her husband (Adalbaldus, the grandson of Gertrude of Hamay), her three daughters and her son (Maurontus); Bertha of Blagny-sur-Ternoise, with her father (Rigobert) and her daughters (Deotilla and Gertrude). For individual twentieth-century biographies, see the BSS; for the saints' older Latin biographies, Van Der Essen Etude critique.

[21] Amalbertus is a saint of Beauvais, where his festival is celebrated on May 20 (BSS I.914-5 by G.B. Proja).

[22] BSS IV 676, auct. Pietro Burchi.

[23] AASS Sept. VI p. 700.

[24] Vita Geremari AASS Sept. VI cc. 20-24 pp. 702-703; Vita Eligii ed. Levison, MGH SRM IV, II.37 pp. 721-722; Van Der Essen Etude critique pp. 324-328.

[25] The bleeding nostril miracle continues: "...ecce nebula descendit de caelo et circumdedit totum locum, ubi construendum erat monasterium, et cum nebula superna uox, dicens: Electi Dei, ecce iste locus metuendus est; quadraginta anni uoluti sunt, ex quo Dominus hunc locum benedixit et sanctificauit et fideli suo Geremaro destinauit..." (cc. 25-26, p. 703).

Appendix 2

Transcriptions of Unpublished Texts Concerning Romanus

A. THE MANUSCRIPT WITNESSES

Only two copies of Fulbertus' biography of Romanus have survived. One of those copies is outstanding for its clarity and grammaticality, that is, the copy in Paris BN lat. 13.090.[1] The codex is one of the artificial collections of the *membra disiecta* of St.-Germain-des-Prés.[2] The Romanus folios (ff. 112v-124v) came to St. Germain from the abbey of Bec, most of whose holdings were destroyed by a terrible accident in the early seventeenth century.[3] The only other surviving fragment from the nearly-destroyed legendary of Bec whence came the BN lat. 13.090 folios now forms ff. 114-128 of BN lat. 13.092,[4] like BN lat. 13.090 a collection of fragments made at St.-Germain-des-Prés. Delisle[5] and Krusch[6] both dated the BN lat. 13.092 fragments to the twelfth century, while Delisle (paradoxically) and Cornelius Van Beek[7] both placed the BN lat. 13.090 fragments in the thirteenth century. Meanwhile, the compiler of BN lat. 13.090 made a note in the manuscript itself dating the folios to the eleventh century.[8] I would date the Bec legendary to the mid-twelfth century.

---

[1] For a description see L. Delisle, *Inventaire des manuscrits latins conservés à la Bibliothèque Nationale sous les numéros 8823-18.613* (Paris, 1863-1871) and CCHP.

[2] F. Dolbeau "Anciens possesseurs des manuscrits hagiographiques latins conservés à la Bibliothèque Nationale de Paris" *Revue d'Histoire des Textes* 9 (1979) pp. 225-226.

[3] Across the top of f. 114r a hand has written "Beccensis coenobii."

[4] A *vita* (BHL 8762 without the preface) and translation of St. Walaricus followed by a fragment (essentially just the *incipit*) of the *vita Silvestri*.

[5] Delisle, *Inventaire.*

[6] B. Krusch, MGH SRM 4 p. 159; see also Wilhelm Levison "Conspectus Codicum Hagiographicorum," MGH SRM 7 (Hannover, 1920) p. 650 (552).

[7] C. Van Beek *Passio Sanctarum Perpetuae et Felicitatis* (Noyon, 1936); a fragment of the *passio* succeeds the legend of Romanus in the codex.

[8] The note reads: "no. 11 du xi s. env." (see f. 110r).

We cannot imagine that the text in BN lat. 13.090 represents the *vita Romani* precisely as it left the pen of Fulbertus two centuries earlier. However, the copy of the *vita Romani* in the Bec legendary is closer to the text of Gerard's abridgement in the Ivory Book of the cathedral of Rouen (Rouen BM 1405 (Y. 27) pp. 62-85; BHL 7313a) than it is to any other copies of the abridgement in use in Normandy. The Rouen cathedral copy of Gerard's abridgement would have been made directly or indirectly from the "libri Gerardi" which he himself had sent to Rouen in the tenth century;[9] the readings of the Rouen cathedral copy of the abridgement should be relatively good witnesses to Fulbertus' tenth-century narrative, from which the abridgement was made. The consistent agreement between the twelfth-century Bec legendary copy of the *vita Romani* and the eleventh-century Rouen cathedral copy of the abridged version implies that the Bec transmission was a privileged and reliable one.

If it were possible, I would do nothing but transcribe the Bec witness to Fulbertus' *vita Romani*. However, the Romanus folios now in BN lat. 13.090 were damaged in the Bec library accident, rendering the upper corners of each page nearly impossible to read. At least one folio of the *vita Romani* has been lost completely. It is therefore impossible to print a simple transcription of the manuscript. Instead, the various passages affected by the damage to the Bec library collection have to be supplied from the other extant copy of Fulbertus' *vita Romani*, a less reliable copy in Evreux BM 101 (folios 17v-29v), a manuscript of the late eleventh century.[10]

Evreux BM 101 presently contains 202 folios, but the original production (ff. 1-160) constituted the October-December portion of a multi-volume legendary set, of which I have not been able to identify any of the other volumes. The community whose sanctoral most nearly matches the contents of the early portion of Evreux BM 101 is St. Wandrille of Fontenelle.[11] The monks of Fontenelle came to Rouen in 1053 and witnessed there the duelling reliquaries of Romanus of Rouen and Nigasius of St. Ouen. It seems logical that the Fontenelle community, interested perhaps in investigating the dispute over precedence in the town between the

---

[9]   See above, pp. 159-165.
[10]   Henri Omont *Catalogue Général des Manuscrits des Bibliothèques Publiques de France. Départements* I (Paris, 1885).
[11]   Compare the thirteenth-century Breviary of St. Wandrille in Rouen 207 (A.505).

abbey and the cathedral, would have procured at that time copies of the major available writings concerning those two saints; Evreux BM 101 contains not only the *passio* of Nigasius and Fulbertus' *vita Romani* but also the only surviving copy of the early-eleventh-century *miracula Romani* (fols. 29v-35r) sponsored by archbishop Robert. The Fontenelle legendary, produced sometime after the community's trip to Rouen in 1053, was in the hands of the canons of the cathedral of Evreux by the thirteenth century.[12]

The Fontenelle transmission of the *vita Romani* represents a distinct tradition from the one preserved at Bec. Although the Bec legendary was not copied until half a century or more after the Fontenelle legendary, the readings of the Fontenelle legendary appear to diverge more than do the Bec readings from Fulbertus' original text, because they are so frequently non-sensical; only on a small number of occasions are the readings of the Bec legendary difficult to make sense of. Consider the following examples, in which the *siglum* "B" stands for the Bec legendary and "E" for the Evreux manuscript; reference is made to the folio numbers in the transcription below:

Folio 113r—B: talibus ex studiis; E: talibus ex tudiis
Folio 113r—B: apud improbos plus nocuisse inuidiam, quam apud beniuolos profuisse gratiam; E: om. gratiam
Folio 113r—B: ne transgredi ea deberem; E: me transgredi ea deberem
Folio 113r—B: tu ne ad lucem ueniant [gesta Romani] dampnosa taciturnitate prefocare contendis; E: tu ne ad lucem uenias...
Folio 114v—B: cathedram pontificalem tunc suo tempore regendam suscepit; E: cathedram pontificalem tunc suo tempore regenda suscepit
Folio 115r—B: cuius rei nuntio turbatus rex; E: cui rei nuntio turbatus rex
Folio 115v—B: mox ut...intellectuales annos attigerit; E: mox ut...intellectuales animos attigerit

---

[12] The table of contents (f. 1), a note relative to the lending out of the manuscript (f. 200) and the contents of the appendix (folios 161-200) all confirm the Evreux cathedral chapter's possession of the codex. There is no other church on either side of the Channel where Edmund of England, Katherine of Alexandria, Thomas of Canterbury, Maximus and Venerandus of Evreux and Swithun of Winchester were all venerated. For calendars of Evreux, see the ebroican breviaries in BN NAL 388, of the fifteenth century, or BN lat. 1270, of the fourteenth century.

Folio 116r—B: lucernam occiduis nationibus; E: lucernam occi nationibus.

Old library catalogues and older historical works confirm the existence of several now-lost manuscripts of both the biography and the miracle collection. Yet another transmission of the *vita Romani*, distinct from the Bec and Evreux ones, was represented in a copy which was in the monastery of St. Ouen of Rouen at the beginning of the eighteenth century, when it was used by Martène.[13] Three more lost copies of the Fulbertine *vita* are attested at Bayeux,[14] Séez (with the cathedral *miracula*)[15] and Rouen itself.[16] It is unfortunate, therefore, but necessary that I complete the text of Fulbertus' *vita Romani* as witnessed in the Bec legendary from the often non-sensical Evreux manuscript, and transcribe the *miracula Romani* from the latter codex as well. I have not attempted to "correct" the readings of either manuscript, but have printed a transcription of the texts as they were actually read.

The apparatus to the transcription effectively contains a transcription of Gerard's abridgement, provided so that the reader can compare Fulbertus' original biography with Gerard of Brogne's abbreviated version. Where significant portions of the Fulbertine *vita* were omitted by Gerard, the omissions are indicated by printing Fulbertus' text in italics as well as

---

[13]   "Fulberti archidiaconi prefatio in vitam sancti Romani" (= BHL 7313a/b) ed. Martène and Durand *Thesaurus Novus Anecdotorum* I.181-183 (Paris, 1717). The St. Ouen version follows Evreux 101 and BN lat. 13.090 with equal frequency (five and six times respectively); however, there are sixteen readings unique to the St. Ouen copy.

[14]   The Benedictine Jean Raulin (1443-1514), who devoted sermons 72 and 73 of his *Sermones de festivitates sanctorum totius anni* (published posthumously by Le Prévost in 1530) to Romanus, used the full version of Fulbertus from a "Lectionary of Bayeux."

[15]   Codex no. 27 of Dom Julien Bellaise's 1683 catalogue of the library of St. Martin of Sées contained a "vita...Romani arch. Rothomag. [sub Lothario Chodovei filio-supralin] auctore Fulberto. Eiusdem miracula." (folio 71; the catalogue is printed by B. de Montfaucon *Bibliotheca Bibliothecarum* II [Paris, 1739] p. 1249).

[16]   There is a number of verbatim citations to an "antiquus lectionarius ecclesie Rothomagensis" in F. Farin's 1659 *La Normandie Chrestienne* and in F. Pommeraye's 1662 *Vie de Saint Romain*. Those same authors' citations for Romanus' post-mortem miracles match the readings preserved in an early-seventeenth-century Bollandist notebook, taken "ex legendario antiquo dictae [Rothomagensis] cathedralis ecclesiae" (Brussels BR 8919 [3485] ff. 76r-80v).

by noting the text of the abridgement in the apparatus. The version of Gerard's abridgement chosen for transcription is an eleventh-century copy from the Ivory Book of the cathedral of Rouen, Rouen BM 1405 (Y.27) pp. 62-85 (BHL 7313a).[17] The cathedral manuscript has been designated with the *siglum* "R" for Rouen.

Another *rouennais* version of Gerard's abridgement is to be found in Rouen BM 1406 (Y.41), the Black Book of St. Ouen (produced at the abbey between 1090 and c. 1093), folios 36r-46v.[18] This version of the abridgement is somewhat more abbreviated than the one in Rouen BM 1405 (BHL 7313a) and has been given a separate BHL number (7313b).[19] The greater abbreviation is essentially a matter of a single passage, omitting all of Fulbertus's opening sketch of early Christian history; in most other regards BHL 7313b follows BHL 7313a, and must therefore have been made from a copy of Gerard's abridgement, perhaps even directly from the "libri Ger-

---

[17] For descriptions of the codex, see Omont, *Cat. Gen.* I and CCHR; for discussions of the contents and the date of compilation of the collection, see Lifshitz "*Acta Archiepiscoporum*." There are a number of extant copies of Gerard's abridgement; however, I have resisted the urgings of Leonard Boyle to produce "critical editions" (Leonard Boyle, "Optimist or Recensionist?: 'Common Errors' or 'Common Variations'" in *Latin Script and Letters* eds. J.J. O'Meara and B. Naumann [1976]). An attempt at a critical edition, whose apparatus contains all the "variant readings" from the extant manuscript witnesses, can be found by the interested reader in Lifshitz, "The Dossier of Romanus of Rouen" pp. 160-232.

[18] For a description see CCHR, *Cat. Gen.* I.

[19] Another copy of BHL 7313b, made from the St. Ouen version in Rouen BM 1406, is contained on fols. 201r-208v of the present Paris, Ste. Gen. 556, a twelfth-century legendary from the canons regular of Beaulieu in the Maine. For a description, see the *Cat. Gen.* The codex forms the September-October portion of a multi-volume legendary set, of which only the May-August part, now Ste. Gen. 555, has been identified as originally from the region of Le Mans, and probably for the use of the canons regular of Beaulieu (F. Dolbeau "Un exemple peu connu de conte hagiographique: La passion des saints Pérégrin, Mathorat et Viventien" AB 97 [1979]). I would add to Dolbeau's arguments that the contents of the legendary match the sanctoral of one of the very few non-Norman witnesses to a cult of Romanus: a fifteenth-century Breviary of Beaulieu, now Ste. Gen. 2627. Furthermore, both the copy of BHL 7313b in Ste. Gen. 556 and the version of his office in BN lat. 1302, a fifteenth-century Breviary of Mans, contain an identical variant attested nowhere else. Both read: "Hi uero a sancto Remigio Remensi archipresule per uerbum sacre doctrine conuersi atque baptismatis latice renati ueri exinde *feruere* cultores."

ardi" at Rouen. Because the St. Ouen copy diverges marginally farther from the Bec Fulbertine *vita Romani* than does the cathedral copy, and omits an entire passage up front, I have preferred to transcribe the cathedral copy in the apparatus. The St. Ouen *miracula Romani* are transcribed from this manuscript.

To summarize: for the *vita Romani*, the transcription follows the twelfth-century Bec copy in Paris, BN lat. 13.090 (= B), except where that witness is damaged or lacunary. The transcription then follows the eleventh-century Fontenelle copy now in the Evreux cathedral codex, Evreux BM 101 (= E). I print in italics whatever passages of the *vita Romani* were omitted in Gérard's abridgement. Gerard's substitute passages are transcribed in the apparatus from the Rouen cathedral copy of the abridgement in Rouen BM 1405 (Y.27) (= R). In addition, the *fécampois* readings for Romanus' office (= BHL 7312) are also indicated in the apparatus, according to the tenth-century Fécamp codex Paris BN lat. 1805.[20]

After the series of abridgements from Fulbertus' biography, the early-eleventh-century *rouennais* cathedral *miracula Romani* (BHL *vacat*) are transcribed from Evreux BM 101, and the late-eleventh-century St. Ouen *miracula Romani* (= BHL 7319b) are transcribed from Rouen BM 1406 (Y.41), fols. 49r-50v. The text of 7319b in Rouen 1406 is mutilated at the end; however, only a finite verb and the doxology seem to be missing. It is evident that another text began almost immediately on the next folio, which has been incompletely excised.

B. FULBERTUS' BIOGRAPHY OF ROMANUS

Incipit prefatio apologetica scriptoris in uita beatissimi Romani archiepiscopi /fol. 112v/ *Dominis et confratribus suis sancte Rothomagensis ecclesie matris filiis Fulbertus peccator salutem.*

Quod a uobis fratres et domini mei totiens rogatus, historicam uitam beati patris /fol. 113r/ *nostri Romani ingenioli mei stilo illustrare quod inquam totiens*

---

[20] For the relationships among the Fécamp and Rouen readings and the full biography by Fulbertus, see above, pp. 165-166. A "critical edition" of the various copies of the Fécamp office (BHL 7312) can be found in Lifshitz "The Dossier of Romanus of Rouen" pp. 300-332.

rogatus, obstinatius huc usque recusaui, non simplex causa me dehortabatur, ex eo uidelicet quod nequaquam artis peritia suffultus, ad opus hoc me minus idoneum sentiebam, ideoque tantam operis sarcinam a peritissimis uiris pretermissam arripere metuebam, ne nobilis materia rustico stilo exarata uilesceret, si forte in manus peritorum incideret grammaticorum. Instabat et alia causa, que ab exequutione dominicalis mandati uestri, animum hesitantem deterrebat, ea scilicet quod nostris id temporibus certis experimentis compertum tenemus, talibus ex studiis apud improbos plus nocuisse inuidiam, quam apud beniuolos profuisse gratiam. Non irrationabiliter igitur, ut putabam, uiribus onus impar assumere detrectabam, cum mihi frater quidam ueteris amicicie gratia notissimus superueniens, paulo seuerioribus me dictis cohercuit. Nam et his inter alios crebris me exhortationibus de fraternis mandatis ne transgredi ea deberem circumuenerat, eo maxime quo talibus obsequiis certior ut fatebatur maneret spes retributionis.

*Unde simulato motu indignationis paulo inestuans, "Usquequo te," inquit, "degener et ignaue mollis desidia, et dissolute mentis deicit hebitudo. Usque adeo intra antra silentii clausum seruas, quod multo melius ad publicum efferri profuisset? Nonne tu idem es, qui ex uerbo cuiusdam sapientis crebro huiusmodi uerbum insonabas 'sapientia abscondita et thesaurus occultus que utilitas in utroque?'[1] Quid tu ergo non uides, quanto noxie recusationis reatu constringeris, dum ea que reserando plerisque fuerant profutura, tu ne ad lucem ueniant dampnosa taciturnitate prefocare contendis? Non potest sane non astringi impietatis flagitio, qui congesta frumenta ne publicis usibus proficiant tempore famis abscondit. Quod cum ita sit, quero a te, quenam tibi pernitiosi silentii restat expiatio, dum tanti patris gesta insignia, que prouehendas mentes suo exemplo ad arduam uirtutum uiam incitabant, dum ea inquam ne ad edificationem moralis exercitii compareant, tanto annisu comprimere intra claustra silentii elaboras. Sed te fortasse haud equo dicis pulsari iuditio, qui nec sacris dero-/*fol. 113v/*gasse legibus, ne publicis deprehensus es obstitisse usibus. Quo contra et ego.*

"Sane uterque michi equo pede claudicat, et qui nocitura infert, et qui profutura denegat, cum in utroque crimen sit, et noxia inferre, et utilia subtrahere. Hunc, itaque, michi reum esse. Haud merito fateor, quicumque est ille, qui quod ad apprehendendam uirtutum arcem me utiliter informare poterat, hoc inuida michi tenacitate abscondit. Michi inquam, immo tantis, quantis ad instruendas mentes salutaria exempla prodesse potuerant. Nam ut exempli gratia tibi loquar, quotiens uirorum illustrium gesta in memoriam posterorum transcribimus, quid

---

[1] Ecclesiasticus 20:32.

aliud facimus, nisi ut ita dicam quedam incitamenta uirtutum proponimus, quibus imbelles animos et inertia torpentes, ad spiritualis militie certamen accendamus? Et enim plerosque intra mundi huius aream conspicimus, quorum enerua brachia ab exercitatione uirilis operis turpis ligat ignauia, quos nimirum si fortia gesta uirorum et triumphales coronas quis eis precantauerit, uideas quasi alios ex aliis factos, seu laudis amore, seu adquirende beatitudinis zelo ad ardua queque egregie uirtutis opera studio feruenti prorumpere. Unde et ego quondam amicus, sed iam non amicus, nisi maturius noxie reluctationis reatum dilueris, iam iudicialis censure in te lapidem primus intorqueo, pro eo quod totiens a fratribus rogatus, apostolici patris nostri Romani memoranda gesta scribere adhuc etiam dissimulas, nec attendis, quia dum hec ab humanis auribus abscondis, quorum exemplo a somno mortalis inertie ad uite melioris lucem excitari poterant, dum hec inquam abscondis, adiutor procul dubio calamitatis eorum exsistis, quia uidelicet horum ignauiam propositis uite magne exemplis uelut quodam salubri antidoto mederi potueras. Audi qualiter Isaias dum a uerbi ministerio cessaret, illustratus superno lumine, ex uoce penitentie se ipsum reprehendit dicens 'Ue michi quia tacui, ue michi quia tacui'[2]

"Tibi plane non opus est exponi quod ex te ipso sepe audiui, quia licet ad beatam uitam sermo exhortationis quantulamcumque excitet emulationem, propensius tamen informande mentes ad spiritualem militiam subrogantibus animantur exemplis, in tantum ut uite mollioris cultum uelut pestem noxiam abdicantes, per /fol. 114r/ aspera queque et ardua uite artioris itinera gradiendo, eorum laborent adscisci sociis coronis, quorum magnis prouocantur exemplis. Ne ergo loquendo te longius teneam, tu te recte egisse memineris, si huius patris nostri gesta insignia, in quantum rerum fides ad nostram noticiam et incorrupta ueritas attulit, si inquam in memoriam posterioris eui scriptor mandata reliqueris."

Tali fratris ipsius inuectiua obiurgatione cohercitus, dum ad refragandum ratio haud sana suppetebat, uiribus quamlibet imbecillis onus impositum suscepi, non artis industria confisus sed inobedientie prime culpam expiaturus. Super quo caritatem uestram omnium exposco ne incultum opus extra domesticos parietes efferri sustineatis, ne si in manus peritorum grammaticorum casu aliquo incideret, fatua unius inertia, in uestram omnium redundet infamiam. Alioquin, de titulo operis eradi melius fuerat nomen auctoris.[3] Ualete.

---

[2]   Isaiah 6:5.

[3]   Cf. Sulpicius Severus's *vita* of Martin of Tours: "intra domesticos parietes cohibere decreveram....titulum frontis erade ut...pagina...non loquatur auctorem" (ed. Jacques Fontaine *Sources Chretiennes* 135 pp. 248 and 250).

Incipit uita sancti Romani archiepiscopi Rothomagensis et egregii confessoris Christi[4]

Glorificatus[5] a patre Dei filius, dum assumptam in se nostre mortalitatis naturam, iam gloria immortalitatis[6] uestitam, in paterne maiestatis dexteram sublimare disponeret, ne grex dominicus corporali presentia pastoris destitutus, hostili turbaretur incursu, electis de mundo pastoribus eum regendum commisit, qui peruigili eum circumspectione contra insidias immundorum spirituum munirent, et contra insurgentes persequentium impetus pro eo stare non formidarent. Hinc duodenus apostolice legionis extitit chorus, animarum uidelicet preelecti iudices, qui haurientes aquas de ipso uiuifico fonte saluatoris primitiuam ecclesiam nouo fidei fundamento[7] stabilierunt, qui etiam Christi euangelium diffusis per orbem terre gentibus enuntiare non destiterunt, quousque prostratis per uaria supplicia corporibus, mortem quam in magistri passione didicerant sustinere, immo gaudenter excipere non recusarent. His triumphalis martyrum successit exercitus, qui et ipsi Christi nomen uiriliter fatentes, usque ad mortem pro fidei defensione certauerunt. Post hos catholicus ordo doctorum[8] Christi ecclesiam regendam suscepit, qui et apostolice confessionis fide solidati dum hanc contra pseudo apostolos et insurgentes hereses defendere uiua auctoritate, /fol. 114v/ contenderent, excitauerunt contra se reges et tyrannos, qui ex his alios exilio dampnatos, alios publice cesos uariis contumeliis affecerunt. Ex his alii in pace ecclesie fide et conuersatione insignes, doctrina et exhortatione subiectis sibi plebibus ad celum eundi ducatum prebuerunt. De quorum collegio uir iste[9] apostolicus[10] beatus uidelicet[11] Romanus Rothomagensis ecclesie cathedram pontificalem tunc suo tempore regendam suscepit, ad quam non uoluntarius neque ambitiosa cupiditate, sed ui regia, immo diuino et angelico preordinante oraculo uocatus

---

[4]   Decimo kalendarum Nouembris, depositio sancti Romani Rothomagensis archiepiscopi R
  [5]   Lectio i R
  [6]   in mortalitatis R
  [7]   testamento R
  [8]   d. o. R
  [9]   om. R
  [10]   om. R
  [11]   om. R

accessit, qui partibus occiduis uelut nouum sydus ad discutiendas[12] errorum tenebras clarus emicuit.

De cuius ortu breui quidem *sed digna relatu expositione loquuturi, paterni sanguinis lineas attingamus.*[13] Tradunt siquidem ueterum historie a Sicambrie partibus gentem quandam aduenisse, *gentem bello insuperabilem atque robustam, quam Romani crebris incursionibus exagitantes, dum uiribus inexpugnabilem experirentur, composito federe in amicitiam et regni societatem ex senatus consulto receperunt, cuius freti auxilio de angusto regno magnum fecerunt imperium.*[14] *Nam gentes indomita feritate tumentes perdomuerunt, quibus iura et leges imposuerunt. Hos, denique, quos remotior plaga orbis celabat ignotos, et ad quos nec fama Romani nominis peruenerat, hos inquam uectigales et tributarios sibi fecerunt, atque ita sociis signis adiuti, gentibus ignotis Romane potentie terrorem infuderunt. Horum regio sanguine*[15] uir quidam intra fines Gallie extitit oriundus, felicis presagii nomine Benedictus, qui militiae actibus egregium in regno Gallie nomen adquisierat tempore Ludouii regis gloriosi.

Hic est Ludouius, quem de pagano christianum fieri fors bellica coegit. Porro huic erat coniunx Clothildis nomine, regio non minus genere orta, sed in Christo salutari fonte regenerata. *Que dum uirum a gentilitatis errore temptaret auertere, ferus animus uitale consilium aspernatus, in regine contumeliam transferebat, cecus ille, qui non uidebat de proximo superuenturum diem ineuitabilis periculi, nisi maturius conuersus ad nomen illud confugisset, quod paulo ante impugnabat. Siquidem Alemanni facta irruptione in regnum ipsius stragem hominum multam dederunt,* /fol. 115r/ *nulla sexus aut etatis miseratione preter quos indulta uita seruabant ad spem redemptionis et pompam captiuitatis. Cuius rei nuntio turbatus rex haut expectatis militaribus copiis suis, cum paucis*

---

[12] addiscutiendas *R*

[13] relatu dignum nobis exponere uidetur *R*

[14] Cf. pseudo-Fredegar (MGH SRM 2 esp. p. 46) and the Liber Historiae Francorum (MGH SRM 2 esp. pp. 242-245).

[15] In regnum Galliae que modo Francia nuncupatur. Hi uero a sancto Remigio Remensi archipresule per uerbum sacre doctrine conuersi atque baptismatis latice renati ueri exinde fuere cultores. Ex eorum uero nobili genere *R*; Igitur temporibus Lotharii incliti regis Francorum filii Hlodouii gloriosissimi principis extitit uir quidam nomine Benedictus in regno Galliarum que modo nuncupatur Francia, ob gloriosissimos uiros et robustissimos bellatores, qui ex Sicambrie partibus Domino ducente peruenerunt in has regiones et a sancto Remigio Remensis sedis archipresule per uerbum sacre doctrine conuersi sunt atque baptismatis latice renati ueri exinde fidei catholice fuere cultores. *BHL 7312*

irruit super eos, qui pauci a multis milibus circumsepti facile confodiebantur. Uidens rex miserabilem cedem suorum, seque auxiliaribus turmis destitutum, preter paucos qui lateri eius inherebant, desperata euadendi facultate inter arma hostilia in uocem huiusmodi erupit: "O Deus unice potestatis et maiestatis immense, quem regina Clothildis colit, confitetur et adorat, adesto michi in presenti angustia, ne de interitu meo inimicus hic exultet exercitus. Tu enim michi ab hodierna die solus eris Deus, et ueneranda potestas."[16]

Ad hanc uocem celitus immisso terrore, concussi aduersarii ad fuge presidium se uniuersi contulerunt, uictoria cessit regi et Francis. Letus rex insperato sibi rerum successu, domum se uictor recepit, moxque a beato Remigio Remensium episcopo diuinis innouatus sacramentis, filiis ecclesie est aggregatus. Nobis paululum ab incepto narrationis ordine secedere hec fuit ratio, ut in rege isto discat etiam quisque peccator, ne inter extrema pericula desperandum de misericordia conditoris, qui inter armatas legiones, inter hostiles enses iam iam moriturus, uno supplici uoto, non solum euasit, sed etiam uictoriam quam non audebat optare promeruit, cui satis esse poterat, si uel incolumis euasisset, ne dum de uictoria cogitaret. Huic successit in regnum Lotharius paterne claritudinis haud degener filius, sub quo puer insignis Romanus alto[17] parentum sanguine[18] natus emicuit, de quo sic ueritas se habet.

Porro[19] is[20] cuius mentionem paulo ante prelibauimus Benedictus, uir erat in cunctis se sobrie agens. Nam bello strenuus, consilio prouidus, maximam apud palatinos uirtutis gloriam, sed[21] uberiorem apud regem familiaris gratie sibi locum parauerat. Et quamuis difficile sit in prosperis carere inuidia, hic tamen quia de fide ac beniuolentia haud quaquam[22] imminuerat, omnes sibi mentis benignitate deuinxerat, ut secundo plebis rumore, sub rege pater patriae nominaretur. Uerum cum tanto infra aulam regiam polleret honore, hoc uno infortunii genere anxius tenebatur, quod

---

[16] Cf. Alcuin's *vita* of Vedastus: "O Deus unice potestatis et summae maiestatis, quem regina Hlothild colit, confitetur et adorat, concede mihi hodie de inimicis meis uictoriam, nam ex hac die tu solus mihi eris Deus et ueneranda potestas" (MGH SRM 3 ed. Bruno Krusch c. 1 BHL 8506-8 p. 417).

[17] alta *R*

[18] prosapia *R*

[19] *om. R*

[20] igitur *ad. R*

[21] et *ad. R*

[22] quaque *R*

filium non habens, alieno censum seruabat /fol. 115v/ heredi. Hoc impatientis desiderii estu anhelus uenerandus heros, sibimet ingratus paululum displicebat, dum mente[23] ipsius hec mordacis cure meditatio exulcerabat cui post exitum suum alta rerum patrimonia, cui regia beneficia, cui etiam longus ordo famulorum, cedere in ius hereditarium deberent. Erat[24] namque illi uxor, ingenuis et ipsa orta natalibus, que coniugalis pudicitie[25] dignitate ceteras tunc suo tempore matronas preibat et exemplo, sed longeue sterilitatis incommodo anxiabatur. Ambo igitur preter cetera pietatis opera quibus attentius inuigilabant, super hoc singulariter uigiliis et orationibus insistebant, ut sibi Deo propitio filius nasceretur, qui et patrem supportaret annosum, et matri auferret sterilitatis opprobium. Nam et pater crebris expeditionibus cum rege in hostem, et armorum bellica sarcina perfractus, iam uite remissioris otio delectabatur, unde se longe facere a militaribus negotiis[26] querebat. Verumptamen,[27] inanis eorum esse non potuit supplicatio.

Mittitur illis insperati gaudii nuntius, angelus scilicet de celo, qui sub nocte uiro consolationis uerba intulit ita dicens: "Ne paueas electe Dei neque formides, ecce ego tibi a Deo[28] missus sum. Ne ergo suspectus uerearis fantasie spiritu illudi, ego sum angelus ille, qui uestra bona studia, et orationes Deo optuli, que diuinis grate[29] conspectibus proximo tempore implebuntur. Nam et ego tibi uotiuum nuntio gaudium, quia Felicitas uxor tua pariet tibi filium, *cui uite illustris prerogatiua nomen adquiret Romanum.*[30] Hunc tu immunem ab omni labe corruptionis uite[31] seruare memento, quia ipsum necdum genitum superna prouidentia ad regimen sancte ecclesie et patrie illuminationem preordinauit electum.[32] Hunc ergo mox ut maternis ablactatus uberibus intellectuales annos attigerit catholicis uiris erudiendum committes. *Futurum est enim, ut Christi ecclesia peruersis*

23 mentem *R*
24 Lectio ii *R*
25 pudiciae *R*
26 *om. R*
27 quia deuota *ad. R*
28 a Deo tibi *R*
29 diuine gratie *R*
30 a Deo electum nomine Romanum *R*
31 *om. R*
32 *om. R*

heresibus·impugnetur, quas suo ille tempore uiuifica dampnabit auctoritate." Sic
fatus, continuo in celum sese recepit,[33] *quem uir Domini longo intuitu intra patentis etheris ianuam prosequutus est.* Certus itaque de angelico oraculo uir
inclitus, uxorem diligenter excitat, sciscitatur an de uisione et alloquutione
celestis nuntii aliquid sensisset. Quod cum /fol. 116r/ penitus abnegasset,
aperuit illi omnem iocunde uisionis ordinem.

Unde generosa matrona diuino oraculo congratulata, *quod intra se et
ipsa celabat, uiro suo manifestare curauit, non sine suspirio dicens: "Quid nam o
mi karissime ulterius tibi sileo stuporis noui miraculum, quod et michi comparuisse paulo ante hos dies contigerat? Ego plane ipsam que hanc istam octaua
precesserat noctem totam insomnem agebam, totaque in hac ipsa meditatione
uersabar, hoc sane peccatis meis imputans, quod conclusisset Dominus uentrem
meum, ne fructus ex me aliquando comparuisset. In qua cum attentius persisterem,
leui ut fit somno ludificante, neque me uigilare nec penitus obdormisse michi
uidebar, cum de improuiso uisus est michi astitisse uir quidam inestimabilem
uultus claritatem preferens, qui niuei candoris habitum gerens iniecta manu pectus
et uentrem tactu leni pertrectabat, cum uerbo huiusmodi: 'Procul o procul hinc
emula abesto sterilitas, ut nouo partu impregnetur iocunda uentris ubertas.' Mox
amotam manum insequitur ignea procedens de utero meo facula, que longa per
auras uia discurrens Neustriam usque regionem superueniens stationem accepit,
eamque circumfusa luce undique complectens submota caligine totam irradiauit.
Huius rei si quod est numinis prefinitum misterium mi karissime pandere tibi ue-
rebar, quia ut sumus misere mulieres, curiosa semper fatuitate denotamur."* Hic
uir prudens ex antecedentibus consequentia comparans, animaduertit se a Deo
uisitatum.

*Unde uxorem intra claustra silentii usque ad tempus que uiderat seruare
premonuit, ne uulgi auribus misterium hoc ullo modo patuisset. Adquiescit mulier
sobrio uiri consilio.*[34] Fiunt interea propensius orationes pro expectatione
heredis de celo promissi, fit elemosinarum largior distributio. Ecce iam noua
Sara[35] diu sterilis et *desperata recepit muliebria, miratur tumescentis uteri*[36]
nouum prodigium, sed querit occultum esse noui conceptus gaudium.

---

[33] Sic fatus continuo in celum sese recepit *crossed out R*
[34] Orationibus et elemosinis cunctisque bonis operibus amplius insudauit R
[35] Genesis 17:15-22, 21:1-7.
[36] cui iam desierant muliebria concepit. Miratur nescientis uteri *R*; "cui" and
"nescientis" are both written over erasures in R which could easily be "desperata"
and "tumescentis."

Quid ultra? Iam tempus aderat, et ecce felix puerpera filium edidit, gaudium parentibus quidem,[37] sed lucernam occiduis nationibus. O felix mater, lacta uouum Isaac, tuum de repromissione[38] filium, sed qui aliquando genitali uerbo editos filios euangelico lacte /fol. 116v/ enutriat, quos de filiis seculi regenerante fide efficiat filios Dei.

Crescit[39] itaque puer, traditur catholicis uiris, imbuitur uberius diuinis scripturis. Quem breui tempore doctrina et eruditione, anteriores suos preire omnes mirabantur. Fulgebat in eo non simplex uirtutum gratia. In corde etenim illius sinceritas, et legis plenitudo. In ore ipsius ueritas erat, et pulchritudo.[40] Uerum diuini dogmatis pregustata dulcedine, *mox uite sanctioris uiam apprehendit, in qua profectu cotidiano coetaneos suos eatenus transcendit, ut eo tempore nulli secundus estimaretur. Ita nominis ipsius fama celebrior per uniuersas urbes Gallie, etiam usque in aulam regis, uirtus egregie adolescentie pernotuit.*[41] Rex etiam ipse illustris iuuenis fama delectatus, iam de eius quem nec dum nouerat institutione precogitat. Mittitur ergo legatio, que ex mandato regis iuuenem ad palatium uenire quantotius moneat. Quod iuuenis strenuus primo quidem spreuit, utpote qui soli Deo uacare studens populosas urbes et regiam frequentiam declinare malebat, sed reputans ex uerbis apostoli "Omnem animam subdi debere sublimiori potestati, et maxime regie maiestati,"[42] licet egre, ad regiam se confert presentiam, quem rex summo cum honore suscipiens, inter primos palatii suis iussit interesse

---

[37] q. p. R

[38] promissione R

[39] Lectio iii R

[40] *om.* R; purae eloquentiae magnitudo R

[41] Quanto plus scientiae ac sanctimonie pollebat copiis, tanto magis humilitati operam dabat omnibusque se affabilem prebebat, nullum se inferiorem existimans, illud cogitando Salomonis: "Quanto magnus es, humilia te in omnibus" [Eccles. 3:18]. Et quia "Deus superbis resistit, humilibus autem dat gratiam" [James 4:6, paraphrasing Proverbs 3:34], sanctitatis eius fama circumquaque fragrante, ad regias aures uirtus tam egregie adolescentiae peruenit. R; Factus ergo diuinarum scripturarum opimus agnitor, quanto plus sanctimonie pollebat copiis, tanto magis humilitati operam dabat, omnibusque se affabilem prebebat, nullum se inferiorem existimans, illud cogitando Salomonis "Quantum magnus es, humilia te in omnibus. Et quia Deus superbis resistit, humilibus autem dat gratiam. BHL 7312

[42] Cf. Romans 13:1 "Omnis anima potestatibus sublimioribus subdita sit, non est enim potestas nisi a Deo," and 1 Peter 2:13-14 "Subiecti igitur estote omni humanae creaturae propter Deum, sive regi quasi praecellenti."

consiliis.

Iam nouus Danihel[43] in aula Babilonica deseruiens, omnibus sobrietatis et mansuetudinis prebebat exemplum. Mirabantur cuncti singularem sapientie et consilii ipsius altitudinem, *sed rex precipue illius prudentiam, et discretam circa singula spectabat actionem.* Felicem omnes illam predicabant[44] ecclesiam, cui talem a Deo rectorem habere olim contingeret. Felicem clerum et populum, cui superna prouidentia talem ac tantum preordinasset pastorem. *Quod gratum sane regi et acceptum erat, et alto corde recondebat eorum sententiam, obseruans quam mox oportunus se locus exibeat, quo tantam Christi lucernam competenter ualeat sublimare, sed consilium hoc summa dissumulatione uiro sancto celabat. Alta etenim mente reconditum seruabat, quam sepe numero idem uir Domini Romanus zelo indignationis aduersus eos infremuisset, quos ambitionis studio ad pontificalem* /fol. 117r/ *honorem se ingerere considerabat, de quo facto episcopos et abbates quamplurimos in sui odium commouit.*[45]

Contigit[46] interea, ut Rothomagensis archiepiscopus sicut se habet ineuitabilis sors mortalium, diem supremum[47] subisset,[48] unde inter ciues[49] et conprouintiales uiros de substituendo pastore generalis commotio facta est, quoniam ut se habet in talibus negotiis, eligentium uota in diuersum trahebant, dum alii alios pro uoluntate sua ad culminis huius apicem attollere conabantur. Tali altercatione ecclesia per aliquod tempus sine pastorali regimine manebat, cum uir quidam altioris ingenii conuocatis ciuibus dampnare cepit tantos ciuilis[50] discordie motus, dicens non ex Deo sed potius contra Deum esse[51] quod temeritas humana hanc sibi preripiebat

---

[43]   A Judean deported to the court of Nebuchadnezzar, where he served the king after the Babylonian conquest of Israel and Judah; see the Book of Daniel.

[44]   predicebant R

[45]   Uenerabatur namque sincero affectu a rege obtimatibusque cunctis necnon et ab episcopis ceterisque sancte matris ecclesie ordinibus ueluti pater modestus, quoniam iugis in eo fulgebat eloquii facundia et consilii magnitudo. R; Uenerabatur namque sincero affectu a rege optimatibusque cunctis necne et ab episcopis, uariisque ordinibus sancte matris ecclesie ueluti pater modestus, quoniam iugis in eo fulgebat eloquii facundia, consilii magnitudo in omnibus. *BHL 7312*

[46]   Lectio iiii R

[47]   d. s. *om.* R

[48]   *emended from* obisset B.

[49]   conciues R

[50]   *supralin. over crossed-out* cuus R

[51]   *over illegible erasure* R

electionem, quam singulariter suo[52] reseruandam iudicio ille[53] institue-
rat, per quem regnum et sacerdotium constant, sicut Scriptura refert dicen-
te Domino: "Non constitues super te regem nisi quem ego elegero,"[54] et
sicut apostolus ait: "Nec quisquam sumat[55] sibi honorem, nisi qui uocatur
a Domino tanquam Aaron."[56] "Unde, o ciues, stultum ualde immo perniti-
osum est de electione pontificis, diuini examinis non expectare iudicium,
de cuius singulariter dono ligandi atque soluendi pontificalis attribuitur
potentia. Meum igitur si adquiescitis consilium est, ieiuno et oratione diuinum super hoc querere responsum. Credo enim nec uana fides,[57] non
diu suspensi tenebimur a Dei uoluntate, quin reuelatione aut quouis ora-
culi responso ad certum rei prouehamur."

His dictis, laudatur a cunctis uiri sententia, fit ex discordibus animis
grata concordia. Postremo in hanc unam sententiam omnium coiit assen-
sus, ut ex consilio senis continuato tridui ieiunio, diuinum expectarent in-
dicium. Sane haud inanis eorum facta est expectatio. Nam expletis indicti
ieiunii diebus, *cuidam uite uenerabilis uiro per uisum dictum est susceptam a
Deo plebis humilem supplicationem: "Irent ergo quantotius ad regem, ut pretermissis aliis omnibus, hunc singulariter deposcerent dari sibi ecclesie rectorem, cui
denominatum ab eo urbis loco instat uocabulum, quo mundani esse arcem constat
imperii. Hunc a Deo uocatum, et antequam nasceretur electum, qui ut precursor
Domini ad parandam illi plebem perfectam ex nomine est prenuntiatus." Facta
igitur hac /fol. 117v/ uoce, uir prefatus seniorem illum qui ciuibus consilium
dederat silentio euocauit, et que sibi dicta fuerant diligenter exposuit. Letus ille
quamquam de persona incertus, conuocatis ciuibus, auditum pandit oraculum, qui
omnes animis exultantibus gratias Deo dederunt. Fit itaque ex hoc inter eos
discussio, quis tali censeretur uocabulo. Uerum pretaxati imperii nomen diu
uentilantes, tandem animaduertunt uirum Dei Romanum diuino portendi oraculo,
qui regis in aula a cunctis sanctimonie et ueritatis testimonium habens, hoc solus*

---

52   Deus *ad. R*
53   *om. R*
54   Cf. Deuteronomy 17:14-15.
55   sumit *corrected supralin. to* sumat R
56   Hebrews 5:4.
57   est quod *ad. R*

nomine intra fines Gallie censebatur.[58]

Nec mora. Mittitur ad regem legatio cum litteris, in quibus regi[59] significatum est de obitu pontificis, et de ciuili discordia pro eligendo successore, et de reformata ex angelico oraculo concordia, per quod oraculum uirum Dei Romanum deberi sibi archiepiscopum addidicerant. Hinc cleri et populi specialis apud regem fit intercessio, ne Christi ecclesia quesiti patroni fraudetur subsidio. Hinc ad episcopos qui tempore ipso regiis adherebant consiliis, hinc ad primos palatii Rothomagensium ciuium fit magna supplicatio, ut regem ne aduersetur petitioni eorum, quam maxime ad sua uota inflectere studeant. *Quid plura? Legationem rex placabiliter suscepit. Gaudet de oportuno euentu, quo uirum sibi dilectum sublimare preoptabat, sed multo amplius, quod Dei super hoc uoluntatem premonstratam audierat. Unde et litteras diuini responsi indices penes se seruare maluit, per quas uirum corriperet, si refutaret officium.*

Fit itaque inter palatinos proceres de uiro sancto communis assensio, sed quod non sine dolore est dicendum, soli tunc episcopi contraire nitentes, regem ab eius electione temptabant auertere, eo solo quod uita huius longe dissimilis ab eorum conuersatione uidebatur. Nam et hoc ad ignominiam et opprobrium suorum futurum esse non ignorabant, si uir tantus pontificalis honoris apicem quandoque adipisceretur, cui necdum sacerdotalis ulla suffragabatur auctoritas, et tamen uitam reprobam et mores eorum carpere non uerebatur. Unde captiosa fraude regem adeuntes dissuadere incipiunt, ne illorum improuido adquiescat consilio, qui nesciunt iunioris etatis uirum nequaquam suscipi debere ad regimen animarum. Rex autem alta pruden-/fol. 118r/*tia suspectam deprehendens ipsorum inuidiam, longe alia uia eorum remordebat sententiam, dicens non debere tantum etatem hominis attendere, quantum uite religionem et prudentiam considerare. Interea uir sanctus alias intentus, nichil omnino quod de illo tractabatur persenserat. Uerum rex accitum hominem leni suadet affatu, ne refutare debeat quod ipse imperat, et regni proceres acclamant, immo quod superna dispositio preordinat. "Ne te," inquit, "karissime suspensum teneam, Rothomagensis sedis archiepiscopus uita excessit,*

---

[58] Fit tanta cleri ac populi de pastoris electione concordia, ut omnes Romanum uirum sanctum unanimiter sibi eligendum acclamarent pontificem. Hoc omnis sexus, hoc omnis etas, hoc omnium uoluntas fieri debere testabatur, ut tanti meriti uir eorum fieret rector, qui eos uie recte dogmate nutriret. Tali ergo diuini amoris instinctu agitante, regis ad aures uniuerse plebis clamor uniuocus intimandus decernitur. *R*

[59] *supralin. B*

unde eiusdem urbis clerus et populus unanimiter te sibi dare poscunt pastorem,
quod et michi beneplacitum esse constat. Uolo ergo et regio iussi impero, ut deso-
late ecclesie tu curam suscipias, et ouile dominicum pastorali sollicitudine foueas,
ut iuxta apostolicum uerbum cum uenerit pastor pastorum, de fideli administrati-
one recipias immarcescibilem glorie coronam."[60] *Ad hec uerba regis uir Domini*
ab alto cordis suspirans, "Quidnam est," inquit, "rex bone, quod ais? Unde hoc tibi
subripi potuit, ut pretermissis tot catholicis patribus et apostolico honore dignis,
me indignum et nullius meriti uirum tam regie ciuitati preferendum estimares,
tamquam infra regnum tuum multo altiores et magis strenuas nequeas inuenire
personas, per quas Christi ecclesia nobiliter regi et consultioribus institutis ualeat
ordinari? Et enim quo tibi abest Laurentius ille flos et decus ecclesie? Quo tibi
Egidius, uir in omni doctrina, et sapientia conspicuus? Ubi amisisti Florianum,
uirum parsimonie et uirtutum flore pollentem? Quid tibi enumerem uiros glorio-
sos optime imperator, quos tibi mater Gallia, uberioris doctrine priuilegio adorna-
tos enutriuit?" Cui uenerandus heros respondens "Ego," inquit, "Laurentium non
sperno, Egidium non improbo, non ceteros quos predicas abhominor, sed omnes
hos in te unum conspicio. Horum sane omnium sapientiam, horum parsimoniam,
horum moralium uirtutum multiplicem gratiam in te unum inuenio. Unde non
erroris sed rationis consilio agitur, quod his pretermissis, te potissimum ad regi-
men sancte ecclesie eligo. Tibi ergo summopere cauendum est ne in quo regie pote-
stati nostre obstinatius resistis, dei ordinationi resistas."[61]

Ad hec uir sanctus "Scio," inquit, "et fateor, domine mi rex, quia anima om-
nis sublimiori potestati subdita esse debet, et sic a deo ordi-/fol. 118v/natum est,
sed in hac re Dei potius electio fuerat expectanda. De cetero non debet hominum
ducatum suscipere, qui nescit homines bene uiuendo preire, ne qui ad hoc eligitur,
ut eorum culpas corrigat, quod resecari debeat ipse committat. Et necesse est ut his
qui preest sollerter attendat, que uel qualia subditis prebeat exempla, ut tantis se
sciat uiuere, quantis se nouit preesse, quia quot regendis subditis preest, ut ita
dicam tot solus animas habet, de quibus sibi apud districtum iudicem ratio redden-
da est. Hec michi precipue causa tanti honeris sarcinam fugere, potius quam am-
plecti hortatur." Ad hec ista rex: "Nichil," inquit, "tibi plane reliquum est quod ex-
cusare debeas, tu ipse uitam et sobrii pastoris conuersationem docte expressisti. Et
quoniam super huiusmodi electionem Dei uoluntatem querendam iudicas, ecce tibi
litteras diuine uocationis interpretes." Tunc sumptas litteras quas penes se habebat,

---

[60] 1 Peter 5:4.
[61] Cf. Romans 13:1.

legendas illi tradidit. Quas perlegens ut uenit ad locum ab angelo denuntiate electionis, nichil ultra resistere presumens, eleuatis oculis in celum ait: "Domine Jesu si est ex te consilium istud, fiat uoluntas tua. Nam licet me imparem tanto honeri sciam, tibi tamen qui facis infirmis posse quod precipis comitto me, et quod subeundum imponis officium." Et conuersus ad regem, "Nichil," inquit, "tibi o rex bone ultra resisto."

Letus rex continuo baculum illi contulit pastoralem, fit communis per amplam regiam leticia. Nec mora. Assumptis rex secum episcopis et regia frequentia, electum Dei famulum ad sedem denominatam perducit. Uidere erat quanta exultatione ciues et extramurani, omnis preterea sexus et etas procedunt obuiam pastori a Deo sibi donato, quante in celum laudes et gratiarum saluatori referebantur actiones. Sed cuius tam ferreum pectus, ut pre gaudio lacrimari non posset, cum audiret etiam pueros clamantes et dicentes "Benedictus qui uenit in nomine domini?"[62] *Is nimirum Pharisaicus liuore succensus a laude saluatoris, Hebreorum pueros deterruisset. At tamen isti non Hebreorum pueri, uerum in laude non degeneres ab eis, Hebreorum Dominum in famulo suo prophetali uersu magnificabant, sicut ipse Dominus ad discipulos ait: "Qui recipit si quem ego misero, me recipit."*[63] *Porro ii non alio spiritu, quam quondam* /fol. 119r/ *pueri Hebreorum incitabantur. Nam et hic uenerandus Dei famulus se in nomine Domini uenisse manifestis indiciis comprobauit, quia mox confirmatus in sede pontificali, templa idolorum ubicumque reperta sunt a fundamentis eruit, statuas comminuit, mercationes quas in regno ecclesie pro sacris ordinibus inoleuisse comperit, simul cum ipsis auctoribus extirpauit exemplo saluatoris, qui mox a turbis laudatus, a pueris acclamatus templum introiuit, uendentes et ementes ab eo eiecit, et cathedras nummulariorum euertit.*[64]

---

[62] Mt. 21:9; Mk. 11:10; Lk. 13:35.
[63] Cf. Mt. 10:40-41; Mk. 9:36; Lk. 9:48.
[64] Matthew 21:12.

Quod audiens rex placabiliter suscipit nimium gratulatus, quod in eius electione quem sublimare preobtabat, diuina pietas uniuerse plebis animos accenderat. Fit itaque inter palatinos proceres de uiro sancto communis assensio, qui omnes unanimiter regi consulunt, ne grex Christi suo fraudetur desiderio, sed diuina protinus ad effectum ducatur electio. Quo rex gratulatus consilio, conuocatis tam episcopis quam abbatibus baculum illi contulit pastoralem. Intronizatus ergo pontificali apice, uniuersis hinc inde exultantibus usque ad Rothomagensem cum multitudinis uocibus laudum perducitur urbem. In ingressu uero eius quanta exultatio uniuersorum occupauerit mentes, nemo eloquentium ualet explicare sermone. Nam adest ouans plebs copiosa, Deo odas omnimodis referens, pro largitate pietatis sue

Erat[65] iuxta urbem ipsam a septentrionali latere, lapideo opere constructa in modum amphiteatri muralis machine altitudo, in qua subterraneum speleum angustum iter introeuntibus prebebat.[66] Domus illic subterranea, latebrosis fornicibus cingebatur. Hanc "domicilium Ueneris," propter scortantium usus apellabant. Uerum desuper intra ambitum muri exterioris spaciosa patebat area, in cuius medio[67] fanum artifici opere constructum eminebat, in quo ara editiori loco stabat, et desuper titulus Ueneris. De quo loco aiebant sepe inmundorum spirituum murmur auditum, *et quasi ad aggregatum concilium de longinquis terre partibus conuentum statutum, in quo rationem operum suorum pro se quisque reddere cogebatur, et pro magnitudine scelerum altius quisque honorabatur, pro inertia uero uerberibus afficiebatur. Post fanum huiusmodi sub obscuro quodam loco spelunca horribilis erat, introrsum quidem spaciosa, sed angusta fauce inestimabilem profundi altitudinem celabat.* Sed neque uisu hominis aduerti poterat, quia hiatu ipso sulphureus uortex tetros uapores exalabat, et intolerabiles fetores, cum quibus flamme piceus[68] horror erumpens, uicine urbis edificia seuo sepe uastabat incendio, multos uero fumifero necabat odore.

Temptari ciues hortabantur, qualis aut quantus intus latebat abyssus. Multi funibus intromissi exanimes retracti sunt. Aiebant denique quendam hiatum tartareum ibi latere. Collecti sepe homines dum propius accedere nequirent, congestam harenam a longe iactantes, ethneam fossam implere temptabant, sed congestio nichil proficiebat. Nam ab imo ui quadam tamquam impulsu turbinis resorta ferebatur in auras, /fol. 119v/ *ex his dispersa mollius ad terram defluebat. Admouebant lapides grandes, quos precipiti iactu intromissos, in crastinum reiectos uidebant igne perustos. Uidentes itaque se inanem concepisse laborem, desistere a labore tanto deliberant, et relicta urbe externam habitationam querere. Incubuerat*

---

senes uidelicet atque iuuenes, pueri quoque pro modulo sui sensus altissonis uocibus dicebant "Benedictus qui uenit in nomine domini," iuxta quod Psalmista inquit "Ex ore infantium et lactentium perfecisti laudem" [Psalms 8:2]. [*colored initial M*] Postquam uero pontificalem adeptus est sedem, illius urbis populi caterua mox inito consilio uenerunt necessitate coacti, petieruntque unanimiter solotenus strati beatum pontificem ut eorum subueniret calamitati. *R*

65   enim *ad. R*
66   *emended in ms. from* prebeat *R*
67   *om. R*
68   picee *R*

enim[69] illis et alia ex parte id est a latere meridiano aquarum crebra inundatio, que expulsis habitatoribus domos et alta palatia optinens per totam urbem spatiabatur. Et hoc binis[70] aliquotiens[71] ternis mensibus sine
sui imminutione peragebat. Turbati ciues et suburbani dicebant mutatio-
nem regni, aut mundi consummationem hoc portendi diluuio, quod neque
ex lunari cursu agebatur, cuius[72] inspiratione estum maris crementum aut
diminutionem sui sumere phisici dicunt.

Conueniunt igitur omnes ad[73] uirum Dei, deplorantes tante calamitatis deformitatem. Quibus pater uenerandus[74] "Oportet nos," inquit, "filii
huiusmodi delubrum uidere, de quo[75] prima nostris auribus insonuit
querimonia." Assumptis itaque secum clericis suis et ciuibus, processit ad
locum. Quem cum eminus inspiceret, ait "Non est fratres minimum genus
miserie ingruentia mala tolerare, et malorum causas ignorare. Quid enim
conflagrationem sodomorum, aut fauillas gomorreorum cinerum quisquam
habet mirari, qui criminose gentis usum execrabilem semel audiuit, et
bestialem scelerate plebis insaniam didicit?[76] Quos enim bonum nature
a bestiali sensu et furentis impetu libidinis cohibere non potuit, hos celestis
indignatio inaudito exemplo dampnauit. Uobis ergo fratres mei uerendum
ualde est in quantum ex delubro hoc comminantis incendii manifesta signa
fas est intueri, uerendum est inquam[77] ne prefate gentis criminosus usus
aliquo modo serpat[78] in uobis, unde simili exemplo eterne combustionis
penam subeatis. Sed nos oportuno tempore, ex eo uobiscum sumus loquuturi. Nunc quod instat manus uestras Domino[79] consecrate, et hanc spur-
citie domum et uenerinum[80] titulum a fundamento diruite, ne pars aduersa ad habitandum sibi sedem relictam esse gaudeat. Habetis me socium

---

[69] quoque R
[70] *in margin* B
[71] a. b. R; aliquotiens *ad.* R
[72] quasi *ad.* R
[73] *om.* R
[74] u. p. R
[75] nunc *ad.* R
[76] Genesis 19.
[77] u. e. i. *om.* R
[78] lateat R
[79] D. m. u. R
[80] uenerium R

operis, si manus apponitis.

Dum hec pontifex loquebatur, audiebatur intra execrabile fanum quidam quasi strepitus murmurantium, et ad fugam cohortantium. Quem /fol. 120r/ cum astantes attentius auscultarent, unus qui execrande legionis princeps habebatur, in uocem huiusmodi erupit. "Quid nobis et tibi Christi sacerdos? Quid nos a sedibus nostris extorres fieri, et inhabitabilem orbis plagam querere cogis? Tu quidem inique hodie a sedibus nostris exturbas, suscitabo et ego tibi gentem aduersam ab extremis finibus maris et ignotis insulis, que tuos quoque a propriis laribus eiectos, externe regionis sedes querere, aut certe intra proprios lares externis Dominis famulari compellet. Sed ne in hoc calamitatis terminus herebit. Nam et ego ossa tua et aliorum seruorum Dei pro metu superuenture gentis a sedibus propriis remota, inuitam exilii peregrinationem assumere, et girouaga deportatione faciam per alienas regiones sedes sibi querere. Tempore illo libeat tibi perpendere, quantam tibi beatitudinis palmam de nostra eiectione lucratus es."

Hic presul uenerandus aduersus tartareum monstrum indignatus, ait "Non est ualde mirandum, si tu nequissime contra homines erigeris, cui non potuit angelice dignitatis natura sufficere, nisi erectis signis te similem altissimo conferre presumeres. Unde tibi digne contigit miser, ut pro ausu temeritatis in hunc caliginosum aerem deiectus, inter inmundas scortantium officinas, gratam nequitie tue sedem deligeres. Sed quid tibi et genti huic de qua futurum gentis nostre exterminium tanto faustu comminaris? Porro gens ista, Christo debetur. Hec sane prefinitu sibi a Deo sue reparationis terminum spectat, nec ei intercludi poterit predestinate uia salutis. Et ut cumque erratica intentio ipsius festinet ad peruadendas sedes aliene hereditatis, hec ipsa tamen ipsius intentio meliori exitu consummabitur, quia tibi a seculo tuo renuntiatura mox dominicis imbuetur sacramentis. Locus autem quem barbarica feritate peruasura est illi erit effectiua causa insperate salutis, quia Christi nomen quod alias necdum audierat ibi mox audiet, auditumque fideliter credet, et creditum magnifice recolet, et ita fiet de gente adultera genus electum, gens sancta, populus adquisitionis, annuntians uirtutes eius qui eum de tenebris uocauit in ammirabile lumen suum, qui aliquando non populus, nunc autem populus Dei, qui non consecutus misericordiam, nunc autem misericordiam consecutus. Ecce /fol. 120v/ quantum nequitie tue fructum adquisitum reportabis de gente quam susciturus es, ad exterminandam gentem nostram. Gens sane ista mox ut in Christo regenerata dominicis fuerit imbuta sacramentis, ossa nostra de cunctis terre partibus ad quas translata esse audierit, summa cum ueneratione ad sedem propriam reportabit. Sed nos quid ultra te nequissime sustinemus? Iam ergo peruasam sedem otius linque spiritus inmunde, et eo usque cum legione tua effuge, quo tibi patent sedes tartaree, aut eam inhabitabilem celi plagam

delige, quo non habitatio est hominum aut animantium horum que ad usus morta-
lium finxit prouidentia conditoris. Nam hic residendi tibi ultra non datur pote-
stas."

Sic fatus, ille dux et signifer, triumphale signum crucis exerens castra inimica peruadit. Et introgressus mox ut[81] infandum titulum cepit euer-tere, *mirabile uisu, innumera demonum legio relicta sede, longo ordine cum hor-rendo ululatu, se in altum aera extendit. Unde qui presentes talia intuebantur, Deum glorificabant, et familiarem patronum magnifice efferebant. Quibus uener-andus pontifex ait, "Ecce iam fratres non ludificante somno neque per falsas imagi-nes, sed uisu conspicuo infernales legiones et diabolica castra contuiti estis, ex qui-bus certum experimentum uobis nisi bruta animalium pectora gestatis, sumere fas est, quanta uobis et urbi pericula ex eorum affinitate instabant. Quibus sane licet sit nocendi semper prompta uoluntas, non tamen semper efficax est noxie uolunta-tis potentia. Uerum ubi luxus et ganea et cetera usus fornicarii opera a uobis non tolluntur, ipsi uos noxie habitationis locum illis exibetis, nec ipsi uobis uim tan-tum inferunt, quantum ipsis uos potestatem et locum seuiendi ex reprobo usu at-tribuitis. Ex quo uobis iure uox illa dominica per increpationem ingeritur, que Iudee insolentiam exprobat dicens, 'non audiuit populus meus uocem meam, et Israhel non intendit michi, et dimisi eos secundum desideria cordis eorum, ibunt in adinuentionibus suis.'[82] Deinde subiungit, 'Si populus meus audisset me, Is-rahel si in uiis meis ambulasset, pro nichilo forsitan inimicos eorum humiliassem et super tribulantes eos misissem manum meam. Inimici uero Domini mentiti sunt ei, et erit tempus eorum in secula.'[83]* /fol. 121r/ *Contestor igitur uos ex nomine ipsius cuius uox hec per prophetam intonat, sit tandem uobis pudor talibus domi-nis subiugali famulatu militasse, et ab hoc uenerio usu conuersi quantotius ad diuina presidia confugite. Ueternosas Niniuitarum offensas matura conuersio pre-ueniens expiauit, et imminentis ruine cladem, urbs peritura euasit.[84] Manus ergo uestras sicut paulo ante dixeram iam nunc Domino consecrate, ut emendandi erro-ris uia prima in demolitionem sacrilege ueneris uertatur."* Necdum uir sanctus *uerba compleuerat, et ecce animis feruentibus qui astabant*[85] facta irruptione, castra inimica peruadunt, et inuisam Ueneris domum funditus euertunt,

---

[81] *om. R*

[82] Psalms 80:12-13.

[83] Psalms 80:14-16.

[84] Cf. Jonah 1:2 ff; 3:2-10; 4:11.

[85] ipsi uero qui astabant animis feruentibus *R*

nec preter muri exterioris ambitum lapidem super lapidem relinquunt.

Nec[86] multum tempus abfuit, cum ciues et extramurani populi ab instanti clade liberati, iam spe meliore suo quisque labori insisteret, ut sepe contigit, ubi tranquilla serenitas humanas leuat sollicitudines, repentina aquarum inundatio ab occiduo mari exestuans circumiacentem urbis planitiem superfuso diluuio occupauit, cui ab orientali plaga infusus aquarius[87] marino estu adiutus,[88] ad alta usque urbis menia intumescens erupit, *ex quo sane diluuio habitatores prope deprehensi uix euaserunt, nimirum qui prima noctis uigilia sompno grauati, nulla rerum aduersa incursione solliciti, dulci in pace quiescebant, cum subitus clamor ad aures quiescentium perueniens, re inopinata turbatos ciues exterruit. Qui raptim sumptis paruulis suis et rebus quas casus obtulerat, ad montes quibus urbis menia cingebantur confugiunt, quibus ex locis conspiciunt domos et alta palatia seuiente uastari diluuio, hoc solo pereuntium rerum dampna consolantes, quod furentis diluuii saltem incolumes euasere pericula.*

Forte aberat uenerandus pontifex. Et enim apud regiam sedem pro causis ecclesie detentus immorabatur, ubi missus a ciuibus illi superueniens nuntius contestatur urbem omnem furentis aquarii uasto teneri diluuio. Turbatus animo uir Domini infectis rebus celeranter a sede regia digreditur, et ad liberandam sedem suam et peruasa arua festinus occurrit. /fol. 121v/ Quam cum eminus feruente estu circumseptam teneri conspiceret, suspirans immoque trahens a pectore uocem, "Quidnam est," inquit, "dominator Domine, quid ego seruus tuus tale commerui, ut urbem et plebem michi comissam inaudito uideam periclitari diluuio? Numquid tu olim per temet ipsum iurasti, quod aquis diluuii genus humanum perdendum nequaquam ultra iudicares?[89] Tibi olim subseruiuit uasta maris profunditas, prebens iter gradienti populo tuo. Tuo Iordanis alueus paruit imperio, refrenato gurgite calcabiles exhibens arenas.[90] Iube obsecro infestantis aquas diluuii retrouersas in maternum pelagi sinum usque cohiberi, ne nostros fines ultra populaturus turbidus amnis excedat."

Sic fatus, crucem dominicam quam pre oculis semper gestari faciebat arripiens, seuientes undas perrumpit intrepidus, que mox precipiti refugio uelut metu

---

[86] Lectio vi *R*
[87] infusio aquarum *R*
[88] adiuta *R*
[89] Cf. Genesis 6:5-9:19.
[90] Cf. 2 Kings 2:7-8 and 2:12-14.

perterrite, a facie ipsius non sine impetu relicta urbe et relictis agris quos male occupauerant effugere ceperunt. Instabat fugientibus aquis uir sanctus, et calcatius morantes urgebat, donec per patentes portas erumpentes preterfluentis Sequane alueo sese infuderunt. Quibus uir apostolicus in ipso portarum introitu ne ultra in euum procederent, terminum constituit, quod et has usque in hodiernum seruare manifestis uidemus indiciis, simili quantum ad naturam elementi quodam modo exemplo sed dispari euentu sub Heliseo.[91] *Ibi namque Helie pallio tacte aque a se diuise propheticis plantis siccum iter prebuerunt, et mox in se refuse arentem semitam operuerunt, hic autem a se nequaquam diuise, sed tota mole ipsa in se collecte a facie persequentis effugerunt, nec postmodum relicta arua repetierunt.*

Stupebant interea super his qui ad montana confugerant, mirantes imperiosam hominis auctoritatem, dum uiderent insensibile elementum refugis undis ipsius parere iussis. Uideres ad uirum Dei e diuerso turbam omnem confluere, et sublatis ad celum manibus Deum et Dominum ex presenti facto collaudare, ipsum quoque uirum apostolicum nouis in celum preconiis attolere. Uerum in hoc se male habere proclamabant, quod sedibus antiquis se ulterius credere non audebant, ne rediuiuo intercepti diluuio una nocte uniuersi perirent[92] *Alias igitur /fol. 122r/ sedes quamlibet procul positas, querere se oportere dicebant. Quibus uenerandus pontifex paterno affatu, immo prophetico spiritu prelocutus, respondit, "Nolite filii karissimi nolite turbari, nec uobis ultra timeatis huiusmodi aquas superuenturas esse. Aque iste prelocuntur uobis aduersarum gentium quandoque piraticum superuenturum exercitum, qui uestre huius regionis fines occupatos, inaudita feritate perdomabit, et posteros uestros per tempus et per*[93] *spatium temporis, suo subiugabit dominio. Uerumptamen apud misericordem Dominum hoc uobis optinui, ut uestris istud non fiat temporibus. Illud autem scitote, quoniam gens illa de qua loquimur gentilitatis errore adhuc detenta, mox ut Christi nomen audierit, catholice fidei cultum arripiet, et populum sibi subiectum multa in pace confouere persistet. Nunc ergo agite, et sedium uestrarum atria confidenter repetite, certi quia ea nequaquam ultra marina uexabit inundatio."*

Non multo denique tempore elapso, uenerandus heros dum canonicis sanctionibus optemperans sue diocesis ecclesias perlustraret, forte quoddam ad castrum peruenit, in quo templum artifici opere constructum prisca percoluerat gentilitas. Hic prisci erroris nulla estimans resedisse uestigia, ex more orationis causa

---

[91]   2 Kings 2:1-15.
[92]   *emended from* preirent B
[93]   *supralin.* B

aliquantulum uoluit immorari. Qui antequam ab equo dissiluisset, altitudinem templi curiosius intuens, uidit teterrimam spirituum inmundorum turbam alta templi fastigia persidentem, et quasi repugnandi studio ne hostibus in interiora atria uia patesceret, ad resistendum festinantem. Rogat igitur socios commeantes, si forte huiusmodi aliquid uiderent. At illi nichil se preter templi[94] eminentem molem intueri respondent. Imperat domnus presul sacerdotes templi presentes adesse. Qui uocati, mox conueniunt. Querit ab his quenam ibi religio seruabatur, uel cuiatis nomine titulus hic insignis habebatur. At illi trementes hesitare, pallescere, ipsa uultus speties singulorum manifesta signa dabat, quod ad deceptionem uulgi potius quam religionis ueritatem templum hoc dicatum consistebat. Quod uir sanctus intelligens, conuertit se, ut prophane edis interiora conspiceret.

Mox de summo tecti culmine uox obscena obgrunniens, in uerba huiusmodi erupit, "Quid tu hic Romane, quid tu hic? Tu ne et nos /fol. 122v/ hinc quoque eicere uenisti, sicut et fraternam legionem nostram moderno tempore a sede sua eiectam ad inhabitabilem plagam coegisti?" Iam non ultra passus horrentis monstri indigna uerba, execrabile templi uestibulum introgressus ianuam impulit, que mox displosis repagulis corruens, grandem quidem dedit sonitum, sed liberum astantibus patefecit introitum. Iam fantastica demonum apparent ludibria, que ad subuersionem animarum in auratas deorum imagines pretendebant. Mira res. Ad has dum uir sanctus feruente zelo pertenderet, repente ad terram omnes corruerunt. Tollitur in celum usque clamor aruspicum et ululatus demoniorum, e contra letabundus clamor christianorum. Fit inter hec pro direptione auri et argenti quibus statue tegebantur, militum grandis concertatio. Quos uir sobrius ne prophani auri anathemate contaminarentur, serenissima increpatione cohercuit, de hinc omnes a nefanda templi ede procul iussit amoueri. A quo dum se ipse paulo longius amouisset, eleuatis in celum oculis tacita paululum oratione subsistit, de hinc dexteram contra execrabilem edem erexit. Mox uelut celestis fulminis ictu atritum, totum illud enorme edifitium quadam terre hiantis uoragine subsedit, non sine ammiratione astantium, qui tantam in homine uidebant uirtutem, ut tam arduam machinam solo impulsu orationis consterneret, et constratam solotenus complanaret.

Iam uicine regionis populos, uirtutis huius nuntia fama permouit. Nam et ipsi cateruatim currentes conquassati delubri miraculum uidere festinabant, qui et ipsi proclamabant se simili arte demonum et dolo sacerdotum ludificari, quibus pro cultu diuinitatis Mercurii et Apollinis statuas impudici sacerdotes erexerant. "Iret

94 *supralin.* B

ergo domnus presul festinus ad discutiendas talium deorum officinas." Audiens hec
pontifex egregius arrepto itinere ad locum uulgi ore signatum impiger progreditur.
*Et ne uerbis immorer, in aduentu ipsius templum omne quo statue deorum stabant
ruens inpreceps soluitur in puluerem. Quo in loco, Christi ecclesiam ex proprio
censu fundatam constituit.*[95] */fol. 25v/ Muros Ierico, circumportata archa testamenti
Domini, corruisse olim didicimus.*[96] *Quo ex facto nobis pro portionalis quedam
ratio rerum quodammodo similitudinem parit. Nam si iuxta moralem uite actionem electorum corda archam Domini dici fas est, uir iste sanctus uere archa Domini erat, que dum elatam mundi huius superbiam intonantibus tubis, id est sa-
cerdotali auctoritate predicationis, prosternebat, muros Iericho, id est superba infi-
delitatis obstacula, destruebat. Unde non mirandum ualde est, si templa idolorum
in aduentu ipsius pre formidine non modo non stare sed etiam ruere cogebantur.
Sed ne stilus noster inter ruinas iericho subruatur, iam illum alias inflectere con-
amur.*[97]

---

[95]   BN 13.090 is here missing three folios; the transcription follows Evreux BM
101, beginning on fol. 25v.

[96]   Joshua 6:1-21.

[97]   Quod multo pridem tempore creberrime facere consueuerat. Hac uero diluuii
inundatione omnes exterriti, beati pontificis presentiam unanimiter eiulando aggre-
diuntur et ut tante calamitatis pestem ab eis auertat, nimiis gemitibus suppliciter
deprecantur. Quorum infelicitati uir Dei miserando compatiens, terre prostratus,
pro filiorum tribulatione ut clementissimus pater, Domino lamentabili prece suppli-
cat ut tam execrabile malum a ciuitate et populo suo auertat. Cumque ab oratione
surgeret, inuocato Christi nomine cum triumpho crucis, aquarum incursui ne amplius, limitem transgrediendo, loca christianorum deuastet sed infra suum se alue-
um compescat imperauit. Nec mora; creatura iusto iudicio mox facture dictis paruit,
factura enim factori obtemperare non neglexit. Sic aqua in se ipsam reuersa, ulterius paccata [*emended in ms. from* peccata] sua permisit manere confinia. Denique,
cuncta sui episcopatus circumiens loca, uerbi Dei semina per audientium corda
spargebat, inquirens si fortasse aliqua Deo exosa a quoquam gererentur. Et si inueniebat delinquentem, modeste corrigebat. Sin autem sedule commonebat ne a bonis
recederent et mala omnimodis deuitarent. Perscrutatus interea omnia sue diocesis
locorum abdita, quodam in loco demonum repperit fana Mercurii scilicet Iouis
atque Apollinis miro compta opere, que Dei nutu ita subuertit ut nec lapis super
lapidem remaneret. Ubi autem quoddam demonum culture edificium constructum
audiebat, nec mora, ab imis destruebat ac templa Christi ibidem locabat. Atque ut
bonus pastor in omnibus se componebat satagebatque uigili cura ne aliquam sui
gregis ouem atrox lupus deuiando a Christo raperet, sed potius proficerent ut
quandoque uiderent Deum Deorum in Sion salutis et glorie. R; Denique cuncta sui
episcopatus circumiens loca, uerbum Dei semina per audientium spargebat corda,

Instabant denique dies quadragesimalis obseruantie, quos uniuersalis
ecclesia artioris uite disciplinis exemplo maiorum seruandos edocuit. Hos
uir iste, sobrietatis et pudicitiae amator, ea sibi deinde ceteris, ea inquam
discretione indixerat, ut, nec caro ipsa ultra quam nature possibilitas exigit
per abstinentiam attereretur nec per alimentorum indulgentiam mens ex
carnali delectatione incontinentie lapsum incurreret. Ceterum in elemosinarum largitione se eo studiosius exhibebat, quo se[98] constitutum subsidio-
rum[99] temporalium dispensatorem recolebat. Nam et plerosque dum ex elemosinarum largitione glorie inanis fauore conspiceret delectari, hos ratione
et consilio ab appetitu laudis compescebat, dicens ut dum necessaria indi-
gentibus exhiberent, tanto humiliter prebuissent, quanto et aliena esse in-
telligebant que dispensabant. Sic misericordes admonebat ne sub ostentu
largitatis ea que possidebant inutiliter spargerent, ne de impenso munere
pietatis fieret popularis appetitio fauoris, sed omnino nesciret sinistra quid
faceret dextera, uidelicet ut quod faciebat amor Dei, non corrumperet aut[100]
perderet[101] cupiditas seculi. Quos autem prodiga effusione insultius sua
largiri uelut contuitu miserationis conspexerat, hos interim lenitatis uerbo
ab immoderato usu compescebat, ut ex equalitate rerum familiarium sup-
plerent indigentiam miserorum, ne dum animus largitoris ferre inopiam
nesciebat, sibi si[102] cuncta necessaria exhauriendo subtraxisset occasionem, contra se /fol. 26r/ impatientie postmodum exquisisset,[103] et dum
minus equanimiter inopiam toleraret premisse largitatis merces periret, et

---

inquirens si fortasse aliqua gerentur a quoquam Deo exosa. Et si inueniebat delinquentem modeste corrigebat. Sin autem sedule commonebat ne a bonis recederent
et mala omnimodis deuitarent. Perscrutatus interea omnia sue diocesis locorum
abdita quodam in loco demonum repperit fana Mercurii scilicet Iouis atque Apollo-
nis miro compta opere, que Dei nutu ita subuertit, ut nec lapis super lapidem remaneret. Ubi autem quoddam demonum culture edifitium audiebat constructum
nec more ab imis destruebat ac templa Christi ibidem locabat atque ut bonus
pastor in omnibus se componebat. Satagebatque uigili cura ne aliquam sui gregis
ouem trux lupus deuiando a Christo raperet, sed pocius proficerent ut quandoque
uiderent Deum deorum in Sion salutis et glorie. BHL 7312

[98]   a Domino *ad. R*
[99]   quoque *ad. R*
[100] uel *R*
[101] proderet *R*
[102] si sibi *R*
[103] exquireret *R*

adhuc mentem deterius murmuratio subsequens perderet. O uirum his nostris temporibus necessarium, uirum inquam insigni laude predicandum, cuius actio ab omni parte circumspecta, nullus[104] calumpniantium morsibus unquam patuisse uisa est, bonos semper ad meliora cohortans,[105] malos a malis reuocans, bonos ne se de benefactis extollant, malos ne in malis suis perdurantes, suppliciis infernalibus pereant. Talibus studiis attentius inherens, uir iste apostolicus creditas sibi oues a Domino, uerbo et exemplo ad pascua uite tendere commonebat. Sed nos, quoniam uniuersa ipsius facta insignia stilo colligere nequimus, ad propositum redeamus.

Peractis[106] siquidem ieiuniorum quadragesimalium diebus, superuenit dominice cene sacratissima dies, dies uidelicet propiciationis et reconciliationis, dies qua mors interitum et uita accipit principium, dies uero[107] in qua fit gaudium de assumptione uocatorum et leticia de absolutione penitentium, quos ipse intra uiscera misericordie complexus, ipsa eadem die intra gremium sancte matris ecclesie reconciliatos admisit. Super quibus uberiore pietatis affectu inlacrimatus, omnium qui astabant infletum corda commouit, dum uiderent eum inter peccantes uelut peccatorem, inter lugentes lugentium peccata deflere, paterno affectu singulos commonere ne iteratis excessibus se ultra ab ecclesie matris communione alienarent. Uenturis deinde ad beate regenerationis lauachrum, fit ex more sanctificandi olei et chrismatis consecratio, et cetera sacramentorii[108] ordinis officia iuxta competentem diei reuerentiam. Nec minus dominice passionis die congruis officiis expleto, dies ille magnus sabbati illuxit quo regenerantis ecclesie fecunda uirginitas filios suos fidei sacre primitus[109] imbuendos in adoptionis sortem[110] spectabat ascribi.

Unde memorandus pater, confectum biduano corpus ieiunio pro expectatione sollempnis officii, orationibus in horam usque nonam protraxit. Cum intelligens[111] a meridiano feruore cursu deciduo tendere solem ad uesperam, erexit se ab oratione *et deflexis casu ad leuum cellule latus oculis,*

---

[104] nullis *R*
[105] cohartans *R*
[106] Lectio vii *R*
[107] *om. R*
[108] *emended from* sacramentorum *R*
[109] primitiis *R*
[110] fortem *R*
[111] intellegens *R*

uidit teterrimam monstri horrentis umbram. Quamdiu intuitus, intellexit sacrosancta ipsius diei officia diabolicis infestanda prestigiis. Crucis tamen signo perterrita, de cellula exire fera bestia compellitur. Conuocatis tamen ad se fratribus, uenerabilis pater ait "Cautius uos agite, fratres mei. Ecce enim diabolus ecclesie huius atria circumuolans, agendis officiis insidiaturus peruigilat. Quo contra et ego uos summam premoneo adhibere diligentiam, ne nobis in aliquo rerum casu nocuisse hodie aduersarius insultet."

Iam hora uenerat qua, peractis omnibus que primo agenda[112] instabant, domnus pontifex sacrandis fontibus astabat. Ut ergo uentum est ad locum quo sanctificatis[113] aquis infudenda chrismalis fuerat benedictio, minister /fol. 26v/ cuius hoc erat officium, alias forte intentus, chrismale sacrum exhibere non meminit. Qui requisitus dum a clericis, causaretur quod domnum episcopum et omnem clerum simul et populum pro expectatione chrismatis solus ipse turbaret artatus. Nimium precipiti cursu ad locum quo crismalis ampulla seruabatur turbata mente progreditur, quam incautius rapiens, dum ad fontes tendere festinat, lubrico fusus pauimento uitream testam superfusus corporee molis attritu comminuit, ex qua chrismalis benedictio uorantibus arenis penitus absorta, spem nullam restitutionis prestabat. Turbati omnes et pre ceteris episcopus, quid nam agerent inter se hesitabant. Nichil sane sibi minister reseruauerat ex quo effusi liquoris dampnum etiam presenti in necessitate reformare quiuisset, quippe qui per uniuerse diocesis ecclesias distribuendo totum penitus consumpsisset. Iam animaduertit uir Deo plenus hoc maligni spiritus insidiis esse factum, qui bonorum omnium inuidus, uocatis ad fidem gentibus regenerationis uiam preuertere nitebatur.

Unde circumstantibus moderata increpatione dicebat: "Numquid non ego uos fratres hodierna die sollitos esse premonui, hoc ipsum protestatus quia diabolus nostra hodie gaudia perturbare moliebatur? Sed iam non querimonia, sed consilio indigemus." Iubet itaque effusi liquoris sibi locum ostendi, ubi mox corpore prostrato, orationi incubuit. Nec mora. Erexit se domnus episcopus et preces sentiens exauditas,[114] iubens uitrea fragmina recolligi ut constrato marmore resilientes minutie sparsim iacebant. Quas collectas, manibus uir sanctus amplectens, in antique forme speciem mox consolidauit. *De hinc*

---

[112] agendo R
[113] *emended from* sanctificans R
[114] preces sent. exaud. erexit se R

reformati uasculi patulum os solo applicat hoc ipso loco quo, effuse benedictionis, casus acciderat. Res mira et inaudito exemplo attollenda. Uideres dispersos olei riuulos et guttulas passim iacentes cogi in unum corpus, et ascendentem uirgulam per angustum oris aditum, intra concauum uentris umbonem se recipi. Ad instar lactis quod, pressis ouium uberibus, in lineam coactum mos est pastoribus mulctris inducere, preter quod illud ab alto ad imum defluit, istud ab imo in altum conscendit. Quante uero ex presenti facto in celum laudes efferebantur impossibile est explicari. Sed de oleo sub manu Helisei[115] *crescente, nescio quis de uulgo in aurem mihi susurrabat. Uerum enim uero si personarum dignitatem et ministrorum maiestatem salua ratione conferre liceat, alias non inuenio quo de signorum magnitudine, concertationibus debeamus inseruire. Cum unius eiusdem Dei qui in ambobus operatus est hanc et illam perpendo uirtutem, preter quod ibi audiuimus prestita uasa non ex collisis reformata, hic uidemus uitrea fragmina ex attritus minutiis in integritatis antique decorem restituta. Illic ex subsistente oleo quamlibet /fol. 27r/ paruo amplioris summe creuisse liquorem. Hic ex penitus effuso et ut ita dicam, iam non subsistente recuperatum. Illic per manum femineam uasis infusum, hic non natura famulante libero ascensu intra ollam uitream reconditum. Sed nos in derogationem prophetice uirtutis nequaquam ista prelibauimus, cui sane post magistrum incomparabilibus miraculis prisca redundant uolumina.*

Unum interim, licet plura suppeditant, narro miraculum, quod uir sanctus summa dissimulatione celare conabatur, ut fame popularis auras magnitudo signi ne quandoquidem attingeret. Sed irrito conatu silere temptauerat quod Dei prouida dispensatio manifestum esse uolebat. Eodem fere tempore, dominice ascensionis dies instabat et ipse ex consuetudine dominica acturus officia processit ad ecclesiam, ubi a clero et populo expectabatur. Ordinatis itaque, que solenni apparatu dies festus exigebat, officiosa religione missa celebratur. Ut autem euangelice lectionis uerba minister expleuit, ipse domnus presul uerbum ad populum ex more facere instituit, in quo de presentibus, de futuris, de fidelium gloria, de eternitate sanctorum, de suppliciis iniquorum nec mortale sonans, iuxta audientium capacitatem sic sacrum dispensabat eloquium, ut cogitationes singulorum, ipse solus et occulta cordium inspicere uideretur, unde omnium corda in lacrimas et alta suspiria commouebantur.

Ex hinc, sacramentoria archana prosecutus, eloquar aut sileam? Sane quo mentis tendebat intentio, sublime a terra corpus satis ostenderat. Tribus sane conuersationis intuentibus, uisum est totum corpus ipsius in sublime aeris appensum

---

[115] 1 Kings 17:8-16.

teneri. Quod uidentes, dum intra se altius stuperent, apparuit illis et aliud iocunde uisionis miraculum. Quo ipsi in excessu mentis effecti, ab alto cordis erumpentibus suspiriis, eo usque increpuerunt ut ceteris aut foret incertum magnum et mirabile fuisse quod uidisse, se alta precordiorum suspiria testabantur, non de nihilo esse quod procul a se distantes, tamen uno eodem hore momento, uno eodemque uisionis ictu impulsi, ab intimis penetralibus suspiria emiserant. Nam ubi ad locum uentum est quo propriis manibus sacrum calicem paulo altius a mensa eleuarat, apparuit super caput eius ignis flammea speties fulgurantis, et e medio ignis dextera hominis benedicens tanquam ad suscipiendum libantis hostias porrecta comparuit.

Quod Christi sacerdos preter se nulli comparuisse estimans, eterno claudi silentio meditabatur. Sed dum prefatis fratribus totum corpus uisionis pernotuisse isdem referentibus intellexit, paulo mente concussa, summa auctoritate denuntiat ne in uita sua ulli mortali res ista patuisset. Querit ab his an et ipsi quoque emissam sibi de celo uocem audissent. Quod dum nequaquam audisse faterentur, ait "Uel in hoc solo uos secretorum meorum /fol. 27v/ fidos custodes habebo, quod inauditum finem uisionis per aures uulgi non disseminabitis." Quem finem cum sibi exponi sub obtestatione paterne caritatis exposcerent, "Cogitis me," inquit, "filii, immo sortis humane ineuitabilis conditio que uocationis mee diem accelerat, cogit me hec ista que poscitis explicare, sed uos alicui ne quandoquidem exponatis. Nam mox ut dextera Domini, quam ipsi uos uidisse testificamini, sese a uisu nostro intra globum igneum recepit, uox continuo subsecuta huiusmodi constans inquit 'Esto famule meus nec frangant te certaminis tui premia diu expectata, neque dimoueat ab incepto labore senio uicta debilitas. Proximo tempore uenio tibi, ut de mundi huius uoragine cenulenta tollam te et inter electorum sacerdotum agmina constituam in regno patris mei, ubi est copiosa merces sanctorum. Ibi de dextera quam uidisti, accipies palmam perhennis glorie et stolam iocunditatis et felicitatis eterne. Sed et in hoc interim suscipio preces tuas, ut quecumque et pro quibuscumque petieris, procul dubio impetrata reportes. Nam et sancta que instanti tractas officio, proximo itidem tempore reposita tibi, gaudebis in regno meo.' Ex his igitur uerbis dominicis, certos uos esse uolo aut diu differri diem uocationis mee."

His auditis, fratres uersis in luctum gaudiis et sauciis dolore cordibus, a fletu continere haud quaquam poterant. Quos pater pius benigne consolatus, "Deponite," inquit, "fratres mei, huiusmodi dolorem nec uobis molestum sit me ex huius peregrinationis exilio eo quo me Christus uocat adire. Et enim de uocatione mea nequaquam uos turbari oportet, quem in nullo uobis defuturum spes manet haud incerta. Affui uobis corporali huc usque presentia; adero uobis apud internum iudicem opitulatione continua. Seruite Domino in timore et exultate ei cum tremore, apprehendite disciplinam ut et ego de uestro et uos de meo quandoque consortio in superna Ierusalem gaudere ualeamus." Suspectum igitur uocationis sue tempus preueniens, uir Domini artius se contemplationis sancte studiis insere-bat. Unde ciuium frequentiam spernens, remotioris celle habitationem delegit, in qua dum hiemali quodam tempore solitarius sacras per acturus uigilias assurgeret, sumptam temporis et loci occasionem, malignus spiritus ad callida nequitie sue uertit argumenta.

Nam assumpta feminei sexus specie, longe adhuc ab oratorio quo sanctus Domini Romanus pernoctabat, tremula uoce clamare cepit se miserandam, se infe-licem, que capta et spoliata a latrunculis uix manus eorum euaserat, que per auia lustra ferarum sub algenti nocte modo errabunda effugit, cui nec apud agrestes feras fida restant latibula, nec apud homines nature memor patet hospitalitas. Talibus inestuans querimoniis, callida pestis simulato algore, labris trementibus, hostium celle pulsare cepit dicens "O, si hic miseris mortalibus /fol. 28r/ prestatur miseratio. O, si hic uagos et egenos indulta fouet hospitalitas, o, quicumque es loci huius habitator, si Christi nomen audisti, audi Christum dicentem hospes fui et non collegistis me. Ergo si in membris suis se suscipi Christus recognoscit, quid tu intolerabili gelu me cruciandam arces ab hospicio tuo? Quid tu non audis apo-stolum dicentem 'Hospitalitatem nolite obliuisci?'[116] Sed nimirum dum habita-torem ex nomine non appello, non curat ignote causam persone. Uerum enim uero quendam uenerabilis uite uirum hoc in loco habitare aiebant, uirum misericordie operibus deditum, nomine Romanum, qui inter cetera sancte exortationis documen-ta hanc precipue uirtutem haberi monebat, ut aduenas et peregrinos colligere et, sumptibus necessariis, perfouere meminissent. Hic, si presens adesset, non me pate-retur gelide noctis horrore cruciari. Reum et enim se iure estimaret, si quod ille uerbis suadet, actu ipse implere refugeret. Quam enim excusationem sibi pararet in illum magni iudicii diem, quando impios et immites et qui claudunt uiscera sua ab egeno et paupere, uidebit a ianua uite repulsari? Sed absit ab aliquo mortali hoc credere, ut uir tante sanctitatis hanc unam captiuam miserabili mortis genere pati-atur perire. Uerum dum ego captiuitatis mee erumnas deploro, nescio cuius uocem ab intus interim audio. Nimirum hic est de quo loquor, ille Dei electus Romanus; hunc, ergo, appellare iuuat. O electe Christi sacerdos, quid tu non audis infelicem mulierculam ad hostium tuum clamantem, que capta et spoliata a latrunculis, dum manus eorum uix euado, etiam ab umbraculo culminis tui crudeliter repellor? Haccine erat olim uox tua que ex lectione apostolica suadebat hospitales esse sine

---

[116] Hebrews 13:2.

murmuratione?[117] *et per quam testabaris quosdam placuisse angelis hospitio receptis?*[118] *Surge, ergo, presul Domini et aperi michi, ut et tibi Christus aperiat ianuam uite. Surge, inquam, obsecro, certissime sciens quia in susceptione mea Christum suscipis, qui te intra ianuam beatitudinis olim non ut hospitem sed ut heredem Dei et coheredem sibi recipiat."*

His tandem querimoniis uir sanctus immemor doli ad misericordiam mouetur, et personam intromitti decreuerat, dum ancipiti cogitatione mente pulsatus, dubitare cepit quid ageret. Hinc quia sexus huius consortium aspernabatur, hinc quia misericordiam non prestari quoddam genus impietatis fore estimabat. Tandem uicit propositum pietas; recipitur hostis ex femina. Inquiritur fallentis monstri simulata captiuitas, et captiue miserandus casus et euasionis euentus. Iam inquirentis uerba callidus hostis ad prestigia nequitie sue coaptans, crinibus expansis, pectus detegit, precandidam forme speciem pretendit, transformans se in lucem feminei decoris. Hinc proprius se admouens in amplexum recipi oscula libari /fol. 28v/ impudenter consorte stratu confoueri deposcit. Iam prestigiatoris sidias uir Dei animaduertit nec enim ultra dissimulare dolum spiritus poterat inmundus. Quid tamen ageret? Aliquandiu sese inuucem conspicientes, silentium tenuerunt, cum miles Christi intra se cepit meditari, quo de honestationis genere a cellula hostem impurum eiceret, uolens illum si fas est diris modis torquere. Et ecce angelus Domini superueniens, uniuersa celle hostia et laquearia nec[119] */fol. 123r/ non et tecti superioris patentia culmina crucis signo muniuit, de hinc latronem arreptum mirum in modum cedens undique urget, undique coartat, ut nec per hostium per quod introgressus fuerat, nec summi tecti culmina ferali bestie pateret exitus, sed per inmundas cloacas digno sibi exitu effugere compelleretur.*

Tandem discessu hostis securus uir Domini, dampnare in se leuitatis culpam uehementer cepit, cur soluto grauitatis antique proposito femineum sexum quamlibet deceptus hospicio suscepisset. Tum uero pugnis tundi pectus uideres innocuum, miserum se clamare, dira inprecari, indigne ferre se pastoralis insigne regiminis, qui uel ex deceptione primi parentis satis edoceri potuerat, quam sint uitanda presertim tali in conuentu feminee suasionis blandimenta. Tali estu conscii doloris accusantem se, idem qui hostem malignum extruserat angelus, ne se tanto dolore excruciet, consolari cepit dicens, "Merito electe altissimi, merito inquam compun-

---

[117] 1 Peter 4:9.

[118] Hebrews 13:2.

[119] From here until the end the transcription again follows Paris BN lat. 13.090, taking up on fol. 123r.

geris, quod sexus corruptibilis quamlibet speciem mentitam, sub umbra culminis tui intromittendam credidisti, sed uicit te pietas, uicit mortalibus haut deneganda miseratio. Repara igitur uirilis animi robur, resume aduersus temptatoris occulti insidias prudentie et sobrietatis constantiam, hoc pro uero intelligens, quia iuxta serpentem positus diu non eris illesus. Preterea de uocatione tua que proximo tempore futura instat sollicitus, subiectam tibi Christi familiam ut pastor uigilantissimus premunire, uel instruere contra huiusmodi fallentis hostis prestigia, dum uita presens subinstat ne differas."

His uerbis angeli recreatus, et de uocatione sua certior factus, fratres monasterii ad se iussit conuocari, quibus primum de instanti obitu, de hinc de insidiis quas a diabolo perpessus fuerat pro edificatione sua intimabat, ne et hii de familiaris peste consortii se corrumpi aliquando permisissent. Iam tempus aderat, cum uerus Israhel ab Egipti erumnis ad promissa regna uocatus,[120] peracti certaminis premia fuerat percepturus. Unde dierum labentem cursum mente preoccupans, hunc ipsum quem per /fol. 123v/ angelum didicerat exitus sui diem sollicitus expectabat. Fit igitur rerum mobilium in pauperes Christi larga distributio, fit per ecclesias Dei sub testamento prediorum multa distratio. Factum est autem quadam nocte dominica dum membra debilia nocturnis fessa uigiliis, tenui sompno recreare uoluisset, sensit se quibusdam intra uiscera regnantis morbi aculeis perurgeri, et iccirco diem illam et sequentem ebdomadam pro expectatione exitus sui psalmis et orationibus usque in sequentis sabbati horam nonam continuabat. Qua hora dum dolorem ad uitalia crebris persensit ictibus pulsare, conuocatis ad se fratribus, iubet sibi oleo sancto corpus egrum perungi.

De hinc paucis quidem sed salutaribus eos monitis instruere cepit dicens, "Ecce fratres mei et filii karissimi, non est ut cernitis dissimulandi libertas, non remorandi potestas, soluendum nobis est nature mortalis debitum, eundum nobis est quo Christus et alia nos uita longe melior inuitat. Nec uobis molestum esse debet, si nos eo properamus, quo certa manet requies laborum, quo sanctis reposita est eterne felicitatis beatitudo.[121] Unum est[122] quod uobis peruigili mente

---

[120] For the calling of the "old" Israel out of Egypt, see Exodus.

[121] Sicque pristino restituta decori ampulla, eiusdem qui fusus fuerat chrismatis confestim referta est liquore. Unde circumastantes plebes Domino laudum rependerunt munera, qui eis tante sanctitatis cesserat pastorem, ut uelut Helisei meritis, ita et istius oramine, uas fractum redundaret olei liquore. {*Compare BHL 7312: Mox miro dictu omni pristino restituta est decore crismatis referta liquore. Unde circumadstantes plebs Domino rectori laudum rependerunt munera qui eis tante sanctitatis cesserat pastorem, ut uelut Helisei merita in Galgala ita et istius oramine uas fractum redundaret olei*

obseruandum instituo, uidelicet ut pacem et unanimitatem manere inter
uos recognoscat ille qui ex hoc mundo transiturus ad patrem, electis suis

---

liquorem.} [lectio viii] Ergo quia ad fidem tante sanctitatis uiri corroborandam, plura
de miraculis inscripsimus oportet, ut ad illud diuinum quod cetera super eminet
stilum uertamus. Quod uir sanctus summa dissimulatione celare conabatur ut fame
popularis aura magnitudinem signi ne quandoquidem attingeret, sed irrito conatu
silere temptauerat quod Dei prouida dispensatio manifestum esse uolebat. Quadam
namque die dum diuina celebraret misteria, ubi ad locum uentum est quo propriis
manibus sacrum calicem paulo altius a mensa eleuarat, apparuit super caput eius
ignis flammea species fulgurantis et e medio ignis, dextera hominis benedicens tanquam ad suscipiendum [*emended from* suscipiandum] libantis hostias porrecta comparuit. Sed peractis officii sollempniis, conuocari iubet quosdam quos in diuinis se-
cretis pre ceteris familiares habebat, quibus uisionis secreta aperiens: "Iam pro certo
fratres," inquit, "filiolique mei in Christo nosse uos uolo, tempus resolutionis mee
instare, quoniam licet haud exigentibus mee paruitatis meritis, debita missarum
celebrans sollempnia merui dexteram dei conspicere. Unde subnixe fraternitatis
uestre ex oro clementiam, ne cuiquam huius oromatis pandatis inditium quo ad
usque me uideatis morte resolutum. Et quia Dei dextera que mihi apparuit regnum
celorum designatur, tempus me migrandi ad Dominum instare per hoc certissimum
uobis habeatur." Sua ergo de uocatione securus, beatus Romanus die noctuque ab
oratione mentem non reflectebat, sed quanto uiciniorem nouerat exitus sui diem,
tanto magis iugiter bonorum operum studiis inseruiebat, ac efficatius orationi uaca-
bat. Quodam autem tempore hiemali dum sacer ille, scilicet antistes Romanus, solus
pernox orationi uacaret, accedens inimicus ante fores ubi intus beatus Romanus
orabat. Astitit femineam habens speciem, cupiens temptare uersutia sua beatum uirum, inquiens ad illum "Sancte et electe Dei Romane, aperi mihi ianuas cellule tue
meque famulam Dei, fatigatam longo itinere, intromitte domum. Quoniam nimbri
frigore premor, ueste nudata. Sed sanctus Domini omnino talia spernens consortia,
aure quidem mulieris captabat uocem sed mente ex toto recusabat, indignum fore
infra precordia cogitans sui pectoris, tali se iungere socio. Tunc mulier per dirum
a pectore mouens luctum, cepit clamare "O Romane sacer Christi, tu Christo reddi-
turus es rationem ob animam meam, que a frigoribus e corpore meo cogitur exire.
Nec tu eris in hoc insons nec criminis expers in me, qui claudens tua limina, non
me permittis intrare." Cumque sanctus ille undique anxius staret, tandem pietate
commotus, uocantem hostem introuenire decreuit. Sed postquam delusor diabolus
ad ignem est calefactus, dilatans crines sui capitis usque ad pedes, cum illecebrosis
colloquiis sancti animum uellet corrumpere. Beatus Romanus crucis uallatus munimine, antiqui hostis insidias triumphali fidei superauit certamine. [Lectio viiii *margin*] Denique cum appropinquasset exitus sui dies, fidelium conuocata copia, cuncta
que possidere uidebatur in mundo egenis et aduenis uiduis et orphanis larga manu
distribuit, nihil sibi reseruans ex omnibus, ne transituro e mundo aliqua contagii
macula inueniretur, in eo illud cogitans psalmiste "Dispersit, dedit pauperibus; iu-
sticia eius manet in seculum seculi, cornu eius exaltabitur in gloria" [Psalms 112:9-

dicebat, 'Pacem relinquo uobis, pacem meam do uobis.'[123] Scitis namque quia redemptor humani generis in mundum ueniens, per celestem et angelicam creaturam pacem hominibus bone uoluntatis indixit,[124] rediturus ad patrem per se ipsum pacis inuiolabile pignus seruandum instituit. Summa ergo uigilantia uos attendere premoneo, quanta animaduersione plectendi sunt qui odia in corde retinent, rixas excitant, discordias[125] serunt, quando nec munus eorum ad altare recipitur, nisi primum frater offensus, fiat digna satisfactione placatus."

"Pensandum ergo ualde est quantum malum sit discordie, pro qua etiam et alia bona facta a Domino reprobantur. Considerate uolatilia celi quomodo ea que unius generis sunt sese socialiter uolando non deserunt, sicut et ipsa[126] bruta animalia que gregatim /fol. 124r/ pascuntur, que si sollerter aspicimus nimirum sibi concordando irrationalis natura, indicat quantum malum per discordiam rationalis natura[127] committat, dum uidelicet ista rationis intentione perdit quod illa naturaliter custodit. Uos natura rati-

---

10]. Sicque ut filios carissimos allocutus est eos tali sermone: "Dominus meus Jesus Christus, cui a primeua etate seruiui pro uiribus, uocare me est dignatus. Pro sua pietate ut pro quantitate mei laboris iam mihi reddat felicis glorie premium. Unde paterno affectu uos moneo, dilectissimi, ne a recti itineris tramite deuii respiciatis retro quod absit; immo, de die in diem magis augmentantes sincere uiuatis, quoniam iuxta Pauli uocem apostoli, 'Unusquisque propriam recipiet mercedem secundum suum laborem' [1 Cor. 3:8]. Si quis uero, quod absit, aliter egerit, uestro pio refoueatur exemplo. Unusquisque quod sibi fieri non uult, alii ne faciat, ne atrox inimicus qui non nostra tollere querit sed ut feriat in nobis caritatis amorem, aliquod inueniat periculi malum, unde decepti perire possitis. Quoniam ego pastor hactenus uester, iam amplius non ero. R {*Compare BHL 7312: Unde paterno uos affectu moneo, uos dilectissimi, ne a recto itineris tramite deuii respiciatis retro quod absit; immo, de die in diem magis augmentantes sincere uiuatis, quoniam iuxta Pauli uocem apostoli, "Unusquisque propriam recepiet mercedem secundam suum laborem." Si quis uero, quod absit, aliter egerit, uestro pio refoueatur exemplo. Unusquisque quod sibi fieri non uult, alii ne faciat, ne trux inimicus qui non nostra tollere querit sed ut feriat in nobis caritatis amorem, aliquod inueniat periculi malum, unde decepti perire possitis. Quoniam ego pastor hactenus uester, iam amplius non ero.*}

122 ergo *ad.* R
123 John 14:27.
124 *emended from* induxit B
125 discordia R
126 cetera R
127 indicat...natura *in margin* R

onales genuit, uidete ne dotale priuilegium nature per discordie malum adulteretis, sed iuxta apostolum 'solliciti sitis seruare unitatem spiritus in uinculo pacis, dum in uno ipsius corpore prescripti estis, qui in scissura mentium non habitat.'[128] Uerumptamen hanc ea discretione uos moneo seruare fratres mei, ut cum quibus eam fundare debeatis sollerter caueatis, scientes quia si peruersorum nequitia in pace iungitur, profecto eorum malis actibus[129] robur augetur, quia quo sibi in malitia magis congruunt, eo se robustius bonorum afflictionibus illidunt. De talibus uero hec uos seruare ammoneo, ut quid[130] facti sunt diligere, et quod facti non sunt increpare studeatis, perpendentes uidelicet, quando ab increpatione malorum cessatur, quanta culpa cum pessimis pax teneatur, dum Dauid sanctus hoc uelut in hostias Deo optulit, quod contra se pro Domino prauorum inimicitias excitauit. Unde et dicit, 'Nonne qui oderunt te Domine oderam, et super inimicos tuos tabescebam? Perfecto odio oderam illos; inimici facti sunt michi.'"[131]

"Ecce iam fratres ecce iam uocor a Domino, sermone uos longe tenere ultra[132] non debeo. Uos ipsi scitis qualiter uobiscum conuersatus sum ab initio ordinationis mee, non aurum, aut[133] argentum, aut omnino que uestra fuerant, sed uos ipsos quesiui. Non in uos tyrannicam dominationem exercui, sed ut ipsi michi testes estis paterno uos affectu percolui. Non de singularitate potentie intumui, sed prelationis culmen ex communi nature conditione censendum estimaui. Enimuero si rexi uos non ut decuit, rexi tamen ut noui et potui. Uos recturus a Christo accepi, Christo uos regendos restituo. Ne longum faciam, ipsi uos committo, qui salutari uos lauit baptismate, et proprio redemit sanguine, Christo Jesu Domino nostro qui unus cum patre et spiritu sancto uiuit et regnat Deus per inmortalia secula seculorum. Amen."

Ita fatus[134] collegit se in lectum suum, quem cinere et cilitio constratum /fol. 124v/ pro festiua mollitie habere consueuerat, ex quo sanctam celo animam reddidit, ubi fruitur gaudens et exultans societate angelorum,

---

128 Ephesians 4:3.
129 *emended from* actionibus B
130 quod R
131 Psalms 138:21-22.
132 u. t. R
133 non R
134 *emended from* factus R

optinetque palmam perhennis glorie, et stolam iocunditatis eterne. Preterea ad eius transitum gloriosus occurrit sanctorum[135] numerus, cum quibus ab omni labe integer[136] sequitur agnum uirginee castitatis auctorem Dominum Jesum Christum. De obsequio funeris ipsius quia sufficienter eloqui non ualeo, silere potius quam ueritatis lineam pretergredi estimaui, quia ad illud quantus ordo psallentium, quanta turba occurrit lamentantium, estimari quidem potest, numerari non potest. Transiit autem dominica nocte,[137] decimo uidelicet kalendarum nouembrium die, *sepultusque est primo ab urbe miliario, in oratorio quodam suo, quo in loco in honore beati Gildardi quondam eiusdam sedis archiepiscopi fundata constat ecclesia, ubi diuina uberius prestantur beneficia ad laudem et gloriam Dei et Domini nostri Iesu Christi, cui est honor, uirtus, et potestas, cum Patre et Spiritu Sancto, per omnia secula seculorum. Amen.*[138]

Explicit uita beatissimi Romani Rothomagensis archipresulis.

C. The Cathedral Miracles of Romanus

/fol. 29v/ ...Explicit uita. Item incipiunt miracula.

Si rerum nobis causas perpendere libet, sicut ex luce reuerberata, lux refunditur, ita quodammodo ex miraculis signa oriuntur. Huius rei exemplo satis esse putamus quendam euentum, uisu et auditu terribilem, sed fide et oratione probabilem, quem sane non humanis auctoribus sed elementis protestantibus constat nobis didicisse. Instabat siquidem beati Ro-

---

[135] s. o. R
[136] i. l. R
[137] d. n. *om.* R; e mundo *ad.* R
[138] Tunc accipientes corpus eius sanctissimum, sepelierunt eum cum omni diligentia. Ubi diuina gratia eum deuote petentibus plurima prestantur beneficia, auxiliante Domino nostro Iesu Christo, cui est honor et gloria in secula seculorum. Amen. R; Tunc accipientes corpus eius sacrum sepelierunt cum omni diligentia ubi multarum beneficiarum miracula Domini pandit magnificentia per seruum suum Romanum usque in hodiernum diem, ipso auxiliante cui est honor, gloria et imperium per infinita seculorum secula. Amen. *BHL* 7312.

mani depositionis dies, quam fratres monasterii solennibus uigiliis preue-
/fol. 30r/nientes, nocturnis studiosius perstabant officiis. Ad quem uenerandus presul Rotbertus sacras et ipse acturus excubias conuenerat. Uentum
forte fuerat ad locum, quo prefati patris liber uite editus commemorat,
sicut in anteriori uisione audiuimus, olim sibi dum dominicis instaret
sacramentis, de summo uertice dexteram Domini comparuisse, qua ex reuelatione intellexit uir Deo plenus uocationis sue tempus instare, sicut et ipse
mox conuocatis fratribus exposuit. Sibi quidem ad gaudium, illis uero ad
lamentum, sibi quia ad eum uadit, illis quia amittunt solatium egregii
pastoris. Hoc in loco prefatus prefatus presul aliquandiu hesitans, his qui
astabant, et precipue cuidam seniori quem in disciplinis liberalibus magistrum habuerat, sic ait: "Quamquam de meritis huius uenerandi patris
nostri sit nefas dubitare care magister, locus tamen iste fateor scrupulosis
sepe cogitationibus flucture dubiam mentem impellit, an sicut paulo ante
presens historia presonuit credibile sit summi redemptoris dexteram con-
spicabilem apparuisse, ut Christo semel celo recepto, homini corporeo
quamlibet sancto, quamlibet mundo fas fuerit, dexteram Dei uisu conspicuo intueri."

Ad hec uir ille uelut ictu saucius alte suspirans, et quasi amisso spiritu moderata increpatione cohercuit dicens: "Quid mi karissime tale cogitare
potuisti? Immo si uanis cogitationibus impugnamur, quid usque ad offen-
sionis uerba impelli potuisti? Sed esto, inusitato rei exemplo turbatus,
hesitationis foueam incidisti. Uel anteriorum patrum exemplo doceri potueras, quibus uetus prodit historia reuelatam Domini gloriam sepe comparuisse, quem innixum scale quondam generosus ille patriarcha conspexerat,
dum uncto deorsum lapide ascendentes et descendentes angelos conspiceret, in prefiguratione predicatorum, qui sursum sanctum caput ecclesie
Dominum uidelicet contemplando debent appetere, sed deorsum quoque
ad membra illius miserando descendere.[1] Nam et Isaias nondum incarna-
tum Dominum, super solium excelsum sedentem se uidisse testatus est.[2]
Sic et Micheas Dominum sedentem, et illi omnem celi militiam assistentem
uidit, cum profano regi Achab ultio digna incubuisset, ad quem decipien-
dum per pseudo prophetas spiritus mendax mittebatur.[3] Siquidem et ille

---

[1] Genesis 28:10-20.
[2] Isaiah 9:6-7, 11:1-16.
[3] 1 Kings 22:19-23

prothomartyr Stephanus dum saxea grandine lapidum premeretur, filium hominis a dextris Dei stantem se uidisse profitebatur.[4] Procul igitur, procul absit a te mi domine huiusmodi dubitatio, neue istud libeat ad publicas aures proferre, quod nefas est solummodo."

Ad hec episcopus increpantis uerbum patienter ferens, "Fateor," inquit, "uenerande magister, ita esse nec est quod aperte rationi contraire debeam. Sed quia rerum similium exemplo me fregisti, rerum similium te erga me indulgentia uenialis promoueat. Licuit sane Thome apostolo, de Christo usque ad ostensionem uulnerum dubitare.[5] Licuit et Petro de carcere resoluto de ductu angelico dubitare, /fol. 30v/ dum somno ludificante omnia fieri estimaret, donec in se reuersus, rei ueritatem intelligeret.[6] Ignosce itaque michi uenerande magister, quia non ut famam patris eximii attenuarem hec ista protuli, sed quia in hoc miserandi sumus, quod ex nostrorum diffidentia meritorum erga sanctos Dei falsa sepe opinione monemur, ut quod nobis impossibile constat, illis quoque in quibus Christus operatur impossibile estimemus." Ad hec ille respondit: "Ignosco mi domine, et Deus utinam ignoscat, sed nec ad iniuriam suam prolatum beatus confessor uerbum huiusmodi accipiat, ne et tu in sortem eorum iudicandus appareas qui imminente dominice passionis hora, emissam super Christum paternam uocem dicebant tonitrum esse. Quin potius si fas nobis est signum de celo querere, utinam ad fidei huius auctoritatem propitius Deus manifesta signa moueat, iuxta illud quod Dominus in Exodo ad Moysem ait, 'Si non crediderint,' inquiens,'nec audierint filii Israel sermonem signi prioris, credent uel uerbo signi sequentis.'"[7]

Necdum uerba compleuerat, et ecce repentina aeris choruscatio et fragor intonuit, quo omnes qui ad laudes uigilabamus, ex elementorum solutione mundi interitum superuenisse fatebamur, cum nulla tempestatis signa, sed omnia eque serena paulo ante comparuissent. Nobis preformidine in terram corruentibus, quid aliud restabat, nisi celi commotis uirtutibus extremi iudicii presentem horam expectare? Iam hora transierat, et ecce uerendi luminis illa choruscatio que tota ecclesie spatia a summo usque deorsum occuparat, in unum se radium collegit, et recta uia sese in feretrum

---

[4]   Acts 7:59-60.
[5]   John 20:24-29.
[6]   Acts 5:18-19.
[7]   Exodus 4:8.

quo sacra ossa quiescunt spetie mirabili nobis spectantibus infudit, ut lucis huius residua signa forinsecus nulla comparuissent, ac si patenter elementa testarentur, quod corda humana credere recusabant. Unde id nostris temporibus prefigurata non incongrue uidetur uox illa prophetica: "Illuxerunt choruscationes tue orbi terre, commota est et contremuit terra,"[8] dum humanis cordibus dubitationis nocte caligantibus, in testimonium patris nostri choruscantis luminis fulgur illuxit, quamquam iuxta spiritualem intelligentiam, in rota mundi uoce predicantium intonante, miraculorum choruscantes terrena corda incredulorum commouissent.

Quid ultra? Nos rerum specie mirabili stupefacti, diu nos inuicem contuentes silentium tenuimus, spectantes utrum nam hanc terribilem speciem, terribiliorum rerum consummatio continuo sequeretur. Enimuero resumpto cursu, non sine formidine laudes ad finem usque transegimus. Quibus expletis, quis enumerare sufficiat, quam multe questiones super rerum euentu, quam dissone sententie promouebantur? Tandem uenerandus pontifex uerbum quod inter se et magistrum conferebant hac ipsa hora qua lux cum /fol. 31r/ tonitruo emicuit, fratribus aperuit, quod uerbum sane uim quidam altioris intelligentie et antique auctoritatis assumens, ad firmamentum prefate reuelationis competenti ratione coaptauit. "Si," inquit, "Babilonicus tyrannus, dum inter profana conuiuia, uasa Domini sacra pollueret, manum scribentis in pariete ad interpretationem festinantis sed uindicte uidere potuit,[9] quis iure dubitandum fore iudicet, si uir iste apostolicus dum inter agenda diuina mysteria artius intentus, interne mentis oculos in ipso uultu conditoris defigeret, si inquam desuper apparente sibi dextera redemptoris hoc intelligere celitus commoneretur, quod manus Domini manu ipsius semper superposita, quodcumque benedixisset et illa benedicebat, que etiam de manu ipsius et oblata susciperet, et mox de mundo exituro dignanter occurreret, ne certe malignorum spirituum occursum paueret, sed laboris sui mercedem certus hac ipsa dextera remunerante expectaret? Nam dum ad opprobrium Iudeorum mortem Christi insensibilia saxa doluerunt,[10] dignum sane uideri debet, ut contra incredulitatem nostram in testimonium huius patris nostri mundi elementa occurrant."

Sed neque hoc silendum arbitror, quod senioris cuiusdam uiri relatu

---

[8] Psalms 76:19.
[9] Daniel 5:5.
[10] Mt. 27:51.

compertum addidici. Porro uir iste, et dignitate et officio sacre edis prefecturam moderanter agebat. Huic quoniam ceteros ante uenire noctu ad laudes necdum pulsatis signis familiaris fuerat consuetudo, sciscitari curiosius cepi, si quid memoria dignum in ecclesia aliquando uidere sibi contigisset. Quod cum multa dissimulatione fateri refusisset, tandem importunitate mea uictus, unum michi hoc retulit, quod a me quoque tegi silentio flagitabat. "Quod tibi," inquit, "refero, non ludificante somno frater, sed uisu conspicuo me uidisse profiteor."

"Dominica siquidem quadam nocte de somno excussus, dum ex more procedere ad ecclesiam festinarem, astitit michi quidam uir deterrens me, ne deberem seniores inquietari. Cuius dum uultum discernere nequirem, aut de quibus fratribus aieret penitus ignorarem, mira res repente somno reprimente in extasim rapior, et uidebam me ad ecclesiam, tanquam solenni die procedere. Quam cum introgressus oculos uersus orientalem plagam intenderem, eloquar aut sileam? Sane uisu mirabile, sed dictu delectabile uidi et uere uidi circa ipsam aram in modum corone uiros sacerdotales, pontificalibus circumamictos infulis sedentes. Quibus reuerenter circumsedentibus, unus forte qui astabat medius, ceteris quasi cure officialis exhibebat ministerium. Qui a tergo respiciens, ut me intuitus est, uultu paululum seuero specie me increpantis perterruit, cur iniussus intrare presumpsissem."

"Sed quid impudens ego dicerem? Continuo tremens ac stupens solotenus corrui, fulgur oculorum et uultus speciem angelicam ferre non ualens. Porro uir ille miseratus, ne timeam /fol. 31v/ hortatur. Ad quem ego sumpta audatia, sic aio: 'Conuentum istum mi dise non curiositas, non sane temeritas me introire persuasit, sed rerum penitus ignarus, de introitu offensionem aliquam contrahere non metuebam. Sed postquam aut nescius aut insolens huc ueni, non me ignorare uelit dominus meus si fas est querere, qui sunt isti seniores, uel quid huc collecti aduenerunt.' Qui ait: 'Isti sunt apostolici rectores, qui presentem ecclesiam quondam in uita sua rexerant, per quos et regnum istud multa in pace floruit, et plebs subdita longa incolumitate uiruit, quibus adhuc quoque cura est de loco et publica salute non modica.'"

"A quo cum singulorum nomina exponi michi deposcerem, 'Satis,' inquit, 'satis tibi esse potuerat impune abisse a loco quem introgressus offenderas, ne dum istorum nomina que iam in libro uite titulis aureis scripta refulgent, tibi exponi iubeas. At uero quia super hoc te tanto anxium intueor, ille quem ad dexteram altaris conspicis, ueneranda canitie abbicantem, hic est domnus Mellonus, qui ex mellea caritatis dulcedine, congruum sibi sortitus est uocabulum. Ille alter quem sanguineis rosis interlucente corona laureatum uides, hic est beatus Nigasius, qui unus ex nobis sub persecutionis tempore materiali gladio cesus occubuit. Ille autem angelice dignitatis uultu et oculis stellantibus prefulgens, hic est dominus noster Audoenus,[11] qui tempore suo aduersus Arrianam perfidiam et Priscillianam heresim ceterorumque christiani nominis aduersariorum, bella non modica miles infatigabilis peregit, quos et diuini dogmatis gladio spirituali, et signorum potentia uictoriosus Christi athleta, mutos reddidit penitus et elingues. Felix adhuc Rothomagensis hec ciuitas, tanti patroni suffulta uicino munimine. Ille autem qui proxima sede recumbit, uenerandus extat Ansbertus, qui et doctrina precipuus, et miraculis choruscus effulsit.'"

"Sic enumeratis singulis stellantis corone sessoribus, cum beati Romani mentionem mundum audissem, hunc ipsum qui michi loquebatur uere beatum Romanum fore arbitrabar, eo certius, quo uelut patrem familias domus ceteris astare, tanquam ad mystica rerum ordinanda persperam. Hunc ergo familiari ausu interrogans, 'Tu ne es,' inquam, 'uenerande pater noster ille aduocatus Romanus, qui solus hunc nobis locum seruare maluisti?' At ille: 'Ne me,' inquit, 'hunc esse, dixeris. Nam ut eum uideris, non erit tibi opus inditio alieno. Satis tibi erunt signa manifesta, uultus sole clarior, stellis micantior, oculi siderea luce et gemmis stellantibus rutilantes, ceruix lactea, gene rosee, frons niue candidior, ut nichil de perfecta resurrectionis gloria deesse uideatur.' Cui et ego: 'Quid,' inquam, 'mi domine hunc abesse dicam, quem presentius adesse decuerat? An locum istum deseruisse fatear?' Tunc uenerandus heros: 'Non ut times,' inquit, 'locum istum domnus Romanus deseruit, sed famili-/fol. 32r/arius ceteris preest, seruat atque custodit. Et enim non longum abesse uidebis. Est plane intra sacrarium, cum quo et ex pontificali ordine uiri, qui ei ad ornandum sacris uestibus famulantur, nec non leuitice dignitatis et sequentis ordinis non ignobiles persone, qui continuo addexterabunt eum ante presentem aram ad sacra dominica peragenda, quia hinc hodie nequaquam sumus abituri, donec sumpta benedictione ab eo, gratissimum ab eo uale reportemus, qui et ipsius edictum expectamus, quam mox ad diuinum huiusmodi concilium occurrere debeamus.' Cui et ego: 'Quem igitur te pater esse dicimus, qui

---

[11] hic...Audoenus *om. ms.*; supplied from Ste. Gen. 131, an early-thirteenth-century lectionary of the collegial church of St. Lô in Rouen, containing readings for Romanus' June translation (fols. 90r-92v) and October octave (fols. 246v-249v) which are based on these *miracula*.

me sic alloqui dignatus es?' 'Uictricius,' inquit, 'dicor, cognomento firmissi-
mus, quem tali nomine fratres iccirco appellari maluerunt, quia in causis
iudicialibus non persone metus, aut amor, a uero umquam auertere preua-
luerunt. Unde et apostolica sedes, et cetera per subiectum orbem concilia,
ab hac nostre humilitatis sede responsa, in causis dubiis postulare consue-
uerant. Sed nec illud firmum aut consummatum fatebantur, quodcumque
nostre sanctionis titulo caruisset.'"

"Cum hec ille pater egregius exponeret, ecce ab interiori sacrario mira
odoris fragrantia nostris se naribus tanta infuderat, ut omnia aromata odoris suauitate uinceret. Subsequitur mox acies ordinata cum crucibus, cum
cereis, et turibulis, cum textis euangelicis. Ipse autem in extremo agmine,
duobus a dextera et leua famulantibus uiris pontificalibus, ipse inquam
beatus pontifex Romanus incedebat, uultu et habitu incomparabili, de cuius specioso decore nec cor meditari, nec lingua eque ualet effari, quippe
cum uelut ille quondam Israhelitice plebis ductor Moyses descendens de
monte incedebat, in cuius faciem populus deorsum expectans intendere
non poterat propter gloriam uultus eius, quam ex consortio diuini colloquii
assumpserat. Quid ultra? Mox illi aduenienti, omnis circumsedentium
chorus assurgit, cum uoce huiusmodi: 'Uir iste in populo suo mitissimus
apparuit,'[12] quam cum uersu usque in finem psallentes, usque ad ipsum
altare perducunt. Uerum orationi paulo immoratus, dum se erigeret, pacis
osculum a dextris et a sinistris fratribus stans ipse libauit, et sic ad aram
progreditur, ceteris missam incipientibus in hec uerba: 'Sancti tui Domine
benedicent te.' Ut autem uentum est ad locum offertorii, singuli panem et
uinum ex ordine offerebant. Iam hora benedictionis instabat, et ipse domnus Uictricius eleuata uoce ceteros ad benedictionem iubet inclinari, de
hinc sacramentis celestibus communicari. Ita officiis expletis, curiosius ex-
plorabam, quo se hec daret turba sanctorum. Nam ut 'Ite missa est' excla-
matum est, ipse domnus Romanus paululum orabat, ceteris reuerendum
silentium agentibus. Ut autem se ab altari remouit, ecce omnes illum
medium obeuntes, in prefatum sacrarium deducunt."

"Ego a foris diu expectans, dum exire /fol. 32v/ neminem aut intrare
postmodum intueor, suspenso pede ad sacrarium tremulus progredior, et
diligentius introspiciens, ex uacua cella uniuersos abisse conspicio uel rep-
perio. Quo ex facto, me stupor altus conterruit, quod exitum, aut uesti-

12 Numbers 12:13.

gium, sed neque signum aliquod deprehendere potui, preter quod ex residua odoris fragrantia satiari non poteram." De quibus quid conicere debeam, penitus addubito, nisi quia cum hos apud Deum presentes esse, certissima fide constet, inter hos qui amicti stolis albis secuntur agnum quocumque ierit, hanc ipsam tamen sacri celebritatem officii, hunc conuentum concilii mortalibus innotescere uoluerunt, ut intelligeremus eos locum quem temporaliter rexerant, hunc presentibus eos patrociniis, nisi nostris offensionibus arceantur gubernare.

"Duo ab urbe Rothomagensi leuitico ordine fratres, tercius adiacentis Colonie quidam uenerabilis presbiter, condixerant sibi pariter Ierusolimis dominicum inuisere sepulchrum. Arrepta igitur peregrinatione, superatis alpibus Romane urbis menia usque perueniunt, haut dignum estimantes apostolorum sacra limina insalutata preterire. Huc de remotis terre partibus uirorum se numerosa turba infuderat, qui et ipsi expetita peregrinatione hanc ipsam adibant felicis patrie regionem, que nati saluatoris nutricia tellus extitit, que moriente condoluit, que resurgenti mortuos suos testes resurrectionis exhibuit. Quesitis igitur altrinsecus partium causis, mox inuicem confederati progrediuntur ab urbe, hinc Adriatici maris littora feruentibus animis expetunt, hinc naues honerarias quamplures forte reperiunt, quam mercibus onustas, in ulteriora littora exposituri naute parabant. Harum unam que expeditior uidebatur, tres quos prefati sumus fratres conscendunt, alias alii pro se quisque sortiuntur. Uentis itaque ad uota spirantibus, haut mora statione soluta, omnes simul naues prospero cursu maris alta tenebant.

Et iam medium ferme pelagus peregerant, cum hec una que fratres memoratos uebebat, repentino turbinis impulsu agitata, incredibilis iacture casum miserabilem incurrit. Nam cum cetera maris equora circumquaque tranquilla serenitate radiarent, huc toto ab ethere collecta nimborum infusio, huic uni carine uehementius incubuit. Erat sane miserabile intueri, ratem uiolentis turbinis sinu interceptam, nautis eluctantibus nequaquam posse expediri. Compulsi extremis malis naute ipsi, desperata arte, raptim sumptis mercibus quod uile quod preciosum multis ex terris collegerant, nulla damni consideratione marinis inferunt gurgitibus. At nec sic quidem rebus amissis, nauicula periculis eximitur, cui ex aduerso austro ingruit procella nigrescente aere formidabilis. Sicque inualescente uentorum turbine, nunc in celum erecta, nunc in abyssum /fol. 33r/ dimersa, modo ex tumentis pelagi tanquam muralii machine uallante crepidine, circumflua tandiu agitatione fatigatur, donec hiantis abyssi profundo recepta, imis subsedit arenis, non sine manifesta tamen presentis Dei custodia. Porro nunc seuientis pelagi hinc inde crebris pulsibus nauicula ipsa quatiebatur, nunc uero elemento cameratis fluctibus operiebatur, sane incredibili rerum miraculo, quod sub aquis uehementibus uiuere homines potuissent. Enimuero miserabile mortis genus illis fuerat mori non posse, quos longo cruciatu tenebat non imaginaria mortis expectatio. Cetere interea naues prosperiore freto cursum suum accelerabant, longeque reductis oculis morantes socios contemplantes, dum nec signa ulla conspiciunt, perisse inter fluctus arbitrantur. At uero naute inte inter uite et mortis discrimina constituti, murmure incusabant se suscepisse uiros sacrilegos quos diuino iudicio damnatos, nec terra sustinere, nec pelagus poterat portare. Aut reuera quicquid illud fuisset tale aliquid infra se conuehisse, quod contra Dei uoluntatem maris elementa ferre nequiuerant.

Fratribus ipsis presentis mortis formidine consternatis, et si ratio non defuisset, qua leuigatio fraudis obiecta dissoluerent, tamen quia in huiusmodi patentibus naufragiis non suppetit ocium de iudicialibus causis, ubi potius de uita et morte cogitatur, nulla calum dabant responsa, sed tantum labiis trementibus de celo non uite auxilium, sed celerem interitum postulabant, cum unus eorum in uocem erumpens, sanctum Romanum acclamare cepit. Nam his sanctum Romanum speciali memoria, cotidiana celebritate percolere consueuerat, quem et hoc ipso die tanto impensius preuenisse meminerat, quanto illi presentius de marina iactatione timor incubuerat. Is ut familiarem patronum inclamauit, sicut ipse fratribus qui adhuc supersunt sub fide Christi et non sine lacrimis sepe contestatus est repente intra patentis etheris secreta uidit uirum inestimabili luce choruscum, cum precibus huiusmodi dominum maiestatis compellantem: "Si est dominator Domine ut hos famulos tuos quos passionis tue locum requirentes seua maris tempestas intercludit, ut hos inquam longe a ciuitate sancta et tabernaculo tuo noxialis quedam arceat criminum magnitudo, fiat illis rex bone repulsa hec uel malorum presentium euasione tolerabilis, ut indulto sibi uite beneficio, uotis quandoque purioribus uoluntarii exilii pro tuo nomine resumant peregrinationem, et ne antiquus hostis si quid in eis attemptare molitur, hoc ad sue artis nequitiam transcribat, quod hos qui sanctificantis aque gaudent se fonte renatos, hos pelagi seuientis insultet se perdidisse naufragio. Fiat quinpotius in presentibus periculis manifesta sacramenti tui potentia ut unda que /fol. 33v/ te auctore fuit illis uia salutis in adoptionis gratiam, fiat te rectore eis portus saluationis ad uite custodiam. Assit ergo illis obsecro summe Deus saluantis dextere tue cita opitulatio, ut furentis ponti dimotis terroribus et uictricem manum tuam laudare, et me seruum tuum in periculis suis non inaniter uocasse meminerunt, et illis in hoc preuentum mortis accelerasse diabolus insultet, quod te rectorem maris et abyssi fatentes, tete auctorem uite eo loco requirunt, ubi Deus immortalis fieri dignatus mortalis pro mortalibus, morte tua hereditarie mortis cyrographum euacuasti, et unde resurgens a mortuis, lege mortis triumphata, in dexteram paterne maiestatis residens, uiuorum et mortuorum omnium dominator existis."

His dictis, uox continuo redditur, quam licet uicine mortis horrore circumfusus frater ille, uelut aure tenuis sibilum hausit in hunc modum: "Fuerat tibi dilecte meus sub ipso caduci eui tempore pro caris tuis in dubiis casibus formidandum, nunc iam regi tuo adherentem, quid te super sortem eorum metus exagitat, quos egregia tibi meritorum uirtus adquisiuit, ne casibus aduersis liceat aliquid super his quibus te patronum constiterit opitulari? Enimuero est et erit salua tibi semper meritorum prerogatiua, ut quicquid nomini tuo attributum indubitata fides poposcerit, superna sanctione donetur. Uerbi huius experimentum mox tibi prebebit de marinis gurgitibus reddita nauis ad superos, si ceteras que secundis uelis portum festinant apprehendere, mox ipsa omnes ante uolans optatam sedem preoccupauerit." Nec mora, beatus Romanus de improuiso in posteriorem partem carine uisus est consedisse, et summotis unde seuientis cumulis, ratem ab arentibus arenis extorsisse, de hinc constrato equore, baculo quo in mundano pelago nauem ecclesie gubernauerat, hoc ipso ratem adeo uisus est impulisse, ut quantum infra diei spatium libero cursu socie classes confecerant, hoc totum intra hore spacium transuolans, et eas quasi uisio pertransiens, multo ante tempore optato in littore stationem acciperet.

Nec multum temporis affuit, cum ceteri iam iam portum et ipsi tenentes amissos socios lamentabili sermone recitarent, mirabile quidem sed ueridico dictu, offendunt in littore socios, quos seuo estimarant perisse naufragio. Nec tamen presumunt credere quod uident, sed somnium putant, donec euentus sui exposito ordine certos reddunt quod dubios acceperant. Fit communis de alter utrum salute leticia. Paratis itaque omnibus que reficiendis forent necessaria, dum ille unus cui inter fluctuosas uoragines dimerso prefata patuerat reuelatio, dum ille inquam se ab esu carnis abstineret, et ceteri causam curiosius perquirerent, ille cordis ab alto suspirans sic ait: "Uiuit Dominus qui me inter undas seruatum de profundo abyssi liberauit, /fol. 34r/ quia caro et omne quo inebriari potest os meum non introiet donec seruatori et gubernatori meo sanctissimo Romano de ereptione mea in loco quo sanctissimum corpus eius quiescit gratiarum referam actiones, quem pro redemptione nostra hodie tremendam Domini maiestatem hisce oculis compellasse perspexi." Quod et factum est. Nam is ceptum iter expeditius peragens, mox ut solutis uotis a sancto sepulchro regressus natale solum attigit, neque ad dexteram neque ad sinistram declinans, non salutationibus attendens, non amplexus, non oscula amicorum suscipiens, directo cursu ad ecclesiam beati Romani tetendit. Ibi centies flexis genibus, milies labris solum prementibus satiari nequiuerat. Ex ore ipsius nisi laudes, nisi gratiarum actiones Deo et patri suo Romano audiri poterant. Ab ipso die quicumque repentinus celi fragor aut choruscatio aut ruine strepitus quilibet fieret, mox sanctus Romanus in ore ipsius uelut familiare presidium erat.

Beati patris Romani depositionis dies natalis transierat, et octauas ipsius deuota fratrum congregatio, continua celebritate prosequendo, festiuis laudibus percolebat. Horum unus ut se habet instabilis hominum fortuna, rebus exhaustis attenuatus, dum quadam die sacris expletis misteriis, domum et familiam uisitasset, et consumpto censum nichil quod ad uictum sibi apponeret penitus inuenisset, uicinorum et amicorum beniuolentiam experiendam animo deliberabat. Qui omnes a se uacuum illum remiserunt. Tum miser ille dolore et alto pudore confusus, dum nusquam superesse uidet qui sibi miserationem prestaret, domum sese recepit, et in lectum se turbata mente proiecit. Ibi mens stimulis cogitationum incutientibus quiescere non poterat. Uertebat se in latus aliud, nichil emendatius proficiebat. Sic eger animo diu uolutando, sollicitudinum morsus repellere a se nequiuerat.

Tum uero adactum corde dolorem in modicus animi ultra non ferens, a lecto sese furibundus excussit, et alte suspirans in uocem huiusmodi erupit: "Ut quid infelix presentem tibi lucem contigit uidisset? Quid tibi miser nasci profuerat, cui uitam erumnosam infausta natiuitas pariebat? Age ergo infelix, adime tibi dulces somnos, et horas placide quietis, occurre laudibus impiger matutinis, serua insomnes uigilias noctis, et alimentorum securus infatigabiliter diurnis persiste officiis. Et cum inoffense debitum cursum expleueris, tunc tunc expecta, dum tibi coruis ministrantibus ut Helie necessaria ferantur alimenta,[13] aut ut Danieli Abbacuc propheta angelo

---

[13] 1 Kings 17:2-6.

portante tibi perferat grata pulmenta.[14] Ecce Romane pater, ecce quanto
aput te stat nostre seruitutis impensa! Nam quid nobis ultra restat abs te
expectare, qui nec hodierna subsidia corporis famulo tuo prebes egenti?"
Talia retractando per patentem casesamentis[15] inops deambulabat, cum
/fol. 34v/ mente recepta sese reprehendens, cogitare anxius cepit, ut ad beatum Romanus recentem conuitiorum offensam ementurus ire deberet, et
sic de instanti necessitate indulgentiam postularet.

Propero itaque gressu monasterium adiit, ibi totum se in lacrimis ef-
fundens orationi incubuit. Primum errati ueniam poscit, postmodum de
hac que altius urebat necessitate uberius exorauit dicens: "O gloriose Christi confessor, si uerum est te quondam effuso oleo fracte ampulle minutias
in solidum reparasse, et indempnem sacre benedictionis liquorem conser-
uasse, ita et huic famulo tuo uirtutis tue ostende potentiam, et affluentem
gratie tue confer habundatiam, ut sicut in uita tua esurienti pauperum col-
lati dapibus satiaueras, ita et egenti seruo tuo quem undique miserabilis
coartat angustia, sufficientem uictualis alimonie prebeas hodie portionem,
qua me et miseram familiam que me ieiunis faucibus expectat, uel ad presentem diem ualeam sustentare." His dictis, ab oratione surrexit, atque sub-
iunxit, "Tibi pastor egregie, tibi me et familiam hodie et consilium meum
committo." Sic effatus, uersus domum uicinos iterum expetiturus ire dispo-
nit.

Necdum a monasterio excesserat et ecce uir quidam regionis ignote
per patentem portam introgressus nullo comite, conuerso uultu ad altare
uelut incedit, habitu quidem peregrino, sed ornatu precioso. Ceterum uultu et statura egregiam preferebat dignitatem. Quem dum frater ille curiosius obseruaret, an aliquid offerret ad altare, quod suis usibus necessarium
foret, ille nichil ad hoc intendit, sed ipso motu uenerandi capitis fratrem
sibi propius assistere iubet. Quem moderata lenitate an esset presbiter
requirit, quo missam ei celebraret. Cui cum ita esse respondisset, et se ad
officium promptius exhibuisset, mox illi uenerandus erops quinque solidos
nummorum de pera sua eductos latenter contulit. Letus frater ille fameli-
cus, petitionis indulte conscius, lacrimis pre gaudio obortis, toto corpore
ad Deum et ad indeficientem largitorem suum conuersus gratias egit, de-
hinc ad uirum faciem otius conuertit, uolens uidelicet sciscitari, quisnam

14   Daniel 14:33-39.
15   *corrected to* casatamentis E

ille foret egregius herops, qui tantam sibi miserationem fecisset. At ille nusquam comparuit.

Stupefactus presbiter, miratur hominem sibi tam recente sublatum. Qui sursum ac deorsum cursitans dum attentius ex uiatoribus perquirit, an hominem tali uultu et tali habitu uspiam conspexissent, nec signum ab his aliquod audire potuit. Sed et homines qui pro foribus monasterii multo ex die ociosi consederant, huiusmodi hominem nequaquam intrasse aut exisse testabantur. Tum presbiter quo se uertisset ignorans, desperata inuentione querere hominem ultra desistit, mirans secum quod factum /fol. 35r/ fuerat. Necdum nummos perspexerat, sed artius manu constrictos adhuc seruans, dum intueri diligentius uellet, intra se uehementer cepit hesitare, reputans ne forte fallax demonum astutia in his aliquid attemptasset, quo captioso munere inescatum seductor callidus nefandis insidiis enecasset. Consulturus igitur Dominum super his ire ad monasterium meditatur. Ibi beatum Romanum supplici prece depostulat, ut si ex Deo et ipsius dono factum constaret, ueris indiciis comprobare potuisset. Si autem fantasiam aliquam ars diabolica in his fuisset operata, mox ex inanita ipsius prestigia in nichilum redigerentur. Tunc primum manum extendens et digito contrectans, conspicit nummos flammea nouitate rutilantes, ac si ea ipsa hora subtracti ab igne fuissent. Sed quem nobis datur estimare uirum illum fuisse, nisi ut uerum esse constat uenerabilem patrem nostrum Romanum, qui fratris egentis angustiam miseratus, in presenti facto nobis uoluit ostendere, quanta supplicantibus sibi miseratione dignetur semper adesse?

Explicit uita sancti Romani archiepiscopi Rothomagensis.

D. The St. Ouen Miracles of Romanus

/fol. 49r/ Lectiones in alia translatione ipsius que celebra quintodecimo kalendas iulii.

[Lectio i]

Inter cetera miraculorum insignia que dominus noster ad laudem sui nominis per beatum Romanum post eius transitum uoluit operari, illud precipue commemorari dignum duximus, quod in hac die festiuitatis eius ueraciter factum fuisse cognouimus. Eodem namque anno quo huius gloriosi antistitis caput a galliarum partibus est relatum, et in aecclesia beati Audoeni infra dominice resurrectionis dies honorifice conditum, post solennem /fol. 49v/ sancti spiritus aduentum, ipsius beati Romani quintodecimo kalendas iulii agebatur festum, pro sacri corporis eius translatione priscis temporibus constitutum.

[Lectio ii]

Hac igitur die, quedam mulier in suburbio eiusdem metropolis nomine Fredesendis paruulum habens filium etate trinium, in ede genitoris cum propinquorum et quorumdam hospitum frequentia epulabatur. Adhuc autem illis recumbentibus idem puerulus cum altero grandiusculo foras exiit, et per ortum deambulans ad puteum qui ibidem erat accessit. Cumque paululum se inclinasset, et prono uultu in eum intenderet, maligno spiritu impediente subito titubantibus menbris introrsus cecidit. Aqua uero putei tante erat altitudinis, ut nulli dubium foret quin unius hore articulo submersus occumberet.

[Lectio iii]

Alter uero infans hoc uiso uehementer exterritus fugiit, paternisque laribus se conferens nulli quod acciderat nimio tremore palpitans indicauit. Post prandium igitur mater pueri sui miserabilis euentus nescia ortum ingreditur, et circa os putei consistens dimisso uultu conspicatur pueri iam exanimati corpusculum in aquis iacere supinum et foliis arborum que circa puteum erant usque ad ipsius patuli oris labella opertum.

[Lectio iiii]

Tunc ingenti stupore attonita, et incredibili cordis dolore perculsa, cum gemitu exclamauit: "Sancte Romane adiuua miseram, sancte Romane adiuua perituram." /fol. 50r/ Dein femineo ululatu perstrepere, domus familia ubi hoc auditum est planctibus furere, uicinia undique ruptis sepium obstaculis passim ad hoc infortunii spectaculum concurrere. Extrahitur itaque infans de puteo mortuus, crebro suspenditur, et admoto igno diutius uaporatur, nec quid in eo penitus uitalis spiraculi comperitur. At parentes quamuis de uita pueri foret desperatum, eo tamen maxime dei omnipotentis per beatum Romanum exorabant clementiam, quod tanti reatus improuide commiserant neglegentiam.

[Lectio v]

Igitur cum hec agerentur, et pueri funus pareretur, post aliquot horarum intercapedinem is qui diu extinctus iacuerat diuina uirtute puer resumpto spiritu suspirauit. Ad quem mater ilico accurrens, tenuem in pectore flatum persensit. O immensa benignitas saluatoris, cui beatus Romanus iugiter adhesit puro affectu dilectionis! O mira et magnifica eius pietatis opera que tot uirtutibus in dies renouantur, et nulla temporum uetustate obliterantur. Extemplo enim sub aspectu omnium uelut a somno excitus puer incolumis surrexit, et lugentium mentes in stuporem et gaudium conuertit.

[Lectio vi]

Mox cereus ex more componitur et ad beati Audoeni aecclesiam una cum eodem pusiolo, cumque plebis multitudine properatur. Ostenditur cunctis miraculum, eodem die per beatum Romanum diuinitus operatum. Assignatur /fol. 50v/ paruulus ipso die mortuus et resuscitatus. Unde cenobialis militie ordo pro tam ingenti miraculo diuine iubilationis hymnum modulando concrepauit signa ex more pulsauit, et deum in sancto suo confessore gloriosum uoce simul et corde magnificauit. Ex ea etiam aqua qua preciosum beati caput antistitis perfusum est, agente gratia christi multi a uariis morborum incommodis pristine restituti sunt saluti.

[Lectio vii]

Quedam etenim puella per biennium acerrima decubans egritudine, infra sanctos rogationum dies per ipsum intempesta nocte admonetur, ut ex eadem limpha potum percipiat, ac per hoc sancti confessoris meritum experiri ualeat. Quid multa? Hausta salutifera potione adeo repente conualuit, ut die ascensionis domini una cum populo ad eandem aecclesiam conueniret, gratias ageret, ac festiue processioni seu missarum solenniis interesse gauderet.

[Lectio viii]

Quidam adolescens monastico habitu decoratus et regularibus adprime disciplinis imbutus, repente omnibus menbris dissolutus et pristino uigore destitutus ad eo acutissime passionis molestiam incidit, ut nichil aliud quam presentis uite exitum in proximo uideretur operiri. Hic ergo ubi paululum ex ipso salubri latice prelibauit, preclari patroni sui meritis sospitatem adipisci promeruit. Hec et alia uirtutum insignia dominus et saluator noster ad laudem sui nominis per beatum Romanum incessanter ibidem operari....

Bibliography of Printed Literature

The following bibliography includes all works cited in *The Norman Conquest of Pious Neustria*, as well as literature on which I have drawn for related article-length studies published elsewhere. Only materials available in print are listed in this bibliography.

Acta Apostolica Sedis: Commentarium Officiale XV (Rome, 1923)

Acta Archiepiscoporum Rotomagensium ed. J. Mabillon *Vetera Analecta* II (Paris, 1675); repr. PL 147

"Actus pontificum cenomannis in urbe degentium" eds. G. Busson and A. Ledru (*Archives Historiques de Maine* II; Le Mans, 1901)

Adalbero of Laon *Poème au roi Robert* ed. Claude Carozzi (Paris, 1979)

Adams, Henry *Mont-Saint-Michel and Chartres* (1st edition in private circulation, 1904; cited from the Penguin edition, Harmondsworth, 1986)

Ademar of Chabannes "Chronicon" in MGH SS IV ed. Pertz (Hannover, 1841); *Chronique* ed. Jules Chavanon (Collection de textes pour servir à l'étude et à l'enseignement de l'histoire 20; Paris, 1897)

Addison, James Thayer *The Medieval Missionary: A Study of the Conversion of Northern Europe AD 500-1300* (London, 1936)

Aigradus of Fontenelle, "Vita Ansberti" [BHL 520a/BHL 523] ed. W. Levison in MGH SRM 5

——, "Vita Lantberti" [BHL 4675] ed. W. Levison, MGH SRM 5

Aimoin of St. Germain *Libri quinque de gestis Francorum* ed. J. du Breul (Paris, 1603)

Alcuin of York, Series of Latin Inscriptions in *MGH Poetae Latini aevi Carolini* I pp. 305-312

——, "Vita Audoeni" [BHL 751/752/753] ed. E.P. Sauvage AB 5 (1886) pp. 76-146 and AASS Aug. IV pp. 810-819

——, "Vita Richerii" [BHL 7223-7227] ed. B. Krusch in MGH SRM 4

——, "Vita Vedastis" [BHL 8506-8508] ed. B. Krusch in MGH SRM 3 pp. 414-427

——, "Vita Willibrordi" [BHL 8935], trans. C.H. Talbot in *The Anglo-Saxon Missionaries in Germany; Being the Lives of SS. Willibrord, Boniface, Sturm, Leoba and Lebuin, together with the Hodeoporicon of St. Willibald and a selection from the correspondance of St. Boniface* (London, 1954)

Alexander, J.J.G. *Norman Illumination at Mont-St.-Michel, 966-1100* (Oxford, 1970)

Anderson, Robin *Between Two Wars: The Story of Pope Pius XI (Achille Ratti), 1922-1932* (Chicago, 1977)

Andrieu-Guitrancourt, Pierre "Notes, remarques et reflexions sur la vie ecclésiastique et religieuse à Rouen sous le pontificat de saint Victrice" *Etudes
offerts à Jean Macqueron* (Aix-en-Provence, 1970)

Angenendt, Arnold. *Kaiserherrschaft und Königstaufe: Kaiser, Könige und Päpste
als geistliche Patrone in der abendländischen Missionsgeschichte* (Arbeiten zur
Frühmittelalterforschung 15; Berlin, 1984)

Annales Bertiniani/ Les Annales de St. Bertin ed. F. Grat, J. Vieillard and S. Clé-
mencet (Paris, 1964); *Annals of St. Bertin: Ninth-Century Histories* I trans.
Janet Nelson (Manchester, 1991)

Annales Mettenses priores ed. B. von Simsom (Hannover/Leipzig, 1905)

*Annales regni Francorum 741-829 qui dicuntur Annales Laurissenses maiores et Ein-
hardi* ed. F. Kurze in MGH SRG (Hannover, 1895)

*Annales Vedastini/ Jahrbücher von St. Vaast: Quellen zur Karolingischen Reichsge-
schichte* II ed. Reinhold Rau (Ausgewählte Quellen zur Deutschen Geschichte des Mittelalters 6; Berlin, 1966)

Ardo, "Vita Benedicti abbatis Anianensis" [BHL 1096] ed. G. Waitz in MGH SS
15/1 pp. 200-220

Arnoux, Mathieu "La fortune du *Libellus de revelatione, edificatione et auctoritate
Fiscannensis monasterii*. Note sur la production historiographique d'une
abbaye bénédictine normande" *Revue d'Histoire des Textes* 21 (1991) pp.
135-158

Atsma, Hartmut ed. *La Neustrie. Les pays au nord de la Loire de 650-850* (Colloque historique international; Beihefte der Francia 16/1-2, 1989)

Augustine of Hippo *Aurelii Augustini Hipponeiensis Episcopi Epistulae* ed. A.
Goldbacher (CSEL 34; Prague/Vienna/Leipzig 1895)

——, *Confessions* trans. R.S. Pine-Coffin (London, 1961)

Avril, François *Manuscrits normands, XI-XIIème siècles* (Catalogue of an Exhibition by the Bibliothèque Municipale de Rouen, Musée des Beaux-Arts de
Rouen, Feb-March 1975; Rouen, 1975)

Babcock, W.B. "MacMullen on Conversion: a response" *The Second Century* 5
(1985/86) pp. 82-89

Baedorf, Balthasar *Untersuchungen über die Heiligenleben der Westlichen Normandie* (Bonn, 1913)

Bates, David *Normandy Before 1066* (London, 1980)

——, "Rouen from 900 to 1204: From Scandinavian Settlement to Angevin 'Capital'" in *Medieval Art, Architecture and Archeology at Rouen* (British Archeological Association Conference Transactions (XII, 1993) ed. Jenny Stratford) pp. 1-11

Bauthier, R. H. "L'historiographie en France au Xe et Xie siècles" in "La storiografia altomedioevale," *Settimane di studio del Centro italiano di studi sull' alto medioevo* 17 (1970)

Baylé, Maylis "Interlace Patterns in Norman Romanesque Sculpture: Regional Groups and Their Historical Background" *Anglo-Norman Studies* 5 (1982) pp. 1-20

Becker, P.A. "Der Planctus auf den Normannenherzog Wilhelm Langschwert (942)" *Zeitschrift fur fränzösische Sprache und Literatur* 43 (1939)

Bede *Ecclesiastical History of the English Church and People* eds. and trans. B. Colgrave and R.A.B. Minors (Oxford, 1969)

——, "Vita Cuthberti" [BHL 2021] ed. and trans. B. Colgrave in *Two Lives of Cuthbert* (Cambridge, 1940; repr. 1969)

——, "Vita metrica Cuthberti" [BHL 2020] ed. Werner Jaeger *Bedas metrische vita sancti Cuthberti* (Palaestra 198. Untersuchungen und Texte aus der Deutschen und Englishen Philologie; Leipzig, 1935)

Benedictines of Paris/ Baudot-Chaussin, *Vies des saints et des bienheureux selon l'ordre du calendrier avec l'historique des fêtes* I-XII (Paris, 1952)

Bernard, H. "Bulletins" AM 11 (1981) pp. 290-292; AM 12 (1982) pp. 315-318

——, "Les cathédrales de Thérouanne" AM 10 (1980) pp. 105-135

Bibliotheca Hagiographica Latina eds. Hagiographi Bollandiani I-II and Supplements; Brussels, 1989-1911, 1987

Blin, J.-B.-N. *Vies des saints du diocèse de Séez et histoire de leur culte* (Laigle, 1873)

Bloch, Howard *Etymologies and Genealogies: a Literary Anthropology of the French Middle Ages* (Chicago, 1983)

Boeren, P.C. "Les évêques de Tongres-Maastricht" in Riché ed. "La Christianisation des pays" pp. 25-36

Boniface, Epistolae in *MGH Epistolae Selectae* I

Bonner, Gerald "The Extinction of Paganism and the Church Historian" *Journal of Ecclesiastical History* 35 (1984) pp. 339-357

——, D.W. Rollason and C. Stancliffe eds. *St. Cuthbert, His Cult and Community* (Woodbridge, 1989)

Borias, André "S. Wandrille, a-t-il connu S. Benoit?" *Revue Bénédictine* 89 (1979) pp. 8-28

Bouet, Philippe "Dudon de St. Quentin et Virgile: 'L'Enéide' au service de la cause normande" *Cahiers des Annales de Normandie* 23 (1990) pp. 215-236

Boussard, Jacques "Les évêques en Neustrie avant la réforme Grégorienne (950-1050 environ)" *Journal des Savants* (1970) pp. 161-196

Bouvris, Jean-Michel "L'école capitulaire de Rouen au XIe siècle" *Etudes Normandes* 35 (1986)

Boyer, Régis *Le mythe viking dans les lettres françaises* (Paris, 1986)

Boyle, Leonard "Optimist or Recensionist?: 'Common Errors' or 'Common Variations'" in *Latin Script and Letters* eds. J.J. O'Meara and B. Naumann (London, 1976)

——, "Popular Religion: What is Popular?" (Plenary Address to the 1st International Medieval Congress, Leeds, July 1994)

Branch, Betty "Inventories of the Library of Fécamp" *Manuscripta* 23 (1979)

Breese, Lauren Wood "Early Normandy and the Emergence of Norman Romanesque Architecture" *Journal of Medieval History* 14 (1988) pp. 203-216

Brenk, B. *Tradition und Neuerung in der christlichen Kunst des ersten Jahrtausends* (Vienna, 1966)

Bromer, Peter "*Capitula Episcoporum.*" *Die bischöflichen Kapitularien des 9. und 10. Jahrhunderts* (Typologie des Sources du Moyen Age Occidental 43; Turnhout, 1985)

Brown, Elizabeth A.R. "The Tyranny of a Construct: Feudalism and Historians of Medieval Europe" *American Historical Review* 79 (1974) pp. 1062-1088

Brown, Peter *The Cult of the Saints. Its Rise and Function in Latin Christianity* (Chicago, 1981)

Brown, T.S. "Romanitas and Campanilismo: Agnellus of Ravenna's View of the Past" in *The Inheritance of Historiography, 350-900* eds. C. Holdsworth and T.P. Wiseman (Exeter Studies in History 12; Exeter, 1986) pp. 107-114

Brühl, Carlrichard "Die Geburt des modernen Europa nach 1000" in "Il Secolo di Ferro" pp. 1085-1106

Buck, V.D. "De sancta Childemarca" in AASS Oct. XI pp. 679-684

Bullough, Donald "Alcuin and the Kingdom of Heaven: Liturgy, Theology and the Carolingian Age" in Uta-Renate Blumenthal, ed. *Carolingian Essays* (Andrew W. Mellon Lectures in Early Christian Studies; Washington, D.C. 1983) pp. 1-69

Bulst, Neithard *Untersuchungen zu den Klosterreform Wilhelms von Dijon* (Pariser Historische Studien 2; Paris, 1973)

Bur, M. *La formation du comté de Champagne, 950-1150* (Nancy, 1977)

Camille, Michael *Image on the Edge. The Margins of Medieval Art* (Cambridge, Mass.; 1992)

Campbell, James "Observations on the Conversion of England" *Ampleforth Journal* 78 (1975) pp. 12-26

——, "The Debt of the Early English Church to Ireland" in Chatháin and Richter, eds. *Irland und die Christenheit* pp. 332-347

——, "The First Century of Christianity in England" *Ampleforth Journal* 76 (1973) pp. 10-29

Carlson, Eric Gustave "Religious Architecture in Normandy, 911-1000" *Gesta* 5 (1966)

Carolingian Chronicles. Royal Frankish Annals and Nithard's Histories trans. Bernard Walter Scholz with Barbara Rogers (Ann Arbor, 1970)

Cathelin, J. and G. Gray *Hommes et cités de Normandie* (Paris, 1965)

Cavallo, Guglielmo "Libri scritti, libri letti, libri dimenticati" in "Il Secolo di Ferro" pp. 759-794

Cazelles, Brigitte *The Lady as Saint: A Collection of French Hagiographic Romances of the Thirteenth Century* (Phildelphia, 1991)

Chanson de Roland. Texte original et traduction ed. and trans. Gérard Moignet (Paris, 1989); *Song of Roland* trans. Patricia Terry (Philadelphia, 1965)

Chatháin, Proínséas Ní and Michael Richter, eds. *Irland und die Christenheit/ Ireland and Christendom: Bibelstudien und Mission/ The Bible and the Missions* (Acta of the Conference "Irland und Die Christenheit," Dublin 1984; Veröffentlichungen des Europazentrums Tübingen: Kulturwissenschaftliche Reihe; Stuttgart, 1987)

Chartes de l'abbaye de Jumièges (824-1204) conservés aux archives de Seine-Inférieur ed. J.J. Vernier (Rouen, 1916) 2 vols.

Chibnall, Marjorie "Charter and Chronicle: the use of archive sources by Norman historians" *Church and Government in the Middle Ages* ed. C.N.L. Brooke, a.o. (Cambridge, 1976) pp. 1-17

——, "The Merovingian Monastery of St. Evroult in the Light of Conflicting Traditions" *Studies in Church History* 8 (1972) eds. Cuming and Baker

"Christentum der Bekehrungszeit," *Reallexikon der Germanischen Altertumskunde* (2nd. ed., IV. 5 pp. 510-599

Christian, William *Local Religion in Sixteenth-Century Spain* (Princeton, 1981)

Chronicon Fontenellense ed. J. Laporte (Société de l'Histoire de Normandie; Mélanges, XVe serie; Rouen, 1951)

"Chronicon Rotomagense" ed. Philippe Labbé *Nova Bibliotheca manuscriptorum* I (Bourges, 1657)

Cioffari, P. Gerardo *S. Nicola nella Critica Storica. Le fonti, le vita, la letteratura* (Bari, 1987)

"Circumvectio Taurini" [BHL 7996] ed. P. Boschius, AASS Aug. II pp.650-656

Clanchy, M.R. and Brian Stock *The Implications of Literacy* (Princeton, 1983)

Clarke, C.P.S. *A Short History of the Christian Church, from the Earliest Times to the Present Day* (London, 1929; 2nd ed. 1950)

Clarke, H.G. and Brennan, Mary *Columbanus and Merovingian Monasticism* (Essays from the University of Dublin Colloquium, 1977; British Archeological Reports, International Series 113 (Oxford, 1981))

"Clausula de unctione Pippini regis" ed. B. Krusch in MGH SRM 3

Cochet, J.B.D. *La Normandie souterraine, ou, Notice sur des cimetières romains et des cimetières francs explorés en Normandie* (Brionne, 1854)

Collette, A. *Histoire du Bréviaire de Rouen* (Rouen, 1902)

Columbanus *Le pénitentiel de saint Columban* ed. J. Laporte (Monumenta Christiana Selecta 4; Tournai, 1958)

Coolidge, T. "Adalbero, Bishop of Laon" *Studies in Medieval and Renaissance History* 2 (1965) pp. 1-114

Corblet, Jules *Hagiographie du diocèse d'Amiens* I-IV (Amiens, 1868)

Cristiani, L. "Liste chronologique des saints de France" *Revue d'Histoire de l'Eglise de France* 31 (1945) pp. 5-96

Crosby, Sumner McKnight *The Abbey of St. Denis, 475-1122* (New Haven, 1942) 2 vols.

Crouch, David "Feudalism and the Historians" (Paper presented at the International Congress of Medieval Studies, Kalamazoo 1994)

Daly, William M. "Clovis: How Barbaric, How Pagan?" *Speculum* 69 (1994) pp. 619-664

Davis, R.H.C. *The Normans and their Myth* (London, 1976)

De Bouard, Michel "De la Neustrie Carolingienne à la Normandie féodale: continuité ou discontinuité?" *Bulletin of the Institute of Historical Research* XXVIII (1955) pp. 1-14

De Clercq, C. *Concilia Galliae, 511-695* (CCSL 148A; Turnhout, 1963)

——, *La legislation religieuse franque de Clovis à Charlemagne* (Louvain/Paris, 1936)

De Gaiffier, Baudouin *Etudes critiques d'hagiographie et d'iconologie* (Subsidia Hagiographica 43; Brussels, 1967)

——, "S. Mélance de Rouen, vénéré à Malmédy, et S. Mélas de Rhinocolure" AB 64 (1946) pp. 54-71

De Jong, Mayke "Power and Humility in Carolingian Society: the Public Penance of Louis the Pious" *Early Medieval Europe* 1 (1992) pp. 29-52

De Longpérier, A. "Louis d'Outre-Mer en Normandie. Trouvaille d'Evreux" *Revue Normand* n.s. IV (1869-70) pp. 71-85

——, "Monnaies normandes" *Revue Normand* VIII (1943) pp. 53-61

"De sancto Waningo et fundatione Fiscannensis monasterii" [BHL 8812] in AASS Oct. XI pp. 684-685

"De statu ecclesiae Constantiniensis ab anno 836-1093 - Gesta Gaufredi" in *Gallia Christiana* XI (1759), Instrumenta coll. 218-234

De Vesly, L. *Les fana ou petits temples gallo-romains de la région normande* (Rouen, 1909)

Déchelette, M. *Manuel d'archéologie préhistorique, celtique et gallo-romaine* I-V (Paris, 1931)

Delahaye, Hippolyte *Les légendes hagiographiques* (Subsidia Hagiographica 18; Brussels, 1906)

Delamare, F.A. "Essai sur la véritable origine et sur les vicissitudes de la cathé-drale de Coutances" *Mémoires de la Société des Antiquaires de Normandie* 17 (1840-41) pp. 161-172

Delisle, Léopold "Anciens catalogues des évêques des églises de France" *Histoire Littéraire de la France* XXIX (1885) pp. 421-423

——, "Inscription découverte à Rouen" *Bibliothèque de l'Ecole des Chartes* 50 (1889) p. 508

Delumeau, J. *Le catholicisme entre Luther et Voltaire* (Paris, 1971)

Depping, M. *Histoire des expéditions des Normands et de leur établissement en France au Xe siècle* (Paris, 1844)

Devigne, R. *Le Légendaire des provinces françaises à travers notre folklore* (Paris, 1950)

Devisse, Jean *Hincmar, Archévêque de Reims, 845-882* (Travaux d'Histoire Ethico-Politique xxix.1-3; Geneva, 1975-1976)

D'Haenens, Albert, "Gérard de Brogne à l'abbaye de S. Ghislain" in *Gérard de Brogne*

——, *Les invasions normandes, une catastrophe?* (Brussels, 1970)

Dhondt, Jan *Etude sur la naissance des principautés territoriales en France (IXe-Xe siècles)* (Bruges, 1948)

Dierkens, Alain "Prolégomènes à une histoire des relations culturelles entre les îles Britanniques et le continent pendant le haut moyen âge: La diffusion du monachisme dit colombanien ou iro-franc dans quelques monastères de la région parisienne au VIIe siècle et la politique religieuse de la reine Bathilde" in Atsma, ed. *La Neustrie* II pp. 371-394

——, "Quelques aspects de la christianisation du pays mosan à l'époque méro-vingienne" in *La civilisation mérovingienne dans le Bassin Mosan* (Actes du colloque Internationale d'Amy-Liège; August, 1985)

Dionysiaca. Le Texte Latin des Oeuvres du pseudo-Aréopagite (Recueil Donnant l'Ensemble des Traductions latines des ouvrages attribués au Denys l'Aréopagite) (Bruges, 1937)

Dodwell, C.R. *The Pictorial Arts of the West, 800-1200* (Yale, 1993)

Dolbeau, François "Anciens possesseurs des manuscrits hagiographiques Latins conservés à la Bibliothèque Nationale de Paris" *Revue d'Histoire des Textes* 9 (1979)

——, "Les hagiographes au travail: collecte et traitement des documents écrits (IXe-XIIe siècles). Avec annexe: Une discussion chronologique du XIIe siècle (édition de BHL 5824e)" in *Manuscrits Hagiographiques et Travail des Hagiographes* ed. M. Heinzelmann (Beihefte der Francia 24; 1992) pp. 49-76

——, "Un exemple peu connu de conte hagiographique: La passion des saints Pérégrin, Mathorat et Viventien" AB 97 (1979)

Dopsch, Heinz "Die Salzburger Slawenmission im 8./9. Jahrhundert und der Anteil der Iren" in Chathaín, ed. *Irland und die Christenheit*

Douglas, D.C. "The Norman Episcopate Before the Norman Conquest" *Cambridge Historical Journal* 13 (1957) pp. 101-115

——, *William the Conqueror; the Norman Impact upon England* (London, 1964)

Dubois, Jacques "Les listes épiscopales témoins de l'organisation ecclésiastique" in Riché ed. *La Christianisation des pays* pp. 9-23

Duchesne, Louis *Fastes episcopaux de l'ancienne Gaule* I-III (Paris, 1900)

Dudo of St. Quentin *De moribus et actis primorum Normanniae ducum* ed. Jules Lair (Mémoires de la Société des Antiquaires de Normandie 23; Caen, 1865)

Duft, Johannes "Iromanie, Irophobie. Fragen um die frühmittelalterliche Irenmission exemplifiziert an St. Gallen und Alemannien" *Zeitschrift für Schweizerische Kirchengeschichte* 50 (1956) pp. 244-262

Dumas-Dubourg, Francoise *Le Trésor de Fécamp et le monnayage en Francie occidentale pendant la seconde moitié du Xe siècle* (Paris, 1971)

Dunbabin, Jean *France in the Making (843-1180)* (Oxford, 1985)

Eberhardt, Newman C. *A Summary of Catholic History* 2 vols. (St. Louis, 1961-62)

Ebrard, J.M.A. *Die iroschottische Missionskirche des sechsten, siebenten und achten Jahrhunderts und ihre Verbreitung* (Gütersloch, 1873; repr. Hildesheim, 1971)

Einhard, "Vita Karoli" [BHL 1580] ed. G.H. Pertz, MGH SS 2 (1829) pp. 443-463

Enright, M.J. "Iromanie-Irophobie Revisited: A Suggested Frame of Reference for Considering Continental Reactions to Irish Peregrini in the Seventh and Eighth Centuries" in *Karl Martell in seiner Zeit* eds. J. Jarnut, U. Nonn and M. Richter (Beihefte der Francia 37, 1994)

Epistulae Austrasicae ed. W. Gundlach CCSL 117 (Turnhout, 1957)

Erlande-Brandenburg, Alain *Le roi, la sculpture et la mort. Gisants et tombeaux de la basilique de Saint-Denis* (Exposition de la Maison de la Culture et des Services d'Archives de la Seine-St.-Denis; Paris, 1975)

Ermentarius, "Miracula Filiberti" ed. René Poupardin in *Monuments de l'Histoire des Abbayes de Saint-Philibert* (Paris, 1905)

Ewig, Eugen "Die Christliche Mission bei dem Franken und im Merowingerreich" in Derek Baker, ed. *Miscellanea Historiae Ecclesiasticae* III (1970), reprinted with minor revisions in Schäferdiek ed. *Kirchengeschichte als Missionsgeschichte*, and in Jedin *Handbuch der Kirchengeschichte*

——, *Spätantikes und fränkisches Gallien. Gesammelte Schriften (1952-1973)* ed. H. Atsma, 2 vol. (Munich, 1976-1979)

Fallue, L. *Histoire politique et religieuse de l'église métropolitaine et du diocèse de Rouen* (Rouen, 1850)

Fanning, Steven *A Bishop and His World Before the Gregorian Reform: Hubert of Angers, 1006-1047* (Transactions of the American Philosophical Society 78.1; Philadelphia, 1988)

Farin, François *La Normandie Chrestienne, ou l'Histoire des Archevesques de Rouen* (Rouen, 1659)

Farmer, Sharon *Communities of St. Martin: Legend and Ritual in Medieval Tours* (Cornell, 1991)

Farrall, S. "Sung and Written Epics: The Case of the Song of Roland" *Oral Tradition in Melanesia* eds. D. Denoon and R. Lacey (Hong Kong, 1981)

Festugière, A.J. "Lieux communs littéraires et thèmes de folklore dans l'hagiographie primitive" *Wiener Studien* 73 (1960) pp. 123-152

Fichtenau, Heinrich *The Carolingian Empire: the Age of Charlemagne* (Studies in Medieval History 9; Oxford, 1957; translation by P. Munz of the introduction and cc. 1-6 of *Das Karolingische Imperium. Soziale und geistige Problematik eines Grossreiches*)

Fisher, G.P. *History of the Christian Church* (New York, 1887)

Fliche, Augustin and Victor Martin *Histoire de l'église depuis ses origines à nos jours* (Paris, 1948) vol. VII, *L'église au pouvoir des laïques*

Flint, Valerie I. *The Rise of Magic in Early Medieval Europe* (Princeton, 1991)

Flodoard of Reims, *Les Annales de Flodoard* ed. Philippe Lauer (Collection de Textes pour servir à l'étude et à l'enseignement de l'histoire 39; Paris, 1905)

——, "Historia Ecclesiae Remensis" eds. J. Heller and G.H. Waitz in MGH SS 13 (Hannover, 1881)

Folz, Robert *The Coronation of Charlemagne, 25 December 800* (London, 1974; trans. J.E. Anderson and revised by H. Maas, of *Le couronnement impérial de Charlemagne; Trente journées qui ont fait La France* vol. 2: 25 décembre, 800; Paris, 1964)

Fontaine, Jacques "La culture carolingienne dans les abbayes normands: l'exemple de St.-Wandrille" in Musset, ed. *Aspects du Monachisme*

——, "Hagiographie et politique. De Sulpice Sévère à Venance Fortunat" in Riché ed. *La Christianisation des pays* pp.113-140

——, "Victrice de Rouen et les origines du monachisme dans l'ouest de la Gaule (IVe-VIe siècles)" in Musset, ed. *Aspects du Monachisme*

Förstemann, Ernst *Altdeutsches Namenbuch* (Bonn, 1901)

Fortunatus, "Vita Paterni" [BHL 6477] ed. B. Krusch MGH AA 4.2

Fouracre, Paul "Merovingian History and Merovingian Hagiography" *Past and Present* 127 (1990) pp. 3-38

———, "The Work of Audoenus of Rouen and Eligius of Noyon in Extending Episcopal Authority from Town to Country in Seventh-Century Neustria" *Studies in Church History* 16 (1979; "The Church in Town and Countryside" ed. D. Baker) pp. 77-91

Fourasté, R. "St. Exupère d'Arreau" in *Les saints et les stars* ed. J.-C. Schmitt (Paris, 1979) pp. 101-132

Fournée, Jean *Le culte populaire des saints en Normandie* (Cahiers Léopold Delisle numero spécial, 1973)

———, *Saint Nicolas en Normandie* (Nogent-sur-Marne, 1988)

———, "Quelques facteurs de fixation et de diffusion du culte populaire des saints: exemples Normands" *Bulletin Philologique et Historique du Comité des Travaux Historiques et Scientifiques 1982/1984* (Paris, 1986)

Fournier, Gabriel *Les mérovingiens* (Paris, 1966)

Frémont, Armand *Atlas et géographie de la Normandie* (Rouen, 1977)

Fulbertus of Jumièges, "Vita Aichardi" [BHL 182beta] in *Histoire de Hainault par Jacques de Guyse* (Paris, 1830) vol. VIII pp. 40-137

———, Preface to the Vita Aichardi [BHL 182alpha] ed. L. Surius *De Probatis Sanctorum Historiis* V (1574) p. 239

———, "Vita Romani" ed. F. Lifshitz, "The Dossier of Romanus of Rouen: The Political Uses of Hagiographical Texts" (Ph.D. Dissertation; Columbia University, 1988)

Fulbertus of St. Ouen, "Miracula Audoeni" [BHL 760], AASS Aug. IV pp. 825-837

Ganshof, F.L. "La revision de la Bible par Alcuin" *Bibliothèque d'Humanisme et de la Renaissance* IX (1947) pp. 7-20, in *The Carolingians and the Frankish Monarchy* ed. and trans. Janet Sondheimer (1971)

Gauthier, Nancy *L'évangélisation des pays de la Moselle, IIe-VIIe siècles* (Paris, 1980)

———, "Les premiers siècles des origines aux Carolingiens" in *Le Diocèse de Rouen-Le Havre* ed. N.-J. Chaline (Histoire des Diocèses de France 5, dir. J.-R. Palanque and B. Plongeron; Paris, 1976)

———, "Quelques hypothèses sur la redaction des vies des saints évêques de Normandie" in *Memoriam Sanctorum Venerantes* (Miscellanea in onore di Mons. Victor Saxer; Studi di Antichità Cristiana XLVIII; Vatican City, 1992) pp. 449-468

———, "Rouen pendant le haut Moyen-Age (650-850)" in Atsma ed., *La Neustrie* 16/2 pp. 1-20

Geary, Patrick *Aristocracy in Provence: The Rhône Basin at the Dawn of the Carolingian Age* (Monographien zur Geschichte des Mittelalters 31; Stuttgart, 1985)

——, "Cults Without Impresarios" (Plenary Address to the Sewanee Medieval Colloquium, "Saints and Their Cults in the Middle Ages," April, 1993)

——, *Furta Sacra. Thefts of Relics in the Central Middle Ages* (Princeton, 1978; 2nd ed. 1990)

——, "L'humiliation des saints" *Annales. E.S.C.* 34 (1979) pp. 27-42

——, "The Ninth-Century Relic Trade. A Response to Popular Piety?" in *Religion and the People* ed. J. Obelkevich (Chapel Hill, 1979)

"Genealogium comitum Flandrensium" ed. L. C. Bethmann in MGH SS 9 (Hannover, 1851)

St. Gérard de Brogne et son oeuvre réformatrice (Acts of the Millenary Conference on Gerard's Death, 1959) = *Revue Benedictine* 70 (1960)

Gerberding, Richard *The Rise of the Carolingians and the Liber Historiae Francorum* (Oxford, 1987)

"Gesta abbatum Fontenellensium" ed. G.H. Pertz in MGH SS 2 pp. 271- 301

Gesta sanctorum patrum Fontenellensis cenobii (Gesta abbatum Fontenellensium) eds. F. Lohier and J. Laporte (Rouen/Paris, 1936)

Gesta Normannorum Ducum of William of Jumièges, Orderic Vitalis and Robert of Torigni ed. and trans. E.M.C. van Houts I-II(Oxford, 1992-1995)

Gilliard, Frank D. "The Apostolocity of Gallic Churches" *Harvard Theological Review* 68 (1975) pp. 17-33

Gilmore, Carroll "War on the Rivers: Viking Numbers and Mobility on the Seine and Loire, 841-886" *Viator* 19 (1988) pp. 80-109

Goffart, Walter "The Historia Ecclesiastica: Bede's Agenda and Ours" *Haskins Society Journal* 2 (1990) pp. 29-46

——, *The Le Mans Forgeries: A Chapter from the History of Church Property in the Ninth Century* (Cambridge, Mass 1966)

——, *Narrators of Barbarian History. Jordanes, Gregory of Tours, Bede and Paul the Deacon* (Princeton, 1988)

——, "Paul the Deacon's 'Gesta Episcoporum Mettensium' and the Early Design of Charlemagne's Succession" *Traditio* 42 (1986) pp. 59-93

——, Constantine and the Barbarians" *American Historical Review* LXXXVI (1981) pp. 275-306

Gossiaux, G. "Le lieu de naissance et la famille de S. Gérard de Brogne" *Revue Diocésaine de Namur* 15 (1961) pp. 170-178

Goubert, L. *Notice sur s. Nigaise, apôtre du Vexin* (handwritten by the author, 1867)

Gougaud, L. "Le culte de St. Columban" *Revue Mabillon* XXV (1935) pp. 169-178

Graus, František *Volk, Herrscher und Heiliger im Reich der Merowinger* (Munich, 1965)

Gregory of Tours "Liber in gloria martyrum" (= Libri octo miraculorum 1; ed.

B. Krusch, MGH SRM 1.2 (Hannover, 1884))

——, "Libri decem historiarum" ed. B. Krusch, MGH SRM (Hannover, 1884) 1.1

Grémont, D.-B. "Lectiones ad Prandium à l'abbaye de Fécamp" *Cahiers Léopold Delisle* 12 (1971)

Grenier, A. *Manuel d'archéologie gallo-romaine* I-IV (Paris, 1960)

Griffe, E. *La Gaule chrétienne à l'époque romaine* I-III (Paris, 1964-1966)

Grosset, Charles "Hypothèses sur l'évangelisation du Cotentin: III-Un Poitevin de bonne famille: Paterne" *Revue du Département de la Manche* XV (1973) pp. 41-59

Guillot, Olivier "La conversion des Normands peu après 911. Des reflects contemporains à l'historiographie ultérieur (Xe-XIe s.)" *Cahiers de Civilisation Médiévale* 24 (1981) pp. 101-116 and 181-219

——, "Formes, fondements et limites de l'organisation politique en France au Xe siècle" in "Il Secolo di Ferro" pp. 57-116

——, "A Reform of Investiture Before the Investiture Struggle in Anjou, Normandy and England" *Haskins Society Journal* 3 (1991) pp. 81-100

Guiraud, J. "L'action civilisatrice de S. Colomban et de ses moines dans la Gaule mérovingienne" *Thirty-First Annual Eucharistic Conference* (Dublin, 1932)

Gurevich, Aaron J. *Contadini e santi. Problemi della cultura popolare nel Medioevo* (Turin, 1986; Italian translation of Russian original *Problemy Srednevekovoj narodnoj Kul'tury*, Moscow, 1981)

——, *Historical Anthropology of the Middle Ages* ed. and trans. Jana Howlett (Chicago, 1992)

Gussone, Nikolaus "Adventus-Zeremoniell und Translation von Reliquien. Victricius von Rouen, *De Laude Sanctorum*" *Frühmittelalterliche Studien* 10 (1976) pp. 125-133

Halperin, Samuel William *Italy and the Vatican at War, a Study of Their Relations from the Outbreak of the Franco-Prussian War to the Death of Pius XI* (Chicago, 1936)

Hardwick, C. *A History of the Christian Church: the Middle Ages* (London, 1861; 2nd ed. 1883, ed. W. Stubbs)

Hariulf of St. Riquier "Chronicon Centulense" ed. F. Lot in *Chronique de St.-Riquier* (Collection des textes pour servir à l'étude et à l'enseignement de l'histoire; Paris, 1894)

Haselbach, Irene *Aufstieg und Herrschaft der Karolinger in der Darstellung der sogenannten Annales Mettenses priores* (Historische Studien 42; Lübeck/Hamburg, 1970)

Haskins, C.H. *Norman Institutions* (Cambridge, Mass, 1919)

Hauck, Albert *Kirchengeschichte Deutschlands* (Leipzig, 1896; repr. Berlin, 1952)

Head, Thomas *Hagiography and the Cult of Saints: The Diocese of Orleans, 800-1200* (Cambridge, 1990)

Heene, Katrien "Merovingian and Carolingian Hagiography: Continuity or Change in Public and Aims?" AB 107 (1989) pp. 415-428

Heinzelmann, Martin *Bischofsherrschaft in Gallien. Zur Kontinuität römischer Führungsschichten vom 4. bis 7. Jahrhundert. Soziale, Prosopographische und bildungsgeschichtliche Aspekte* (Beihefte der Francia 5; Zurich-Munich, 1976)

——, *Translationsberichte und Andere Quellen des Reliquienkultes* (Typologie des Sources du Moyen Age Occidental 33; Turnhout, 1979)

——, and Joseph-Claude Poulin *Les vies anciennes de sainte Geneviève de Paris. Etudes critiques* (Bibliothèque de l'école des hautes études, IVe section. Sciences historiques et philologiques 329; Paris, 1986)

Heiric of Auxerre "Vita Germani" [BHL 3458] ed. L. Traube in MGH Poet. Lat. III pp. 428-517

Helgaud of Fleury *Vie de Robert le Pieux. Epitoma vitae regis Rotberti pii* ed. and trans. R.H. Bauthier and G. Labory (Paris, 1965)

Heliand. The Saxon Gospel trans. G. Ronald Murphy (Oxford, 1992)

Heliand und Genesis ed. Otto Behaghel (9th ed., reworked by Burkhard Taeger, Tübingen, 1984)

Hen, Yitzak "Merovingian Liturgy in Cultural Perspective" (Paper presented to the 1st International Medieval Congress, Leeds, July 1994)

——, "Paganism and Superstition in the Time of Gregory of Tours: Une question mal posée" (Paper presented to the 29th International Congress on Medieval Studies, Kalamazoo, May 1994)

——, "Popular Culture in Merovingian Gaul" (Ph.D. Dissertation, Cambridge University, 1994)

Henry-Rosier, M. *S. Colomban dans la barbarie mérovingienne* (Paris, 1950)

Herren, Michael "Classical and Secular Learning among the Irish Before the Carolingian Renaissance" *Florilegium* 3 (1981)

Herschman, Joel "The Eleventh-Century Nave of the Cathedral of Coutances: A New Reconstruction" *Gesta* 22 (1983) pp. 121-134

Herval, René *Origines Chrétiennes: de la IIe Lyonnaise gallo-romaine à la Normandie ducale (IVe-XIe siècles). Avec le texte complet et la traduction integrale du De laude sanctorum de Saint Victrice (396)* (Rouen, 1966)

Hilduin of St. Denis "Passio Dionysii" [BHL 2174-2175] in PL 106 coll. 22-50

Hillgarth, J.N. *Christianity and Paganism, 350-750. The Conversion of Western Europe* (Philadelphia, 1986)

——, "Modes of evangelization of Western Europe in the Seventh Century" in Chatháin, Proínséas Ní and Michael Richter, eds. *Irland und die Christenheit*

Hincmar of Reims, "Ad Carolum regem pro ecclesiae libertatum defensione" in PL 125 col. 1040-1041

——, "Gesta Dagoberti I regis Francorum" [BHL 2081] ed. B. Krusch in MGH SRM 2 pp. 511-524

——, "Opusculum LV capitulorum adversus Hincmarum Laudunensem" in PL 126 col. 325

——, *De ordine palatii* ed. and trans. Maurice Prou (Bibliothèque de l'école des hautes études 58; Paris, 1885); eds. and trans. T. Gross and R. Schieffer (Hanover, 1980)

——, "Vita Remigii" [BHL 7153-7163] ed. B. Krusch, MGH SRM 3

Histoire de l'abbaye royale de St.-Pierre de Jumièges par un religieux Bénédictin de la Congregation de St. Maur (1764) ed. Julien Loth (Société de l'Histoire de Normandie, Publications; Rouen, 1882) 3 vols.

"Historia monasterii Mosomensis" ed. W. Wattenbach, MGH SS 14 (Hannover, 1883)

Hodges, Richard *The Anglo-Saxon Achievement: Archeology and the Beginnings of English Society* (Ithaca, 1989)

Hourlier, Jacques "Les sources écrites de l'histoire montoise antérieure à 966" in *Millénaire monastique du Mont Saint-Michel* 2 vols. (Paris, 1966)

——, "Reims et les Normands" *Mémoires de la Société de l'Agriculture, Commerce, Sciences et Arts du Département de la Manche* 99 (1984) pp. 87-96

Houtin, Albert *La controverse de l'apostolicité des églises de France au XIXe siècle* (Paris, 1900)

Howe, John "The Date of the 'Life' of St. Vigor of Bayeux" AB 102 (1984) pp. 303-312

Howe, N. *Migration and Myth-Making in Anglo-Saxon England* (New Haven, 1989)

Hubert, J. "Sources sacrées et sources saintes" *Comptes-rendus de l'Academie des Inscriptions et Belles-lettres* (1967) pp. 567-573

Huisman, Gerda "Notes on the Manuscript Tradition of Dudo of St.-Quentin's Gesta Normannorum" *Anglo-Norman Studies* 6 (1984)

I, Deug-Su *Cultura e ideologia nella prima età carolingia* (Istituto Storico Italiano per il Medio Evo; Studi storici 146-147; Rome, 1984)

——, *L'opera agiografica di Alcuino* (Biblioteca degli "Studi medievali" XIII; Spoleto, 1983)

"Inventio et translatio Taurini" [BHL 7992 and 7995] ed. P. Boschius AASS August 2 pp. 643-650

Inventio et miracula sancti Uulframni [BHL 8740] ed. Jean Laporte (Mélanges publiés par la Société de l'Histoire de Normandie, 14e séries; Rouen, 1938)

James, Edward "Archeology and the Merovingian Monastery" in Clarke and Brennan, eds. *Columbanus and Merovingian Monasticism*

———, "Cemeteries and the Problem of Frankish Settlement in Gaul" in *Names, Words and Graves: Early Medieval Settlement* ed. P.H. Sawyer (Leeds, 1979) pp. 55-89

———, "Ireland and Western Gaul in the Merovingian Period" in *Ireland in Early Medieval Europe (Studies in Memory of Kathleen Hughes)* ed. Rosamond McKitterick (Cambridge, 1982) pp. 362-381

———, *The Franks* (Oxford, 1988)

Jaud, Léon S. *Filibert, fondateur et abbé de Jumièges et de Noirmoutier, sa vie, son temps, sa survivance, son culte. Etude d'histoire monastique au VIIe siècle* (Paris, 1910)

Joannou, P.-P. *Démonologie populaire-démonologie critique au XIe siècle. La vie inédite de S. Auxence par M. Psellos* (Schriften zur Geistesgeschichte des östlichen Europas; Wiesbaden, 1971)

John of Avranches *Le Liber de officiis ecclesiasticis de Jean d'Avranches* ed. René Delamare (Evreux, 1923)

Jonas of Bobbio "Vita Columbani abbatis discipulorumque eius libri duo" (BHL 1898) ed. B. Krusch, MGH SRM 4

———, "Vita Vedastis" [BHL 8500-8503] ed. B. Krusch in MGH SRM 3 pp. 406-413

Jones, Charles W. *St. Nicholas of Myra, Bari and Manhattan. Biography of a Legend* (Chicago, 1978)

Jonsson, Ritva *Historia. Etudes sur la genèse des offices versifiés* (Stockholm, 1968; Studia Latina Stockhomensia 15)

Jordan, Mark D. "Philosophic 'Conversion' and Christian Conversion: A Gloss on Professor MacMullen" *The Second Century* 5 (1985/86) pp. 90-96

Jordan, Victoria B. "The Role of Kingship in Tenth-Century Normandy: Hagiography of Dudo of St. Quentin" *Haskins Society Journal* 3 (1992) pp. 53-62

Jumièges. Congrès scientifique du XIIIe centenaire (Rouen, June 1954; Rouen, 1955)

Kaiser, Reinhold *Das römische Erbe und des Merowingerreich* (Enzyklopädie deutscher Geschichte 26; Munich, 1993)

———, "Royauté et pouvoir épiscopal au nord de la Gaule (VIIe-IXe s.)" in Atsma, ed. *La Neustrie* I pp. 164-160

Kaminsky, Howard "The Problematics of Later-Medieval 'Heresy'" in *Husitství-Reformace-Renesance: Sborník k 60. narozeninám Frantiska Smahela* edd. J. Pának, M. Polívka and N. Rejchrtová (Prague, 1994) pp. 133-154

Kaufmann, H. *Altdeutsches Namenbuch* (Ergänzungsband; Munich, 1968)

Kelly, Susan "Trading Privileges from Eighth-Century England" *Early Medieval Europe* 1 (1992) pp. 3-28

Kieckhefer, Richard "Imitators of Christ: Sainthood in the Christian Tradition" in R. Kieckhefer and G. Bond eds. *Sainthood. Its Manifestation in World Religions* (Berkeley, 1988) pp. 1-42

——, "The Specific Rationality of Medieval Magic" *American Historical Review* 99 (1994) pp. 813-836

Kienast, Walter *Studien über die französichen Volkstämme des Frühmittelalters* (Stuttgart, 1968)

Köenig, J. "Irlands europäische Mission" *Würzburger Diozese Geschichtsblätter* 45 (1983) pp. 15-25

Koller, Heinrich "Die Iren und die Christianisierung der Bayern" in Löwe, ed. *Die Iren und Europa* vol. 2 pp. 345-373

Krusch, Bruno "Die älteste Vita Richerii" *Neues Archiv* 29 (1904) pp. 15-48

Kupfer, Marcia *Romanesque Wall Painting in Central France: The Politics of Narrative* (New Haven, 1993)

Kurth, Gustave *Etudes franques* (Paris, 1919) 2 vols.

Lafaurie, Jean "Trouvailles de monnaies franques et mérovingiennes en Seine-Maritime, Ve-VIIIe s." *Histoire et numismatique en Haute-Normandie* (Caen, 1980; Cahier des Annales de Normandie 12A) pp. 111-116

Lair, Jules *Etude sur la vie et la mort de Guillaume Longue-Epée* (Paris, 1893)

Landes, Richard "The Dynamics of Heresy and Reform in Limoges: A Study of Popular Participation in the 'Peace of God' (994-1033)" in *Essays on the Peace of God: The Church and the People in Eleventh-Century France* eds. T. Head and R. Landes (Historical Reflections/Réflexions Historiques 14 (1987)) pp. 467-511

Lanfry, Georges "L'église carolingienne Saint-Pierre de l'abbaye de Jumièges" *Bulletin monumental* 98 (1939) pp. 47-66

Langlois, Pierre-Laurent *Recherches sur les Bibliothèques des Archevêques et du Chapitre de Rouen* (Rouen, 1853)

Lanzoni, Francesco "Il sogno presago della madre incinta nella letteratura medievale e antica" AB 45 (1927) pp. 224-241

Laporte, Jean "La date de l'exode de Jumièges" in *Jumièges* I

——, "Etude chronologique sur les listes abbatiales de St.-Riquier" *Revue Mabillon* XLIX (1959)

——, "Fontenelle" *Dictionnaire d'Histoire et de Géographie Ecclésiastique* 17

——, "Gérard de Brogne à S. Wandrille et à S. Riquier" in *Gérard de Brogne*

——, "Les listes abbatiales de Jumièges" in *Jumièges* pp. 435-466

——, "Les origines du monachisme dans la province de Rouen" *Revue Mabillon* XXXI (1941)

——, *St. Riquier. Etude hagiographique* (1958)

Lasteyrie, C. *L'abbaye de Saint-Martial de Limoges* (Paris, 1903)

Lauer, Philippe *Le règne de Louis IV d'Outremer* (Paris, 1900)

——, "Les translations des reliques de Saint Ouen and de Saint Leufroy du IXe au Xe siècle et les deux abbayes de la Croix-Saint-Ouen" *Bulletin Philologique et Historique du Comité des Travaux Historiques et Scientifiques* (1921)

Le Blond, Bernard *L'accession des Normands de Neustrie à la culture occidentale (Xème-XIème siècles)* (Paris, 1966)

Lecroq, Gaston *Les manuscrits liturgiques de l'abbaye de Fécamp* (Extrait du Bulletin de l'Association des Amis du Vieux-Fécamp, 1934; Fécamp, 1935)

Le Goff, Jacques "Culture ecclésiastique, culture folkorique au Moyen-Age: St. Marcel de Paris et le dragon" *Richerche storiche ed economiche in memoria di Corrado Barbagallo* II (Naples, 1970) pp. 53-90; English translation by A. Goldhammer in J. Le Goff *Time, Work and Culture in the Middle Ages* (Chicago, 1980)

Legris, Canon "L'exode des corps saints au diocèse de Rouen" *Revue Catholique de Normandie* 28 (1919) pp. 125-136, 168-174 and 209-221

——, *Les premiers martyrs du Vexin, SS. Nigaise, Quirin, Scivicule, Pience* (Evreux, 1913)

——, "Les vies interpolées des saints de Fontenelle" AB 17 (1904) pp. 265-306

Le Maho, Jacques, "Bulletins" in AM 17 (1987) pp. 213-214; 18 (1988) pp. 333-334; 19 (1989) pp. 301-303; 20 (1990) p. 389; 21 (1991) p. 326; 22 (1992) pp. 462-463

——, "Le groupe épiscopal de Rouen du IVe au Xe siècle" in *Medieval Art, Architecture and Archeology at Rouen* (British Archeological Association Conference Transactions (XII, 1993) ed. Jenny Stratford) pp. 20-29

Le Maître, Philippe "L'oeuvre d'Aldric du Mans et sa signification (832-857)" *Francia* 8 (1980) pp. 43-64

Le Patourel, J. "Norman Kings or Norman 'King-Dukes'?" in *Etudes Yver: Droit privé et institutions régionales* (Rouen, 1976) pp. 469-479

Leroquais, Victor *Les bréviaires manuscrits des bibliothèques publiques de la France* I-V (Paris, 1934)

Levalet, Daniel "The Cathedral Church of St. André at Avranches" AM 12 (1982) pp. 107-153

Levillain, Léon "De l'authenticité de la *Clausula*" *Bibliothèque de l'Ecole des Chartes* 88 (1927) pp. 20-42

Levison, Wilhelm "Die Iren und die Fränkische Kirche" *Historische Zeitschrift* 109 (1912) pp. 1-22; repr. *Aus rheinischer und fränkischer Frühzeit* (Düsseldorf, 1948) pp. 247-262

——, "Zur Kritik der Fonteneller Geschichtsquellen" *Neues Archiv* 25 (1899/1900)

Licquet, M. *Histoire de Normandie depuis les temps les plus reculés jusqu'à la conquête d'Angleterre en 1066* 2 vols. (Rouen, 1835)

"Libellus de revelatione, aedificatione et auctoritate Fiscannensis monasterii" in PL 151 coll. 699-724

Lifshitz, Felice "A Real and Present Danger: Demonic Infestation in the Tenth Century" (paper presented to the International Congress of Medieval Studies, Kalamazoo, May 1994)

——, "The *Acta Archiepiscoporum Rotomagensium*: A Monastery or Cathedral Product?" AB 108 (1990) pp. 337-347

——, "Beyond Positivism and Genre: 'Hagiographical' Texts as Historical Narrative" *Viator* 25 (1994) pp. 95 -113

——, "Des femmes missionnaires. L'exemple de la Gaule" *Revue d'Histoire Ecclesiastique* 83 (1988) pp. 5-33

——, "The Dossier of Romanus of Rouen: The Political Uses of Hagiographical Texts" (Ph.D. Dissertation, Columbia University, 1988)

——, "Dudo's Historical Narrative and the Norman Succession of 996" *Journal of Medieval History* 20 (1994) pp. 101-120

——, "Eight Men In. Rouennais Traditions of Archiepiscopal Sanctity" *Haskins Society Journal* 2 (1991) pp. 63-74

——, "The Encomium Emmae Reginae: A Political Pamphlet of the Eleventh Century?" *Haskins Society Journal* 1 (1990) pp. 39-50

——, "The 'Exodus of Holy Bodies' Reconsidered: The Date of the Translation of Gildardus of Rouen to Soissons" AB 110 (1992) pp. 329-340

——, "The Migration of Neustrian Relics in the Viking Age: The Myth of Voluntary Exodus, the Reality of Coersion and Theft" (forthcoming, *Early Medieval Europe*)

——, "La Normandie carolingienne" (forthcoming, *Annales de Normandie*)

——, "The Politics of Historiography: Bishops versus Monks in Eleventh-Century Rouen" (Paper presented to the Modern Languages Association, December 1994)

——, "The 'Privilege of St. Romanus': Provincial Independence and Hagiographical Legends at Rouen" AB 107 (1989) pp. 161-170

——, "Saint Romain de Rouen: missionnaire franc dans la Normandie des vikings" in *La France à l'Ouest: Voix d'Ouest en Europe, Souffles d'Europe en Ouest* (Actes du Colloque International d'Angers, May 1992; Angers, 1993) dir. G. Cesbron pp. 23-30

Liutgar, "Vita Gregorii abbatis Traiectensis" [BHL 3680] in MGH SS 15/1 ed. O. Holder-Egger pp. 66-79

Livre du millénaire de la Normandie, 911-1911 (Paris, 1911)

Logié, Paul "Jumièges and St. Riquier" in *Jumièges* I pp. 199-207

Lohaus, Annethe *Die Merovinger und England* (Münchener Beiträge zur Mediä-
   vistik und Renaissance Forschung 19; Munich, 1974)
Loomis, C.F. *White Magic. An Introduction to the Folkore of Christian Legend*
   (Cambridge, Mass., 1948)
Lopez, Robert S. "An Aristocracy of Money in the Early Middle Ages" *Speculum*
   28 (1953) pp. 1-43
———, "Still Another Renaissance" *American Historical Review* 57 (1951-52) pp. 1-
   21
———, *The Tenth Century: How Dark the Dark Ages?* (New York-Chicago-S.F.-Lon-
   don, 1959)
Lot, Ferdinand *Etudes critiques sur l'abbaye de Saint-Wandrille* (Bibliothèque de
   l'Ecole des Hautes Etudes 204; Paris, 1913)
Lotter, Friedrich "Legenden als Geschichtsquellen" *Deutsches Archiv* 27 (1971)
———, "Methodisches zur Gewinnung historischer Erkenntnisse aus hagiographischen Quellen" *Historische Zeitschrift* 229 (1979) pp. 298-356
Loud, G.A. "The 'Gens Normannorum'-Myth or Reality?" *Anglo-Norman Studies*
   4 (1982; Proceedings of the Battle Conference, 1981; ed. R.A. Brown) pp.
   104-116
Löwe, Heinz ed. *Die Iren und Europa im Früheren Mittelalter* (Acts of the International Colloquium, "Die Iren und Europa," Tübingen, 1979; Stuttgart,
   1982) 2 vols.
Luisello, Bruno "Il mito dell'origine troiana dei Galli, dei Franchi e degli Scan-
   dinavi" *Romanobarbarica* 3 (1978) pp. 89-121

MacMullen, Ramsey *Christianizing the Roman Empire, AD 100-400* (New Haven,
   1984)
———, "Conversion: a historian's view" *The Second Century* 5 (1985/86) pp. 67-81
Malnory, M. *Quid Luxovienses monachi, discipuli sancti Columbani, ad regulam
   monasteriorum atque ad communem Ecclesiae profectum contulerunt* (Paris,
   1894)
Manselli, R. "La religione popolare nel medio evo: prime considerazione meto-
   dologiche" *Nuova Rivista Storica* 58 (1974)
Marcus, Robert *The End of Ancient Christianity* (Cambridge, 1990)
Marnell, William *Light from the West. The Irish Mission and the Emergence of Mod-
   ern Europe* (New York, 1978)
Martin of Braga *Martini episcopi Bracarensis Opera Omnia* (Papers and Mono-
   graphs of the American Academy in Rome 12; New Haven, 1950) ed.
   C.W. Barlow
Masson, André *L'église abbatiale de S.-Ouen de Rouen* (Paris, 1927)
Mayr-Harting, Henry *The Coming of Christianity to England* (London, 1972)

McEvoy, James J. "The Relationship Between Neoplatonism and Christianity: Influence, Syncretism or Discernment" *The Relationship between Neoplatonism and Christianity* eds. Thomas Finn and Vincent Twomey (Dublin, 1992)

McKitterick, Rosamund *The Carolingians and the Written Word* (Cambridge, 1989)

——, "The Diffusion of insular culture in Neustria between 650-850: The implications of the manuscript evidence" in Atsma ed. *La Neustrie* II pp. 395-432

——, "Frauen und Schriftlichkeit im Frühmittelalter" *Weibliche Lebensgestaltung im Frühen Mittelalter* ed. H.W. Goetz (Cologne and Vienne, 1991) pp. 65-118

——, "The Scriptoria of Merovingian Gaul" in eds. Clarke and Brennan, *Columbanus and Merovingian Monasticism*

McNeil, J.T. and H.M. Garner eds. and trans. *Medieval Handbooks of Penance* (Columbia Records of Civilization; New York, 1938; repr. 1990)

Mesnel, J.-B. *St. Taurin, premier évêque d'Evreux. Les saints du diocèse d'Evreux* I (Evreux, 1914)

Meyer-Sickendiek, I. *Gottes gelehrte Vaganten. Auf die Spuren der irischen Mission und Kultur in Europa* (Munich, 1980)

"Miracula Audoeni" [BHL 761] AASS Aug. IV pp. 837-839

Misonne, Daniel "Un écrit de S. Gérard de Brogne relatif à une relique de S. Landelin" AB 83 (1965)

——, "Gérard de Brogne et sa dévotion aux reliques" *Sacris Erudiri* 25 (1982)

Montfaucon, B. de *Bibliotheca Bibliothecarum* (Paris, 1739)

Moore, Robert I. *The Formation of a Persecuting Society: Power and Deviance in Western Europe, 950-1250* (Oxford, 1987)

Morlet, M.-T. *Les noms de personne sur le territoire de l'ancienne Gaule du VIe au XIIe siècle. I: Les noms issus du germanique continental et les créations gallo-germaniques* (Paris, 1968)

Mulders, J. "Victricius van Rouaan. Leven en Leer" *Bijdragen. Tijdschrift voor Philosophie en Theologie* XVII (1956) pp. 1-25 and XVIII (1957) pp. 19-40 and 270-289

Müller, Wolfgang "Der Anteil der Iren an der Christianisierung der Alemannen" in Löwe, ed. *Die Iren und Europa* vol. 2 pp. 336-340

Munro, C.D. *Translations and Reprints from the Original Sources of European History* (Philadelphia, 1899)

Murphy, G. Ronald *The Saxon Savior. The Germanic Transformation of the Gospel in the Ninth-century Heliand* (Oxford, 1989)

Musset, Lucien "L'aristocratie normande au XIe siècle" ed. P. Contamine in *La noblesse au Moyen Age, XIe-XVe siècles. Essais à la mémoire de Robert Boutrouche* (Paris, 1976) pp. 71-96

——, ed. *Aspects du Monachisme en Normandie (IVe-XVIIIe siècles)* (Actes du Colloque Scientifique de l'Année des abbayes normandes, Caen 1979; Bibliothèque de la Société de l'Histoire Ecclésiastique de la France 15-16; Paris, 1982)

——, "Ce qu'enseigne l'histoire d'un patrimoine monastique: Saint-Ouen de Rouen du IXe au XIe siècle" *Aspects de la société et de l'économie dans la Normandie médiévale (Xe-XIIIe siècles)* (Cahier des Annales de Normandie 22; Caen, 1988)

——, "Les conditions financières d'une réussite architecturale: les grandes églises romanes de Normandie" *Mélanges offerts à René Crozet à l'occasion de son 70e anniversaire* (Poitiers, 1966) pp. 307-314

——, "De S. Victrice à S. Ouen: La christianisation de la province de Rouen d'après l'hagiographie" in Riché ed. *La Christianisation des pays entre Loire et Rhin* pp. 141-152

——, "Les destinés de la propriété monastique durant les invasions normandes (IXe-XIe s.). L'exemple de Jumièges" in *Jumièges* vol. I pp. 49-55

——, "Les domaines de l'époque franque et les destinées de la régime domaniale" *Bulletin de la Société des Antiquaires de Normandie* 49 (1942-45)

——, "L'époque ducale" in *Histoire de Rouen* dir. M. Mollat (Rouen, 1979; Histoire des Villes dir. P. Wolff)

——, "L'exode des reliques du diocèse de Sées au temps des invasions normandes" *Bulletin de la Société Historique et Archéologique de l'Orne* 86 (1970) pp. 3-22

——, "Les invasions scandinaves et l'évolution des villes de la France de l'Ouest" *Revue Historique de Droit Français et Etranger* 43 (1965)

——, "Monachisme d'époque franque et monachisme d'époque ducale en Normandie: Le problème de la continuité" in Musset, ed. *Aspects du Monachisme en Normandie*

——, "Recherches sur les pélerins et pelerinages en Normandie jusqu'à la Première Croisade" *Annales de Normandie* 12 (1962)

——, "La Renaissance urbaine des Xe et XIe siècles dans l'Ouest de la France: problèmes et hypothèses de travail" in *Etudes de civilisation médiévale (IXe-XIIe siècles): Mélanges offerts à E.-R. Labande* (Poitiers, 1974) pp. 563-575

——, "Le Satiriste Garnier de Rouen et son milieu (début du XIe siècle)" *Revue du Moyen Age Latin* 10 (1954) pp. 237-266

——, "Sur la connaissance du grec et de l'écriture runique en Normandie sous Richard II: une erreur d'attribution" *Annales de Normandie* 3 (1953) pp. 84-87

Nécrologe de l'abbaye de St.-Taurin d'Evreux ed. A. Porée (Caen, 1889)

Nelson, Janet "Carolingian Royal Ritual" in D. Cannadine and S. Price eds. *Rituals of Royalty. Power and Ceremonial in Traditional Societies* (Cambridge, 1987) pp. 137-180

——, "Inauguration Rituals" in P.H. Sawyer and I.N. Wood eds. *Early Medieval Kingship* (Leeds, 1977) pp. 50-71; reprinted in J. Nelson *Politics and Ritual in Early Medieval Europe* (London, 1986) pp. 283-308

——, "Perceptions du pouvoir chez les historiennes du Haut Moyen Age" in *Les femmes au Moyen Age* ed. Michel Rouche (Paris, 1990) pp. 77-85

Noble, T.F.X. *The Republic of St. Peter: The Birth of the Papal State, 680-825* (Philadelphia, 1984)

Nortier, E. *Les bibliothèques médiévales des abbayes bénédictines de Normandie* (Caen, 1966)

Notger of St. Gall "De Carolo magno" ed. Pertz in MGH SS 2; trans. L. Thorpe in *Two Lives of Charlemagne* (Hardmonsworth, 1969)

Odo of Cluny "Vita Geraldi comitis Aurillacensis" [BHL 3411] in PL 133 coll. 639-704

Orderic Vitalis *The Ecclesiastical History of Orderic Vitalis* I-VI ed. and trans. Marjorie Chibnall (Oxford, 1968-1980)

Orselli, Alba Maria "Santi e Città. Santi e demoni urbani tra tardoantico e alto medioevo" in "Santi e Demoni"

Orsi, Robert *The Madonna of 115th Street: Faith and Community in Italian Harlem, 1880-1950* (New Haven, 1985)

Palanque, Jean-Rémy *S. Ambroise et l'Empire Romain* (Paris, 1933)

Parente, F. "L'idea di conversione da Nock ad oggi" *Augustinianum* 27 (1987) pp. 7-25

Parisse, "Princes laïques et/ou moines. Les évêques du Xe siècle" in "Il Secolo di Ferro" pp. 449-513

"Passio Nigasii" [BHL 6081] ed. Goubert, *Notice sur s. Nigaise*

Paulinus of Nola *Sancti Pontii Meropii Paulini Nolani Epistulae* ed. G. de Hartel (CSEL 29; Prague/Vienna/Leipzig, 1894)

Penco, Gregorio "Le figure bibliche del vir Dei nell'agiografia monastica" *Benedictina* XV (1968) pp. 1-13

——, "L'imitazione di Christo nell'agiografia monastica" *Collectanea Cisterciana* 28 (1966) pp. 17-34

——, "Significato e funzione dei prologhi nell'agiografia Benedettina" *Aevum* 40 (1966) pp. 468-478

Périn, Patrick "A propos de publications recentes concernant le peuplement en Gaule à l'époque mérovingienne: la 'question franque'" AM 11 (1981) pp. 125-145

———, and Laure-Charlotte Feffer *Les Francs* I-II (Paris, 1987)

———, "Les objets vikings du Musée des Antiquités de la Seine-Maritime" *Recueil d'études en hommage à Lucien Musset* (Cahiers des Annales de Normandie, 23, Caen 1990) pp. 161-188

Philippart, Guy *Les légendiers latins et autres manuscrits hagiographiques* (Typologie des sources du Moyen Age Occidental 24-25; Turnhout, 1977)

Picard, Jean-Charles *Le souvenir des évêques. Sépultures, listes épiscopales et culte des évêques en Italie du Nord des origines au Xe siècle* (Bibliothèque des écoles françaises d'Athènes et de Rome, 268; Rome, 1988)

Picard, J.M. "Structural Patterns in Early Irish Hagiography" *Peritia* 4 (1985)

Pietri, Charles, "Remarques sur la topographie chrétienne des cités de la Gaule entre Loire et Rhin des origines au VIIe siècle" in Riché ed. *La Christianisation des pays*

———, "Saints et démons: L'héritage de l'hagiographie antique" in "Santi e demoni" pp. 74-82

Pigeon, E.-A. *Histoire de la Cathédrale de Coutances* (Coutances, 1876)

———, *Vies des saints des diocèses de Coutances et Avranches* I-II (Coutances, 1876)

Platelle, Henri "L'oeuvre de S. Gérard à S. Amand" in *Gérard de Brogne*

Pommeraye, François *Histoire de l'abbaye royale de S. Ouen* (Rouen, 1662)

———, *Histoire des Archevesques de Rouen* (Rouen, 1667)

———, *Vie de Saint Romain* (Rouen, 1662)

Pothier, Dom "Note sur la musique sacrée en Normandie au onzième siècle" *Mémoires sur la Musique Sacrée en Normandie* (Vienne, 1896)

Potts, Cassandra "Normandy or Brittany? A Conflict of Interests at Mont St. Michel (966-1035)" *Anglo-Norman Studies* 12 (1990) pp. 135-156

Poulin, Joseph-Claude "Entre magie et religion. Recherches sur les utilisations de l'écrit dans la culture populaire du haut moyen age" in *La culture populaire au Moyen-Age* ed. Pierre Boglioni (Actes du colloque de l'Institut d'études médiévales, Université de Montréal, April 1977; Montreal, 1979) pp. 123-143

———, *L'idéal de sainteté dans l'Aquitaine carolingienne d'après les sources hagiographiques (750-950)* (Quebec City, 1975)

Praet, D. "Explaining the Christianization of the Roman Empire. Older theories and Recent Development" *Sacris Erudiri* 23 (1992-93) pp. 5-119

Prentout, Henri *Etude critique sur Dudon de St.-Quentin et son Histoire des Premiers ducs Normands* (Mémoires de l'Academie Nationale des Sciences, Arts et Belles-Lettres de Caen; Caen, 1915)

Prinz, Freidrich "Die Rolle der Iren beim Aufbau der merowingische Klosterkultur" in Löwe, ed. *Die Iren und Europa*

———, *Frühes Mönchtum im Frankenreich. Kultur und Gesellschaft in Gallien, den*

Rheinlanden und Bayern am Beispiel der monastichen Entwicklung (4. bis 8. Jahrhundert) (Munich-Vienna, 1965)

———, "Zum fränkischen und irischen Anteil an der Bekehrung der Angelsachsen" *Zeitschrift für Kirchengeschichte* 95 (1984) pp. 315-336

Prost, Bernard *Le trésor de l'abbaye St. Bénigne de Dijon* (Dijon, 1894)

Raulin, Jean *Sermones de festivitates sanctorum totius anni* (Bayeux, 1530)

Receuil des actes de Charles II le Chauve ed. George Tessier (Chartes et Diplômes Relatifs à l'Histoire de France, 8-10; Paris, 1943-1955)

Receuil des actes de Charles III le Simple ed. Philippe Lauer (Chartes et Diplômes Relatifs à l'Histoire de France 9A; Paris, 1940-1949)

Receuil des actes de Robert I et de Raoul ed. J. Dufour (Paris, 1978)

Receuil des actes des ducs de Normandie (911-1066) ed. Marie Fauroux (Mémoires de la Société des Antiquaires de Normandie 36; Caen, 1961)

Receuil des actes du roi Eudes ed. R.-H. Bauthier (Paris, 1967)

Receuil des chartes de l'abbaye de Saint-Germain-des-Prés ed. Réné Poupardin (Paris, 1909-1910)

Renaud, J. *Les Vikings et la Normandie* (Ouest-France, 1989)

Renoux, Annie "Fouilles sur le site du château ducal de Fécamp (Xe-XXe siècles): Bilan provisoire" *Anglo-Norman Studies* 4 (1982) pp. 133-152

———, "Le monastère de Fécamp pendant le haut moyen âge (VIIe-IXe siècles). Quelques données historiques et archéologiques" in *Les abbayes de Normandie* (Actes du XIIIe Congrès des Sociétés Historiques et Archéologiques de Normandie, Caudebec-en-Caux 1978; Rouen, 1979) dir. André Dubuc pp. 115-133

"Revelatio ecclesiae sancti Michaelis" [BHL 5951] in Thomas Le Roy, *Livre des curieuses recherches du Mont-Sainct-Michel* ed. Eugène de Robillard de Beaurepaire (Mémoires de la Société des Antiquaires de Normandie 29; Caen, 1876) Appendix II pp. 856-863; AASS Sept. VIII pp. 76-78

Richard, Jean-Claude "Les 'miracula' composés en Normandie aux XIe et XIIe siècles" *Positions des Thèses, Ecole des Chartes* (1975) pp. 183-189

Riché, Pierre, ed. *La Christianisation des pays entre Loire et Rhin, IVe-VIIe siècles* (Actes du Colloque de Nanterre, May 1974 = *Revue d'Histoire de l'Eglise de France* 62 (1976))

———, "Columbanus, His Followers and the Merovingian Church" in Clarke and Brennan eds. *Columbanus and Merovingian Monasticism* pp. 59-72

———, *Education et culture dans l'occident barbare (VIe-VIIIe siècles)* (Paris, 1972)

———, "La 'Renaissance' intellectuelle du Xe siècle en Occident" *Cahiers d'Histoire* XXI (1976) pp. 27-42

Richer of Reims *Histoire de France, 899-995* ed. and trans. Robert Latouche (Classiques de l'Histoire de France auMoyen Age 12 and 17; Paris, 1930)

Ridyard, Susan J. *The Royal Cults of Anglo-Saxon England: A Study of West Saxon and East Anglian Cults* (Cambridge, 1988)

Rimbert, "Vita Anskarii" [BHL 544/545] in *Quellen des 9. und 11. Jahrhunderts zur Geschichte der hamburgischen Kirche und des Reiches* (Darmstadt, 1968)

Roblin, Michel "Fontaines sacrées et nécropoles antiques, deux sites fréquents d'églises paroissiales rurales dans les sept anciens diocèses de l'Oise" in Riché, ed. *La Christianisation des pays entre Loire et Rhin* pp. 235-251

Rojdestvensky, Olga *Le culte de Saint Michel et le Moyen Age Latin* (Paris, 1922)

Roosens, H. "Reflets de christianisation dans les cimetières mérovingiens" *Les Etudes Classiques* LIII (1985) pp. 111-135

Rouche, Michel "Les Saxons et les origines de Quentovic" *Revue du Nord* 59 (1977) pp. 457-473

Rougé, J. "Topos et realia: La tempête apaisée de la Vie de Saint Germain d'Auxerre" *Latomus* 27 (1988)

Ruotger, "Vita Brunonis Coloniensis" [BHL 1468] ed. Irene Ott in MGH SRG n.s. 10 (Weimar, 1951)

Russell, James C. *The Germanization of Early Medieval Christianity. A Sociohistorical Approach to Religious Transformation* (Oxford, 1994)

Russell, Jeffrey Burton *Lucifer. The Devil in the Middle Ages* (Ithaca, 1984)

Ryan, J. "The Church in the Sixth Century" in *Mélanges Colombaniens* (Actes du Congrès International de Luxeuil, July 1950; Paris, 1951)

Saas, Jean *Notice des manuscrits de l'Eglise Metropolitaine de Rouen* (Rouen, 1746)

Salin, Edouard *La civilisation mérovingienne d'après les sepultures, les textes et le laboratoire* I-IV (Paris, 1949-1951)

Salzman, Michelle Renee "Aristocratic Women: Conductors of Christianity in the Fourth Century?" *Helios* 16 (1989) pp. 207-220

Sanford, Eva "The Study of Ancient History in the Middle Ages" *Journal of the History of Ideas* 5 (1944) pp. 21-43

Santyves, P. *En marge de la légende dorée* (Paris, 1987 reed.)

Sauvage, E.P. "Elenchi episcoporum Rotomagensium" AB 8 (1889) pp. 406-427

Sawyer, Peter H. *Kings and Vikings. Scandinavia and Europe, AD 700-1000* (London, 1982)

Schäferdiek, Knut ed. *Kirchengeschichte als Missionsgeschichte II: Die Kirche des Früheren Mittelalters* I (Munich, 1978)

——, "The Irish Mission of the Seventh Century: Historical Fact or Historiographical Fiction?" in *The End of Strife* (Papers from the Colloquium of the Commission Internationale Ecclésiastique Comparée, U. of Durham, Sept, 1981) ed. D. Loades (Edinburg, 1981)

Scheibelreiter, Georg *Der Bischof in merovingische Zeit* (Vienna, 1983)

Schmitt, J.-C. "'Religion populaire' et culture folklorique" *Annales E.S.C.* 31 (1976) pp. 941-953

Schmitz, G. "Das Konzil von Trosly" *Deutsches Archiv für Erforschung des Mittelalters* 33 (1977) pp. 347-356

Schröder, Isolde *Die westfränkischen Synoden von 888 bis 987 und ihre Überlieferung* (MGH Hilfsmittel 3; Munich, 1980)

Searle, Eleanor "Fact and Pattern in Heroic History: Dudo of St. Quentin" *Viator* 15 (1984) pp. 119-137

——, *Predatory Kinship and the Creation of Norman Power (840-1066)* (Berkeley, 1988)

Semmler, Joseph "Die Aufrichtung der Karolingischen Herrschaft im nördlichen Burgund im 8. Jahrhundert" *Langres et ses évêques, VIIIe- XIe siècles. Aux origines d'une seigneurie ecclésiastique* (Actes du Colloque Langres-Ellwangen, June 1985; Langres, 1986 dir. G. Viard)

"Sermo de adventu santorum Wandregiseli, Ansberti et Uulframni in Blandinium" [BHL 8810] ed. N.-N. Huyghebaert in *Une translation de reliques à Gand en 944* (Brussels, 1978)

Shopkow, Leah "The Carolingian World of Dudo of St. Quentin" *Journal of Medieval History* 15 (1989)

Simonetti, M. *La crisi ariana nel IV secolo* (Rome, 1975)

Smith, Julia "Oral and Written: Saints, Miracles and Relics in Brittany, c. 850-1250" *Speculum* 65 (1990)

——, *Province and Empire. Brittany and the Carolingians* (Cambridge, 1992)

Smyth, Alfred P. *Scandinavian Kings in the British Isles, 850-880* (Oxford, 1977)

Spear, David "Les archidiacres de Rouen au cours de la période ducale" *Annales de Normandie* 34 (1984)

——, "Les chanoines de la cathédrale de Rouen pendant la période ducale" *Annales de Normandie* 41 (1991)

——, "Les dignitaires de la cathédrale de Rouen pendant la période ducale" *Annales de Normandie* 37 (1987)

——, "Les doyens du chapitre cathédral de Rouen durant la période ducale" *Annales de Normandie* 33 (1983)

Spencer, Mark "Dating the Baptism of Clovis, 1886-1993" *Early Medieval Europe* 3 (1994) pp. 97-116

Spiegel, Gabrielle *The Chronicle Tradition of St. Denis: A Survey* (Brookline, Mass, 1978; Medieval Classics: Studies and Texts 10)

——, *Romancing the Past: The Rise of Vernacular Prose Historiography in Thirteenth-Century France* (Berkeley, 1993)

Stafford, Pauline *Unification and Conquest. A Political and Social History of England in the Tenth and Eleventh Centuries* (London, 1989)

Stancliffe, Clare "Cuthbert and the Polarity Between Pastor and Solitary" in Bonner et. al. eds. *St. Cuthbert*

——, *St. Martin and His Hagiographer* (Oxford, 1983)

Stephen of Rouen *Le Dragon normand et autres poèmes* (Rouen, 1884)

Strzelczyk, Jersy "Irische Einflüsse bei den Westslawen im Frümittelalter" in Chatháin, ed. *Irland und die Christenheit* pp. 445-460

Sullivan, Richard R. *Christian Missionary Activity in the Early Middle Ages* (Variorum Collected Studies Series CS 431; Great Yarmouth, 1994)

Sulpicius Severus, *Sulpicii Severi Opera* ed. C. Halm (CSEL 1; 1866)

Swarzenski, Hans "The Role of Copies in the Formation of the Styles of the Eleventh Century" *Studies in Western Art I: Romanesque and Gothic Art* (Acts of the 20th International Congress of the History of Art, New York, 1961; Princeton, 1963) pp. 7-18

Tabacco, Giovanni "Agiografia e demonologia come strumenti ideologici in età carolingia" in "Santi e demoni"

Tabuteau, Emily Zack *Transfers of Property in Eleventh-Century Norman Law* (Chapel Hill, 1988)

Tatlock, J.S.P. "Geoffrey and King Arthur in Normannicus Draco" *Modern Philology* 31 (1933-34)

Tessier, Georges *Le baptême de Clovis: 25 décembre (Trente journées qui ont fait la France* 1; Paris, 1964)

Thacker, Alan "Lindisfarne and the Origins of the Cult of St. Cuthbert" in *St. Cuthbert, His Cult and Community* eds. Bonner, et. al.

Theis, Laurent "Dagobert, St.-Denis et la royauté française au moyen âge" in Bernard Guenée ed. *Le metier d'historien au moyen âge. Etudes sur l'historiographie médievale* (Paris, 1977) pp. 19-30

——, *Dagobert. Un roi pour un peuple* (Paris, 1982)

Tilliette, Jean-Yves "Les modèles de sainteté du IXe au XIe siècle d'après le témoignage des récits hagiographiques en vers métriques" in "Santi e demoni"

Tougard, Alfonse "La Vie de St. Romain" *Société des Bibliophiles Normands* 60 (Rouen, 1899)

"Translatio Ebrulfi, Ansberti et Evremundi" [BHL 2379] ed. Jean Mabillon in ASOSB saec. V

"Translatio Geremari" [BHL 3442/3443] ed. J. Perierus, AASS Sept. VI

"Translatio Leutfredi" [BHL 4900] ed. W. Levison in MGH SRM 7

"Translatio Nigasii et socii" [BHL 6084] eds. Martène and Durand, *Thesaurus Novus Anecdotorum* (Paris, 1717) vol. III cols. 1677-1682

"Translatio Regnoberti et Zenonis" [BHL 7062] ed. Papebroch, AASS May III pp. 620-624

"Translationes Audoeni" [BHL 756 and 757] eds. E. Martène and V. Durand, *Thesaurus Novus Anecdotorum* III cols. 1669-1682 (Paris, 1717) and AASS August IV

Usuard, *Le martyrologe d'Usuard. Texte et commentaire* ed. Jacques Dubois (Subsidia Hagiographica 40; Brussels, 1965)

Vacandard, Elpidius "Saint Victrice, évêque de Rouen (IVe-Ve s.) *Revue des Questions Historiques* 37, NS 29 (1903) pp. 379-441

——, *Vie de S. Ouen, évêque de Rouen (641-684). Etude d'histoire Mérovingienne* (Paris, 1902)

Van Beek, Cornelius *Passio Sanctarum Perpetuae et Felicitatis* (Noyon, 1936)

Van der Essen, L. *Etude critique et littéraire sur les Vitae des saints mérovingiennes de l'ancienne Belgique* (Brussels, 1907)

Van der Straeten, Joseph "L'auteur des vies de S. Hughes et de S. Aychadre" AB 88 (1970) pp. 63-73

——, "La Vie inédite de S. Hughes, évêque de Rouen" AB 87 (1969) pp. 232-260

Van Gennep, A. *Manuel de folklore français contemporian* (Paris, 1937)

Van Houts, Elizabeth M.C. "Historiography and Hagiography at Saint-Wandrille: The 'Inventio et Miracula sancti Uulfranni'" *Anglo-Norman Studies* 12 ed. Marjorie Chibnall (Proceedings of the Battle Conference, 1989; Woodbridge, 1990) pp. 233 -251

——, "Scandinavian Influence in Norman Literature of the Eleventh Century" *Anglo-Norman Studies* 6 (1984) pp. 109-121

——, "Women and the Writing of History in the Early Middle Ages" *Early Medieval Europe* 1 (1992) pp. 53-68

Van Uytfanghe, Marc "La Bible dans les Vies des saints mérovingiennes. Quelques pistes de recherche" in Riché ed. *La Christianisations des pays* pp. 103-111

——, "L'hagiographie: un 'genre' chrétien ou antique tardif?" AB 111 (1993) pp. 135-188

Van Werveke, H. "Saint-Wandrille et Saint-Pierre de Gand (IXe et Xe siècles)" *Miscellanea Mediaevalia in memoriam Jan Frederik Niermeyer* eds. D.P. Blok, A. Bruckner, et. al. (Groningen, 1967)

Vansina, Jan *Oral Tradition as History* (Madison, Wisconsin, 1985)

Vauchez, André *La Sainteté en occident aux derniers siècles du moyen âge d'après les procès de canonisation et les documents hagiographiques* (Rome, 1981)

Vezin, Jean *Les scriptoria d'Angers au XIe siècle* (Bibliothèque de l'école des hautes études, IXe section, Sciences historiques et philologiques 322; Paris, 1974)

Victricius of Rouen *De laude sanctorum* ed. Jacobus Mulders (CCSL 64; 1985)

"Vie de Saint Romain" ed. A. Tougard *Société des Bibliophiles Normands* 60 (Rouen, 1899)

Vieillard-Troiekouroff, M. "Les monuments religieux de Rouen à la fin du VIe siècle d'après Grégoire de Tours et Fortunat" in *Centenaire de l'abbé Cochet (1975)* (Actes du Colloque International d'Archéologie, Rouen, July 1975; Rouen, 1978) vol. III pp. 511-520

Vion, Claude and Paul Massein, "Les témoins liturgiques du culte de saint Aychadre" in *Jumièges* I pp. 365-370

"Vita Aichardi" [BHL 181] in AASS Sept. V and ed. Levison MGH SRM 5

"Vita Ansberti" [BHL 519] ed. Sauvage in AB I (1882) pp. 178-191

"Vita Aquilini" [BHL 655] ed. B. Bossue in AASS Oct. VIII pp. 505-510

"Vita Audoeni" [BHL 750] ed. W. Levison in MGH SRM 5

"Vita Audomari" [BHL 763/764] in AASS Sept. III pp. 396-399

"Vita Audomari" [BHL 767/768] in AASS Sept. III pp. 402-403

"Vita et miracula Austrebertae" [BHL 832/836/837] ed. J. Bollandus in AASS Feb. II

"Vita Condedi" [BHL 1907] ed. W. Levison, MGH SRM 5

"Vita Condedi" [BHL 1908] ed. Victor de Buch, AASS Oct. IX pp. 354-355

"Vita Corbiniani" [BHL 1947] in *Bischof Arbeo von Freising und die Lebensgeschichte des hl. Korbinian* eds. H. Glaser, F. Brunhölzl and S. Benker (Munich-Zurich, 1983)

"Vita Eligii" [BHL 2474] ed. B. Krusch, MGH SRM 4

"Vita Eremberti" [BHL 2587] ed. W. Levison, MGH SRM 5 pp. 653-656

"Vita Ermenlandi" [BHL 3851] in MGH SRM 5 pp. 684-710

"Vita Filiberti" [BHL 6805/6806] ed. W. Levison, MGH SRM 5 (1910)

"Vita Genovefae" [BHL 3335] ed. B. Krusch, MGH SRM 2 (Hannover, 1896)

"Vita Gerardi" [BHL 3422] ed. L. de Heinemann, MGH SS 15.2 (Hannover, 1888)

"Vita Geremari" [BHL 3437] ed. J. Perierus in AASS Sept. VI

"Vita Geremari" [BHL 3441] ed. B. Krusch in MGH SRM 4

"Vita et translatio Gildardi" [BHL 3539/3540] ed. A. Poncelet in AB 8 (1889)

"Vita Hugonis" [BHL 4032] = c. 8 of the "Gesta abbatum Fontenellensium"

"Vita Hugonis" [BHL 4032a] ed. J. Van der Straeten, "La Vie inédite de S. Hugues" in AB 87 (1969) pp. 232-260

"Vita et miracula Leutfredi" [BHL 4899 and 4901] ed. J.-B. Mesnel, *Les saints du diocèse d'Evreux VI: Leufroy* (Evreux, 1922)

"Vita Martialis prolixior" [BHL 5552] ed. W. Gray de Birch in *Vita sanctissimi Martialis: The Life of St. Martial by Aurelianus* (London, 1877)

"Vita Richerii" [BHL 7245] ed. A. Poncelet in AB 22

"Vita Rimberti" [BHL 7258] ed. G. Waitz in *Vita Anskarii auctore Rimberto; accedit Vita Rimberti*, MGH SRG 55 (Hannover, 1884) pp. 81-100

Vita Sturmi des Eigil von Fulda ed. P. Engelbert (Marburg, 1968)
"Vita Vigoris" [BHL 8608-8613] ed. De Smedt in AASS Nov. 1 pp. 297-305
"Vita Uulframni" [BHL 8738] ed. W. Levison in MGH SRM 5
"Vita Wandregiseli" [BHL 8804] ed. B. Krusch in MGH SRM 5
"Vita Wandregiseli" [BHL 8805] in AASS July V ed. P. Boschius
"Vita Willehadi" [BHL 8898] in MGH SS 2 pp. 379-384 ed. H. Pertz
"Vitae patrum iurensium Romani, Lupicini, Eugendi" ed. B. Krusch in MGH SRM 3
Vogel, Cyrille *Les 'Libri Paenitentiales'* (Typologie des Sources du Moyen Age Occidental 27; Turnhout, 1978)
Vogel, Walther *Die Normannen und das fränkische Reich bis zur Gründung der Normandie (799-911)* (Heidelberger Abhandlungen zur mittleren und neueren Geschichte 14; Aalen, 1973)
Von Campenhausen, H.F. *Ambrosius von Mailand als Kirchenpolitiker* (Berlin and Leipzig, 1929)
Von den Steinem, W. *Chlodwigs Übergang zum Christentum; eine quellenkritische Studie* (Libelli 103; Darmstadt, 1969; reprinted from *Mitteilungen des Österreichischen Instituts für Geschichtsforschung* XII. Ergänzungsband, 1932 pp. 417-501)

Wallace-Hadrill, J.-M. *The Frankish Church* (Oxford, 1983)
——, *The Long-Haired Kings, and Other Studies in Frankish History* (London, 1962)
Ward, Benedicta *Miracles and the Medieval Mind* (Philadelphia, 1982)
Ward-Perkins, Bryan *From Classical Antiquity to the Middle Ages: Urban Public Building in Northern and Central Italy, AD 300-800* (Oxford, 1984)
Warner of Rouen, "Satire de Garnier de Rouen contre le poète Moriuth (Xe-XIe siècle)" ed. Henri Omont in *Annuaire-Bulletin de la Société de l'Histoire de France* XXXI (1894) pp. 193-210
Wehrli, Christoph *Mittelalterliche Überlieferungen von Dagobert I* (Geist und Werk der Zeiten; Arbeiten aus dem Historischen Seminar der Universität Zürich 62; Bern and Frankfurt, 1982)
Weidemann, M. "Bischofsherrschaft und Königtum in Neustrien vom 7. bis zum 9. Jahrhundert am Beispiel des Bistums Le Mans" in Atsma, ed. *La Neustrie* I pp. 161-193
Werner, J. "Frankish Royal Tombs in the Cathedrals of Cologne and St. Denis" *Antiquity* 38 (1964) pp. 201-216
Werner, K.F. "Conquête franque de la Gaule ou changement de régime?" in *Childéric-Clovis, rois des Francs, 482-1983. De Tournai à Paris. Naissance d'une nation* (Paris, 1983)

————, "Le rôle de l'aristocratie dans la Christianisation du nord-est de la Gaule" in Riché, ed. *La Christianisation des pays entre Loire et Rhin* pp. 45-72

————, "Quelques observations au sujet des débuts du 'duché' de Normandie" in *Etudes Yver: Droit privé et institutions régionales* (Rouen, 1976) pp. 691-709

White, L. Michael *Building God's House in the Roman World. Architectural Adaptation among Pagans, Jews and Christians* (Baltimore, 1990)

White, Stephen D. *Custom, Kinship and Gifts to Saints: The Laudatio Parentum in Western France, 1050-1150* (Chapel Hill, 1988)

Wieland, Gernot "Geminus Stilus: Studies in Anglo-Latin Hagiography" in *Insular Latin Studies: Papers on Latin Texts and Manuscripts of the British Isles, 550-1066* (Papers in Mediaeval Studies 1; Toronto, 1981) ed. Michael W. Herren pp. 113-133

Wightman, Edith *Gallia Belgica* (Berkeley, 1985)

William of Jumièges *Gesta Normannorum Ducum* ed. Jean Marx (Rouen, 1914); *Gesta Normannorum ducum of William of Jumièges, Orderic Vitalis and Robert of Torigni* I-II ed. and trans. E.M.C. Van Houts (Oxford, 1992-1995)

William of Malmesbury *Gesta Regum Anglorum* ed. W. Stubbs (Rolls Series 90; London, 1887)

William of Poitiers *Histoire de Guillaume le Conquérant* ed. and trans. Raymonde Foreville (Classiques de l'Histoire de France au Moyen Age 23; Paris, 1952)

Willibald "Vita Bonifatii" (BHL 1400) ed. H. Pertz in MGH SS 2 pp. 333-353

Wollasch, R. "Gerard von Brogne im Reformmöchtum seiner Zeit" in *Gérard de Brogne*

Wood, Ian "Pagans and Holy Men, 600-800" in Chatháin ed. *Irland und die Christenheit* pp. 347-360

————, "Saint Wandrille and its Hagiography" *Church and Chronicle in the Middle Ages. Essays presented to John Taylor* eds. I. Wood and G.A. Loud (London, 1991)

————, "The Vita Columbani and Merovingian Hagiography" *Peritia* 1 (1982) pp. 63-80

Wormald, F. "Some Illustrated Manuscripts of the Lives of the Saints" *Bulletin of the John Rylands Library* 35 no. 1 (1952) pp. 250-262

Wright, Roger *Late Latin and Early Romance in Spain and Carolingian France* (Classical and Medieval Texts, Papers and Monographs 8; Liverpool, 1982)

Young, Baily "Paganisme, Christianisation et rites funéraires mérovingiens" AM 7 (1977) pp. 5-81

Yver, Jacques "Autour de l'absence de l'avouerie en Normandie: notes sur le double theme du developement du pouvoir ducal et de l'application de la réforme grégorienne en Normandie" *Bulletin de la Société des Antiquaires de Normandie* 57 (1963-64)

——, "Les bases du pouvoir ducal en Normandie" *Revue Historique du Droit Français et Etranger* 4e séries, XXVIII (1951)

Zettel, Horst *Das Bild der Normannen und der Normanneneinfälle im westfränkischen, ostfränkischen und angelsächsischen Quellen* (Munich, 1977)

Zimmer, H. "Über directe Handelsverbindungen Westgalliens mit Irland im Altertum und frühen Mittelalter" part III, *Sitzungsberichte der Königlich Preusissischen Akademie der Wissenschaften* XIV (1909) pp. 543-580

Ziolkowski, Jan *Jezebel: A Norman Latin Poem of the Early Eleventh Century* (Studies and Sources Relating to the Middle Ages and the Renaissance 10; Humana Civiltas 10; N.Y., 1989)

Zoepf, L. *Das Heiligen-Leben im 10. Jahrhundert* (Leipzig, 1908)

Index of Persons, Texts and Places

Note: Only those individuals who are treated in the present study in their capacity as venerated saints are designated by the abbreviation "St."